Gender and the Quest
in British Science
Fiction Television

CRITICAL EXPLORATIONS IN SCIENCE FICTION AND FANTASY
(a series edited by Donald E. Palumbo and C.W. Sullivan III)

1 *Worlds Apart? Dualism and Transgression
in Contemporary Female Dystopias* (Dunja M. Mohr, 2005)

2 *Tolkien and Shakespeare: Essays on Shared Themes and Language*
(Ed. Janet Brennan Croft, 2007)

3 *Culture, Identities and Technology in the* Star Wars *Films: Essays on
the Two Trilogies* (Ed. Carl Silvio, Tony M. Vinci, 2007)

4 *The Influence of* Star Trek *on Television, Film and Culture* (Ed. Lincoln Geraghty, 2008)

5 *Hugo Gernsback and the Century of Science Fiction* (Gary Westfahl, 2007)

6 *One Earth, One People: The Mythopoeic Fantasy Series of Ursula K. Le Guin,
Lloyd Alexander, Madeleine L'Engle and Orson Scott Card* (Marek Oziewicz, 2008)

7 *The Evolution of Tolkien's Mythology: A Study
of the History of Middle-earth* (Elizabeth A. Whittingham, 2008)

8 *H. Beam Piper: A Biography* (John F. Carr, 2008)

9 *Dreams and Nightmares: Science and Technology in Myth and Fiction*
(Mordecai Roshwald, 2008)

10 Lilith *in a New Light: Essays on the George MacDonald Fantasy Novel*
(Ed. Lucas H. Harriman, 2008)

11 *Feminist Narrative and the Supernatural: The Function of
Fantastic Devices in Seven Recent Novels* (Katherine J. Weese, 2008)

12 *The Science of Fiction and the Fiction of Science: Collected Essays on SF Storytelling
and the Gnostic Imagination* (Frank McConnell, ed. Gary Westfahl, 2009)

13 *Kim Stanley Robinson Maps the Unimaginable: Critical Essays* (ed. William J. Burling, 2009)

14 *The Inter-Galactic Playground: A Critical Study
of Children's and Teens' Science Fiction* (Farah Mendlesohn, 2009)

15 *Science Fiction from Québec: A Postcolonial Study* (Amy J. Ransom, 2009)

16 *Science Fiction and the Two Cultures: Essays on Bridging the Gap Between
the Sciences and the Humanities* (ed. Gary Westfahl, George Slusser, 2009)

17 *Stephen R. Donaldson and the Modern Epic Vision: A Critical Study
of the "Chronicles of Thomas Covenant" Novels* (Christine Barkley, 2009)

18 *Ursula K. Le Guin's Journey to Post-Feminism* (Amy M. Clarke, 2010)

19 *Portals of Power: Magical Agency and Transformation in Literary Fantasy*
(Lori M. Campbell, 2010)

20 *The Animal Fable in Science Fiction and Fantasy* (Bruce Shaw, 2010)

21 Illuminating Torchwood: *Essays on Narrative, Character and Sexuality
in the BBC Series* (ed. Andrew Ireland, 2010)

22 *Comics as a Nexus of Cultures: Essays on the Interplay of Media, Disciplines
and International Perspectives* (ed. Mark Berninger, Jochen Ecke, Gideon Haberkorn, 2010)

23 *The Anatomy of Utopia: Narration, Estrangement and Ambiguity in
More, Wells, Huxley and Clarke* (Károly Pintér, 2010)

24 *The Anticipation Novelists of 1950s French Science Fiction:
Stepchildren of Voltaire* (Bradford Lyau, 2010)

25 *The* Twilight *Mystique: Critical Essays
on the Novels and Films* (ed. Amy M. Clarke, Marijane Osborn, 2010)

26 *The Mythic Fantasy of Robert Holdstock: Critical Essays
on the Fiction* (ed. Donald E. Morse, Kálmán Matolcsy, 2011)

27 *Science Fiction and the Prediction of the Future: Essays on Foresight
and Fallacy* (ed. Gary Westfahl, Wong Kin Yuen, Amy Kit-sze Chan, 2011)

28 *Apocalypse in Australian Fiction and Film: A Critical Study* (Roslyn Weaver, 2011)

29 *British Science Fiction Film and Television: Critical Essays* (ed. Tobias Hochscherf, James Leggott, 2011)

30 *Cult Telefantasy Series: A Critical Analysis of* The Prisoner, Twin Peaks, The X-Files, Buffy the Vampire Slayer, Lost, Heroes, Doctor Who *and* Star Trek (Sue Short, 2011)

31 *The Postnational Fantasy: Essays on Postcolonialism, Cosmopolitics and Science Fiction* (ed. Masood Ashraf Raja, Jason W. Ellis and Swaralipi Nandi, 2011)

32 *Heinlein's Juvenile Novels: A Cultural Dictionary* (C.W. Sullivan III, 2011)

33 *Welsh Mythology and Folklore in Popular Culture: Essays on Adaptations in Literature, Film, Television and Digital Media* (ed. Audrey L. Becker and Kristin Noone, 2011)

34 *I See You: The Shifting Paradigms of James Cameron's* Avatar (Ellen Grabiner, 2012)

35 *Of Bread, Blood and* The Hunger Games: *Critical Essays on the Suzanne Collins Trilogy* (ed. Mary F. Pharr and Leisa A. Clark, 2012)

36 *The Sex Is Out of This World: Essays on the Carnal Side of Science Fiction* (ed. Sherry Ginn and Michael G. Cornelius, 2012)

37 *Lois McMaster Bujold: Essays on a Modern Master of Science Fiction and Fantasy* (ed. Janet Brennan Croft, 2013)

38 *Girls Transforming: Invisibility and Age-Shifting in Children's Fantasy Fiction Since the 1970s* (Sanna Lehtonen, 2013)

39 Doctor Who *in Time and Space: Essays on Themes, Characters, History and Fandom, 1963–2012* (ed. Gillian I. Leitch, 2013)

40 *The Worlds of* Farscape: *Essays on the Groundbreaking Television Series* (ed. Sherry Ginn, 2013)

41 *Orbiting Ray Bradbury's Mars: Biographical, Anthropological, Literary, Scientific and Other Perspectives* (ed. Gloria McMillan, 2013)

42 *The Heritage of Heinlein: A Critical Reading of the Fiction Television Series* (Thomas D. Clareson and Joe Sanders, 2014)

43 *The Past That Might Have Been, the Future That May Come: Women Writing Fantastic Fiction, 1960s to the Present* (Lauren J. Lacey, 2014)

44 *Environments in Science Fiction: Essays on Alternative Spaces* (ed. Susan M. Bernardo, 2014)

45 *Discworld and the Disciplines: Critical Approaches to the Terry Pratchett Works* (ed. Anne Hiebert Alton and William C. Spruiell, 2014)

46 *Nature and the Numinous in Mythopoeic Fantasy Literature* (Christopher Straw Brawley, 2014)

47 *J.R.R. Tolkien, Robert E. Howard and the Birth of Modern Fantasy* (Deke Parsons, 2014)

48 *The Monomyth in American Science Fiction Films: 28 Visions of the Hero's Journey* (Donald E. Palumbo, 2014)

49 *The Fantastic in Holocaust Literature and Film: Critical Perspectives* (ed. Judith B. Kerman and John Edgar Browning, 2014)

50 Star Wars *in the Public Square:* The Clone Wars *as Political Dialogue* (Derek R. Sweet, 2016)

51 *An Asimov Companion: Characters, Places and Terms in the Robot/Empire/Foundation Metaseries* (Donald E. Palumbo, 2016)

52 *Michael Moorcock: Fiction, Fantasy and the World's Pain* (Mark Scroggins, 2016)

53 *The Last Midnight: Essays on Apocalyptic Narratives in Millennial Media* (ed. Leisa A. Clark, Amanda Firestone and Mary F. Pharr, 2016)

54 *The Science Fiction Mythmakers: Religion, Science and Philosophy in Wells, Clarke, Dick and Herbert* (Jennifer Simkins, 2016)

55 *Gender and the Quest in British Science Fiction Television: An Analysis of* Doctor Who, Blake's 7, Red Dwarf *and* Torchwood (Tom Powers, 2016)

Gender and the Quest in British Science Fiction Television

An Analysis of Doctor Who, Blake's 7, Red Dwarf *and* Torchwood

Tom Powers

Foreword by Matt Hills

CRITICAL EXPLORATIONS IN
SCIENCE FICTION AND FANTASY, 55
Series Editors Donald E. Palumbo *and* C.W. Sullivan III

McFarland & Company, Inc., Publishers
Jefferson, North Carolina

LIBRARY OF CONGRESS CATALOGUING-IN-PUBLICATION DATA

Names: Powers, Tom, 1972–
Title: Gender and the quest in British science fiction television : an analysis of Doctor Who, Blake's 7, Red Dwarf and Torchwood / Tom Powers.
Description: Jefferson, North Carolina : McFarland & Company, Inc., Publishers, 2016 | Series: Critical explorations in science fiction and fantasy ; 55 | Includes bibliographical references and index.
Identifiers: LCCN 2016035247 | ISBN 9781476665528 (softcover : acid free paper) ∞
Subjects: LCSH: Science fiction television programs—Great Britain—History and criticism. | Doctor Who (Television program : 1963–1989) | Doctor Who (Television program : 2005–) | Blake's 7 (Television program) | Red Dwarf (Television program) | Torchwood (Television program) | Heroes on television. | Sex role on television. | Television—Production and direction—Great Britain.
Classification: LCC PN1992.8.S35 B75 2006 | DDC 791.45/615—dc23
LC record available at https://lccn.loc.gov/2016035247

BRITISH LIBRARY CATALOGUING DATA ARE AVAILABLE

ISBN (print) 978-1-4766-6552-8
ISBN (ebook) 978-1-4766-2693-2

© 2016 Tom Powers. All rights reserved

No part of this book may be reproduced or transmitted in any form or by any means, electronic or mechanical, including photocopying or recording, or by any information storage and retrieval system, without permission in writing from the publisher.

Front cover: (top, left to right) Peter Capaldi as the Twelfth Doctor, Paul Darrow as Kerr Avon, Craig Charles as Dave Lister and John Barrowman as Captain Jack Harkness (BBC/Photofest); background image © 2016 iStock

Printed in the United States of America

McFarland & Company, Inc., Publishers
 Box 611, Jefferson, North Carolina 28640
 www.mcfarlandpub.com

For my wife Amanda

Acknowledgments

I would like to thank Thomas J. Slater, whose synergistic advising on my dissertation led to the creation of this book, as well as my dissertation committee members, John Branscum and Christopher Orchard, who gave me valuable advice and encouragement. Moreover, I appreciate Alexis Lothian, for introducing me to queer theory; Hugh Ormsby-Lennon, for supporting my early musings on *Red Dwarf*; Marc Schuster, for his insightful feedback on my manuscript; and Don Z. Block, for his kind words. I am also grateful to Donald E. Palumbo, who helped me to refine this work for publication, and Matt Hills, for providing such a thoughtful foreword.

Table of Contents

Acknowledgments	viii
Foreword: The Challenges of Regeneration (by Matt Hills)	1
Introduction: Doctor Who, Blake's 7, Red Dwarf *and* Torchwood: *Gendered Heroic Quests*	11
One: The Phenomenological Meanings of BBC Cult SF Headquarters and Objects	21
Two: The Rise, Fall and Nostalgic Embers of 1980s *Doctor Who*	42
Three: The CNC Implications of *Blake's 7*'s Stylized Retro-Future	79
Four: What a Smegging Quest! The Journey of *Red Dwarf* and Its Fandom	108
Five: Everything's Constantly Changing: Sex and Death on *Torchwood*	147
Six: *NüWho*'s Quest to Stay Relevant with Its Fans	186
Conclusion: Encoders and Decoders Shaping the Destinies of Four Cult SF TV Sagas	221
Appendix: Televised Works	233
Chapter Notes	245
Works Cited	259
Index	265

Foreword: The Challenges of Regeneration

by Matt Hills

In one sense, this book reverses the (theoretical) polarity of Henry Jenkins's seminal study of cult/telefantasy TV and its fans, *Textual Poachers*. Where Jenkins largely dispensed with Stuart Hall's influential encoding/decoding model—to focus instead on Michel de Certeau's model of "poaching"—Tom Powers intriguingly inverts that decision. In the pages that follow, then, we get a return to Hall's approach, albeit one that is revised in order to better capture the temporality of long-running media franchises—or, at least, of TV shows that their fans refuse to let fade away via "post-object fandom" (Williams, *Post-Object*). As Powers thoughtfully muses in his conclusion: "One constant has been present [across these case studies]—time…. Time is … ever present in an always-evolving decoding sense as the four fan cultures … continue to build upon their DIY cultural productions that celebrate, criticize and recreate their televised objects of affection."

Putting media fans' and brands' temporalities back into the encoding/decoding model in this way means admitting that a synchronic, singular focus on moments of determinate decoding is far too limited a way of thinking. As Jonathan Gray has pointed out in his own reworking of Hall's approach: "I propose, therefore, that we talk not of encoding/decoding, but of encoding/redecoding, and of reading through. Both reading and the text are a continual journey *through*, a continuance of motion, and while there might be determinate moments, there are always potentially more determinate moments to come" (34). And both this and Powers's highly productive return to fans-as-decoders work to address the very reasons why Jenkins had initially rejected Hall's well-established theory:

de Certeau's notion of "poaching" differs in important ways from Stuart Hall's ... formulation (1980). First, as it has been applied, Hall's model of dominant, negotiated, and oppositional readings tends to imply that each reader has a stable position from which to make sense of a text rather than having access to multiple sets of discursive competencies by virtue of [a] more complex and contradictory place within the social formation. Hall's model ... suggests that popular meanings are fixed and classifiable, while de Certeau's "poaching" model emphasizes the process of making meaning and the fluidity of popular interpretation [Jenkins 33–34].

In his analyses of the British cult telefantasies *Doctor Who*, *Blake's 7*, *Red Dwarf* and *Torchwood*, Powers effectively takes forward Jonathan Gray's call for a focus on "redecoding," and thus counters the notion that popular meanings are somehow "fixed and classifiable" rather than marked by (contested) fluidity over time. Indeed, Powers argues not just for a focus on fans' (re)decodings over the years—happening between media texts' proposed or actual reimaginings—but also for a consideration of how fannish (re)decodings can relate to new encodings of, say, official *Doctor Who* or *Red Dwarf*. Gray has noted how his own rebooting of Hall's work leads to a series of research questions: "After all, a lot revolves around the *potential* of texts to be kept alive, and this model requires work on issues as disparate as ... which texts or types of texts are particularly long lasting and why; which texts are prone to frequent decodings ... and why; which *people* are more or less likely to redecode" (35).

There are some new explorations of these issues on display in this volume: clearly, cult TV offers one type of textuality that is prone to frequent (re)decoding across weeks, months and years, as fans revisit eras or series, rewatching their favored objects. And within the fan world (akin to the "art world" theorized by Howard Becker, where what it means to be a fan, and who gets to be a true fan, replaces analogous questions addressed towards the identity of "the artist") texts' *"potential"* to be kept alive is surely maximized—part of being a long-term, dedicated fan means precisely redecoding, campaigning, and evangelizing for the return of a reinvigorated version of the beloved fan object (see, e.g., Jones on international *X Files* fandom).

In this book, Tom Powers seeks, crucially, to reconnect the specificity of fans' decoding and producers' subsequent (rather than prior) encodings, positing a feedback loop of sorts; a relationship that can sometimes be mutually reinforcing and sometimes problematic for both parties. As the author points out in chapter one: "I will be discussing ... iterations of what I ... call encoding/decoding/encoding—or EDE." Encoders and decoders may be institutionally separated at any given moment of textual production and consumption, but they remain in a constrained and enabled dialogue.

By way of illustrating how fans' voices and decodings can constrain producers' subsequent encodings, Powers, in his introduction, focuses on "the reciprocal pull oscillating between ... encoders and decoders in any of these four unique media situations," terming this "the *Continuum of Nostalgic Continuity* (CNC)" (see also Harvey 97). Such a thing sounds almost science-fictional in its own right, as if it could be a part of the hyperdiegetic worlds of *Doctor Who*, *Blake's 7*, *Red Dwarf* and *Torchwood*. But more importantly, the CNC points to how these different fandoms negotiate the challenge of brand regeneration (Lury 8), as their shows are reinvented or enter the realms of production development and speculation (Gwynne). The CNC amounts to a cluster of fan (re)decodings which work, communally and collectively, to demarcate what the fan object should be. This is an authenticating and possibly even essentializing fan view (Hills, *Triumph* 5), laying out what *Doctor Who* must contain, without which it forfeits its own identity and textual authenticity, or stipulating what *Torchwood* should be. As Powers observes in the latter case at the end of chapter five:

> While *Torchwood*'s future as a continuing television narrative is undetermined at present, a strong feeling exists amongst online fandom that ... the series should return to its fundamental Cardiff roots and earlier emphasis on character-based and pansexual storytelling.... [T]his mindset may seem creatively and economically suicidal, but, after all, *Torchwood* ... will most likely find the future means for success via its ... fans.

Fans' desire to recreate "true" *Torchwood* or "true" *Red Dwarf* can result in an encoding CNC template for producers which either restricts the regendering of these shows' heroic quests, or leads to conflict between producers and (sections of) fandom. Another of Powers's exemplars, *Doctor Who*, has become embroiled in production, media and fan debates around the gendering of its title character. At the same time, it is not inevitable that fans' construction of a CNC will result in a backward-looking, regressive or reactionary model of the "true" text being reproduced—despite a vocal minority attacking *Battlestar Galactica* for its noughties' regendering of Starbuck as a female character, the franchise was ultimately strengthened and modernized by this move, being successfully repositioned as "quality TV." There are evidently key encoding/decoding/encoding moments where any given TV show has the chance to undergo dramatic and radical reimagining—points at which it is rebranded, and where new production communities take over from prior creative teams. The EDE circuit that Powers examines across his case studies (or even EDEDE; the circuit extends ever onwards in actuality) is not necessarily one where the same encoders are involved at successive determinate moments. As Mark Wolf has rightly observed in his study of imaginary worlds: "Fans who are serious about contributing canonical material to a world can become employees or freelancers, or in some cases, even the torchbearers assigned to continue a world (as is the case with lifelong *Doctor Who* fan Steven Moffat…). However … the majority of … [fans] are on the lower end of the hierarchies of authorship" (280).

This highlights the fact that TV's fan-decoders can cross over into the roles of producer-encoders, becoming what Suzanne Scott has termed "fanboy auteurs" (51), although this extradiegetic quest is very often (problematically) gendered too. It may be tempting to draw general conclusions from such movements between fannish decoder and official encoder—perhaps suggesting that hybridized producer-fans are always-already placed within both production and fan communities or discourses—but we need to remain conscious of the highly unusual status of the fan-turned-"torchbearer" who assumes creative control over a franchise. Such cases tend to be strongly publicized in contemporary media culture—whether we look at BBC TV's *Doctor Who* being taken over by Chris Chibnall in 2018, or Disney's *Star Wars* having been reinvigorated in 2015 by J.J. Abrams—no doubt because such semiotic maneuvers can work to reassure fans not only that the CNC will be honored, but also that any changes made will remain sensitive to, and cognizant of, fans' constructions of textual authenticity. Yet the "fanboy auteur" does not reflect the cultural and industrial positions of "ordinary fandom" (used in a variant context by Sandvoss and Kearns 93). While fans with appropriately high levels of cultural and media-industry capital can become candidates for these industrial blurrings of fan and official producer, the vast majority of fans are not, and will not ever be, in such a situation themselves. The "Showrunner Dream" is, we might say, no less ideological than the American Dream, holding out a promise of "making it" that remains restricted to a very small elite.

Powers's focus on the encoding/decoding/encoding circuit also engages with cases where the same specific producer has maintained generally cordial relations with fandom over time—e.g., Doug Naylor working on *Red Dwarf*—and instances where production teams have given way to successor "torchbearers" drawn from fandom themselves, as with *Doctor Who*. Derek Johnson has analyzed how media franchises are not simply concerned with "world-building," i.e., creating an expansive diegetic universe that fans can learn about as well as expanding via non-canonical productivity (Jenkins, *Convergence* 114–15), but also with "world-sharing among creative workers and communities" (Johnson 109).

What Johnson labels "multiplied production" can "be successive ... or significantly after" (122), with different producers separated by long periods of time tending to characterize reboots/reimaginings. But such EDE dialectics do not only respond to fans' "continuum of nostalgic continuity": new producers also aim to display their creative autonomy through novel encodings. If *all* that producers are creating is "fan service," or an explicit emulation of past texts, then their work risks being positioned as wholly reactive and derivative, lacking in any claim to auteur status or any articulation with industrially valued discourses of TV art and creativity. The fan continuum of nostalgic continuity therefore inevitably interacts with what might be considered an *industrial continuum of nostalgic creativity*, partly harking back to a more paternalistic and sequestered era of media production where fans and producers were not as significantly and symbolically proximate as they are today (thanks to social media, fandom's cultural mainstreaming, and industry discourses of branding/engagement). As Derek Johnson indicates,

> [R]elations [between producers] have shaped the shared use of franchise worlds within these intra-industrial contexts—chiefly in the desire of different production communities to both take pleasure in a tradition of creativity and establish their own unique identities and ... creative viewpoints. What has resulted are practices that acknowledge the use of shared worlds while also pushing for recognition of a difference that [has] allowed production communities to make meaningful claims to creative and professional distinction [123].

That is, new producers want to make their authorial mark on rebranded franchises, at the same time as acknowledging fan discourses (this was just as true for *Doctor Who*'s producer in the 1980s, John Nathan-Turner, as it was for showrunner Russell T Davies in 2005). Even when a producer is a "fanboy auteur," then, they will still aim to integrate CNC fan service with an artistic autonomy or authorial distinctiveness likely to challenge at least some fannish received wisdoms (see Hills, "Expertise").

But if fan-decoders can become producer-encoders, what of the situation where official encoders become aligned with fan-decoders? Powers analyzes *The Five(ish) Doctors Reboot*, a low-budget production which featured on the BBC's Red Button as part of *Doctor Who*'s fiftieth anniversary celebrations, as well as being available online and then as part of a Collector's Edition Blu-ray set. This mockumentary about former *Who* actors Peter Davison, Colin Baker and Sylvester McCoy attempting to appear in the anniversary special "The Day of the Doctor" was directed by none other than Davison himself, who had previously appeared in the show as the Fifth Doctor (1981–84). Davison had also directed videos for the major U.S. fan convention, Gallifrey One, including one apologizing for his absence from the event. On this note, Powers writes in chapter two,

> This video [for Gallifrey One 2010] ... represents an interesting hybrid production in which an encoder-actor is collaborating with decoders to produce a quality fan-produced work, whose satiric tone would be echoed in *The Five(ish) Doctors Reboot*.... Can one, however, consider Davison ... Baker, McCoy, and [Paul] McGann, as fans of *Doctor Who*?... [C]an four actors ... be fans of themselves? More paradoxically, does Davison's ... [work here] serve as the ultimate act of narcissism, or is he articulating the inherent power wielded by contemporary participatory culture in being able to lower and blur the traditional barriers standing between ... encoders and decoders?

There are many questions here, to be sure, though it seems persuasive that the line between encoding and decoding is eroded through such fan-targeted paratexts (Hills, *Doctor Who* 48–50). Is Davison's convention skit best considered as a "fan-produced work," though? It may be necessary to distinguish between different meanings of fandom in such examples (Ross 260). Professional actors can certainly perform fan identities by aligning themselves with paying convention-goers (Geraghty 110), as well as experiencing the emotional attachments of fandom—both to communities and texts. But still, the *Doctor Who* fandom of Peter Davison can again be distinguished from that of "ordinary" fans—Davison combines his fandom with industry "insider" status and media capital. Such hybridity cannot disqualify or invalidate his "fan" alignment, to be sure, but it undoubtedly colors and modifies it. As such, the questions raised by Powers compel us to consider how fandom cannot be considered as one cultural entity (if it ever could!), but instead needs to be analyzed in relation to its intersectionality with other (professional/media world) performances of self.

Observing how the former Doctors appearing in *The Five(ish) Doctors Reboot* wear a "mix of proper and commercial costumes [i.e., merchandised T-shirts]" that "signifies their newfound roles as fan-actors," Powers also draws our attention to the temporal trajectories of professional actors, for whom these TV series can sometimes correspond to jobs from many, many years ago. Davison, Baker and McCoy thus occupy a liminal position—their regular convention attendance may contribute to the allegiance they feel towards long-term *Doctor Who* fans, yet, despite their industry "insider" positioning, they simultaneously remain at a distance from the current production of *Doctor Who*, forming part of previous production teams. *The Five(ish) Doctors Reboot* is thus more than merely fan-pleasing satire, since it also captures the phenomenological position of being a former Doctor, both privileged in industry/fan terms and yet secondary to the show's contemporary production.

If *Doctor Who* has been subjected to a vast array of canonizing academic study, while *Torchwood* has attracted reasonable attention by virtue of being a *Doctor Who* spinoff (see Ireland and Williams, *Torchwood*), then *Blake's 7* and *Red Dwarf* have perhaps been unfairly downplayed in scholarship. Each show generates much fruitful analysis here, however, with *Blake's 7* being addressed in part though the "post–Gauda Prime" genre of fan fiction where fans imagine what comes after the cataclysmic events of the show's final episode "Blake." Powers, in chapter three, suggests that while "[o]ccupying a nebulous space between fan fiction and a proper place in *Blake's 7* spinoff narratives, *The Logic of Empire* perhaps represents the finest example of encoding/decoding/encoding I can offer." Made available as a cassette tape more than fifteen years after the end of *Blake's 7* on TV, and written by Alan Stevens and David Tulley, *The Logic of Empire* is not an official, canonical BBC production. Despite this, it features leading actors from the original series (Paul Darrow, Jacqueline Pearce, Gareth Thomas, Peter Tuddenham) and is effectively endorsed by *Blake's 7*'s series four producer, Vere Lorrimer, who contributes to the liner notes: "I was associated with all four seasons of Blake's Seven. I am proud to be associated with this audio play" (Lorrimer). Regardless of such "nebulous" interplay between fandom and (former) official producers and star actors, *The Logic of Empire* remains legally non-official. By contrast, Peter Davison's production of *The Five(ish) Doctors Reboot* became legally official when BBC Wales agreed to fund it—so there are discursive regimes of branding and intellectual property which continue to distinguish very keenly and precisely between these textual states.

Powers additionally analyses how *Blake's 7* "remains in a limbo state.... [T]he majority of [licensed Big Finish audio/novelized] tales are caught in a CNC vortex as they cater to fans' sentimental feelings about the original series, so their potential influence in helping to jumpstart a reinvigoration of *Blake's 7* fandom is rather limited." The implication here is that fandom can sometimes be its own worst enemy, essentializing an "authentic" version of the fan object which "may consequently disrupt any potential encodings of a reboot."

And yet producers can, and do, still find ways to playfully and purposefully renovate such shows, observing the industrial continuum of nostalgic creativity as well as the fannish CNC. This has very much been the case for *Red Dwarf*, which returned after a period of dormancy with *Back to Earth*, a meta-fictional story in which the show's characters entered a version of "our" everyday world. Given *Red Dwarf*'s status as SF comedy, it was able to integrate this gambit with canonical status, even suggesting that the program's TV audiences and fans had been created as a result of the "actual" crew's adventures. Powers suggests that *Back to Earth* constitutes a commentary on the brand's ongoing viability, and it is certainly the case that cancelled TV shows moving from "post-object" to rebooted/continued status often seem to focus self-reflexively on their own previous fan audience and prior version(s). Indeed, one conclusion of Powers's work is that "in order for a dormant science fiction brand to achieve a successful media revival, encoders may be required to include ... the original cast, a true continuation of its heroic quest, and a synergistic relationship with its decoders." We may also need to address intervening changes in industrial context, and how shows are required to engage with such developments: for example, when *Doctor Who* came back in 2005, it needed to function as a coherent brand, and also to operate in relation to norms of "televisuality" established by U.S. quality-cult TV.

Sometimes referred to as "NüWho," the BBC Wales' incarnation of the series has recently addressed criticisms of its gendered heroic quest from fans and critics alike. The character of the Master—a key antagonist for the Doctor—has thus been regendered as the female "Missy" (or "Mistress"), while Series Nine ended with the Doctor's companion, Clara Oswald (Jenna Coleman), taking on a Doctor-like role with a female companion of her own, Ashildr (Maisie Williams). Tom Powers, in chapter six, rightly notes that these characters "represent a completely feminized iteration of travelers and time machine—a progressive encoding step on [showrunner Steven] Moffat's part, [and] one that may signal future versions of *Doctor Who*." The interesting issue which this raises, however, is the extent to which Moffat's scriptwriting decisions here can be read as encoding choices premised on fans,' journalists,' and academics' critical decodings of *Who*'s gendered limitations. Is "Hell Bent" (Series Nine, episode 12) a producer's response to his vocal critics? Circuits of encoding-decoding-encoding (and so on) may sometimes correspond to what Sharon Marie Ross calls an "obscured" invitation to tele-participation (4), i.e., rather than the most recent encoding being explicitly positioned as a response to prior fan decodings—which would position Moffat's work as reactive fan service rather than autonomous TV authorship—the industrial continuum of nostalgic creativity works to obscure this relationship. The result is that showrunners such as Moffat can be discursively positioned as proactive, valued creators rather than as responsive, derivative media workers taking their cue from audience tastes and cultural politics. Perhaps, then, it isn't only fans who have to navigate the challenges and potential inauthenticities of regenerated TV shows via the CNC, but also media producers who have to negotiate new challenges of regenerated encoding/decoding possibilities, sometimes obscuring or masking an EDE circuit in favor of strengthening professional and production discourses of creative autonomy.

Tom Powers's book proffers an invaluable guide to this terrain, bringing a revisionist encoding/decoding model back into studies of SF TV and media fandom, astutely relating this to critical readings of gender and sexuality, and arguing, in his conclusion, that fan "decoders are the ones who ultimately serve as the true stewards of these series' fantastical narratives." By contrast, changing "torchbearers" and multiple "production communities" might represent only temporary embodiments of the media's encoding power, sometimes partaking of fan discourses (Booth 102), but nevertheless still remaining distinct from the fan world and its assorted communities and cultures.

WORKS CITED

Becker, Howard S. *Art Worlds: Updated and Expanded 25th Anniversary Edition.* Berkeley: University of California Press, 2008. Print.
Booth, Paul. *Playing Fans.* Iowa City: University of Iowa Press, 2015. Print.
Geraghty, Lincoln. *Cult Collectors: Nostalgia, Fandom and Collecting Popular Culture.* London: Routledge, 2014. Print.
Gray, Jonathan. *Watching with The Simpsons.* New York: Routledge, 2006. Print.
_____. *Show Sold Separately.* New York: New York University Press, 2010. Print.
Gwynne, Owain. "Fan-Made Time: *The Lord of the Rings* and *The Hobbit.*" Eds. Kristin M. Barton and Jonathan Malcolm Lampley. *Fan CULTure: Essays on Participatory Fandom in the 21st Century.* Jefferson: McFarland, 2014. 76–91. Print.
Harvey, Colin B. *Fantastic Transmedia.* Basingstoke: Palgrave Macmillan, 2015. Print.
Hills, Matt. *Doctor Who: The Unfolding Event—Marketing, Merchandising and Mediatizing a Brand Anniversary.* London: Palgrave Macmillan, 2015. Print.
_____. "The Expertise of Digital Fandom as a 'community of practice': Exploring the Narrative Universe of *Doctor Who.*" *Convergence* 21. 3 (2015): 360–374. Print.
_____. *Fan Cultures.* London: Routledge, 2012. Print.
_____. *Triumph of a Time Lord.* London: I.B. Tauris, 2010. Print.
Ireland, Andrew, ed. *Illuminating Torchwood: Essays on Narrative, Character and Sexuality in the BBC Series.* Jefferson: McFarland, 2010. Print.
Jenkins, Henry. *Convergence Culture: Where Old and New Media Collide.* New York: New York University Press, 2006. Print.
_____. *Textual Poachers: Television Fans and Participatory Culture.* New York: Routledge, 1992. Print.
Johnson, Derek. *Media Franchising: Creative License and Collaboration in the Culture Industries.* New York: New York University Press, 2013. Print.
Jones, Bethan. "The Fandom Is Out There: Social Media and *The X Files* Online." *Fan CULTure: Essays on Participatory Fandom in the 21st Century.* Eds. Kristin M. Barton and Jonathan Malcolm Lampley. Jefferson: McFarland, 2014. 92–105. Print.
Lorrimer, Vere. Liner notes. *The Logic of Empire.* Magic Bullet Productions, 1998. Audiocassette.
Lury, Celia. *Brands: The Logos of the Global Economy.* London: Routledge, 2004. Print.

Ross, Sharon Marie. *Beyond the Box: Television and the Internet.* Malden: Blackwell, 2008. Print.

Sandvoss, Cornel, and Laura Kearns. "From Interpretive Communities to Interpretative Fairs: Ordinary Fandom, Textual Selection and Digital Media." *The Ashgate Research Companion to Fan Cultures.* Eds. Linda Duits, Koos Zwaan and Stijn Reijnders. Farnham: Ashgate, 2014. 91–106. Print.

Scott, Suzanne. "Who's Steering the Mothership? The Role of the Fanboy Auteur in Transmedia Storytelling." *The Participatory Cultures Handbook.* Eds. Aaron Delwiche and Jennifer Jacobs Henderson. New York: Routledge, 2013. 43–52. Print.

Williams, Rebecca. *Post-Object Fandom: Television, Identity and Self-narrative.* London and New York: Bloomsbury Academic, 2015. Print.

_____, ed. *Torchwood Declassified: Investigating Mainstream Cult Television.* London: I.B. Tauris, 2013. Print.

Wolf, Mark J.P. *Building Imaginary Worlds: The Theory and History of Subcreation.* New York: Routledge, 2012. Print.

Matt Hills is a professor of media and journalism at the University of Huddersfield. The author of six books, including *Fan Cultures* and *Doctor Who: The Unfolding Event*, he has published widely on media fandom, cult film and TV, and *Doctor Who*.

Introduction: Doctor Who, Blake's 7, Red Dwarf and Torchwood: Gendered Heroic Quests

Since the early Saturday evening of November 23, 1963, at 5:16 p.m., when the British Broadcasting Corporation premiered the first episode of *Doctor Who*, "An Unearthly Child," the dualistically synergistic and antagonistic connection between BBC science fiction (SF) television producers and viewers has been a thriving, living process that has not only shaped the history of television but also how fans perceive themselves in relation to a media text. Indeed, many of the children and adolescents who grew up watching this show in its first run, which ended in 1989, were involved in the continuation (i.e., survival) of its brand during "The Wilderness Years" (1989–2005) and in its eventual revival as writers and producers.[1] During *Doctor Who*'s second decade, in 1978, the BBC debuted a more adult piece of SF television, *Blake's 7*, which offered an intersection point between traditional and queer fandom (if the two can even be remotely separated), with its characterizations of such interesting gendered characters as the heroic Blake, Avon, and Vila and their villainous counterparts, Servalan and Travis. Another quite playful—but equally critical fandom—arrived a decade later with the BBC SF sitcom, *Red Dwarf*, and its fan culture, Smegheads, who have adored and resisted the various iterations of the show to the present day. Yet all of these fandoms could be viewed as setting the stage for the second invasion of BBC SF shows, which would experience unprecedented transatlantic and global success. Heralded by the 2005 critically and economically effective reboot of *Doctor Who*, followed by its spin-off, *Torchwood*, this wave of BBC shows, through the myriad platforms of social media, are constantly renegotiating and blurring the boundaries between corporate/creative producers and viewers/fans.

In his classic cultural studies piece "Encoding/decoding," sociologist and Birmingham School critic Stuart Hall provides a breakdown of the interactive relationship between entertainment producers/creators and their viewers/fans. On the encoding/decoding process, Hall writes,

> [T]he broadcasting structures must yield encoded messages in the form of a meaningful discourse. The institutional-societal relations of production must pass under the discursive rules of language for its product to be "realized." This initiates a further differentiated moment, in which the formal rules of discourse and language are in dominance. Before this message can have an "effect" (however defined), satisfy a "need" or be put to a "use," it must first be appropriated as a meaningful discourse and be meaningfully decoded. It is this set of decoded meanings which "have an effect," influence, entertain, instruct, or persuade, with very complex perceptual, cognitive, emotional, ideological, or behavioural consequences [130].

With this passage, Hall points out the reciprocal relationship shared between producer-encoders and fan-decoders in which they shape what constitutes "meaningful discourse." In other words, while encoder-BBC SF television producers may have the intention to create media products such as *Doctor Who*, *Blake's 7*, *Red Dwarf*, and *Torchwood* that generate "meaningful discourse," this process cannot be fully realized until the respective fans decode these creative productions according to their own definitions, needs, and critical appraisal. More specifically, these series exemplify both decoders and encoders searching for definitions of heroic identity through the lens of gender and sexuality. On the one hand, when the encoding process has been successful, the shows flourish critically and commercially, and fan cultures find a voice for their own gender and sexual roles. On the other hand, when the gendered and sexualized heroic encoding achieves a negative effect in failing to satisfy fan expectations, which occurs in all four of my case studies, the shows are subject to widespread fan criticism. For instance, with the case of 1980s *Doctor Who*, which was subject to significant fan resistance, ratings gradually slipped, and the series ultimately was cancelled, while *Red Dwarf* and *Torchwood* have experienced negative critical reception, which may have slowed down the production of future seasons of these shows.[2] With *Blake's 7*, however, the company Big Finish produces audio and print merchandise spin-offs, and positive online fan support for a revival of the brand exists, but any proposed reboot that reimagines the show and does not continue its established continuity has been met with skepticism and opposition.

While what I am stating here applies to practically any TV show as viewers' levels of appreciation inevitably depreciate over a given course of time according to a number of variables[3] until a series is cancelled or retired, I am arguing that my four BBC cult SF shows under discussion represent modern heroic mythologies that transcend their roots as transitory media entertainment. Even if *Doctor Who, Blake's 7, Red Dwarf,* and *Torchwood* go off the air for a time, fan productions keep these brands alive, adding a legacy quality to them that entices encoder-producers interested in reviving any of their specific cult SF brands. To articulate this process, I am developing my own terminology by calling the reciprocal pull oscillating between encoders and decoders in any of these four unique media situations the *Continuum of Nostalgic Continuity* (CNC). Since a consistent (or slightly paradoxical[4]) continuity is important to fans of all four of these shows' developing or suspended mythologies, characters' personalities, gendered traits, and histories must be understood and maintained by the current or potential producer-encoders. Nostalgia, then, a powerful factor operating throughout this continuum, has been keeping these brands alive in the form of both decoder fan productions (original fiction, art, videos, blogs, cosplay, and conventions) that do not merely advance their economic and corporate influences and new encoder-produced seasons of some of the shows,[5] which, to a noticeable degree, cater to fan desires and expectations. At the same time, this nostalgia-focused and fueled adherence to these shows' mythologies locks them into somewhat rigid forms that cannot be significantly rebooted or reimagined. This book therefore argues that both the producer-encoders and the fan-decoders of *Doctor Who, Blake's 7, Red Dwarf,* and *Torchwood* are continually engaged in an ongoing act of media synergy and conflict that distinctively shapes and stalls their gendered heroic SF mythologies.

To focus my encoding/decoding understanding of the gendered heroic quests embarked upon in my four televised objects of study, I will, whenever it is pertinent to my discussion, be relying upon the heroic monomyth that Joseph Campbell develops throughout *The Hero with a Thousand Faces*. In this work, Campbell provides a classic formula representing the mythological adventurer's rite of passage: "separation–initiation–return." He writes, "*A hero ventures forth from the world of common day into a region of supernatural wonder: fabulous forces are there encountered and a decisive victory is won: the hero comes back from this mysterious adventure with the power to bestow boons on his fellow man*" (30). Although in a narrative sense, the worlds of *Doctor Who, Blake's 7, Red Dwarf,* and *Torchwood* may, at times, deal with any of the following SF tropes—the past, the future, body horror, or alien threats—they are allegorical and literal signs of the times. In short, "*the world of common day*" in which they are produced is reflected in the encoders' gendering and sexualization of the shows' characters (and of the worlds from which they emerge—like

Doctor Who's Gallifrey and versions of a futuristic Earth). In terms of the Campbellian "boons" these heroes (and, sometimes, villains) bring back to their respective civilizations, they work on a twofold level through the encoding/decoding of their quest narratives. On a heroically encoded textual level, for example, the Doctor often helps his female companions find their voices as heroes; the traditionally heroic Roj Blake temporarily defeats the evil Federation by the end of Series B; *Red Dwarf*'s Arnold Rimmer learns what it takes to be a masculine hero in the seventh season of the show; and *Torchwood*'s omnisexual Captain Jack, in the 2011 BBC/Starz coproduction, *Miracle Day*, sacrifices his cherished mortality to help humanity lose their problematic immortality. Through these plot elements, the shows could be either reaffirming or challenging traditional visions of gendered heroism inherent in many SF television shows and movies (i.e., the masculine hero saves the day with a helpful female at his side). Viewers then decode these texts through responses of joy, disgust, admiration, anger, dissatisfaction, confusion, or curiosity toward the televised heroic journeys.

Returning to *Doctor Who*, which debuted in 1963 with its remit to be a children's educational program, one can continue to explore it encoding roots. Cognizant of the show's power to shape young minds, creator Sydney Newman and producer Verity Lambert chose to cast an authoritative figure in their leading man with William Hartnell, who, at the time, had been best known for playing tough army sergeants. Hartnell's First Doctor, although an eccentric alien who travels the universe in a time-traveling police box that is infinitely bigger on the inside than outside, is an older gentleman who could readily fit the bill for an older, British empowered man of respect—a businessman, teacher, or politician—for this time period.

In the following two and a half decades of *Doctor Who*, depending on the incarnation (or actions in certain episodes) of this alien outsider who travels time and space and his respective relationships to his companions, the Doctor would both reinforce and reject British patriarchal and imperialistic values in his gendered behaviors and actions. More importantly, in relation to different production eras of the show, its fans either celebrate and empathize with the Doctor and his companions' characterizations, or actively campaign against these encoding choices. With this book, I will examine two of the show's eras, the latter 1980s and the present, to show what happens when fan resistance to the gendered encoding of the Doctor's ongoing heroic quest either helps the show succeed or fail in terms of lost ratings and fandom goodwill. In short, I will be arguing that *Doctor Who* fans' clout as critical decoders of these two iterations of the show more or less grants them the power of being de facto encoders of the series as well.

Although *Doctor Who* is ostensibly a child's show, the program does manage to provide a counterculture figure in its lead hero at times. For example, the Third Doctor allies himself with the hippie scientific commune, the Nut Hutch, in "The Green Death," and the Sixth Doctor vocally denounces the corruption of his people in part thirteen of "The Trial of a Time Lord." However, the encoding of the adult-viewer centered *Blake's 7* definitely provides a more rebellious, counterculture vision of BBC British heroism in its depiction of a band of thieves and convicts wielding a powerful alien starship, the Liberator, to fight against the corrupt Earth-run Federation. At the same time, the show depicts hypermasculinity in the form of the rivalry between Roj Blake, a magnetic resistance leader, and Kerr Avon, a near-sociopathic computer thief, and overt sexuality via the lead characters' various romances. Queerness likewise manifests itself with the sometimes androgynous Servalan and her sadistic leather-clad henchman, Travis. Over the years, *Blake's 7* fans, through slash fiction,[6] have decoded these depictions of sexuality to find queer overtones, thus adding their own interpretations of *Blake's 7*'s gendered heroic quest, which, at the same time, have alienated other members of fandom. Consequently, this ongoing decoding debate over whether or not the show serves as a kitsch, kinky period piece encapsulating late 1970s BBC SF perhaps affects the legacy and potential revival of this series. To properly reboot the series in an encoded manner that satisfies viewers and fans of the original *Blake's 7*, the latent sexuality must be present in the storytelling. However, since SF-fantasy television has progressed to the point where hetero and queer sex itself can be graphically depicted onscreen in shows such as *Torchwood* and *Game of Thrones*, *Blake's 7*'s once-innovative and playful presentation of such themes may appear passé.

Complementing and deviating from *Doctor Who* and *Blake's 7* is *Red Dwarf*, which is unique in the sense that it both serves as a sitcom and as an SF adventure. In its portrayal of Dave Lister, the last surviving human three million years in the future; Arnold Rimmer, a hologram of Lister's dead bunkmate; Cat, a humanoid descended from cats; and Kryten, their domestic robot, the show provides a mocking look at male British heroism and the heroic quest as these four mediocre-intelligence-level, posthuman males stumble their way through a chaotic universe not governed by empires or major economic structures. Like *Doctor Who* fans, *Red Dwarf* fans, depending on the tone of a specific series, either embrace or criticize the show. In other words, when the series deviates from its initial premise of comically looking at the last surviving human and his companions, it is widely criticized by fandom, which leads *Red Dwarf* co-creator Doug Naylor to change his encoding of the show's heroic quest. In short, the asymmetry of the fans' relationship to the *Red Dwarf*'s producers creates an imbalance in fandom's favor, meaning, in some ways, these decoders have become the show's encoders.

When compared with 1980s *Doctor Who* fans, whose essentially destructive efforts toward criticizing Nathan-Turner's encoding of the show (in)directly contributed to its demise, or *Blake's 7* fans' hyper-loyal adherence to the show's history, which could affect the critical reception of a potential revival—both manifestations of CNC—*Red Dwarf* fans are similar in demanding that their beloved core characters remain masculine and in charge of their ever-continuing heroic quests, whether they are drama- or comedy-based. On the one hand, these strong-willed efforts on the decoders' part may hinder the encoders' creative efforts toward invigorating a stale brand by adding new characters or narrative wrinkles to their specific SF television mythology, which could, in turn, hinder the act of attracting new viewer demographics, particularly in the potential form of younger, female, and LGBTQ fans. On the other hand, if the CNC-fan-generated influences on the encoding of a brand assure the commission of future series of a show and subsequent support in the form of positive online reviews and increased revenue (via DVD and spin-off merchandise sales) for the corporation producing the media product, one can contend that the synergy occurring between encoders and decoders has been mutually satisfying.

Soon running on a parallel track with the rebooted *Doctor Who* (2005) was the 2006 spin-off series *Torchwood*, featuring a group of top-secret paranormal/alien investigators headed by the polyamorous Captain Jack Harkness. In a similar manner to *Blake's 7*, *Torchwood's* heroic encoding proves that the show's producers are unafraid to kill off its lead characters on a regular basis. The only constant characters are Jack and Gwen Cooper, the former representing (at least in *Torchwood*) queer sexuality and the latter, heterosexuality and a heteronormative lifestyle away from the team. In reaction to *Torchwood's* open portrayal of queerness, LGBTQ fans have connected with the show, as seen in their scholarly and fan-based productions, most strikingly in the form of cosplay. At the same time, their decodings of the show's encoding of its gendered heroic quest have demonstrated their resistance to the series as it gradually deviates from the original premise of being set in Cardiff and featuring a queer romance between Jack and Ianto Jones, who was controversially killed off in *Torchwood: Children of Earth*. Like the encoding/decoding issues affecting the potential revival of *Blake's 7*, fan reception and criticism of *Torchwood* has had an effect on the possibility of a fifth season.

With the eighth season of the rebooted *Doctor Who*, the Doctor is now portrayed by Peter Capaldi, who is the same age as William Hartnell when he played the First Doctor in 1963. Because he is significantly older than David Tennant and Matt Smith, who played the Tenth and Eleventh Doctors, Capaldi's casting created fan criticism that the show is simply reinforcing traditional British patriarchal values. Despite the growing fan and media demand for a female actor in the role, the encoding of the gendering of the Twelfth Doctor's heroic quest has been striving to create another viable male vision of the Doctor—in this situation, one who both intentionally frustrates yet ultimately endears himself to his massive fan base.

Regarding the inherent power harnessed by a show's participatory fan culture, especially in the case of these *Doctor Who* fans, where the Continuum of the Nostalgic Continuity's devotional and gravitational pulling toward the past is being potentially overwritten by demands for new interpretations of a five-decade old patriarchal brand, one can turn to the work of adaptation theory scholar Linda Hutcheon, who writes, "We can be told or shown a story, each in a range of different media. However, the perspective, and thus the grammar, changes with the third mode of engagement; as audience members, we interact *with* stories in, for instance, the new media, from virtual reality to machinima" (22). Hutcheon's definition of this third mode of engagement articulates the difference between a reader who privately consumes a text and then formulates an opinion that is kept to oneself and one who discusses his or her thoughts with others in public, via mail, and eventually, over the telephone, which, of course, only offers a limited communicative means of voicing pleasure or criticism of a given text. Of course, with the proliferation of participatory fan cultures on the Internet, the opportunity to interface with other readers or television/movie viewers via discussion boards or instantaneous messaging shifted the balance of power between encoders and decoders. In other words, instead of the producer-corporate-encoders viewing the decoder-reader-viewers as compliant consumers, they are often obligated (or forced through fan and media-induced pressure) to acknowledge shared mass fandom criticisms of a particular book, episode, or movie installment of their object of devotion. Consequently, in some cases, this understanding of an organized fandom's displeasure toward a print or media product can lead to significant changes in the encoding direction of a brand with the hope of appeasing the reader-viewer-decoders with the ultimate goal of regaining lost critical and economic (i.e., revenue) support.

In her 2012 preface to the second edition of *A Theory of Adaptation*, Hutcheon, furthermore, comments upon this growing threat of fan decoding efforts to media conglomerates' (e.g., the BBC) hegemony over a property:

> Fan-generated content has exploded in recent years, and not only online, of course. Yet, when fans can remake their favourite films on minimal budgets ("sweding") and then distribute them on *YouTube*, who is in control? When they can adapt and thus personalize a video game to suit themselves, should its creators greet this with "cease and desist" letters or with joy at the free publicity? Fan loyalty can obviously translate into sales, but it can also pose a threat to control and ultimately to economic gain. When fans can not only view but remix, interact with, and share content, an argument can be made that individual agency has trumped textual fidelity, and with that, ownership rights. For better or worse, the new media are participatory media [XXV–XXVI].

With Hutcheon's thoughts in mind, one can declare that when the SF hero reflects the fans' value-driven and preformed expectations for gendered heroism, a show such as *Red Dwarf* or *Torchwood* delivers a satisfying completion (or partial fulfillment) of the hero's quest and can shape fandom's identity formations as their loyalty has been earned by a particular BBC brand. However, when fans believe the depicted heroism has become inadequate and/or offensive, they may reject the televised narrative and assert their quite vocal individual agency in the form of such participatory media as online zines, instant tweets, vidding, or original extrapolative fiction, which, in turn, serve as their counter-identity markers. When these forms of resistance have gathered enough contributors or followers, their combined critical efforts can be picked up by the news media, which may shape a negative portrayal of a brand's fandom to the non-fan community. This process can be seen in July 2009, when *Torchwood: Children of Earth* co-plotter James Moran received abusive tweets and death threats after Ianto Jones was killed off in "Day Four," which had been written by John Fay. When the media picked up this story, a vision of *Torchwood* fans as obsessive, rude, and potentially dangerous thus was formulated and promulgated.

In understanding Hutcheon's thoughts on the power of readers and viewers, one should also refer to Michel de Certeau's seminal definition of the operative cultural studies term, poaching, as found in *The Practice of Everyday Life*: "[R]eaders are travellers; they move across lands belonging to someone else, like nomads poaching their way across fields they did not write, despoiling the wealth of Egypt to enjoy it themselves" (174). Equally useful in understanding how fans feel comfortable appropriating, remixing, and mashing up media properties are de Certeau's thoughts on the actions of the reader: "[H]is place is not *here* or *there*, one or the other, but neither the one nor the other, simultaneously inside and outside, dissolving both by mixing them together, associating texts like funerary statues that he awakens and hosts, but never owns. In that way, he also escapes from the law of each text in particular, and from that of the social milieu" (174). Although de Certeau is talking about readers being able to escape "the law of each text," one can reverse this assertion by exploring what happens when their identities become inexorably linked to a text. For example, what happens when *Red Dwarf* fans take personal offense to encoding decisions made by the producers in latter series of the show? At the same time, *Doctor Who* or *Torchwood* cosplayers, depending on the particular convention venue, location, or time, may "remix" the texts of heroes, villains, and monsters together from their objects of devotion when sewing/constructing new costumes for each different persona they choose to embody.

Building on Certeau's theories, media scholar Henry Jenkins, writing on the subject of fan communities in *Textual Poachers*, declares, "Organized fandom is, perhaps first and foremost, an institution of theory and criticism, a semistructured space where competing interpretations of common texts are proposed, debated, and negotiated and where readers speculate about the nature of the mass media and their own relationship to it" (86). Essential in Jenkins's formulation of fans' readings and criticisms of a text is the theme of them discovering their own identities via these very media texts under oftentimes rigorous scrutiny—a theme that this book enthusiastically explores.

Mikhail Bakhtin's thoughts on reader reception and interpretation of a text is likewise useful in this work's discussion of various fan appropriations of such lucrative BBC media properties with transatlantic/global appeal as *Doctor Who, Blake's 7, Red Dwarf,* and *Torchwood*. In *The Dialogic Imagination*, Bakhtin, commenting on the process of "[t]he dialogic orientation of a word among other words" (275) occurring in the text of a novel, claims,

> [N]o living word relates to its object in a *singular* way: between the word and its object, between the word and the speaking subject, there exists an elastic environment of other, alien words about the same object, the same theme, and this is an environment that is often difficult to penetrate. It is precisely in the process of living interaction with this specific environment that the word may be individualized and given stylistic shape [276].

Extended to the subcultural sphere of BBC SF fan cultures, Bakhtin's thoughts of the elasticity of the *alien* word (a phrase which takes on a doubled meaning when applied to media SF worlds) articulates how each fan responds uniquely to his or her adored or despised source text. When, for instance, 1980s *Doctor Who* fans rebel against what they may consider a marginalizing, offensive text, Umberto Eco's definition of a "guerilla solution" for one's television viewing habits may become useful: "What must be occupied, in every part of the world, is the first chair in front of every TV set.... The battle for the survival of man as a responsible being in the Communications Era is not to be won where the communication originates, but where it arrives" (142). Although Eco wrote these words in 1967, they still apply to our multichannel, multiplatform genre television viewership. From a simple critical tweet to one's friends regarding a disappointing element projected in a favorite TV show to a full-length fan novel one posts online in order to correct the self-conceived "wrongs" one sees occurring in a given mythology arc that took a beloved character in a "disappointing" direction, one can realize Eco's call to action in the form of "fan guerilla warfare."

With these useful media theories in complementary play, my first chapter explores how Hall's encoding/decoding formulation works through the philosophical lens of phenomenology in relation to *Doctor Who*, *Blake's 7*, *Red Dwarf*, and *Torchwood*.

Chapter One

The Phenomenological Meanings of BBC Cult SF Headquarters and Objects

A blue police box that travels the totality of time and space; an appropriated alien starship that initially appears to be flying in the wrong direction; a red mining ship immense in length; and an underground lair that is a cross between a World War II bomb shelter and a high-tech lab—these settings are the mobile transports and headquarters that house the SF worlds of *Doctor Who*, *Blake's 7*, *Red Dwarf*, and *Torchwood*. Naturally, the gendered quest of many a mythological or SF hero involves a form of transport. In search of the Golden Fleece, Jason and his masculine compatriots travel aboard the Argo; the four still-effeminate children in *The Lion, the Witch and the Wardrobe* find passage to magical Narnia through a simple clothes wardrobe; the Wicked Witch of the West, arguably of the antifeminist tradition, rides a flying broomstick in *The Wizard of Oz*. All of these iconic images, either mobile or stationary, both shape and represent the gendered heroic or villainous characteristics of their users.

To aid in this understanding of how objects reflect gendered heroic identity in the four BBC shows under discussion, one can "turn" toward philosopher Edmund Husserl's work on phenomenology. In his work *Ideas*, Husserl expounds upon his phenomenological relationship to the world surrounding him:

> [W]hen consciously awake, I find myself at all times, and without my ever being able to change this, set in relation to a world which, through its constant changes, remains one and ever the same. It is continually "present" for me, and I myself am a member of it. Therefore this world is not there for me as a mere *world of facts and affairs*, but, with the same immediacy, as a *world of values*, a *world of goods*, a *practical world* [92–93].

For Husserl, humanity is caught within a paradoxically changing yet unchanging world. Correspondingly, *Doctor Who*'s TARDIS and *Red Dwarf*'s massive mining ship represent settings that both change and stay relatively the same during the duration of their shows. Applying Husserl's thoughts, one could say these two objects possess not only a utilitarian quality but an identity-shaping power as well. For example, although the Doctor's interior TARDIS space represents a mobile home and hearth to which he can retreat when he is not adventuring, its police box exterior becomes part of the identity he projects to the external world, especially when his eleventh self refers to himself as "a madman with a box." Likewise, for Dave Lister, the Red Dwarf represents a vessel through which he can voyage across the universe to search for Kristine Kochanski, his shipmate, yet it also shapes his identity in a posthuman world as it represents his home in lieu of an absent Earth.

On the qualities of the latter effect of objects, Husserl also writes,

> Without further effort on my part I find the things before me furnished not only with the qualities that befit their positive nature, but with value-characters such as beautiful or ugly, agreeable or disagreeable, pleasant or unpleasant, and so forth. Things in their immediacy stand there as objects to be used, the "table" with its "books," the "glass to drink from," the "vase," the "piano," and so forth. These values and practicalities, they too belong to *the constitution of the "actually present" objects as such*, irrespective of my turning or not turning to consider them or indeed any other objects [93].

It is in this "turning" in which one orients oneself to objects in the phenomenological methodology. In Sara Ahmed's application of Husserl's ideas toward what may be declared a heteronormative orientation, objects that are meeting places for the family, such as a table, possess straight edges that reflect the hierarchical lifestyle positioning of those sitting around it. However, Ahmed points out,

> Objects, as well as spaces, are made for some kinds of bodies more than others. Objects are made to size as well as made to order: while they come in a range of sizes, the sizes also presume certain kinds of bodies as having "sizes" that will "match." In this way, bodies and their objects tend toward each other; they are oriented toward each other, and are shaped by this orientation. When orientation "works," we are occupied. The failure of something to work is a matter of a *failed orientation*: a tool is used by a body for which it was not intended, or a body uses a tool that does not extend its capacity for action [51].

In this passage, Ahmed has effectively modified Husserl's approach to phenomenology by threading it through a queer lens by arguing that bodies that have failed to orient towards hetero bodies have done so on account of their gay sexual identities. This refinement can be granted another level of understanding in combination with Hall's encoding/decoding model. From an encoding standpoint, the various authors of *Doctor Who*, *Blake's 7*, *Red Dwarf*, and *Torchwood* bring their own gendered identities and backgrounds to their characterization and scripting of heroism in their assigned episodes of each series. If their vision of sexuality is predominately heteronormative, as seen in the various series of *Red Dwarf*, the straightness of the table at which they possibly write[1] matches their psychological and cultural (i.e., nature-nurture) predispositions for reinforcing straightness in their characters' choices and behavior. Conversely, if the authors/producers are gay, in the case of *Doctor Who* showrunners John Nathan-Turner and Russell T Davies, or straight and sympathetic to LGBTQ concerns in the example of showrunner Steven Moffat, who notably questioned heteronormativity as a given (or as a concept) when he created the interspecies lesbian couple, Madame Vastra, a Silurian, and Jenny, a human, with the Series Six episode "A Good Man Goes to War," this literal and figurative table represents a straight-edged object from which the author deviates in a creative sphere to craft alternate perspectives on sexual lifestyles.

Yet, as in the case of Moffat, who likewise demonstrates his orientation toward the straight edges of his writer's table when he offers traditional *Doctor Who* couplings with the Eleventh Doctor's companions, Amy Pond and Rory Williams, and the Twelfth Doctor's Clara Oswald and Danny Pink, traditional heteronormative values can be reinforced to a sexually diverse viewing audience. Regardless of one writer's gender and sexual orientation, the encoder-writer's table is always flexible in concept, and this potentiality, in regard to future SF television productions, will allow for new expressions of hetero, queer, and a diverse number of bisexual and posthuman natures in between.

Perhaps, then, the decoding end of this theoretically informed conception of the writer's table accurately represents a multitude of fan genders and sexualities. After all, when one statistically compares the select several dozen BBC showrunners- and writers-encoders composing *Doctor Who*, *Blake's 7*, *Red Dwarf*, and *Torchwood* to thousands, even millions, of fan-writer decoders, the potentiality for a greater societal gendered and sexual variety exponentially increases. Oriented toward or away from the edges of these encoders' literal and figurative tables, hetero and LGBTQ decoders will compose online reviews, original fiction, or blog musings that reflect either their acceptance or resistance to the episodic productions of their chosen SF television objects of devotion or revulsion.

The TARDIS: The Doctor's Hearth, Closet, or Pick-Up Vehicle?

In "An Unearthly Child," *Doctor Who*'s debut episode, the opening shot depicts a British patrol officer walking across the screen. Soon accompanying this organic representative of law and order in Great Britain at this time is an ostensibly inanimate object that the officer could likely utilize to call for backup assistance, or even, if necessary, as a temporary measure to detain prisoners within its structure—a police box. For millions of viewers, this object was still a familiar sight on London streets, a reassuring public signifier of law, order, trust, and safety. In a simple sense, it is an upright rectangular shape, painted blue, with a light atop it. Offering a phallic rendering of its form may be too basic, but the police box nonetheless provides a masculine shape reflective of an era in which predominately male police officers patrolled London streets.[2]

Within the narrative of "An Unearthly Child," Coal Hill School teachers Ian Chesterton and Barbara Wright travel to their enigmatic pupil Susan Foreman's address to find out it is actually a junkyard. Finding a police box in the middle of the junkyard, Barbara remarks on its vibrational properties while Ian declares, "It's alive!"—signaling to the audience that, in a greater sense, the fantastical object should be regarded as a character in its own right. The Doctor soon arrives upon the scene and denies any knowledge of Susan, but once Barbara and Ian hear the teenager's voice coming from inside the police box, they run into this vessel under the mistaken impression that he is perhaps holding the girl hostage. Of course, once they enter the object, they quickly discover that it is substantially bigger on the inside than the outside as it houses a control room with a hexagonal console and a revolving time rotor that is contained within a glass-like casing. An argument regarding Susan staying in the twentieth century then ensues between the two teachers and the Doctor, leading him to purposely hit a series of switches across the console, sending the group back in time to 10,000 BC. Subsequently, by the close of the adventure, the Doctor, functioning as a quasi–Prometheus, has restored the primitive Tribe of Gum's lost knowledge of drawing fire to them. In this instance, the Doctor's action is rather appropriate if one considers his very TARDIS control room to represent an encoded reflective hearth by which conservative British family values are affirmed and reinscribed to early-evening, all-ages family viewers who have gathered around in middle-class living rooms to witness the Doctor and his pseudo-family's televised weekly adventures.

In the subsequent season one episodes depicting the quartet's series of travels across time and space, the Doctor assumes the leader role while Ian, Barbara, and Susan serve as his three companions. But this dynamic also lends itself to that of an identifiable heteronormative family. As played by William Hartnell, the First Doctor is a grandfather, who, for never-revealed reasons, has been given charge of his granddaughter. At the same time, although he is an older gentlemen, he is not beyond flirting with the aging Aztec female Cameca and unwittingly becoming betrothed to her by sharing a ritualistic cup of cocoa in "The Aztecs" (1964).

From this gendered trajectory, the Doctor serves as the patriarchal head of his TARDIS family unit, with Ian and Barbara, both single yet straight, as his surrogate children, who assist the time traveler by looking out for and instructing their "adopted" daughter, Susan, in the ways of romance. With this extended-family dynamic in mind, a phenomenological rendering of the primary TARDIS space shown to early 1960s British viewers offers a reinforcement of heteronormative values in a domestic setting. Arguably, the TARDIS's roundels form an enveloping maternal backdrop to their adventures, in that their brightly glowing yet comforting orbs can be seen as an extension of the circular shapes of a female's breasts and pregnant belly. At the same time, the six sharp lines of the TARDIS console itself, in an application of phenomenology, reinforce contours of straightness. In other words, their hexagonal, rigidly sharp edges mirror the "straight" reproductive commitments of heterosexuality to which the Doctor, Barbara, and Ian subscribe.

At the conclusion of the six 1964 serials commonly known as "The Dalek Invasion of Earth," the Doctor double locks the exterior TARDIS doors to Susan, thus stranding her in the futuristic Dalek-devastated London of 2164. This time, the TARDIS, which Susan claims she named in "An Unearthly Child," now serves as an impenetrable fortress denying her access to her "family" as the Doctor forces her to stay with her new love, David Campbell, a resistance fighter who had been struggling against the Daleks. During his farewell speech to Susan from the interior of the TARDIS control room, he optimistically tells his granddaughter, "One day I shall come back. Yes, I shall come back. Until then, there must be no regrets, no tears, no anxieties. Just go forward in all your beliefs and prove to me that I am not mistaken in mine." On a simple level, the Doctor is saying that both of them (and the audience, by extension) must follow their dreams. However, from a more complicated gendered perspective, he is coercing Susan into going "forward" (i.e., in a *straight* line) in a heterosexual, Western culture vision of a nine-to-five reproductive lifestyle with a human as he retains the freedom to travel all of time and space, with or without companions—or lovers. Even more problematic is his promise to "come back" and check on Susan someday, which can be construed as his reminder to carry out the reproductive demands of her chosen hetero lifestyle.[3] In an early 1960s Britain, which was on the cusp of a massive youth social change, the Doctor's choice words and speech, spoken from the safety and security of his technological hearth in an address performed toward the viewers' perspective, can be seen as behavior that encodes traditional British cyclical family values of marital love and subsequent reproduction. At the same time, they are curiously alien, and anti-extended family in tone, as he rationalizes abandoning Susan on a future Earth so that she can properly love her chosen mate. But the act of heterosexual love being the catalyst for a companion's departure from the Doctor continues when Barbara and Ian later leave together at the conclusion of "The Chase" (1965) in a manner heavily hinting that they are reiterating the classic romantic narrative trope of the couple living happily ever after. As a result, the six pronounced straight-lines of the TARDIS console have been symbolically successful in pointing out the eventual heteronormative trajectory of the show's original supporting cast.

When *Doctor Who*'s 1973–74 production team had the Third Doctor first grant a feminine identity to the TARDIS by referring her to as "old girl" in "The Time Warrior," they were following the established British naval tradition of granting ships female names. For the Doctor, it is a term of endearment, reflecting his admiration for the TARDIS when she functions according to his technical expectations for her. In a way, she has been elevated to the position of nonhumanoid companion. But she later takes on a more distinct maternal role in the opening season nineteen adventure, "Castrovalva," which features twenty-nine-year-old Peter Davison[4] debuting in the role of the Fifth Doctor. Caught in a post-regenerative crisis, this addled Doctor is in search of the palliative Zero Room. To accomplish this goal, he acts like a wounded child wishing to return to his cybernetic mother's bosom or womb, casting off his older-looking predecessor's several layers of burgundy-hued clothing as he dons the soft, white-tan colors dominating the youthful garb of an English cricketer.[5] When he finally finds his destination—the Zero Room, which is visually depicted as an open space with large roundels lit with pinkish-gray hues— the Doctor, who immediately regains his former composure in this space, is soon levitating on his back to gain necessary sleep. At the same time, through telepathic communication, which is somehow facilitated by the TARDIS, he is once more directing his companions, Tegan and Nyssa, in a controlling (i.e., patriarchal) manner to which they and the viewers are accustomed by utilizing their respective coordinative and technical skills to keep their newfound "family" together. Paradoxically, the blending of the Zero Room's maternal scenery tells viewers that this heroic iteration of the Doctor is more sensitive and vulnerable. As a result, the TARDIS has effectively been reencoded as a feminized, mother-like caregiver.

Although Peter Davison had attracted a strong female fandom from playing veterinarian Tristan Farnon in another BBC drama, *All Creatures Great and Small*, and his character of the Fifth Doctor was surrounded by young, beautiful female companions in the form of Tegan, Nyssa, and Peri, producer John Nathan-Turner instituted a "no hanky-panky" rule in the 1980s TARDIS. This encoding choice lasted throughout Nathan-Turner's tenure as producer until the show's cancellation in 1989. Without barely a hint of overt heterosexual encoding, the Fifth, Sixth, and Seventh Doctors, then, altogether function as a backward-looking recapitulation of the sexless British establishment hero. Put another way, in the era of the 1980s, when the SF masculine lead of television and films[6] is frequently being encoded as a virile male, the Doctor preserves his relatively family-friendly roots as a hero, who, while once capable of heterosexual reproduction as he is a grandfather, seems to be symbolically retaining his former elderly impotence by never engaging in romantic or sexual liaisons with any of his companions, female guest stars, or villains.

From this eliding of sexuality in an era when fantasy action heroes regularly romanced women,[7] one can ask, "Does *Classic Who*[8] suggest that the TARDIS is the Doctor's closet, thereby hinting at his repressed homosexuality, or is he simply a sexless hero?" This question, of course, will be discussed in greater depth with the following chapter, which points out that when *Doctor Who* becomes more colorful (i.e., arguably queer) in this flamboyant 1980s production period, with the bright garbs of the Fifth, Sixth, and Seventh Doctors, which complement the tone of many of the stories and their production design, the show's ratings generally decline until its cancellation in 1989. As fans have argued over the years, Nathan-Turner's gay lifestyle indicators of admiring light entertainment performers and producing Christmas pantomimes irrevocably affected the encoding of his *Doctor Who* era. Likewise pertinent to this gradual loss of viewership were the fan group who produced the fanzine *Doctor Who Bulletin*, which published such incendiary headlines as "JN-T Must Go Now," "BBC Solicitors Act for JN-T," and "And the 'New' Producer is ... John Nathan-Turner,"[9] which were picked up and promoted by the British media. For that reason, this chapter will explore if this and other instances of fan resistance articulated their belief that the Doctor failed to either represent and/or resist his traditional dualistic role of British imperial and counterculture hero. Put another way, I will look at what happens when the Doctor's gendered heroic quest becomes one that is decidedly less masculine than that of the first four Doctors. Via the Continuum of Nostalgic Continuity, I am also considering how a 2013 BBC online production, *The Five(ish) Doctors Reboot*, which was directed by Peter Davison, relates to contemporary encoding/decoding views on this era, which, in many ways, has been queered by current showrunner Steven Moffat (in the sketch "Time Crash") and by the fans themselves via slash fiction productions.

Returning to the image of the TARDIS, a general survey of TARDIS images under the key term "TARDIS dress" shows how the upright, phallic blue box exterior has been reworked to express the more delicate, rounded contours of the female form. Initially, through convention cosplay and DIY (Do it yourself) and DIO (Do it with others) sewing efforts, contemporary female *Doctor Who* fans have, one can rather confidently argue, correctly decoded the TARDIS's exterior police box shell as signifying femininity.[10] This is not to say that female *Doctor Who* fans during the late 1970s and the 1980s did not interpret the TARDIS as a feminine object. But, as many historical photos of those era capture predominately male *Doctor Who* fans dressing up like the Doctor, and his male companions, UNIT[11] allies, and enemies, amongst a sundry of what amounted to early cosplay decoding efforts, a totalizing verdict could be cautiously rendered that *Classic Who* fandom was phallocentric and reinforced the patriarchal-encoded foundation of the show. For these male fans, straight or gay, the first seven incarnations of the Doctor served as embodiments of a foppish heroism, of a male who was on a mission to not just repeatedly save all of creation but also to better understand his own gendered identity.

The Liberator and the Scorpio: Luxury Versus No-Frills Living on *Blake's 7*

In *Blake's 7*'s first episode, "The Way Back," which aired on January 2, 1978, the audience was introduced to a seemingly unlikely hero: Roj Blake. Amnesiac in regard to his past as a freedom fighter, Blake immediately upholds the "refusal" quotient of Joseph Campbell's heroic call to action formula. However, a friend from his former life, Bran Foster, reminds him of his past, which reawakens his memories and motivates him to attend a resistance meeting, which turns out to be a setup by the corrupt, totalitarian Federation. During Blake's subsequent trial, he is framed not as a rebel, but as a child molester. Unlike *Doctor Who* of this era, which, despite its often frightening scenarios, offers a somewhat trustworthy adult figure in the form of the Fourth Doctor, who travels around with a fellow Time Lord, Romana, and a mechanical dog, K9—all child-friendly fare—*Blake's 7* presents a lead who is unfairly being accused of sexually corrupting children. With this grittier character encoding, Terry Nation (*Blake's 7*'s creator), producer David Maloney, script editor Chris Boucher, and the various directors of the show's episodes established and entertained a target audience that was not primary children but older viewers.

In other words, *Blake's 7* is about inverted encoding SF television formulations or an inverse *Star Trek*, if one will. While the original *Star Trek* presents the adventures of Captain James T. Kirk and his crew, who are serving the benevolent Federation of Planets aboard the starship Enterprise, *Blake's 7* flips this formula on its head by having its titular character and his crew of criminals fighting against a malevolent Earth government, also called the Federation, via the Liberator, an all-powerful alien starship. Even the model design of the Liberator, with its trio of needle-like engines protruding forth alongside its main hull is anti–*Star Trek* via its design. In comparison, the Enterprise's saucer section projects forward, upon its lower hull, and in front of its two port nacelle engines—an image that Liberator designer Roger Murray-Leach was consciously trying to avoid copying. He remarks, "I turned the ship around, so it was drawn to look as though it was going one way, but flew the other way. In fact, if you take the line of flow, the angles go with it to give it a sense of speed, and we turned that around so the 'wings' all canted forwards not backwards" (qtd. in Nazzaro and Wells 14). Murray-Leach's choice of words, "the line of flow," lends itself to a phenomenological reading as the appropriated Liberator houses a predominately male crew (Blake, Avon, Vila, and Gan [Plus, the ship's computer, Zen, and the sentient computer box, Orac][12]) with only Jenna and Cally representing the female members of the group. While these crewmembers do not actively engage in romantic liaisons with one another, there are subtly encoded moments in which heterosexual jealousy is expressed.

Similarly casting a Freudian lens upon the Liberator's design gives the ship a predatory phallic intensity as it wages war against the Federation, which is characterized by its equally phallic pursuit ships and in one of its major leaders, Supreme Commander Servalan, a glamorous yet androgynous female. In order to successfully wage a guerrilla war against these patriarchal warships, the Liberator paradoxically serves as a weapon for peace and destruction as its crew stealthily flies this vessel to free the people of an oppressed Earth and numerous Federation planets but often pragmatically resorts to employing its formidable weaponry as a destructive counterweight to the pursuit ships' masculine retaliatory might.

Murray-Leach's statement that the Liberator "was drawn to look as though it was going one way, but flew the other way" is equally applicable to the encoded sexuality of the crew housed within its peculiarly-designed hull. Regarding the interior of the Liberator, for an appropriated ship used to wage war against an all-powerful galactic government, it is curiously luxurious. Like the six-sided TARDIS console, hexagonal shapes are inherent to the design of the ship's interior, forming passageways and windows. Viewed via phenomenology, these shapes reinforce the straight-edged heterosexual encoding of the crew and remind the viewer that despite these characters' criminal or questionable histories, they are, in the end, traditionally heroic in their actions and gendered identities. For Zen, the ship's computer, who speaks in a deep male voice, Murray-Leach designed a large crescent, dome-like form on the wall, framed by a hexagonal shape. He remarks, "We needed the computer to be omnipresent and could be referred to easily so the characters could address it without just staring into space" (qtd. in Nazzaro and Wells 14). Although Zen serves the Liberator crew, they are oriented in their command chairs to see the flickering lights on his dome flash to the sound of his voice, which reinforces the patriarchal structure of their human chain of command: Blake, followed by his rival, Avon. Additionally, the hexagonal frame surrounding Zen orients him and his masters toward straightness, or heterosexuality.

In addition to his idea of Zen being a prop that could be addressed by Blake's crew, Murray-Leach claims,

> The other concept was the way people might sit or work at their station when they had a choice of how heavy they were in space. Rather than put everyone in chairs, I thought it might it might be fun if we gave them a completely different seating position, which we did. It was almost like a bicycle saddle with a back rest, that you straddled, which led to a quite a few ribald comments, particularly from the female crew [qtd. in Nazzaro and Wells 14].

Although Murray-Leach's commentary on the chair design points out the female crew's perceived suggestive sexuality on the encoding end, the five chairs themselves possess a rather pointed phallic design reinforced by the triangular yellow lighting that rises up behind these objects. As a result, the phallocentric emphasis of the Liberator's exterior is matched by its interior design elements, reinforcing a patriarchal encoding.

In front of the ship's command chairs sits a lounge area akin to a rec-room, where the crew in Series A to C can be often seen sharing friendly banter. Like the TARDIS console room, this set, which one could compare to the permanent, primary standing sets utilized in sitcoms, serves as the stage for the reinforcement of the values that are shared by a group of unlikely friends who essentially function as a family. Through this lens,

Blake, despite his traditional attempts at fighting the Federation, which become increasingly terroristic over the course of Series A and B, could still be viewed as a driven father figure, one who makes tough decisions to keep his criminally inclined crew in order—or going in an ostensibly heroic straight line.

His patriarchal leadership is similarly reflected in the phallic-like shape of the weapons his crew finds aboard the ship inside the teleport chamber. Possessing the destructive firepower of a *Star Wars* blaster, yet more elongated in its blaster tip, like the Doctor's sonic screwdriver, this form of weapon, wielded by both Blake's male and female crew members, turns them toward the phallic overtones of the object's shape while offering an equal playing field in harnessing and releasing its explosive firepower. Yet these weapons are balanced out gender-wise by another object they utilize in this chamber: the rounded teleport bracelets. These objects, which possess a circular feminine shape, reflect their nurturing function as a de facto technological umbilical cord that forms a literal lifeline to the Liberator, since, without them being safely positioned on the crew's wrists, Blake and his comrades cannot either communicate with each other from a distant location or be teleported back to the vessel.

Once Gareth Thomas, who played Blake, and Sally Knyvette (Jenna) departed the series before Series C began, along with their barely-hinted-at romance, Avon became the central character of the show, commanding a Liberator housing young and attractive new crewmembers, Dayna and Tarrant. Thus, the gendered heroic encoding of the show was still centered on characters with heterosexual inclinations,[13] who, whether intended to or not, reflect the family values and antigay policies of a Margaret Thatcher–run 1980s Great Britain. The Liberator itself becomes an extension of Avon, as Servalan lusts to control both the craft and its commander. By once more applying a phenomenological lens, one can argue that the ship's crew is turned toward its straight lines, while their enemy, Servalan, and by extension, her phallic-like pursuit ships, are turned toward the ship as well.

In the Series C finale, "Terminal," which was thought at the time of its March 31, 1980, broadcast to be the conclusion of the series until it was given a last-minute reprieve by the BBC at the end of the episode's transmission, Servalan at last gains control of the Liberator. As she boards the ship with her entourage, however, she is oblivious to the contamination caused by the vessel's exposure to a deadly space cloud. Though the ship is literally bubbling with decay, she resumes her antiheroic journey of taking back her control of the Federation by ordering her boarding crew to set the ship for Earth. After she confidently exclaims the words, "Main drive—Maximum power!" and extends her arms to the level of her head while standing before a command station, the ship begins to break up, one of the phallic-like ship engines spinning off into space. On a basic encoded level, the villain receives her "just desserts" as her coveted object proves to be the apparent means to her demise.[14] Seen through a gendered, phenomenological lens, Servalan's feminine amassing of the ship's power, as she turns toward an object that grants one control of its functions—the command station—results in the sickened object's emasculation—or castration—as the destruction of the fan-beloved vessel is achieved through a series of long shots witnessed by both them and Avon's crew from an underground scientific lair on the planet below. While one can argue that Servalan represents the continuation of a long line of antifeminist villains in that she represents a figure whose very touch corrupts that which it is turned toward, she can also be decoded as a powerful, castrating force that cannot be defeated by her predominately male enemies, whether they are a part of Blake/Avon's crew or the fractured Federation throughout the entirety of the series.

As for the fans' feelings toward the legacy of the Liberator, their decoding efforts are on copious display throughout the Internet. Computer-generated and illustrative images abound on blog and fan sites, often depicting the vessel realistically (as far as a CGI or painted replication of a BBC model can be deemed so) and respectfully. Numerous fan artists even appropriate and augment the Liberator's design by using it as a base from which they create modern extrapolations of its form with both "updated" iterations of its shape and new vessels. As a result, the *Blake's 7* fan base's shared reverence for the Liberator's iconic phallocentric design strongly hints that any modern revitalization—or reboot—of the series should perhaps be cautious by encoding the general original shape of this ship into any reimaged version. In short, like the J.J. Abrams–directed *Star Trek* (2009) reboot and Syfy's *Battlestar Galactica* series,[15] which have incorporated classic design elements for their relative spacecraft in order to satisfy longtime fans, *Blake's 7*'s future producers should potentially follow suit. But the bigger issue arising from this fan-decoder adherence to *Blake's 7*'s classic Liberator design is that it provides another Continuum of Nostalgic Continuity example—in this case, fans' slavish indoctrinated devotion to the original designs for *Blake's 7*, and, by natural extension, its core characters and seasonal story arcs, thereby relegating the show to a time capsule of kitsch BBC 1970s SF. Conversely, this fan-driven devotion to *Blake's 7*'s original Liberator design, on a greater note, could be showcasing the inherent power of decoders in both establishing and demanding a litany of elements that must be included as the nucleus for any successful reboot of a cult SF brand.

In Series D, the fourth and final season of *Blake's 7*, the Liberator is replaced by a substantially smaller ship, the Scorpio. Situated closer together in the plain, predominately gray-and-white interior hull of the Scorpio, which forms a stark contrast to the warm-colored visual luxury of their former craft, Avon's crew find themselves on the run from a renewed Federation. In contrast to the Liberator, this ship does not possess a self-regenerative function, is not vast in size, and, most significantly, does not contain a storeroom of valuable jewels. Replacing Zen is Slave, the Scorpio's sycophantic ship's computer, who addresses each of the crew as "master" and is visualized as tall and phallic-shaped with a rounded, spinning middle section from which it communicates, which simultaneously posits the machine as being "pregnant" with messages for the crew. As for the exterior of the ship, like the Liberator, it possesses a phallic shape aerodynamically designed for acceleration. Furthermore, while the Scorpio, like the Liberator, has a teleport function, it does not supply weaponry for the crew, as they now utilize pistol-like weapons, closer in design to a *Star Wars*–type blaster. But the ship is not their sole living quarters as they utilize the appropriated Xenon Base as both a home and as an ultimately failed meeting place for forming a greater alliance against their powerful enemy, the Federation. As a result, objects, in this final season, while reinforcing the family-like structure of the group, also serve as a failed means to the phallocentric end of defeating Servalan and the rapidly rebuilding Federation, upon which she is desperately trying to resume leadership. In other words, Avon's motley crew's alignment toward heteronormative heroism is not strong enough to defeat the weapons-wielding, leather-clad Federation soldiers who gun them down in the closing moments of "Blake," the finale of the show, which was controversial because the evil faceless Federation soldiers seemingly triumphed over the well-meaning but increasingly outmatched heroes.[16]

Building upon these themes, the third chapter of this book will therefore trace how gender and identity inherent in the characterizations of the rebels and the Federation forces challenge or reflect heteronormative gender roles. It shall likewise connect with the second chapter by showing how *Blake's 7* complements and deviates from *Doctor Who* in its heroic characterizations. Also relevant to this chapter's argument will be *Blake's Junction 7*, an officially-sanctioned fifteen-minute parody film that imagines the *Blake's 7* crew stopping at the contemporary mundane location of a rest stop. Interestingly, Servalan is performed by a male actor, Mackenzie Crook, while Avon and Blake, two ostensibly hetero characters, experience an "awkward" queer moment in a men's room. The gender politics of *Blake's 7* are thus both celebrated and playfully mocked in this production that points out the contemporary camp resonance of the show and which can be compared to chapter two's thoughts on *The Five(ish) Doctors Reboot*. Moreover, this official parody, which was produced by B7 Enterprises, will work well in comparison to *Blake's 7* fan fiction, audio, and video decoding efforts.

Red Dwarf: A Serious Romantic Quest Disguised Under a Male Comedy?

Several years after *Blake's 7* ended its run, *Red Dwarf*, which was created by Rob Grant and Doug Naylor, and made its BBC Two debut on February 15, 1988. While both shows would depict their lead characters becoming the proprietors of large powerful ships, *Red Dwarf*, an SF comedy, offers an unlikely hero in the form of Dave Lister, whose quest is more existential and romantic than political and bellicose like Blake and Avon's. *Red Dwarf*'s city-sized titular ship itself, almost jokingly endless in its lengthy design as the camera pans across its hull in the show's opening and closing credits, is encoded with an immense masculinity. On the Red Dwarf model's design elements, Peter Wragg, a member of the BBC Special Effects Department, comments,

> It had a ram scoop on the front which was like a hoover and collected debris from space. And then we added on things as we went along, feeling that maybe a meteorite had hit it at some stage.... One of the shots I did like was the end closing credits where you move into the front of it, then up over the top, then run along the top of it, then over the end of it and it makes it look as if it's going on for quite a long way [qtd. in Killick 23].

An obvious influence on this closing credits shot is the opening moments of *Star Wars: A New Hope*, in which an Imperial Star Destroyer's massive triangular underbelly is captured in a long shot as it gradually fills the screen in its pursuit of the tiny Rebel Blockade Runner ship. While *Red Dwarf* is similarly employing motion-control special effects to relay the image of the show possessing respectable model work, it is also reminding viewers that its almost-endless presentation of the Red Dwarf ship's exterior in the end credits once more encodes it as a comedic reworking of more dramatic 1980s cinematic fare as presented in the *Star Trek* and *Star Wars* movies of that era. Unlike the more functional male buddy duos of Captain Kirk-Mr. Spock and Luke Skywalker-Han Solo, who interact in the Starship Enterprise and Millennium Falcon respectively, the double act of Dave Lister-Arnold Rimmer, housed in the gigantic Red Dwarf, presents a dysfunctional, neurotic, antiheroic vision of masculinity that is "dwarfed" by their mode of transport. This encoding choice is reinforced by the fact that the Red Dwarf, a Jupiter Mining Corporation ship, as established in the show's first episode, "The End," was built to house hundreds of officers and crew members in order to carry out the rather mundane task of mining minerals in space.

Three million years later, however, as depicted in the same episode, after an accidental radiation leak had long ago wiped out the ship's crew, Dave Lister, the last surviving human, is awakened from stasis by the ship's computer, Holly. From this point, his unplanned heroic quest, prompted by his unrequited love for Kochanski, begins as he seeks a way to be reunited with her. On this quest, he is joined by Cat, who is descended from a race of cats, and later by Kryten, an android who doubles as their caretaker. They are also assisted by the bumbling ship's computer, Holly, who is played by a male actor, Norman Lovett, in *Red Dwarf I–II*, and then by a female actor, Hattie Hayridge, in *Red Dwarf III–V*. With *Red Dwarf VI*, however, Grant and Naylor decided to scale back their setting by separating the crew from the Red Dwarf and placing them in the more intimate environment of the smaller spacecraft, Starbug, a class two, ship to surface vessel. Like the scaled-down craft that is *Blake's 7*'s Scorpio, *Red Dwarf*'s Starbug places Dave Lister and company in situations in which they cannot depend upon the safety and luxury of a large, powerful ship. The Starbug itself, as a mobile object, had to be reoriented, or reencoded, to reflect the crew's new domestic setting, upon which *Red Dwarf* designer Mel Bibby comments, "The cockpit looks the same ... but it's actually much bigger than it was before. [The ship] still has the same basic shape, but there are other sections built in" (qtd. in Howarth and Lyons 120). Additionally, according to Chris Howarth and Steve Lyons, "An airlock, a kitchen and a whole upper floor had to be added" to the Starbug set (120). With this more intimate, yet domestic setting, which is somewhat similar to the former standing sets for the Red Dwarf's various quarters, the characters, although ostensibly bumbling, reluctant heroes, are, at the core, oriented toward objects that encode them with domestic traits that contain equal feminine and masculine gender values. In other words, although Lister may be encoded a slob, he and his crewmates must cook, clean, and sleep in a ship that doubles as their home.

In *Red Dwarf VIII*, the heteronormative-encoded roots of the show are reinforced by the nanobots' resurrection of the long-dead original Red Dwarf crew. Though Lister's desire to find "home"—Earth—had been partially fulfilled in him being reunited (although in an unrequited romance sense) with a parallel universe version of Kochanski in *Red Dwarf VII* and with his crewmates in *Red Dwarf VIII*, he has lost the heroic distinction of being the last surviving human. Fans, nevertheless, were resistant to this encoding choice, which more or less was rectified in *Red Dwarf: Back to Earth* and *Red Dwarf X*, as Kochanski has once more gone missing and the show's default status quo of four male characters being oriented toward an extraordinarily large mining ship has been restored. Whether or not this formula is modified with the upcoming *Red Dwarf XI* and *XII*, remains to be seen as announcements on the encoding choices are released—or leaked—to the media by the show's producers and/or fans. With these ideas in mind, this work's fourth chapter will argue that *Red Dwarf* fans will only accept Lister's (non)heroic quest when it is told through the lens of mostly lighthearted comedy. When compared to the more serious drama of modern *Doctor Who* and *Torchwood* (and, before them, *Blake's 7*), which also include camp elements, a different perspective is rendered concerning gendered heroic quests.

The Hub: *Torchwood*'s Closet

In the debut episode of *Torchwood*, "Everything Changes," Captain Jack and new acquaintance Gwen Cooper step upon a descending lift to the Hub while a cloaking device renders the two future teammates invisible from anyone who is topside the Torchwood organization's underground headquarters. For a hideout, the Hub, in this sense, is akin to Batman's Batcave, a mysterious underground hideout in which the Dark Knight Detective solves crimes and stores his various weaponry, trophies from cases (which include a giant penny and an amusement park dinosaur), and assault vehicles. On the one hand, for Bruce Wayne's crime-fighting alter ego, the dark, murky crevices of his Batcave orient his aggressive masculinity that borders on the side of repressed psychotic violence masquerading as vigilante heroism. Captain Jack's "cave," on the other hand, is more brightly lit with modern, smooth metallic support beams, which could be seen as objects that orient him and other bi-curious members of the team (Ianto, Owen, and Tosh) toward queer desire and romance. At the same time, vestiges of the fantastic, or prehistoric, are made apparent with the Hub's pet pterodactyl, which could represent the truth that the safe underground world of comradery and shared sexual experimentation that Jack has constructed can only exist below the commerce-driven, heteronormative-oriented society of Cardiff topside.

Commenting on the design ethos behind the Hub is the BBC production designer for *Torchwood*, Edward Thomas: "We tried to make the Hub as visually exciting as we could, with all those layers of Victoriana and contemporary modernism, to reflect the history of the organisation. Just as scripts have many layers, it's our job to put many layers into the sets" ("Grand Designs" 20). *Torchwood* indeed is also a "layered" show in terms of its gendered characterizations. Seen through the lens of phenomenology, the encoding of the sets serves as a reinforcement of the lead characters' sexual orientation. Captain Jack, although declaring himself omnisexual, has been depicted as mostly engaging in homosexual parings on *Torchwood*, most noticeably with teammate Ianto Jones. In a few instances, Jack's queer lifestyle is oriented toward his setting. Firstly, he lives in a subterranean bedroom, through which he enters via a hatch. On this design choice, Thomas and *Torchwood* series designer Julian Luxton declare, "Russell [T Davies] always wanted Jack to live in the Hub, but not necessarily have a full-on bedroom. We know from *Doctor Who* and hints about his military past that he's used to sleeping in vehicles and barracks, so the idea of an underground bunk with a submarine-style hatch seemed to fit that. I think we've only ever seen him down there once" ("Grand Designs" 19). In addition to living in his underground bedroom, a metaphor for his queer sexuality, Jack engages in lovemaking with Ianto in the Hub's hothouse, an act which is accidently witnessed by Gwen in the episode "Adrift." Thomas and Luxton likewise offer their thoughts on the design of the hothouse, which debuted in the show's second series:

> We decided this year that there should be somewhere the team could use as a quiet area, where they could have time alone, or talk on a one-to-one basis. So with the old boardroom vacant, we started to think about what would look good—and what could be better than alien flowers? It makes things visually more interesting, and it adds some colour, as well as making it feel a little more private and secluded, like a sci-fi potting shed ["Grand Designs" 16].

As far as choosing the hothouse as the setting for Jack and Ianto's sexual tryst, its "private and secluded" aspects most likely influenced the *Torchwood* production team's encoding decision to use it to stage Gwen's discovery of her two teammates' hitherto "closeted" queer affair.

This vision of the Hub being a place out of time, basically, a spacious queer closet, is further reinforced by the appearance of the turn-of-the-century Victorian bricks and mortuary slabs built in the early twentieth-century. In fact, when Jack himself, unbeknownst to his past self, cryogenically sleeps in one of these slabs for nearly a hundred years, as revealed in the Series Two finale, "Exit Wounds," his queer lifestyle is effectively doubled in its psychological and physical complexity. For the first two series that aired on BBC Two, the encoding of the Hub as the Torchwood team's base of operations and place for friendly banter lent the show a familiar episodic television setting for weekly viewers. Conversely, when *Torchwood* made the jump to the more prestigious BBC One with the five-part miniseries, *Children of Earth*, which aired in July 2009, the Hub (to many viewers) was shockingly destroyed in the first episode. In many ways, this controversial encoding decision begins a gradual shift away from the Cardiff roots of the series, and, in turn, unwittingly generates serious fan criticisms of the show that only grow in intensity when the show experiences unprecedented accelerated media success in its fourth season via an America-centric, BBC/Starz coproduction titled *Torchwood: Miracle Day*.

Considering these fan criticisms, the fifth chapter of this book will equally explore how *Torchwood*'s encoding of queer relationships has generated substantial fan reactions and productions on the decoding end, significantly through cosplay in that its bi male characters represent objects of identification for gay and lesbian fans alike as male characters such as Captain Jack and Captain John have been cosplayed by both sexes. However, gay lifestyle portrayals do not account for a majority of *Torchwood*'s substantial fan base, which will lead to my analysis of how the show transcends a simple queer branding, on both the encoding and decoding ends. Moreover, in a similar manner to *Blake's 7*, the show serves as a counterpoint for *Doctor Who* as it features heroes who are routinely killed off and do not achieve total victories over their foes. The show also, as a counterpoint to *Blake's 7*'s veiled queerness, uniquely presents sympathetic lead queer characters in the form of Captain Jack, Ianto Jones, and Captain John. At the same time, these troubled visions of heroic masculinities are complemented by more altruistic female characters. For a show presenting alternative sexualities, it is worrying that its encoding nonetheless maintains a static vision of the male-dominated heroic quest.

Doctor Who Reborn: *Nü Who*'s Romantic Doctor and Maternal TARDIS

Returning the Doctor to the British airwaves in 2005 as the guilt-ridden PTSD survivor of the obliterated Time Lord race powerfully resonated with viewers of the new series. In stark contrast to the original series, *NüWho*, as it is affectionately called by the fans, presents a dramatically sexualized Doctor who struggles with his free reign as an all-powerful traveler of time and space. However, the answer as to why a prominent number of female fans have embraced this new series of *Doctor Who* is a complex one that could be quickly reduced to two facts: One, the Ninth, Tenth, and Eleventh Doctors are respectful, sensitive, heroic, and, most importantly, romantic interpretations of the Time Lord. Two, the female companions are empowered and well-rounded characters. The formulation of these two reductive points is not to say that some (or mostly all) of these characteristics did not exist in the classic series, but the bottom line concerning showrunner Russell T Davies's and successor Steven Moffat's encoding of the series is that the TARDIS functions as the Doctor's "pick-up" ship (or vehicle) with which he can flirt with such companions as Rose Tyler and Clara Oswald while rejecting the advances of Martha Jones and Amy Pond. In more recent seasons of *NüWho*, against many cynical fans' expectations, the *Classic Who* dynamic of mentor–Doctor traveling through time and space with his platonic companion,[17] has been reinitiated with the Twelfth Doctor's era, which will form the basis for chapter six's discussion.

In that chapter, I will analyze how, amidst a growing media and fan demand for a female Doctor, Moffat chose instead to cast Peter Capaldi, the oldest actor in the lead role since William Hartnell. He has also established Coal Hill School (from "An Unearthly Child") as a semi-regular setting for the show and included, in apparent homage to *Doctor Who*'s original cast, two teachers, Clara and her colleague/love interest Danny Pink, and a student, Courtney Woods, from the school. At the same time, Danny, a former soldier suffering from PTSD, serves as both a rival to Clara's affections and a critic of the Doctor's elitist manner, which he frequently compares to the behavior of an uncaring officer class. The question of whether or not these spatial and casting choices retain the patriarchal roots inherent in the Doctor's heroic quest will inform my discussion of how the show cyclically echoes its original cast dynamic (one Doctor, three companions). Working with John Tulloch and Manuel Alvarado's formulation in *Doctor Who: The Unfolding Text* that the 1963 cast dynamic is echoed in the 1982 season (featuring the Fifth Doctor and his three companions), I will explore how the pairing of the Twelfth Doctor and his several companions continues this cyclical casting pattern in relationship to fan writing, reviews, and other appropriations of Series Eight material.

Prior to Moffat introducing the new (or former) platonic paradigm of the Doctor-companion relationship in the latest series, he had also initiated another layer to the Time Lord's relationship to the TARDIS by commissioning fantasy author Neil Gaiman to write the Series Six entry "The Doctor's Wife." In this story, the TARDIS's essence is poured into a female humanoid form—Idris, whom many fans claim resembles a Tim Burton character with her patchwork clothing and Goth-like hair. Through this human interface, however, the Doctor is able to express his feeling toward his beloved time machine in ways that literally posits her as an attractive companion—or, as with the story's title—his wife. Though this repositioning of the Doctor-TARDIS dynamic is temporary as the episodic nature of the serial's storytelling—and the expected formula of the show— necessitates that Idris dies and the TARDIS's energy rightfully returns to the ship itself, Gaiman and Moffat have reencoded the time machine as something that has feelings for her captain. Moreover, in the episode, Idris reveals that she chose the Doctor instead of the converse being true, which reverses the long-standing encoded and decoded conceit of the Doctor simply absconding from Gallifrey with his appropriated time machine. Put another way, in this new revisionist origin schema, the Doctor's heroic quest has now been initiated by a sentient maternal, time-and-space traveling object that had been first oriented toward him.

Before Gaiman had added this gendered layer to the TARDIS's characterization, Moffat himself, had, with the Eleventh Doctor's debut story, "The Eleventh Hour," revealed that the TARDIS can organically grow itself a new control room. When the Eleventh Doctor beholds his vessel's newest interior iteration, he announces, "Hello, Sexy," before we, the viewers, can see her new metallic and glass-themed interior. Curiously, like the Liberator, which provides Blake's crew with weaponry, the TARDIS supplies the Doctor with his newest sonic screwdriver. Returning to a phenomenological lens, the Doctor is turned toward the female TARDIS console in supplying him with his penis substitute. Put another way, in a more psychoanalytical sense, the female-encoded cybernetic vessel has undone the castration caused by the destruction of his sonic screwdriver's previous model earlier in the episode.

Moffat had also expressed a fannish love of the TARDIS via the Doctor-as-mouthpiece in the climax to his first season as showrunner— "The Big Bang." As the Doctor sits by a sleeping young Amelia Pond before the universe reboots, and he will be seemingly trapped on the other side of it, he gently hopes that she will remember him and his TARDIS, which he poetically waxes about as having "the bluest blue" he has ever seen. Taking into consideration that Moffat was a childhood fan of the show, one can see that this encoding choice dualistically has been generated by the fan–Moffat's lifetime of decoding what the blue of the TARDIS police box represents to him. Whenever appropriate, then, I will be discussing further iterations of what I will call encoding/decoding/encoding—or EDE—in this book.

* * *

On a closing note to this chapter, I would like to mention that analyzing the BBC's corporate and creative encodings of *Doctor Who, Blake's 7, Red Dwarf,* and *Torchwood* across the years spanning 1978–2015 will reveal how, over time, the shows are allowed greater leeway for freer expressions of storytelling and characterization, and yes, gendered heroic identity. In short, such tenets of postmodernism as nonlinear narrative, parody, and pastiche increasingly inform the production ethos of these series. But these changes inevitably generate a more complicated question when it comes to the decoding end of Stuart Hall's resilient media formulation: How does postmodernism affect the formation of fan identity, especially as they celebrate, mirror, criticize, parody, promote, and rework four SF television objects of devotion? More importantly, how do these fans affect the encoding of their favorite shows? My conclusion's thoughts for this book, therefore, will work toward bringing all of my research together to examine how past and present fans, especially socially progressive ones, may be a few steps ahead of more conservative, patriarchy-reinforcing television producers and whether these decoding efforts are pertinent to the encoding inherent in the corporate greenlighting and production of future televised British SF gendered heroic quests.

Chapter Two

The Rise, Fall and Nostalgic Embers of 1980s Doctor Who

Before I begin my discussion of how *Doctor Who* in the 1980s challenged the show's traditions only to eventually be thwarted by the very people—the fans—who should have been supporting its dualistically innovative and tired appropriations of its formula, like Henry Jenkins so bravely before me, I must confess that I am an aca-fan. I truly believe I need to make this distinction as an academic analyzing this period of the show (and in approaching my discussion of *Blake's 7, Red Dwarf,* and *Torchwood* as well) since I lived through the eras (of the Fifth, Sixth, and Seventh Doctors) under discussion, actively watching all of the episodes, attending SF conventions, and discussing the series' turbulent times with fellow viewers. At the time, I was only in grade and then high school, unaware that my adolescent adoration for the show was, in so many ways, preparation for this very work—but that is what this chapter is about—applying my CNC (Continuum of Nostalgic Continuity) theory to 1980s *Doctor Who* in order to analyze how the rich past of the series has shaped both fan reactions to that troubled era in the present (and possibly the future)— for fellow fans/aca-fans, and, most interestingly, those unique fans (the decoders) who have become writing professionals (the new encoders) and currently steer the course of *Doctor Who*.

One of the key players of my discussion, producer John Nathan-Turner, whose queer lifestyle inexorably shaped his encoding of the show, even made an appearance in my life—albeit from the distance of a stage at a spring 1985 Creation convention in Valley Forge, Pennsylvania. JN-T, as he was called by fans, in an era where the stars of the SF convention circuit were primarily the actors of a given beloved cult SF show (e.g., *Star Trek*), reversed this tradition by capitalizing on his powerful producing of the show—and his distinct Britishness, which he playfully married to American culture by actively wearing his trademark loudly colorful Hawaii shirts. Although Sixth Doctor Colin Baker was ostensibly the headlining guest of this convention, JN-T, a trained actor, stood before the crowd jubilantly working them up into a frothing of fannish excitement before premiering season twenty-two's third story, "The Mark of the Rani," which had not yet been broadcast in the States. For me and other fans, JN-T, unlike the producers before him—but very much like his future successors—Russell T Davies and Steven Moffat—would embody an emblematic media face for the show, nearly as important as the leading man playing the Doctor. In marked difference to Davies and Moffat, however, Nathan-Turner, who initially generated a golden age of fandom goodwill as the "Fan's Producer"[1] in the early 1980s with his producing of Peter Davison's era as the Fifth Doctor, would later feel the destructive, media-fueled ire of these same fans in the middle of the decade during Colin Baker's problematic tenure as the Time Lord.

If binaries were to be employed to characterize Nathan-Turner's stewardship of *Doctor Who* from 1980–89, perhaps they would be paired as follows: brilliant/abysmal, stylized/gaudy, groundbreaking/recycled, postmodern/traditional, and straight/queer. All of these paradoxical couplings would overlap and contradict each other in a fluctuating manner within any of the stories broadcast during seasons eighteen to twenty-six (*Classic Who*'s final series), occasionally blurring the lines outlining the Doctor's heroic characterization. In relationship to *NüWho* (2005–present), the episodes, moreover, represent textual barometers against which good storytelling has been measured, as elements of the classic series either resonate in the new show or are buried—or, more accurately—closeted, their components perhaps written off as camp, unheroic, and too feminine or queer. For a show about time travel, the concept of its past saga enacting a pull on its present production and fan reactions ironically and appropriately fits the bill of explaining how twenty-first century *Doctor Who* holds an ambivalent conversation with its critically maligned and continually reassessed older counterpart.

Arguing that 1980s *Doctor Who* is queer, however, since its producer was gay is not an absolute process. None of the Doctors produced by Nathan-Turner—the Fourth, Fifth, Sixth, or Seventh—ostensibly evince behavior that could be considered homosexual or even homoerotic, which makes sense, as the show, despite having an ever-growing all-ages audience, was still being encoded with its 1963 roots of being a children's program. While Tom Baker had been experiencing a fiery courtship with Lalla Ward, who played the second incarnation of his companion Romana[2] onscreen in season eighteen, the two professionally played the parts as fellow Time Lord friends and colleagues. One could, however, make an argument that the Fifth Doctor is either asexual or simply shy[3] in not noticing or displaying any attraction to his comely young companions, Tegan, Nyssa, and later, Peri, as he is, after all, a Gallifreyan, an alien who possesses a different physiology and longer lifespan than a human. On the surface, imagining the acerbic Sixth Doctor romancing Peri[4] or his other female companion, Mel, is not easily supported by the show's scripting or any potential overt actions occurring between them onscreen. Likewise, the Seventh Doctor functions as an avuncular figure to both Mel and Ace, without any sexually suggestive piece of dialogue occurring between him and these younger companions. The obvious bottom line is that, at this point in the history of the show, the Doctor never romanced his companions.

But to simply argue that the Doctor is never encoded as gay or overtly sexual, however, is not to say he cannot be *queered* when it comes to examining slash fiction fan productions, some of which I shall be discussing in this chapter. In fact, Nathan-Turner himself may have rather symbolically posed the question of the Doctor's sexuality by instructing costume designer June Hudson to add two prominent red question marks to the Fourth Doctor's lapels when he exuberantly took over as producer of the show. These question marks, subsequently, were transferred to both the Fifth and Sixth Doctor's costumes and culminated as a full repeated horizontal pattern on the Seventh Doctor's colorful sweater. Of course, they were merchandise markers used for the branding of the show, but they also emphasized the overall mystery of the character, which includes questions involving his past on Gallifrey and whether or not he ever loved and consummated his passions for a woman since his first companion, Susan, refers to him as "grandfather."

Nathan-Turner, nonetheless, did not choose to address any of these fan-generated questions for the character. In fact, with each subsequent Nathan-Turner-cast Doctor, the show takes on a brighter, more eccentric hue, and, in turn, faces more fan resistance or ennui. Since Nathan-Turner was a gay man, a fact known by many of his friends and colleagues, but not picked up on or reported by the *Doctor Who* fan press or the greater media in the 1980s,[5] the obvious question arises: Were the Fifth, Sixth, and Seventh Doctor, on Nathan-Turner's part, closeted representations of queerness? Furthermore, is the character a gay icon? If anything, a number of gay male fans have self-identified with the Doctor not because he is an object for desire but because he represents a societal outsider like themselves. On this note, *Classic Who* fan Martin Warren, who was born in 1970, writes,

There is something to be argued about my experience as a child, then a nascent gay teen, then a fledging queer adolescent, and finally a cognizant gay man about the Otherness of the Doctor and the idea that this might have been attractive. His ability to change yet remain the same, his isolation in the midst of a group that loves him, the push and pull of wanting to belong and yet resisting acceptance [142].

For Warren, the Doctor's emotional, and, by extension, romantic and sexual distance from his companions works as touchstone for his developing identity as a gay man. He continues, "It's all there, writ cringingly large if one wants to read it that way—the psyche of many a gay man, exhibited and performed out loud, an Alien Other. Thankfully, an Other that had positive elements and bestrode the universe, charming millions and defeating baddies (rather than—say—piloting a ship and boldly leading a team of outer space explorers)" (142). Although Warren is not directly stating that the 1980s—or any of the *Classic Who* Doctors are gay—his claim that the Time Lord performing the role of an "Alien Other" embodies the queer fan experience underscores the value of the Doctor's many incarnations rather than any attractive physical qualities. In addition, his oblique jab at *Star Trek*'s actively heterosexual Captain Kirk commanding the Enterprise crew in a machismo-laden manner as embodied by William Shatner serves as a reminder that BBC productions such as *Doctor Who* (and *Blake's 7* or *Torchwood*) represent alternatively gendered heroic quests for their gay fans in the sense that the heroes presented in their televised narratives can be sensitive and not overly masculine in terms of characterization.

Since *Doctor Who* fans did not directly attack Nathan-Turner for his gay lifestyle, could their critical views of his mid–1980s encoding choices have been subconsciously directed at a show that promoted a queer design and celebrity casting ethos[6] better lent to light entertainment productions? Equally, did this growing fan criticism provide a fair reflection of a 1980s *Doctor Who* participatory culture and general television viewing audience, who gradually insisted on more complicated characterizations and sexualities from their leading SF characters? The posing of this question in this chapter will offer a better understanding of why Nathan-Turner and the fans seismically achieved a communications breakdown.

The 1980s Doctors: Heroes or Otherwise?

When John Nathan-Turner became producer of *Doctor Who* with season eighteen[7]—which would prove to be Fourth Doctor Tom Baker's last in the role—the leading man had already been playing the part of the ancient Time Lord for a record-breaking six years. Although Baker's first three seasons as the Doctor, produced by Philip Hinchcliffe, encoded a gothic sensibility in the storytelling, acting, music, and design of the show, his next three, under producer Graham Williams, were more fantasy-driven and playful (mostly due to the fact that the BBC had received notable complaints about stories broadcast during season fourteen).[8] In fact, Douglas Adams's script editing for season seventeen played up *Doctor Who*'s postmodern, self-aware meta aspects by having the Fourth Doctor vocalize a long-standing fan joke of the bulky, pepper-pot-shaped Daleks being unable to climb stairs in "Destiny of the Daleks" and showcasing comedic cameo guest stars John Cleese and Eleanor Bron in "City of Death" discussing the TARDIS as a work of art on display in the Louvre, even in the wake of its near-miraculous dematerialization. Nathan-Turner, however, working with script editor Christopher H. Bidmead, wished to restore a sense of drama to the character and emphasize "hard" over "soft" SF. The results were rather mixed. While the writing, direction, music, and other production values were debatably a notable improvement upon the previous season, Tom Baker's performance of a brooding Fourth Doctor may have lacked the vitality and joyfulness he committed to the role in his previous six seasons.

Baker, nevertheless, through his seven seasons in the role, had succeeded in enchanting both a generation of young and adolescent British and American viewers, the latter first being exposed to the Fourth Doctor thanks to Lionheart Television International[9] securing a national distribution deal with PBS stations in 1978. Nonetheless, in 1983, Baker declined Nathan-Turner's invitation to be included in "The Five Doctors," the show's twentieth anniversary special. Although Baker does actually appear via several scenes in the production that were culled from the BBC-industrial-strike-aborted seventeenth season story "Shada," he does not participate in the celebration proper by interacting with any of the other Doctors, since his character is marginalized in the narrative through a plot point that depicts him as being caught in a time eddy with Romana. Unfortunately, despite this well-intentioned encoding effort on Nathan-Turner's part to include Baker in "The Five Doctors," his absence, for many fans, forms a distinct narrative shortcoming for the story. Writing in 1999, John Kenneth Muir laments on Baker's absence from "The Five Doctors":

> Because of Baker's refusal to participate, the fans missed the only opportunity to see Doctors 2, 3, 4 and 5 in the same production. A reunion show today would be a rather sad thing since Pertwee and Troughton[10] are now dead too. A gathering of

Doctor Whos today would, amazingly, feature Tom Baker as the elder statesman—the oldest living actor to play the Doctor in the series. Would a show uniting Baker, Davison, Colin Baker, McCoy and McGann[11] engender the same nostalgic feelings so evident in "The Five Doctors"? Perhaps ... perhaps not [330–31].

Taking Muir's opinion of Tom Baker serving as elder statesman for *Doctor Who* circa 2000 into consideration, one can look at these words from two directions. One simple view is that Baker's status as the oldest living actor to play the Doctor would be perceived by the fans as making him the only logical choice to fill this venerable position. However, another well-disseminated fandom view at this time claimed that Baker was the only surviving remnant of the so-called golden age of *Doctor Who* spanning the 1960s and 1970s, thus adding a darker hue to his positioning as elder statesman of the show. In this situation, the Continuum of Nostalgic Continuity has enacted a rather negative hold on segments of *Doctor Who* in that they have created an absolute, quintessentially heroic figure in the form of the Fourth Doctor, which does not properly acknowledge subsequent *Classic Who* actors' (Davison, Baker, and McCoy) creative interpretations of the role.

While *NüWho*, depending on what fans one encounters, has either experienced a contemporary golden period during the Russell T Davies era of the Ninth and Tenth Doctors, or recently, with the era of Steven Moffat's Eleventh and Twelfth Doctors, *Classic Who* still experiences a well-contested, fractured division on whether or not Nathan-Turner's Fifth, Sixth, or Seventh Doctors feature in episodes that be considered part of the show's definitive years. One recent manifestation of this division of fan opinion on the Nathan-Turner produced era can be seen in two productions celebrating the show's fiftieth anniversary, both airing on November 23, 2013: "The Day of the Doctor," the "proper" special featuring David Tennant, Matt Smith, and cameos from Tom Baker and Peter Capaldi, and *The Five(ish) Doctors Reboot*, a meta-satirical half hour effort directed by Peter Davison and featuring himself, Colin Baker, and Sylvester McCoy. Although Moffat had initially claimed to the media that he would not be including *Classic Who* Doctors in the special since they would not resemble their younger selves, he ultimately contradicted himself by including Baker at the end of the episode in a "surprise" appearance as "The Curator," an aged character who most likely represents a future incarnation of the Doctor.[12] Fortunately, for the many fans upset by this development, which could also be seen as a snubbing of Nathan-Turner's era as producer of *Doctor Who*, Davison's satiric production, *The Five(ish) Doctors Reboot*, which will be examined in greater detail at the end of this chapter, somewhat fulfilled their expectations and desires to see Doctors Five thru Seven physically participate in the anniversary celebrations.

Returning to 1981, by the end of season eighteen, when the broodingly heroic Fourth Doctor moodily accepts his forthcoming regeneration in "Logopolis," the stage had been set for a dramatically younger Fifth Doctor in the form of Peter Davison, who would inherit three companions whom he did not appear that much older than: Adric, a mathematical genius from Alzarius; Nyssa, who hails from Traken; and Tegan Jovanka, an Australian air stewardess who famously (and perhaps in an unwittingly sexual sense) quips about herself, "I'm just a mouth on legs," in part three of "Earthshock." While innovatively casting a group of attractive young people as the stars of *Doctor Who* may have initially appeared to be an encoding choice that would hint of a newly established potential for romance and flirtation, Nathan-Turner choose to reinforce the show's roots as children's programming by enforcing a "no hanky-panky" rule for his TARDIS crew. At the same time, he would increasingly provide what he called "something for the dads" by having the costume department dress Tegan and Nyssa in more revealing outfits for season twenty, most notably in Nyssa's final story, "Terminus," where the character, who is suffering from heat exhaustion after contracting Lazar's Disease, sheds her clothing down to her slip on the Terminus hospital spacecraft. As a result, Nathan-Turner's growing desire to provide "eye-candy" for male viewers offers an interesting case study on a gay man encoding an all-ages family show with images aimed at eliciting heterosexual desire.

Troubled Masculinities: A Castrated Doctor and Flawed Male Companions

Nathan-Turner, reacting to the near-omnipotent characterization of the Fourth Doctor in the Graham Williams era of *Classic Who*, wished to show the Doctor as being more fallible. This encoding process notably began in Tom Baker's swansong, "Logopolis," when the Doctor, despite managing to defeat the Master by stopping him from destroying the universe with entropy, falls from the Pharos Project radio telescope after his archenemy had locked him out on the structure's gantry and turned it, thereby triggering his regeneration. With the succeeding story, "Castrovalva," which opened season nineteen, the Doctor is presented as suffering from an addled state (or what the fans call post-regeneration trauma) throughout the narrative, his identity only fully coalescing by the tale's closing moments. As discussed in the previous chapter, "Castrovalva" also inverts the traditional gendered heroic expectations for the Doctor and his female companions, in this case, Tegan and Nyssa, as they, along with the feminized TARDIS, become the caretakers/heroes of the story's first two parts. Conversely, Adric, the other (flawed) male hero, has been kidnapped, tied up, and tortured by the Master,[13] who is using the youth's mathematical genius to help set a trap for the Doctor in the form of the fictional world that is the town called Castrovalva.[14]

Three stories later, with "The Visitation," Nathan-Turner appropriated one of Eric Saward's plot choices for the story. Saward comments,

> I didn't like the sonic screwdriver. I thought it had been used badly, especially towards the end of Tom [Baker's] period. It was used to get out of all sorts of situations, and so I thought I'd blow it up, so [the Doctor] wouldn't have it for my story, thinking, somewhere in the TARDIS, there was a drawer full of these things, and he'd take another one out, and he would then go off and use it ["Writing"].

As Nathan-Turner agreed with Saward's view on the frequent narrative misuse of the sonic screwdriver, he consequently made its destruction a permanent development during his tenure as producer. Instead, Nathan-Turner now wanted his lead character to use his intellect and ingenuity in order to escape from a crisis situation—or fail in the attempt in order to encode the itinerant Time Lord as a more realistic masculine hero.

Upon a Terileptil destroying the sonic screwdriver in part three of "The Visitation," the Doctor laments to his alien captor, "I feel as though you've just killed an old friend." On the one hand, from an encoding perspective, this choice emphasizes the organic over the nonorganic or the capably masculine Time Lord's innate superiority to a miraculous technological device, which, in many ways, had decreased the opportunity for him to exert his agency as a hero. Taking a Freudian perspective, on the other hand, could offer the viewpoint that the Doctor has been effectively castrated with the destruction of his all-powerful, penis-substitute sonic screwdriver, which had ensured his heroic virility numerous times in the show's past, starting with the device's 1968 debut in the Second Doctor serial "Fury from the Deep."

Although, arguably, Nathan-Turner's decision helped Davison's Fifth Doctor break the ever-capable heroic mold that had been performed with gusto by his predecessors in the role, particularly with Jon Pertwee's action-man Third Doctor and Baker's bohemian Fourth Doctor, this decision was later undone by succeeding producers. For instance, the 1996 BBC/Fox TV movie[15] gave the Seventh and Eighth Doctor a new sonic screwdriver while modern *Doctor Who* showrunners Russell T Davies and

Steven Moffat have respectively lent playful sexual overtones to the device relating to the Doctor's phallus in the episode "The Doctor Dances," where the Ninth Doctor places his sonic screwdriver in direct competition with Captain Jack's square gun, and "The Day of the Doctor," in which the Tenth, Eleventh, and War Doctor[16] compare the chronologically increasing size of their sonic devices. Taking into consideration the fact that Davies and Moffat grew up as fans of the series, one can suggest that their revision of the sonic screwdriver's signification through a sexualized lens represents them creatively decoding one of the device's more suggestive, or adult, underlying messages via their creative scriptwriting. Thus, pointing out the sonic screwdriver's phallic significance functions as another example of encoding/decoding/encoding (EDE) in play courtesy of *NüWho*, as Davies and Moffat's new encoding of the device inevitably leads to further iterations of participatory culture decoding when fans react humorously or disapprovingly to these comedic "penis joke" scenes in reviews, art, and videos.

With these contemporary *Doctor Who* story examples in play, psychoanalytically viewing the Fifth Doctor's mournful regret in "The Visitation" at the loss of his sonic screwdriver as a form of castration anxiety does not seem like much of an intellectual stretch. Furthermore, if one considers Nathan-Turner's decision to take away the Doctor's sonic screwdriver as an emasculating form of castration, then later producers' choices of restoring this all-purpose-tool object to the Time Lord works as a restoration of his heroic masculinity or as a visually active extension of his enigmatic phallus.[17] Nonetheless, Peter Davison himself was in synch with Nathan-Turner's encoding of his flawed Doctor, as he commented in 1983, "I see my Doctor as well-meaning—although he doesn't always act for the best. But his overriding consideration is still to sort out whatever problem he is faced with as best he can. He may even endanger his companions in doing this. And he always starts out being polite, but usually gets less and less so as disaster looms!" (68). Perhaps, in many ways, Davison, via artistic collaboration with his costars, Nathan-Turner, and the various writers of his era, added a postmodern sensibility to his encoding of the Fifth Doctor's heroic masculinity in the sense that the character's fallible demeanor and behavior questioned the expected dependable nature of the classical hero. Davison's performance choices also set the stage for an evolution of the Doctor as an antiheroic character.

In the forthcoming years of the show, as Colin Baker's Sixth Doctor shows a more erratic, dangerous, sadistic side of the Time Lord, and his successor, Sylvester McCoy, provides a manipulative, gradually more sinister Seventh Doctor, an argument could be posed—based upon declining ratings and a decrease in fandom support—that these encoding markers negatively affected the then-future of the series since it was cancelled in 1989. Conversely, these brave postmodern characterizations have been effectively echoed in *Nü Who*, with the tortured, Last-of-the-Time-Lords survivor Ninth Doctor; the regretful "Time Lord Victorious" Tenth Doctor, who emerges at the end of his era; the occasionally vengeful Eleventh Doctor (as seen in "Dinosaurs on a Spaceship"); the Time-War-scarred, forgotten incarnation who is the War Doctor, and through the recent darker characterization of the Twelfth Doctor. Remarkably, then, for a show about time, some of *Classic Who*'s encoding choices when it comes to the Doctor's heroic qualities, while not particularly right for a certain era—the 1980s—have proven to be ahead of the postmodern curve in crafting a hero/antihero who intrigues and challenges contemporary multiplatform, global viewing audiences.

Fan Fantasies: The Fifth Doctor and His Male Companions

Nathan-Turner, working with script editor and writer Eric Saward, continued his characterization of an imperfectly heroic Fifth Doctor with the penultimate story of *Doctor Who*'s nineteenth season, "Earthshock," whose title was encoded to work as a reference to the tale's conclusion when a space freighter crashes into prehistoric Earth, which, in turn, delivers a more profound "shocking" ending in which Adric is killed off after futilely attempting to undo the Cybermen's three logic codes that had been initially putting the freighter on a crash course for the futuristic Earth. Leading up to this ending had been both the Fourth and Fifth Doctor's troubled relationship with the young Alzarian male, who was a stowaway in the TARDIS at the conclusion of the eighteenth season serial "Full Circle." From an encoded production viewpoint, Adric, played by actor and former *Doctor Who* fan Matthew Waterhouse,[18] was being written out of the show since he had proved to be unpopular with both the series' actors[19] and the fans. Throughout season nineteen, Adric had also been presented as a character who experienced friction with the Fifth Doctor, Tegan, and Nyssa. For example, in "Castrovalva," he was the Master's dupe, and he at first philosophically sided with the alien Monarch against the Doctor and his fellow companions during "Four to Doomsday."

With "Earthshock," however, Adric is encoded as a sympathetic, brave hero. In the beginning of the story, Adric tells the Doctor he wishes to return to his people in E-Space since he feels alienated from the rest of the TARDIS crew. Nonetheless, with part two of this tale, he still manages to help the Doctor, his companions, and a group of soldiers in the year 2526 survive an attack by androids within some Earth caves by smashing one of the mechanical beings' head with a rock. After this moment, Adric is the only one who sticks close to the Doctor when they deactivate a bomb. In a later private conversation with Adric within the domestic technological hearth that is the TARDIS control room, the Doctor expresses his respect for his companion's newfound heroism in these two situations. The Time Lord also agrees to take Adric home to E-Space and admires his companion's calculations for the potential journey, during which this warm exchange takes place:

> THE DOCTOR: Look, uh, I'm sorry about our argument earlier.
> ADRIC: So am I. I overreacted.
> THE DOCTOR: Do you really want to go home?
> ADRIC: No, of course not. There's nothing there for me anymore.

The Doctor and Adric subsequently joke about the boy's apparent useless labor in making the calculations, and then they share a brief affectionate look, which expresses to the viewer that an important textual moment of homosocial bonding has occurred between them. This scene, moreover, serves as a form of emotional foreshadowing when placed in contextual relationship to the story's tragic ending. In the following story, "Time-Flight," a mourning Doctor does not capitulate to Tegan and Nyssa's demand that he travel in time and return to the freighter in order to rescue Adric, claiming that to do so would be a catastrophic choice.

Despite the Doctor's rigid honoring of the laws of time travel, he nonetheless manages to express his guilt for not being able to save his companion in the concluding moments of "The Caves of Androzani." As he is regenerating as a result of contacting spectrox toxaemia, the hallucinating Time Lord sees his companions' heads floating around and speaking to him. Significantly, the final companion head who appears in front of him before an image of the Master turns up to taunt him is Adric's, causing the Doctor to weakly say his name in a questioning manner. This final poignant word thereby reminds viewers of the Doctor's repressed guilt for not saving the boy from his death in "Earthshock."

In terms of Adric's legacy as a companion, fans, to the present day, remain divided upon both Matthew Waterhouse's interpretation of the role and the character's erratic heroic scripting in general. Even the 2004 DVD version of "Earthshock" contains a comedic extra titled "Part Five," in which a clay animation version of Adric is revealed to have survived the freighter's impact into prehistoric Earth only to be eaten in a cave by a dinosaur, which prompts a surviving Cyberman head to say, "Excellent." The creators who commissioned this dark-humored piece for the DVD, the *Doctor Who* Restoration Team, grew up as fans of *Classic Who*. This fact lends an EDE shading to this DVD extra's indictment of Adric's character, especially in light of the fact that the credits list the actor playing Adric as "A Lump of Clay"—an obvious jab at Waterhouse's performance of the role. In addition, Waterhouse himself returned to the *Doctor Who* spin-off media fold itself in 2010 by penning his biography, *Blue Box Boy*, which is curiously written in a third-person manner, perhaps to provide him with a sense of objective distance from his troubled tenure as a companion on the show.[20]

Fan fiction productions have likewise added a decoded perspective of time to Adric's demise, imagining alternate realities in which the Doctor had indeed managed to rescue the adolescent. One slash work in particular, "Saving Adric," composed by a fan with the screen name castrovalva9, adds a romantic/sexual perspective to the Doctor and Adric's homosocial relationship. In this short story, where the Doctor has decided to rescue Adric after all, castrovalva9 writes, "The Doctor would rip apart the universe, modify time, do whatever it took to snatch Adric to safety, and to hell with the consequences. This galaxy could survive without a few dozen random moons and unnecessary planets. What did their existence matter when weighed against the value of Adric's precious life?" Within the quick narrative space of this piece, the Doctor succeeds in rescuing his companion from his time-locked death (only at the price of Rithonia's third moon exploding), prompting castrovalva9 to write, "[T]he Doctor had [Adric] in his arms and was desperately whispering into his hair, 'How long are you going to stay with me?'" The author then adds, "And his hearts surely skipped two beats each when Adric whispered, 'Forever. I'll stay with you forever.'"

Eroticizing the Fifth Doctor and Adric's relationship is not too far of a creative stretch on this writer's part since this version of the Time Lord does not actively reveal his sexuality—hetero, bi, or homo—in any of his episodes. In other words, castrovalva9 adding a sexual dimension to the rather asexual Fifth Doctor's onscreen characterization should be equally shocking or disconcerting to purist *Classic Who* fans who believe that the Time Lord should never be sexually involved with any of his companions, male or female. When viewed through the lens of *NüWho*, however, where the Ninth, Tenth, and Eleventh Doctors, at one point or another, have romanced or kissed a female, the scenario of the character demonstrating sexual traits is not as shocking. What still remains as untouched contemporary encoding narrative territory, at the same time, is the Doctor having a relationship with a male companion. Subsequently, "Saving Adric," in this light, retains a subversive edge that effectively queers a *Classic Who* Doctor-companion pairing and equally resonates with *NüWho* fans who may either support or resist the Time Lord evincing bi- or homosexual traits.

Although Adric had been written out of *Doctor Who*'s ongoing narrative, this encoding choice did not signal the end of Nathan-Turner's desire to feature a younger male companion on the show. With the beginning of the process of commissioning and editing scripts for *Doctor Who*'s twentieth season, Eric Saward had been initially relieved at the prospect of the Doctor only having two companions, Tegan and Nyssa, as this allowed for less scene breakdowns in a given script, which needed to feature material to keep all of the primary cast members interesting to the viewing audience. Nathan-Turner, however, to Saward's dismay, soon informed his script editor that he wanted another male companion to replace Adric, one who would be encoded as a potential traitor. Thus, in the three stories comprising what became known as "The Black Guardian Trilogy," "Mawdryn Undead," "Terminus," and "Enlightenment," the teenage Turlough, who, like the Doctor, hailed from another planet, struck a deal with the malevolent entity, the Black Guardian, to kill the Doctor in return for passage to his home planet. Although it at first appears that Turlough may carry out his villainous task,[21] by the end of "Enlightenment," he rejects the Black Guardian and posits himself as a hero in the Doctor's, and, thereby, the audience's eyes.

Cast in the role of Turlough was actor Mark Strickson. Like Davison before him, who per Nathan-Turner's insistence was contractually obligated to have blond highlights[22] added to his hair, Strickson had to dye his naturally blond hair red so that his appearance did not conflict with his costar's locks. As a result, considering that Nathan-Turner had major input in these attractive male actors' casting, characterization, and cosmetic appearances on *Doctor Who*, one may assert that he was encoding characters who could be demographically desirable to both a hetero and homosexual audience. Indeed, in "Planet of Fire," Turlough's last story, in which he is reunited with his brother and people, Strickson is depicted as wearing an open-buttoned shirt and shorts that substantially show off his bare legs in a fashion formerly reserved for the female companions on the series.

This potential dual sexuality of the two characters is aptly decoded in the *YouTube* fan-generated video "Doctor Who—The Fifth Doctor and Turlough are Bringing Sexy Back," in which user koloSigma1 has provided a video that edits together clips of the two characters interacting in the ten stories in which they appeared. Particularly repeated throughout the video are "Planet of Fire" clips showing Turlough just wearing his swim trunks and a white shirt. Also intermixed in the video are clips of Turlough attempting to kill the Doctor in "Mawdryn Undead" and the two mutually rescuing, talking to, and smiling at one another from several different stories. Moreover, serving as the playful soundtrack for these clips, which could be read as heteronormative or homoerotic depending on the viewer's interpretation, is "SexyBack," Justin Timberlake's Grammy-award-winning[23] 2006 song that contains sexually-explicit lyrics.

Accordingly, koloSigma1's pairing of 1983–84 *Doctor Who* clips with a song written and performed over two decades later lends this humorous and sexually suggestive remix video both a nostalgic and modern feel. The comingling of the two media also celebrates the egalitarian ethos of *YouTube* in that a bottom-up, user-generated work that appropriates top-down, corporate media can exist for *Doctor Who* fandom and greater public consumption. At the same time, its existence on *YouTube*, free of legal repercussions, arguably, serves as free advertising for the BBC and Timberlake's record label, Zomba Recordings/Sony BMG Music Entertainment, and online sites such as *Google Play*, *iTunes*, and *AmazonMP3*, which sell downloadable versions of the song. In short, while efforts such as koloSigma1's resist corporate control of their source material, they likewise laterally, or unwittingly, increase potential consumer consumption of these very products, which exist in DVD/CD/digital purchase form.

The Reluctant Doctor: Refusing the Romantic Call to Action

While slash fiction readings of the Fifth Doctor's complex relationships with his male companions are prevalent in online *Doctor Who* participatory culture's narrative productions, fan writers are also naturally interested in adding a sexual context to his friendships with his female companions, Nyssa, Tegan, and Peri. In both scenarios, hetero and homosexual couplings, this Doctor's youthful appearance quite easily fuels fan fantasies in writing him as an actively romantic and sexual being. However, his encoded onscreen dynamic with Tegan perhaps best offers the most relevant textual evidence for him taking their platonic relationship to the next level. Cases in point: she visually expresses poignant regret at the Doctor inadvertently leaving her behind at Heathrow Airport at the end of "Time-Flight"; Mariner, a member of the Eternals, comments that the image he sees of the Doctor in her mind is "quite intriguing" in "Enlightenment"; and she tearfully leaves the Doctor for the final time at the conclusion of "Resurrection of the Daleks," since she is tired of the bloodshed. In all of these situations, Tegan could be reasonably posited as experiencing unrequited romantic feelings for the Doctor. On this note, fan critic Jackie Marshall asks,

> Was Tegan secretly in love with the Doctor after all? Would it have mattered so much if this had definitely been shown to be the case? It wouldn't have amounted to hanky-panky, and it certainly wouldn't have shattered the Doctor's essential enigma if one single, solitary female had found him fanciable; in fact, bearing in mind that the incarnation in question happened to be "the youngest and sexiest Doctor yet," it seems very strange that no one noticed him in this way [59].

Marshall's critique of Nathan-Turner's encoding choice of denying even the slightest hint of the Doctor or his female companions explicitly expressing romantic feelings for one another is indeed valid when viewed from the perspective that *Doctor Who* in the 1980s had not effectively evolved to meet the storytelling needs of the more mature members of its viewing audience.

For another fan writer who goes by the screen name ToryTigress92, the Fifth Doctor and Tegan's relationship is fertile ground for romantic extrapolation. In fact, the Doctor's decision at the conclusion of "The Five Doctors" to not remain on Gallifrey in order to serve as Lord President of the High Council of Time Lords had inspired her to write "Neutral," in which she envisions the alternate reality scenario of the Doctor making the opposite choice. In this tale, Tegan has remained with him, but the new iteration of their tense relationship, which posits him as a dedicated Lord President and her as his human companion, heatedly reaches a point when she threatens to leave him and return to Earth. Not wanting to lose Tegan's companionship, the Doctor puts on his former clothing and approaches her in this erotically charged passage: "He was dressed in his old cricketing outfit, the stick of celery still resolutely attached to his lapel. All the cool arrogance that had pervaded him had melted away, as if by shedding his Time Lord regalia, he had become someone else. No, not someone else, himself. The Doctor. His blue, blue eyes smoldered as he looked at her." For ToryTigress92, the often fan-criticized, Nathan-Turner dictated cricketer "uniform" for the Fifth Doctor not only signifies his identity as a unique iconoclast who values Earth clothing over Gallifreyan garb of state but also as a familiar identity marker of his "true" self, which, to Tegan, imbues him with a "smoldering" sexuality.

Continuing with this theme of clothing/uniforms metonymically indicating the characters' identities, she next writes, "Tegan was dressed in a similar style to when they had first met, a pencil skirt, blue shirt and heels." Thus, this fantasy-driven romantic scenario reveals ToryTigress92's erotic decoding of the Fifth Doctor and Tegan via their clothing. She soon has the two characters passionately embracing, writing, "All the anger, all the resentment, all the tension that had been between them from the start erupted in that moment, in that one shining moment of touch, of simple communion. And left them trembling in its wake, wiping away everything bar an irresistible need, and an emotion so deep, that it consumed them. Forever." In this passage, noticeably influenced by the literary flourishes of the romance novel, ToryTigress92 has channeled and articulated fan desire for Tegan to consummate her potential romantic feelings for the Doctor.[24]

Since the story was uploaded in 2009, one can easily suggest that *NüWho*, which had already aired the Ninth and Tenth Doctors' romance with human companion Rose Tyler, had influenced her composition of "Neutral." In particular, the climax of "Journey's End" depicts the meta-crisis-generated human version of the Tenth Doctor passionately kissing and choosing to remain on a parallel Earth with Rose. Consequently, when one views "Neutral" in this contemporary context, the Continuum of Nostalgic Continuity is operating through the fact that ToryTigress92 has composed a tale featuring *Classic Who* characters fulfilling long-standing fan desires for them to be lovers. At the same time, this new romantic narrative ground is granted a greater sense of contemporary textual legitimacy since the concept of the Doctor consummating his feelings for one of his female companions has been obliquely realized with *NüWho*.

The Sixth Doctor: Sporadically Cruel and Cowardly

When John Nathan-Turner went to cast Peter Davison's successor in the role of *Doctor Who*'s titular character in 1983, he wanted someone who could prove to be a mercurial, loud, brazen counterpoint to the more soft-spoken, gentle Fifth Doctor. To satisfy these encoding parameters, Nathan-Turner chose Colin Baker, whom he dressed in a colorful costume that he had insisted as being composed in "bad taste." On this costuming choice, Eric Saward comments, "John, at that particular time, wore a lot of Hawaiian shirts, which were works of art to be seen. And some people, cruel people, and I wasn't one of them, said that, really, what he wanted was to reflect his own style of dress in the dress of the Doctor" ("Trials"). Saward's comments have been echoed by Richard Marson, who, in his Nathan-Turner biography, *JN-T: The Life & Scandalous Times of John Nathan-Turner*, writes, "There is a theory that the coat was just a take on John's love of his Hawaiian shirts and that in insisting on dressing Baker in this way, in curling his hair and encouraging him to give an extravagant, theatrical performance, John, was, even if subconsciously, casting himself in the part" (188). While it is true that Nathan-Turner was the prime mover in choosing Baker's costume, which over the years has received widespread criticism for its inappropriateness for the traditional and heroically dependable character of the Doctor, the argument that he was subconsciously encoding his own physical and personality traits into the character is ungrounded by textual evidence and would require somewhat of a psychoanalytical stretch. Baker himself, however, provides this comment on his costume: "In the first year of the television series, it was linked directly to the post-regenerated Doctor. It subsequently became just what he wore, and I am on record repeatedly saying that, I think this whole thing about what the Doctor wears is a distraction" (Wright 66). With this quote, Baker hints how not just the costume but also the unpredictable encoding of his character from the start of his tenure in the role had cast a darker narrative shadow over his Doctor's personality.

In fact, when an addled, post-regeneration Sixth Doctor nearly strangles Peri Brown in part one of "The Twin Dilemma," many viewers lost their trust in the Time Lord's heroic default characterization for the first time in the series' history. The Doctor, unfortunately, instead of sincerely seeking Peri's forgiveness, tells her that he must seek atonement by becoming a monk on the desolate moon Titan 3, with her spending the rest of her mortal life as his young disciple. Offering an online review of "The Twin Dilemma," fan writer E.G. Wolverson writes,

> Personally, I find [S]ixy's initial instability both fascinating and entertaining. Obviously there is a lot of the William Hartnell antihero that shines through in Baker's performance, but there is also a far more ominous side. When the Doctor does the unthinkable and attacks Peri whilst quoting *Lalla Rookh,* a certain line is crossed—the Doctor says it himself; he should have "an in-built resistance to violence" which has clearly been lost in his "renewal."

With this review, Wolverson emphasizes a fundamental flaw in the original encoding of the Sixth Doctor: He comes off as an abuser of women, not as a protector.

However, for a fan writer working according to the screen name, finmagik, this scene contains a fascinating sadomasochistic quality. In his or her short story "The final intimacy," the Sixth Doctor and Peri are depicted as lovers. The two, moreover, as the title indicates, wish to achieve a "final intimacy," which the Doctor defines as "sharing thoughts, memories, sensations, being inside someone else's mind." When the Doctor proceeds to initiate the telepathic process by entering Peri's memories, finmagik writes,

> He was seeing himself as he was now, above her, angry, his hands closed tightly around her neck, choking the life from her. The terror and surprising arousal of that first encounter. He moved on from that memory rather quickly. He went to their other, more conventional, sexual experiences, reliving them from her eyes: all those times in her bed, his bed, the TARDIS console room, the pool, getting warm together after the cold of Necros, a picnic blanket on Bastoria [E]ight, against the wall in the TARDIS corridor ... and finally this time.

For finmagik, the Doctor strangling Peri represents the inaugural step of their latter, "more conventional" sexual intimacies in the alien spaces of the TARDIS and other worlds. But it is his or her argument that Peri was "surprising[ly] aroused" by the Doctor choking her that troubles this story's depiction of the two characters' sexual relationship. While other fan writers may not agree with finmagik's more extreme interpretation of the Doctor and Peri as lovers sharing a complicated sexual past, his or her erotic rendering of "The Twin Dilemma's" "strangulation scene" serves as an interesting representation of the fantasy-driven S/M desires of some *Doctor Who* fan fiction writers.

Returning to the issue of the Sixth Doctor's problematic characterization, one can assert that Nathan-Turner and Saward had equally encoded Peri in a negative manner as his companion. Since the character's introduction to the series, she had been written as a damsel-in-distress. When one considers that *Doctor Who* had introduced more empowered female companions to viewers with the examples of journalist Sarah Jane Smith in 1974; Leela, a Sevateem[25] tribe warrior, three years later; two incarnations of the intellectual, witty Time Lord Romana in the late 1970s/early 1980s; and the strong-willed Tegan in 1981, Peri's embodiment of the typical *Doctor Who* dependent heroine feels like a step backwards. More importantly, many mid–1980s BBC *Doctor Who* viewers had already been accustomed to seeing strong SF heroines in the sixties adventure series, *The Avengers*, and in such 1970s shows as *Sapphire and Steel* and *Blake's 7*, which provided a powerful female villain with Servalan. Today, many fans and media critics argue that one of the key components to the 2005 *Doctor Who* reboot being a modern success involves its strong characterization of the female companion role. This accepted mindset, along with *Nü Who*'s encoding of a markedly more emotional, romantic Doctor, have tonally delimited the show from its 1963–89 predecessor.

For fans of the show familiar with *Classic Who*, however, this argument is not entirely true when it comes to the list of aforementioned strong heroines and with the case of the Seventh Doctor companion, Ace. 1980s companions such as Peri and her successor, Mel, nevertheless embody the weaker *Doctor Who* vision of females. Yet, in marked contrast to season twenty-three and twenty-four's Mel, Peri is often depicted wearing skimpier outfits, making her an object of lust for both the villains and the viewer. On this note, one can consider the following examples: in part one of her debut story, "Planet of Fire," Peri strips down to a skimpy bikini, a fact emphasized by the camera lingering on her nearly bare breasts in a scopophilic manner. Then, in the succeeding serial, "The Caves of Androzani," she is desired by the tortured villain Sharaz Jek; "Vengeance on Varos" depicts the sadistic, lizard-like Sil wishing to transmogrify her body into a bird; "The Two Doctors" shows the gluttonous Shockeye attempting to prepare her for dinner; the despotic Borad in "Timelash" wants to turn her into a mutant like himself, so she can be his mate; and the middle-aged, egotistical chief Necros undertaker Jobel lusts after her in "Revelation of the Daleks." Most disturbingly, "Mindwarp"[26] shows an addled Doctor interrogating a chained Peri on a Thoros Beta beach, a borderline torture scene that all-too easily lends itself to slash fan fiction.

The most egregious transgression against Peri's body takes place, nevertheless, during the final part of "Mindwarp," when the monstrous Lord Kiv steals her very form. His brain successfully transplanted into Peri's body by the scientist Crozier, Kiv awakes, making these observations about his newly appropriated mammal form as the camera pans over actress Nicola Bryant's figure: "Warm, not cold. The body is warm. Oh, wonderful! Legs, toes, toes wiggling. Trunk! Neck, strong. Head, free of pain. Eye sight, colors—warm-blooded sight. Oh, I like this! Now I am she, alive, within this all-so wonderful, wonderful frame!" An enraged King Yrcanos, upon beholding this monstrous (and arguably queered) transformation of his potential lover, who now speaks with masculine inflection of Kiv's former reptilian voice, destroys Peri's body, an act which is later witnessed by a horrified Doctor while he is being placed on trial by the Time Lords. However, part fourteen of "The Trial of a Time Lord" reveals that this sequence in fact had been fabricated by the Valeyard (a future evil manifestation of the Doctor[27]) and that Peri and Yrcanos had fallen in love and she had become his queen. Regardless of this manufactured romantic happy ending for the pair, perhaps one can argue that the Sixth Doctor's consistent inability to protect Peri is indicative of the character's mid–1980s failings to present himself as a proper hero to his viewing audience, many of whom had been growing up with the series.

Doctor Who Producer-Fan Wars

Dissatisfied with season twenty-two, Colin Baker's first full run of episodes in the role as the Sixth Doctor, Michael Grade, the BBC Controller, placed the show on an eighteen-month hiatus in late February of 1985, claiming that it was too violent. When *Doctor Who* returned to the airwaves in autumn 1986 with "The Trial of a Time Lord," a fourteen-part season-long story, the storytelling placed more of an emphasis upon comedy. Although the fans had been initially upset at Grade's decision, their anger and displeasure was eventually refocused upon Nathan-Turner upon the transmission of season twenty-three because they were disappointed with the Doctor's erratic characterization and the series' unfocused umbrella storyline. Perhaps for a better understanding of the social dynamics concerning Nathan-Turner's falling out with the show's fans, one can turn to Pierre Bourdieu's work *Distinction*, where he formulates his structure of the habitus. According to Bourdieu,

> The habitus is not only a structuring structure, which organizes practices and the perception of practices, but also a structured structure: the principle of division into logical classes which organizes the perception of the social world is itself the product of internalization of the division into social classes. Each class condition is defined, simultaneously, by its intrinsic properties and by the relational properties which it derives from its position in the system of class conditions, which is also a system of differences, differential positions, i.e., by everything which distinguishes it from what it is not and especially from everything it is opposed to; social identity is defined and asserted through difference [171–72].

Applying Bourdieu's social structure of the habitus to Nathan-Turner, the encoder-producer, and resistant 1980s *Doctor Who* fandom, the decoder-receivers, is a naturally complex process. From an economic level, both Nathan-Turner, before he achieved wealth and fame from producing and promoting *Doctor Who*, and the fans, most likely were born, raised, educated, and enculturated as members of the British middle class. Moreover, both oppositional sides of this decoding-encoding dynamic grew up as post–1950 BBC license fee payers, with their self-created engrained notions of what constitutes good television. Applying Bourdieu's notion of difference to the differential positions created by Nathan-Turner joining the ranks of encoder-producers when he began working for the BBC as a floor manager in the 1960s, and by the devoted viewer, who amasses subculture capital by uniting with fellow fans in organized *Doctor Who* groups, who, in turn, form a vocalized decoder-receiver gestalt, aids us in understanding the oppositional dynamics oscillating between these two powerful forces. In short, their system of class conditions to which they subscribe in their somewhat synergistic relationship thrives on their encoder-decoder differences.

Within the media space of the shared ecology formed by the production and reception of *Doctor Who* in the 1980s, Nathan-Turner and the fans form two social classes. Within each class in this dualistic antagonism, the conflict of individual versus shared tastes differentiates these two forces. On this note, Bourdieu theorizes, "Taste, the propensity and capacity to appropriate (materially and symbolically) a given class of classified, classifying objects or practices, is the generative formula of life-style, a unitary set of distinctive preferences which express the same expressive intention in the specific logic of each of the symbolic sub-spaces, furniture, clothing, language or body hexis" (173). In classifying Nathan-Turner as a *Doctor Who* producer, once more, one can argue (as journalists and fans often have) that the specific tastes of his private lifestyle as a gay man comingled—or clashed—with his public identity as a BBC producer. (In)famously, he was a lover of musicals and pantomime. Concerning the former, Saward, in an incendiary interview with *Starburst* magazine in September 1986 after he had recently quit his script editor post before production of the show's twenty-third season had ended, made the following remarks:

> I was getting very fed up with the way *Doctor Who* was being run, largely by John Nathan-Turner—his attitude and his lack of insight into what makes a television series like *Doctor Who* work. This had been going on for a couple of years and after being cancelled and coming back almost in the same manner as we were before ... the same sort of pantomime-ish aspects that I so *despised* about the show. I just think it isn't worth it [16].

Saward's frank criticism of Nathan-Turner was a first for the history of the series. In other words, the encoder-script editor had critiqued a fellow encoder to not just the fans but the greater media as well, as represented by *Starburst*, which was being distributed in Great Britain and the United States.

But Saward, ultimately, had not been alone in critiquing mid–1980s *Doctor Who* to the media. On December 6, 1986, *Open Air*, a BBC talk show hosted by Pattie Coldwell, included members of the *Doctor Who* Appreciation Society (DWAS) in its audience, so they could voice their opinions concerning "The Trial of a Time Lord," of which part fourteen had just aired, to the episode's writers, Pip and Jane Baker, and Nathan-Turner, who was participating in the discussion via telephone. In particular, the tension occurring between the producer and one of the show's fervent viewers is quite apparent in the following exchange, as Coldwell talks to both teenaged fan Chris Chibnall[28] and Nathan-Turner. Regarding Coldwell and Chibnall, they share this exchange:

> COLDWELL: Are you happy with the new series, Chris?
> CHIBNALL: It doesn't seem to have much to it. It hasn't improved that much since it went off the air. It could have been a lot better. It could have been slightly better written.

As for Coldwell and Nathan-Turner, they later have this conversation:

> COLDWELL: John, are you surprised by this reaction from the Liverpool *Doctor Who* Appreciation Society's disappreciation, isn't it?"
> NATHAN-TURNER: Yes, it is a little over the top, I think. I don't think we intend to make things over complex. But, at the same time, I do think we attempt to challenge our audience and hence make the plots rather complex ["*Open Air*"].

Interestingly, the act of *Doctor Who* fans turning on their object of affection was notable enough to elicit media interest, particularly from a talk show produced by the very corporation that airs the SF series. Put another way, the variety talk show division of the BBC in late 1986 had encoded this type of programming to critique the encoder of another program by giving the show's decoders a televised soapbox from which to voice their complaints.

However, one can also argue that Coldwell had cleverly manipulated the fans and their views in order to present an argument to the greater BBC television viewing public that the Nathan-Turner-produced season twenty-three was, in fact, a failure. Years later, in a 2005 interview, Michael Grade confesses that he shared Coldwell's implied criticism of the series: "All I did was try to kill [*Doctor Who*] when it was at the BBC. I thought it was horrible, awful. I thought it was so outdated. It was just a little show for a few pointy head *Doctor Who* fans. It was also very violent, and it had lost its magic, and I killed it." For Nathan-Turner, unfortunately, with Saward, Coldwell, Grade, and segments of fandom working against him, his role as an effective producer-encoder of *Doctor Who* had been drastically compromised by both his colleague-encoders and the very fans who traditionally should have been the show's biggest supporters.

In fairly assessing this breakdown in Nathan-Turner's relationship with organized *Doctor Who* fandom, a pertinent question must next be posed: Were the fans justified in leveling such ultimately destructive criticism against the show? In short, as much as the paid producers of a television show are expected to craft and defend their encoding choices, should the unpaid fan decoders on the opposite end of this spectrum be similarly responsible for reemphasizing the "standards" for a given show when the encoding falls short of their expectations? In reality, all criticism, from the very nature of the word, contains an element of caustic, corrosive commentary, which, while potentially delivered by the messenger with the aim of improving the "patient," nonetheless damages the object under review. In other words, some 1980s *Doctor Who* fans may have regarded their criticisms of the show as being akin to an inoculation in the sense that the disease that was identified by their evaluation of the show's flaws should have stimulated Nathan-Turner's recognition of the truth of their words and processed as a form of bad-encoding choices resistance. However, instead of applying such criticism (valid or otherwise) to mid–1980s *Doctor Who* in order to make it a better program, Nathan-Turner regarded the fans' complaints as a form of betrayal. Behind the scenes, he referred to organized fandom as the "barkers," as in barking mad.[29] Ironically, these barkers—or "Dogs of *Doctor Who*"—if one views their act through the lens of a typical *Classic Who* story title, ended up biting the producer-hand that had generously yet unwittingly fed them the very stories and casting/production choices that led to their dyspeptic displeasure.

On the subject of "deadly" *Doctor Who* fans, the authors of *Wallowing in Our Own Weltschmerz: An Auton Guide to the Stories Behind the Stories of the Seventh Doctor* assert in their introduction, "These days the kids with their baggy jeans, MP3s, and iPhones have no idea what it was like to be a fan in the late eighties. Fandom turned its back on *Doctor Who*, led by fanatics who seemed to have forgotten they were fans and had become the enemy. We suspect fandom was a strong contributing factor to *Doctor Who*'s cancellation" (13). In regard to the empowered members of an organized British fan group such as the Liverpool DWAS and the editors and authors of *Doctor Who Bulletin*, who had actively critiqued Nathan-Turner, the authors are correct in assuming that the active participatory *Doctor Who* fan culture had been turning its collective back on the show. As for their conjecture that this resistance and rebellion against the then-current iteration of *Doctor Who* and its controversial producer strongly contributed to its final cancellation in 1989,[30] that speculation remains purely academic.

At the same time, perhaps one should no longer regard such critics of *Classic Who* as fans but as *anti-fans*. As a means of explanation, Jonathan Gray argues, "[F]ans can become anti-fans of a sort when an episode or part of a text is perceived as harming a text as a whole.... Behind dislike, after all, there are always expectations—of what a text should be like, of what is a waste of media time and space, of what morality or aesthetics texts should adopt, and of what we would like to see others watch or read" (73).[31] With Gray's definition in mind, one can argue that, like the character of Omega,[32] a fallen Gallifreyan pioneer who had become villainously insane from being trapped in an anti-matter universe for thousands of years, some fans, as a result of their ruthlessly proffered criticism, had ironically become the antithesis—that is, anti-fans—to their original self-conception as loyal, positive members of *Doctor Who*'s vast 1980s participatory culture.

The Seventh Doctor's Era: Alternate Visions of Gendered Heroism

Even though Grade claimed he was pleased with the encoding changes implemented by Nathan-Turner for season twenty-three, he insisted that Colin Baker could not return for another full season.[33] Thus, Baker was succeeded in the role of the Doctor by Sylvester McCoy, who enthusiastically essayed the seventh and final incarnation of the Time Lord for *Classic Who*. Comedy, however, would still play a major part in this season's encoding of the Seventh Doctor, particularly via the Pip and Jane Baker–scripted "Time and the Rani,"[34] which shows the newly regenerated Time Lord playing the spoons and performing several malapropisms—a trait that would quickly disappear in subsequent stories. In an attempt to invigorate fan and, more importantly, the general BBC viewing public's interest in the show, Andrew Cartmel, who script edited *Doctor Who* for its final three seasons, employed writers new to the series and directed them toward more innovative storytelling.[35]

In point of fact, writer Stephen Wyatt's "Paradise Towers," the second entry in season twenty-four, offers several interesting examples of queer sexuality and heroism. This story provides a parable of what happens to an economically prosperous culture once the majority of the men, "the Inbetweens," go off to fight a foreign conflict ("the Great War") while the remaining populace, referred to as the Youngsters and Oldsters, are sent to live in the high-rise Paradise Towers, which are depicted as dilapidated, dangerous structures whose physical decay matches the fractured society they house, which are populated by rule-book-worshipping Caretakers, several factions of girl gangs, the Kangs, cannibalistic old women, the Rezzies,[36] and one lone Inbetween coward, Pex. Mockingly called "muscle-brain" and "cowardly cutlet" by both the Red and Blue Kangs,[37] since he fled in cowardice from the war by stowing away on the ship that brought everyone to Paradise Towers, Pex provides a textbook example of a male character's hypermasculine overcompensation for his heroic shortcomings.

Before his cowardly past is revealed to the audience in part three of the story, however, Pex debuts in the first part by kicking down the door to the Rezzies' apartment exclaiming, "The name is Pex. I put the world of Paradise Towers to rights."[38] In the following episode, when he shows off his strength to Mel in a Paradise Towers corridor by jumping up and ripping a lamp fixture out of its wall socket and bending its metal bar behind his head, she asks him, "Pex, if you could bend that back into shape and put it where it came from, you might be more use. But you can't, can you?" However, once Pex replies that it is not his "job," Mel has unwittingly succeeded in reaffirming his lack of agency—despite his masculine bravura and physical prowess—to enact true positive change in his world.

In one moment during this story, the Doctor asks the Red Kangs about their knowledge concerning the existence of males in Paradise Towers, and Fire Escape, a member of the girl gang, responds, "Boys? What are boys?" Taking a tongue-in-cheek position in reaction to the puzzling sexuality of the Kangs (and Pex), the *Doctor Who* fan group collectively known as Auton[39] write,

> Although, given that there are men knocking about Paradise Towers, that's a surprising gap in Kang knowledge. Okay, so the [C]aretakers aren't much to look at in their drab grey uniforms with their wide staring eyes, but there's always Pex. Innate cowardice aside, there's no denying he's beefy. Has sexuality been completely erased from the genetic make-up of Paradise Towers? Not if the clothes the Kangs wear are any indication. Let's face it, for all their torn, shabby appearance, those outfits highlight the female form in no uncertain terms. And on the other side of the sexy coin, Pex is clearly dressed to impress. But impress who? [Davidson et al. 37–38].

Although Andy Davidson and his Auton writing colleagues are taking a humorous stance on the sexuality of the Kangs and Pex in this story, they are illuminating a serious shortcoming in the scripting of the young characters who populate this fantasy SF world. Perhaps the "surprising gap" these fan critics are referring to is not actually the Kangs' shared deficient understanding of male anatomy—or a lack of any sexual attraction to men altogether—but an encoding fissure in the production of the very show itself at this juncture in time. After all, under Nathan-Turner's aegis, *Doctor Who* was still being produced as all-ages—or children's—programming. However, as stated, the more adult-viewer-encoded *Blake's 7* had already proven earlier in the decade that BBC audiences were receptive to storylines containing romance and subtle sexual scenes.

Their question as to whom Pex has "dressed to impress" is likewise valid, especially, if judging from the manner in which they have phrased their question, he represents a "closeted" queer character. Through he is in good physical shape and wields a laser gun like any 1980s clichéd cinematic action-hero, other physical indicators—Pex's highlighted, stylized haircut, short, tight, low-cut V-necked shirt, colorful patchwork pants, and the upside-down triangle symbols contained on his necklace and right-arm short shirt sleeve—perhaps hint of an overt-yet-suppressed queer identity. Pex is not alone in representing a veiled queerness in "Paradise Towers," for this theme is similarly expressed through a pair of Rezzies—elderly roommates Tilda and Tabby. These two women's cannibalistic desire to consume Mel also reveals a not-so-subtle lesbian discourse,[40] which is seen in the lustful manner in which the Rezzies repeatedly eye up her body and the S/M bondage overtones inherent in part two's cliffhanger in which Tilda ties Mel up in a black crocheted shawl while Tabby threateningly holds a phallic-like toasting fork to her throat. Unlike Pex's more sensitive portrayal of potential male queerness, this Rezzie couple, ultimately, presents a vision of lesbian sexuality as sadistic and all-consuming of the young, vulnerable, nubile, hetero-female companion who is Mel.

In comparison to the still-evolving-in-terms-of-characterization Seventh Doctor, Pex possesses the physicality this newest incarnation of the Time Lord lacks. Granted, the Doctor, despite his physical shortcomings, manages to use the power of his brain to avoid being executed by the officious Caretakers[41] by outwitting them with the rules contained in their own overwrought rulebook. However, it is Pex who proves to be the true masculine hero at the end of this story when he sacrifices himself to stop a dangerous Kroagnon,[42] who has taken possession of the Chief Caretaker's body. Again, postmodernism has influenced *Doctor Who* in that the ostensible itinerant heroic lead, who is expected to "save the day," watches on the sidelines as the guest substitute-hero achieves his former mission statement for this serial. Interestingly, with the conclusion to "Paradise Towers," Pex and the Doctor are placed on common heroic ground as the now-united Red and Blue Kangs pay tribute to them both. In short, by praising Pex as the "unalive" who, in death, is "brave and bold as a Kang should be" and giving the Doctor a dual-sided scarf that contains both their colors, the Red and Blue Kangs establish a complementary-gendered reciprocity, not only with the males but also between them, when they point out their own tribal form of heroic feminism coexisting in the two men's differing embodiments of masculinity.

Although "Paradise Towers" and the rest of the season twenty-four stories[43] encode the Doctor as a humorous, witty, and rather gentle-hearted manifestation of the Time Lord, the following season would begin to depict him as a dualistic cultural imperialist/anarchist. In a similar fashion to his first incarnation, this newly encoded Machiavellian Doctor now travels with a teenage companion, Ace, whose streetwise attitude and dress style align her with the disenfranchised working-class culture of late 1980s Britain. Synergistically, the Doctor relies on her natural talents as a fighter and her militant application of her homemade cans of explosives, which she deems Nitro 9. Ace, moreover, echoes the role of one of the First Doctor's companions—Ian Chesterton. This version of the Time Lord, however, is equally as bellicose as his young, angry companion as he wields ancient Gallifreyan WMDs, the Hand of Omega and the Nemesis statue, in season twenty-five's "Remembrance of the Daleks" and "Silver Nemesis"[44] respectively, to decimate the Daleks and their home planet of Skaro and the entire Cybermen fleet. Consequently, even in the twilight years of the *Classic Who*, Nathan-Turner and Cartmel are paradoxically resisting and reinforcing dominant Thatcher-Britain jingoistic values. In other words, the Doctor curiously reifies the tenets of latter 1980s England, a military-industrial complex that relies on the apocalyptic threat of nuclear Armageddon to achieve its political goals, by ironically destroying the evil Dalek and Cybermen empires through enacting his own destructive might upon them.[45]

Broadcast in the same season, however, was the postmodern story "The Happiness Patrol," in which the Doctor and Ace land on Terra Alpha, a planet where a sour face can result in any of its citizens being executed. Contra to his bellicose actions in the two narrative stablemates in which he ignited sentient Gallifreyan superweapons, the Doctor simply uses his offbeat humor and the power of his intellect-driven words to foment rebellion on this Earth colony, most especially in part two, when he convinces two guards to "throw away [their] gun[s]." In this sense, he now embodies counterculture principles echoing a late 1960s hippie ethos. In part one, he even shows his acceptance of a queer ethos after Ace points out to him that the blue police box shell of the TARDIS has been painted pink by a Happiness Patrol, and he enthusiastically replies, "Yes, it looks rather good."[46] Audience viewing figures for this and the following final season of *Classic Who*, unfortunately, down a few million from the early 1980s, would reflect the fact that the colorfully-costumed Seventh Doctor's often offbeat, campy and postmodern adventures[47] were not reflective of more conservative British cultural values and dominant viewing habits.

In analyzing the causes for *Doctor Who*'s cancellation in 1989, perhaps a motivating factor had not been viewers or fans' disappointment with Nathan-Turner's latter seasons as producer but audience fatigue in general with the series' adherence to cult television show standards. On this note, fan cultures scholar Matt Hills writes, "The cult form ... typically focuses its endlessly deferred narrative around a singular question or related set of questions. This 'endlessly deferred narrative' typically lends the cult programme both its encapsulated identity and its title" (134). Applying both *Doctor Who*'s title, which functions as the show's fundamental question, and its "unfinished"/unknown lead character to exemplify this process, he argues,

> Over 26 years a fairly comprehensive sense of the Doctor's identity was eventually arrived at, only to be destabilised in the final few seasons (1988–89) where it was hinted that previous programme knowledge was only partial. Threatened with narrative exhaustion, the programme struggled to find a way to "regenerate" the sense of mystery which it had carried since its inception. *Doctor Who* projects its endlessly deferred narrative almost entirely upon the (non-) identity of its (anti)hero [135].

With this passage, Hill points out the paradoxical nature of Andrew Cartmel's valiant attempt at breathing new mythological life into *Classic Who* during its final two seasons despite the fact that the Doctor has been fundamentally encoded with a "(non-) identity." Nevertheless, Cartmel's efforts had ultimately been undermined by the fact that the series, by its very nature of the second word of its title, presents a mysterious character who will never completely reveal his origins or true name. Otherwise, if the Doctor's mystery had been entirely resolved during this era, then his potential heroic journey to come to terms with his true self by generously sharing it with his companions (and the viewers) would have brought the show's narrative to a potentially satisfying and irrevocable conclusion. However, since *Doctor Who* then—and now—represents a corporate television brand, not the creative property of an individual author, the show's "endlessly deferred narrative" will most likely always be encoded, and, by turn, extended, by its current stewards in order to safeguard this lucrative BBC asset's financial earning ability.

Neo Multi-Doctor Reflections on 1980s *Classic Who*

Even though *NüWho* avoided presenting any multi–Doctor stories in its first three seasons, for the short *Doctor Who* 2007 *Children in Need* segment titled "Time Crash," showrunner Russell T Davies asked Steven Moffat to write a story uniting the youthful Tenth Doctor with his predecessor, the Fifth Doctor, played once more by Peter Davison. Because it had been over twenty years since Davison had last regularly acted as the Doctor, he looks noticeably older in his old cricket costume. Moffat, however, utilizing a form of soft science technobabble, has the Tenth Doctor explain that his fifth incarnation's encounter with his future self has shorted out the time-stream differential, hence his older appearance. At the same time, Moffat uses the Tenth Doctor as a mouthpiece to articulate some markedly ageist remarks about his fifth self as he comments on his sagging face, increased stomach girth, and thinning hair. Granted, when viewed from a practical encoding perspective, one can argue that Moffat is employing teasing humor in order to explain to *Nü Who* viewers who may not be well versed in *Classic Who* why the time-displaced Fifth Doctor does not match his appearance as seen in episodes or photos from the early 1980s. Conversely, the writer serves as an apologist by over-explaining the situation, which creates the impression he is overly concerned that *Nü Who* casual viewers and fans who have only experienced two youthful Doctors with Christopher Eccleston's Ninth Doctor and David Tennant's Tenth may not be accepting of Davison's aging Fifth Doctor unless his reintroduction to the show is presented in a sarcastic manner.[48]

Following Davies's lead in sending up *Doctor Who* fans in Series Two's "Love and Monsters," Moffat equally mocks fandom's preoccupation with the actors who have played the Time Lord when the Fifth Doctor does not initially recognize his future incarnation but instead thinks that he is a fan. This misunderstanding leads the Fifth Doctor to exclaim to the Tenth, "Okay, you're my biggest fan. Look, it's perfectly understandable. I go zooming around space and time, saving planets, fighting monsters, and being—well, let's be honest—pretty sort of marvelous. So, naturally, now and then people notice me, start up their little groups." With these words, a certain meta quality shines through the Fifth Doctor's dialogue when one considers that the actor performing the lines has been familiar with the various eccentricities of *Doctor Who* fans for over two decades. In addition, Moffat himself, who had regularly attended *Doctor Who* conventions as a guest in the 2000s[49] before beginning to serve as showrunner in 2009, is also acclimated to the sometimes-obsessive nature of this large and vocal fandom. Certainly, then, his firsthand experiences with decoders have shaped the encoding of this sketch that conflates the sensationalistic qualities of the character of the Doctor with the actors who play him.

"Time Crash" is likewise littered with various references to the Fifth

Doctor's era, as seen in this exchange between the Tenth and his other self:

> TENTH DOCTOR: Where are you now? Nyssa and Tegan? Cybermen and Mara and Time Lords in funny hats[50] and the Master? Oh, he just showed again, same as ever.
> FIFTH DOCTOR: Oh no, really? Does he still have that rubbish beard?
> TENTH DOCTOR: No. No beard this time. Well, a wife.

While the first part of this exchange reflects Moffat's nostalgic admiration for the Nathan-Turner-produced Peter Davison era of *Doctor Who*, the subsequent play on words involving the Master's beard—a slang reference to a gay man's wife or female companion—effectively queers both actor Anthony Ainley's 1980s version of the character and the Davies-scripted/John Simm–performed iteration of the evil Time Lord. In other words, Moffat's problematic reference to Ainley's Master potentially encodes elements of the Nathan-Turner era as queer to *NüWho* viewers who still need to watch those episodes and decode their own assessments of its gendered heroes and villains.

Six years later, when *Doctor Who* showrunner Steven Moffat was presented with the opportunity to include *Classic Who* Doctors in its main fiftieth anniversary celebration, "The Day of the Doctor," he chose, as discussed earlier in this chapter, to only feature Tom Baker in a cameo appearance at the story's conclusion. Then again, although the *Classic Who* Nathan-Turner-produced Doctors played by Peter Davison, Colin Baker, and Sylvester McCoy did not feature in "The Day of the Doctor" except in the form of archived clips from their respective eras and by having their images CGI transplanted upon stand-ins' bodies for a long shot of all thirteen Doctors at the end of the special, they do appear in what more or less amounts to being a meta-multi-Doctor special, *The Five(ish) Doctors Reboot*. To add weight to this argument, one can consider Linda Hutcheon's thoughts on the evolutionary nature of adaptation in relation to a literary or media work over time:

> [A]daptation—that is, as a *product*—has a kind of "theme and variation" formal structure or repetition with difference. This means not only that change is inevitable but that there will also be multiple possible causes of change in the *process* of adapting made by the demands of form, the individual adapter, the particular audience, and now the contexts of reception and creation. This context is vast and variegated [142].

As television audiences have evolved with the changing nature of its technological presentation (from a few available corporate/network channels to cable options and now to multi-digital and online platforms), its variety of storytelling techniques has naturally changed as well. In *NüWho*'s case, the show has embraced self-knowing comedy, particularly snarky humor, as evinced by the Doctor and his companions and enemies. In other words, in a post–*Buffy-the-Vampire-Slayer* television landscape, the 2005 reboot of the show demonstrates postmodern self-awareness of the fact that its SF/fantasy/horror tropes are more than a bit ridiculous at times. Furthermore, the series' fans actively participate in this process of accepting the impossible, of "willingly suspending their disbelief." Since *Nü Who*, in comparison with its 1980s predecessor, possesses the advantages of a considerably greater budget, which is reflected in its sets, costumes, makeup, lighting, special effects, and direction, the show looks more "realistic" and glossy than the episodes produced by Nathan-Turner. For fans of this era—or people discovering it—the process of suspending one's disbelief when viewing these older episodes must oftentimes be doubled on their part in order for them to accept such dated elements as overly bright lighting, more theatrical (i.e., over-the-top) acting forms, and rubber-suited monsters.

Davison was well aware of these facts in his writer-director encoding of *The Five(ish) Doctors Reboot*, the idea for which he formulated after coming to the correct conclusion that Steven Moffat would be writing a multi–Doctor special focusing on the *Nü Who* era, not upon *Classic Who* Doctors. With Moffat's permission, Davison began to craft what he envisioned as an alternate fiftieth-anniversary television celebration focusing on his era and that of any living classic Doctor who agreed to be involved in the production on a potentially unpaid basis.[51] Colin Baker and Sylvester McCoy soon agreed to participate in the production, realized as a mockumentary in which they present themselves as three actors overly desperate to appear in "The Day of the Doctor." Paul McGann, who played the Eighth Doctor, also appears in a few scenes, and *Nü Who* actors David Tennant and Matt Smith make cameo appearances in the thirty-one minute episode, which aired November 23, 2013, on the BBC's online Red Button channel.

Returning to Hutcheon, Davison functions as the "individual adapter" who is in touch with the desires of fans, the "particular audience," whom he believes (or knows) wish to see him and his fellow 1980s Doctors appear together in the proper fiftieth anniversary special. Previously, Davison had filmed two fan-centric videos for the LA-based *Doctor Who* fan-run club, Gallifrey One. The first is a filmed apology to the Gallifrey One 2010 convention attendees for failing to appear at that event due to other professional commitments ("Doctor Who Peter"). The second video, which the Gallifrey One 2011 convention organizers ran for a live audience before

Davison appeared on stage, is a tongue-in-cheek parody that depicts the actor missing that year's convention due to his own procrastination and ineptitude in making his overseas flight to Los Angeles ("Peter Davison"). This video, which features Davison's fellow 1980s costars Janet Fielding (Tegan), Sarah Sutton (Nyssa), and Matthew Waterhouse (Adric) as well as a cameo appearance by Tennant (his son-in-law), also represents an interesting hybrid production in which an encoder-actor is collaborating with decoders to produce a quality fan-produced work, whose satiric tone would be echoed in *The Five(ish) Doctors Reboot*. On this latter production, Davison comments,

> In the end it proved to be hugely popular with fans across the board, but my intention was only to fill a very specific gap in the 50th anniversary celebrations, not to compete with the main event. But I do believe the fact we resisted pressure to take out references and jokes and sometimes even scenes, that wouldn't appeal to across the board, is the secret of its success. We make a joke of it, but we really were doing it for the fans, with the twist that the "fans" included us [Pixley 87].

Can one, however, consider Davison, and, by extension, Baker, McCoy, and McGann, as fans of *Doctor Who*? In other words, can four actors whose bodies and very names are metonymically linked to the show via their representations of different incarnations of the Doctor, be fans of themselves? More paradoxically, does Davison's self-assessment of this production serve as the ultimate act of narcissism, or is he articulating the inherent power wielded by contemporary participatory culture in being able to lower and blur the traditional barriers standing between encoders and decoders?

Perhaps one can complexly label Davison as an *encoder-decoder-encoder* in the sense that, as an actor in the early 1980s iteration of *Doctor Who*, he encoded his vision of the Time Lord through his approach in playing the role. Later, via various convention appearances over the years, he became quite receptive towards fans' love of the show, eventually becoming a fellow decoder through his participation in the two aforementioned Gallifrey One videos. Then, with *The Five(ish) Doctors Reboot*, he becomes an encoder once again through his acting, writing, and directing of the BBC-produced episode. At the same time, despite his claim to not compete against the "main event" that is "The Day of the Doctor," he nevertheless succeeds in crafting an ersatz multi–Doctor tale. Put another way, Hutcheon's opinion that there will be "multiple possible causes of change in the *process* of adapting made by the demands of form, the individual adapter" (142) is realized with *The Five(ish) Doctors Reboot*, which, via the flexible comedic form of parody, serves as a modern adaption of

Classic *Who*'s anniversary celebrations that united several Doctors in a quest-like adventure.

In "The Three Doctors," the opening story of *Classic Who*'s tenth season, Jon Pertwee's Third Doctor meets up with Patrick Troughton's Second Doctor, and the two are advised by William Hartnell's time-eddy-trapped[52] First Doctor in an adventure in which they travel to the anti-matter universe to stop Omega, a long-lost powerful Time Lord, from destroying their universe. Ten years later, "The Five Doctors" presents Doctors One, Two, Three, and Five[53] respectively venturing across Gallifrey's forbidden Death Zone in a quest to enter the Tomb of Rassilon. With "The Day of the Doctor," the Eleventh Doctor is joined by the Tenth Doctor and the War Doctor as they achieve a definitive heroic quest in saving Gallifrey from its apparent destruction during the Time War. Since Davison was provided a copy of the fiftieth anniversary script by Steven Moffat, he was able to compose his own alternate meta-multi–Doctor story that supposedly occurs during the filming of this production. As a result, his parodic quest for his actor–Doctor compatriots involves them venturing to Cardiff, where *NüWho* is produced in order to find a way to be included in "The Day of the Doctor." Indeed, the tale presented in *The Five(ish) Doctors Reboot* ostensibly forms a comedy-tinged mockumentary, but it also represents Davison's clever appropriation of the form of parody to overcome the cosmetic limitations of Baker's, McCoy's, and his older appearances in playing roles essayed by their younger selves. Viewed through Hutcheon's lens, Davison and his marginalized ex–Time Lord company have reacted and rebelled against the ageist "demands of form" that is contemporary BBC television, with its emphasis on youth and beauty, by tapping into the "contexts of reception and creation" by recognizing fan desire and creating a comically self-deprecating multi–Doctor tale (142).

The Five(ish) Doctors Reboot, in a self-aware manner, likewise effectively channels the Continuum of Nostalgic Continuity by referencing several moments from John Nathan-Turner's tenure as producer. For instance, Steven Moffat, who is featured in several scenes in this production, experiences a nightmare in which the floating heads of the aging actors who played companions[54] in *Classic Who* beg him for roles in the then-forthcoming fiftieth anniversary special. This sequence, moreover, mimics the hallucinatory first–POV floating-head sequence that accompanied the Fifth Doctor's regeneration into the Sixth, and both the original and its parodic copy feature Matthew Waterhouse (Adric) performing one of the final lines of dialogue.

McCoy, Davison, and Baker eventually travel to Cardiff and enter the

Doctor Who Experience exhibit, where they find their original prop costumes and subsequently steal and don them, albeit while still wearing the commercial print tee-shirts of their individual shirts/ties/sweaters/waistcoat underneath their purloined clothing. On the one hand, this choice to wear comedic tee-shirts reminds the viewer that these actors are indeed not interacting in a true multi–Doctor special even though they are nearly authentically dressed for the occasion. On the other hand, their mix of proper and commercial costumes signifies their newfound roles as fan-actors, whose participation in *The Five(ish) Doctors Reboot* thereby courageously breaks down the traditional barriers that have been erected between encoder-actor and decoder fan. Nonetheless, the three still give the fans what they would expect when three Doctors meet—competitive yet friendly bickering.

Another CNC moment occurs in *The Five(ish) Doctors Reboot* via the musical cues accompanying Davison, Baker, and McCoy as they visit the *Doctor Who* Experience and then the BBC Wales production facility where *NüWho*, particularly, "The Day of the Doctor," is being produced. Initially, the diegetic music has been lifted from the Roger-Limb scored soundtrack to "Meglos," the second story of the Nathan-Turner produced season eighteen featuring Tom Baker as the Doctor. This style of heavy synthesizer-flavored instrumentals likewise dominated the musical soundscape for the Fifth and Sixth Doctors' eras and was used for some of the Seventh Doctor's stories. For any fan familiar with these four Doctors' eras, the humor of the musical joke is apparent. As the actors enter the BBC building, however, the music suddenly shifts to composer Murray Gold's bombastic orchestra-performed music that characterizes *NüWho*. As a result, the low-key music of *Classic Who*, with its more limited budget, has been effectively counterpointed against the significantly improved musical resources of the new series.

Once inside the *Doctor Who* production area, Davison, McCoy, and Baker discover the current TARDIS control room set being utilized for the Eleventh Doctor's adventures. In a manner similar to the Second Doctor or the Tenth Doctor beholding the newest iteration of their successors' TARDIS interiors in the respective anniversary specials, "The Three Doctors" and "The Day of the Doctor," these three former Doctors comically express their disdain at the newest model. One fan blogger, Chris Morley, comments on this sequence, "You couldn't help but share in their glee when the Doctors three finally got aboard the TARDIS. Those who grew up with them were possibly transported to the first post-regenerative moment each of them stood at the controls. And who didn't chuckle as Davison admitted he missed the 'wobble' of the original set?" For this *Classic Who* fan, Davison's encoding efforts in granting fans a de facto alternative anniversary scene in which Doctors Five to Seven interact in the current incumbent's TARDIS had succeeded in generating appropriate feelings of nostalgia. Morley, however, continues, "Yes, it may all have been a bit naff back then, but for me and countless others it was part of the nostalgia. A shared suspension of disbelief, and a wonderful escape at that. Nobody could blame the Three Stooges of Who for wanting to recapture those glories, even if it was for one last time, onscreen at least. After all, they helped lay the groundwork for New Who." In this section, the blogger articulates some of the more inertia-laden characteristics of the Continuum of Nostalgic Continuity that is cascading through Davison and company's performances in *The Five(ish) Doctors Reboot*, which fundamentally subscribes to the often-propagated notion that 1980s—or *Classic Who* in general—is a camp show that *NüWho* refined, corrected, and thereby redeemed from the ignominy of its 1989 cancellation. Simultaneously, Davison, Baker, and McCoy, from a postmodern perspective, are self-consciously celebrating the budgetary limitations and the sometimes embarrassing storytelling found in their respective eras of *Doctor Who* in order to create a new hybrid subgenre that adds to the show's mythos—the meta, semi-comedic multi–Doctor narrative.

The final joke of *The Five(ish) Doctors Reboot*, which hints that the three ex–Doctors have indeed inadvertently succeeded in making it onscreen in "The Day of the Doctor," is rather problematic. In an earlier sequence in the episode, Baker, McCoy, and Davison had hid from BBC security by placing white sheets over themselves while the ending reveals that their actions made them look like the shrouded Zygons who are seen onscreen via the under-gallery sequence in "The Day of the Doctor." While this ending depicts the trio of actors' apparent good fortune in obliquely achieving their self-inflated heroic quest to honor their fans' wishes, this vision of obscured, whited-out Doctors—in a certain somber sense—may, in reality, serve as *NüWho*'s (or Steven Moffat's) indictment of three Nathan-Turner-encoded eras of *Classic Who*. While Moffat's critique of these Doctors' eras does not necessarily place them in an open-gallery-space queer closet via the sheets, it could very well point to an ageist attitude toward these actors, who do not easily resemble how their younger selves looked when respectively playing the role of the slowly-aging Time Lord. The sheets could likewise represent a "ghosting" of three 1980s-era asexual Doctors, whose lack of a romantic attitude toward—or relationship with—any of their companions could be tantamount to a form of masculine heroic impotence in the eyes of a contemporary multiplatform viewing audience. In other words, Davison may playfully yet seriously indicate in *The Five(ish) Doctors Reboot* that the noticeable absence of new material for his, Baker's, and McCoy's Doctors in "The Day of the Doctor" could signify that their non-sexual Time Lords embody outmoded, translucently encoded characterizations of a character who has been successfully reencoded in *Nü Who* as a complexly sexualized hero.

* * *

As I bring this chapter's discussion of the explosively combative media era of 1980s *Doctor Who* to a close, I would like to present fan writer Greg Cook's interesting assessment of Nathan-Turner's encoding choices during the Sixth and Seventh Doctors' eras:

> When JN-T first became producer, he had clear ideas of how the show should be retooled.... [He] hired Peter Davison because Davison reflected the sort of Doctor JN-T wanted; then JN-T hired Colin Baker because he was different from Davison. No wonder the last five years of JN-T's era seem so uncertain in tone; the producer was intentionally making decisions against his instincts. Such thinking resulted in gimmicks: the longer episodes, the "Trial" season, the comedy of Season 24 (from JN-T, who didn't like the "slapstick" of the later Tom Baker stories).

Cook indeed presents a potentially correct critical formulation of Nathan-Turner's encoding of more than one new Doctor. Simultaneously, his thoughts could be inverted as a positive assessment of the successful format *Nü Who* showrunners have applied to encode more than one original Time Lord: counterpointing the characterization of successive Doctors to keep audiences intrigued with the ongoing evolution of the show. For instance, in his role as showrunner of *Doctor Who*, Russell T Davies had encoded two distinct incarnations of the Doctor—the brooding Ninth and the upbeat Tenth—and his era has been popularly hailed as a classic time for the series, perhaps since the 2005 reboot of the show represented a relatively fresh media product that was still engaged in the process of amassing record numbers of new fans in the United States and on a global scale. Moreover, although *Doctor Who* fan-decoder Steven Moffat has arguably been influenced by Nathan-Turner's encoding of the rather unlikeable Sixth Doctor in his own creation of Peter Capaldi's irascible Twelfth Doctor, who has followed Matt Smith's gentler performance as the Eleventh Doctor, the current *Nü Who* showrunner has effectively worked toward ameliorating the latest Time Lord's rougher characterization over the course of Series Eight and Nine.

With the examples of Davies and Moffat in mind, an argument once more could be made that while *Doctor Who* audiences in the 1980s wanted consistently heroic, trustworthy Doctors as classically essayed by Peter Davison's Fifth Doctor—not Colin Baker's mercurial Sixth Doctor or Sylvester McCoy's clown-then-dark-chess-player Seventh Doctor—Nathan-Turner may have been two decades ahead of his time in attempting to present more challenging interpretations of the show's chameleonic lead character. Regardless of one's critical assessment concerning John Nathan-Turner's legacy as *Doctor Who*'s first gay producer in the 1980s, the fact remains that this era will continue to serve as an experimental encoding and decoding touchstone for what makes the show equally thrive and flounder. Nathan-Tuner likewise reminds current and future showrunners of the dangers inherent in being too close to the decoder-fans. At the same time, this media-savvy man's understanding of the power of meaningfully connecting with *Doctor Who* fandom, in a way, had brilliantly anticipated how instantaneous social media tools such as blogs, *Twitter*, and *YouTube* would radically lower the barriers that had once separated top-down producers and bottom-up fans. In the next chapter, building from these thoughts, I shall be exploring how such current interactive social media works toward both paying homage and in reviving and stalling a potential reboot of another beloved BBC cult TV show—*Blake's 7*.

Chapter Three

The CNC Implications of Blake's 7's *Stylized Retro-Future*

Curiously, in a post–911 and Cold War age, in which so-called contemporary global empires have not always lived up to the idealism imbued in either their democratic or communistic principles, a classic BBC SF television saga—*Blake's 7*—which daringly inverts the *Star Trek* trope of a benevolent Federation with its futuristic totalitarian vision of a united world/galactic government—has not been rebooted. Although this statement may be clouded by this researcher's aca-fan affectionate attitude toward creator Terry Nation's dystopian allegory of antiheroes fighting against a villainous empire, one can say that *Blake's 7* fandom, thanks to the Continuum of Nostalgic Continuity enacting its gravitational hold upon its long-dormant master narrative, may have petrified the show as a kitsch-filled symbol of the time when it was originally broadcast on the television airwaves—1978–81.

One can also consider the case of two other latter 1970s television properties, *Doctor Who* and NBC's *Battlestar Galactica*, which were, during certain points in the fallow years following their cancellations, ridiculed by fans and anti-fans for their more kitsch qualities. Notably, however, both properties were successfully rebooted in the mid–2000s.[1] Since *Blake's 7* attempted to blend dramatic and more offbeat or comedic elements in a similar fashion to those two shows, the lack of a successful attempt at a modern reboot for this long dormant property, which still has a supportive fan base, is rather perplexing.[2] One answer to this problem, which may underscore the fundamental thematic differences occurring between *Blake's 7* and *Battlestar Galactica* and *Doctor Who*, is that Nation's premise involves antiheroes fighting the ultimately undefeatable Federation while the other two shows encode a more traditional heroism with their individual characters struggling against villains who can be more satisfyingly vanquished.[3] Furthermore, since *Doctor Who* and *Battlestar*

Galactica in the 1970s were produced for all-ages audiences whereas *Blake's 7* had been geared at a somewhat older demographic, perhaps it had been easier to sell these concepts to the respective networks who greenlit their reboots, the BBC and Syfy.[4] Regardless of the behind-the-scenes complications over the past two decades surrounding continuing or rebooting *Blake's 7*, one can confidently argue that the classic version of the show itself presents an innovatively gendered heroic quest.

In chapter one, I discussed how *Blake's 7*'s first episode, "The Way Back," encodes a darker SF television saga by introducing a victimized hero in its titular character as he is framed as a child molester in order to discredit him in the eyes of Federation citizenry who may be sympathetic to the resistance movement. Throughout the early part of the episode, Blake, whose memory of his past as a resistance leader has been modified by the Federation in order to reprogram him as a loyal, reformed citizen, refuses his heroic call to action since he cannot recall being one. Applicable to Blake's heroic ennui is Joseph Campbell's elaboration upon what he calls the "dull case of the call unanswered":

> Refusal of the summons converts the adventure into its negative. Walled in boredom, hard work, or "culture," the subject loses the power of significant affirmative action and becomes a victim to be saved. His flowering world becomes a wasteland of dry stones and his life feels meaningless—even though, like King Minos, he may through titanic effort succeed in building an empire of renown. Whatever house he builds, it will be a house of death: a labyrinth of cyclopean walls to hide from his Minotaur. All he can do is create new problems for himself and await the gradual approach of his disintegration (59).

Blake, as a modified member of his "culture," the Federation, is indeed a victim who no longer possesses a real past and lives a clouded existence due to the state-generated propaganda and drug suppressants put in his and his fellow citizens' food. For Blake, who cannot access his memories of being a powerful resistance leader, the "Minotaur" he subconsciously hides from is his past obscured self. His "disintegration," which is potential madness, moreover, awaits him if he cannot reawaken his heroic soul from a mind and body that is all but dead.

Like William Hartnell's initially antiheroic First Doctor, then, he must learn and struggle to define himself as a true hero in the audience's eyes. However, to achieve this narrative goal, Terry Nation crafts a darker, atmospheric first episode that finds a hapless, victimized Blake witnessing a massacre of fellow freedom fighters he cannot remember, being convicted of fabricated charges, and sadly being deported from Earth on a prisoner transport ship, the London, since his defense attorney, Tel Varon, who was on the verge of proving his innocence, has been murdered by Federation soldiers. It is only with the final line of dialogue in "The Way Back"—Blake's defiant promise to a mocking London guard that he will one day return to Earth—that the audience is reassured that he truly embodies a courageous masculine hero, one whose memories of his past life have been successfully reawakened by an appropriately traumatic struggle.[5]

"The Way Back," as a result, functions as a narrative prelude to *Blake's 7*'s format for its first three series: a group of reformed criminals striving against the massive Federation, whose empire is spread out all over the galaxy, via their appropriation of a powerful alien starship, the Liberator. With this thought in mind, a strong argument could be made that the series' second episode, "Space Fall," serves as the proper beginning of *Blake's 7*'s narrative. In the tale, Blake leads an attempt to commandeer the London in order to save its prisoners from potentially being dumped into space by the ship's corrupt crew, so they can save on transportation costs to the prison planet Cygnus Alpha. During this effort, Blake forms a tense alliance with Kerr Avon, a computer mastermind, in order to gain control of the London's central computer. When the London's crew thwarts the efforts of the other prisoners, Blake and company, who have successfully taken over the ship's computer room, are faced with a dilemma: surrender or watch as their fellow escapees are executed.

It is this confined space, serving as the symbolic setting for a heated debate between Blake and Avon, which encapsulates the fundamental conceit of *Blake's 7*'s first two seasons, and, by way of extension, the entirety of the fifty-two episode series. If their escape attempt is successful, then Blake plans on going back to Earth, declaring, "[T]hat's where the heart of the Federation is; I intend to see that heart torn out." Avon, however, replies, "I thought you were probably insane," to which Blake responds, "That's possible! They butchered my family, my friends. They murdered my past and gave me tranquilized dreams." He also tells Jenna Stannis, his fellow escapee, that he will not be properly alive again "until free men can think and speak" and "power is back with the honest man," which reiterates to the audience that he is still crafting his own Campbellian Minotaur—in this case embodied by his reawakened inner idealistic freedom fighter who needs to free *every* oppressed Federation citizen.

As Blake becomes more obsessed with destroying the Federation in Series B, even willing to sacrifice millions of innocents in the episode "Star One" to see his enemy destroyed, Avon's pronouncement on his rival's mental health could indeed be given textual weight. In fact, as a paranoid Avon, who has mostly given up his survival-driven pragmatism by attempting to heroically emulate Blake in Series C and D, eventually comes into contact with his long-lost, scarred mentor in the final episode of the series, "Blake," viewers may have been rather unsure in determining which character is more mentally unbalanced. Additionally, the show, as a whole, could be raising the possibility that prolonged heroic resistance against a superior force, the Federation, could lead even the best of masculine heroes to the edge of insanity.

Before Avon's heroic journey begins, however, in "Space Fall," he voices to Blake and Jenna his practical vision of his reality as an outlaw: "Listen to me: wealth is the only reality. And the only way to obtain wealth is to take it away from somebody else." Although Avon at times in *Blake's 7*'s first two seasons creates the impression he just wants to take the Liberator, the ultimate form of power and capital, and retire to the far reaches of the galaxy, he chooses a more traditional heroic path. This is not to say he is not willing to place his own self before others, as I will discuss later in this chapter. However, for a period of time on *Blake's 7*, he represents a more measured, logical hero than Blake, one who weighs the need for self-preservation against the self-sacrificial tenets of freedom-driven idealism.

Forming the final flexible part of this triadic philosophical argument is Jenna, who essentially functions as the audience surrogate. As Avon continues in "Space Fall," "Wake up, Blake! You may not be tranquilized any longer, but you're still dreaming," she comments, "Maybe some dreams are worth having." Cynically, Avon then asks her, "You don't really believe that?" and Jenna vulnerably replies, "No, but I'd like to." Consequently, in her decision to renounce her gun-running ways and join Blake's heroic crusade against the Federation, Jenna serves as a symbol of the reformed-criminal-turned hero. More importantly, in the following episode, "Cygnus Alpha," one can argue that Blake's masculine heroic influence leads her to concoct the hopeful name "Liberator" for the ship as its sentient computer, Zen, pulls this word from her mind and uses it to vocalize the moniker of the craft to her, Blake, and Avon.

With Vila, the thief, and Gan, the sensitive strongman,[6] being rescued by Blake, Avon, and Jenna at the conclusion of "Cygnus Alpha," and the telepathic Cally joining them in "Time Squad," the fourth episode of Series A, Blake's original seven[7] has been introduced to the show's audience. To balance out this mix of gendered heroism (four males, two females, and a computer with a masculine voice), Nation presents the villainous Servalan and the partially cybernetic Travis in episode six, "Seek–Locate–Destroy." With her short cropped, rather androgynously styled black hair and elegant white dress, Servalan offers a vision of the female villain who straddles the gendered line between masculine and feminine.[8] In fact, one of the episode's scenes depicts her addressing the concerns of one of her officers, Rai, in a way that shows that she is not beyond employing her sexuality to elicit vital information from a male. Sitting next to Rai on a couch in her office, she initially employs a calm, flirtatious tone in order to learn his thoughts on her appointing the disgraced Space Commander Travis to take charge of a mission to apprehend Blake's crew. Upon learning that Rai and certain unnamed colleagues do not wish to serve under Travis because he had massacred Federation civilians during an uprising, she assumes a logical, stern masculine demeanor, rising to stand behind the symbolic command post of her desk to inform him that any act committed against her command will be regarded as treason. As a result of this character-building encoding moment, the audience immediately learns that Servalan straddles—or overlaps—the gendered lines of femininity, masculinity, and androgyny.

Travis, who also debuts in this episode, represents the ultimate archnemesis for Blake. Wearing a tight-black leather soldier's outfit, its collar upturned in a fashionable manner, Travis, played by Stephen Greif in Series A only, is dressed in a costume that has been encoded with both a warrior and a fetish design. On this latter note, costume designer Barbara Lane reveals, "I took [Stephen] to Hardcore Leather on the King's Road, to get his black suit made, because we couldn't find anyone who could work as well with leather as these guys" (qtd. in Nazzaro and Wells 62). This S/M look for Travis symbolically conveys his sadistic feelings toward Blake, whom he wishes to kill for shooting him in the face, leaving him with a disfigurement he masochistically had covered by an unsightly black eye patch,[9] which serves as a reminder to him of the disgrace his enemy caused him. In addition, when paired with Servalan, Travis shows how the main Federation villains of *Blake's 7* have been encoded with a more deviant, perhaps queered sexuality in relation to Blake and company, whose masculinity and femininity are more traditional in terms of appearance and actions. Both characters, moreover, employ the services of Mutoids, former human beings whose memories of their past lives have been erased while their bodies have been technologically augmented with cybernetic implants that are most noticeable in their bulbous head extensions. Dressed in leather like Travis, these posthuman soldiers loyally carry out any order given to them, a situation arguably maintained by their vampire-like reliance on synthetic blood. Furthermore, despite their often exotically attractive appearance in their tight leather uniforms,[10] the Mutoids' very existence subsumes any hetero/homo/bisexual pairings on *Blake's 7*, thus presenting another alternative vision of villain-encoded gender on the show.

When paired with Servalan, however, the sadistic Travis, partially due to being institutionally subservient to his commanding officer, takes on more masochistic characteristics. According to academics Jonathan Bignell and Andrew O'Day, Servalan ruling "over secondary male officers such as Space Commander Travis" works as a "reversal of the binary of male as primary and female as secondary" (174). When one considers that Blake and Avon, on the heroic side of *Blake's 7*'s televised narrative, serve as the primary leaders to the secondary female characters of Jenna, Cally, Dayna, and Soolin, it would seem that the villains of the show present a more positive, progressive vision of gender relations. In short, although these four females assist Blake and Avon in their heroic (and/or mutual survival-driven) endeavors, they are never presented as assuming an active leadership role aboard either the Liberator or Scorpio.

As much as Servalan may appear to represent a more ideal vision of feminine strength on *Blake's 7*, Bignell and O'Day likewise point out,

> [Her] structural position as Blake's main enemy was represented by her unconventionally masculine behaviour. Positive characters conform to gender conventions, while negative characters distort them. The casting of a female actress in the role of the Federation Commander draws attention to the conventionally passive female role in television fiction and in science fiction in particular, and highlights the Federation's conventionally masculine policies of violence and institutionalized aggression [174].

In arguing that Servalan's ambitious, murderous actions throughout *Blake's 7* Series A to D are indicative of a male-dominated Federation, Bignell and O'Day are somewhat correct as Servalan does not take orders from—or compete against—another powerful female who is either politically or militarily involved in her corrupt galactic government. Her rivals are only men, whom she can either manipulate sexually or through sheer force of arms. But to write Servalan off as an extension of the Federation's masculine politics may be to demean her inherent value as a female character whose personal needs separate her from the operating philosophy of an oppressive governmental institution. In an interview with Peter Linford, actress Jacqueline Pearce offers this vision of her performance choices for Servalan: "I saw her as a woman who was very damaged and driven by pain. That can result as manifesting as evil and perhaps it did, but I'm saying that what drove her was not a desire to be evil but a desire to escape from pain, and by keeping oneself invulnerable and getting more and more power, then you can protect yourself" (165). For Pearce, Servalan's constant sadism is a logical, ironic escape from being on the receiving end of other people's cruel actions. Sharing a similar yet less sympathetic view on the encoding of Servalan's villainy, Chris Boucher, the script editor for all four seasons of *Blake's 7*, asserts, "She and people like her, subvert organizations and ideas and movements, not because they have a different view of what they should be, but purely because they can. Servalan was just using the Federation to gratify her own selfish needs, and anyone who got in her way was ruthlessly purged." In reconciling these academic, acting, and writing views on Servalan, one can claim that they celebrate the contradictory and complementary elements of her character, who, in the late 1970s/early 1980s (and even today), complicates and challenges traditional viewer expectations for the roles of SF females and villains alike.

The Blake–Travis conflict ends in the Series B cliffhanger, "Star One," with Travis badly wounding Blake by shooting him in the back. Yet Avon actually delivers the shot that kills Travis, perhaps signaling to the audience that he is *Blake's 7*'s leading-man-in-waiting since Gareth Thomas, who played Blake, had chosen to leave the show. Commenting on this professional choice in an interview with Brian J. Robb, Thomas reasons,

> First, I'd done 26 episodes and felt I couldn't take the character of Blake any further. Secondly, I did believe the series was going a little bit astray. It had started off as *The Dirty Dozen* in Space, with real gutsy characters, but by the end of the second series, it had become tired. The Liberator was this giant spaceship which had this giant room full of wonderful costumes which just happened to fit us all. Things became easy for the characters [162].

For Thomas, the gradual rise of the heroically fanatical Blake over the course of Series A and B, to his apparent victory over the Federation after destroying Star One, their intergalactic communications center, was too easy of a character arc.[11] His successor, Paul Darrow, who played Avon, consequently, had to accept the challenge of stepping in to lead the cast of a show whose titular character has departed. Darrow, however, took a pragmatic approach to his depiction of Avon for Series C of *Blake's 7*, claiming, "Not to sugar coat it, Avon is a back-shooting, murderous grand thief, whose only cause is himself. So, without Blake, we were—I can't resist this—rebels without a cause!" (*You're Him* 85).

Darrow's summation of Avon's role as Blake's successor is not entirely accurate. In point of fact, Avon's ascension to *Blake's 7*'s leading hero begins in the closing moments of "Star One," when he leads the Liberator crew in battle against an invading alien fleet since Blake needs to recuperate from his injuries. Before Blake departs the ship's bridge, however, which equally symbolizes Thomas's departure from the role, he comments to Avon, "[F]or what it is worth, I have always trusted you, from the very beginning." At that moment, this confession presented an emotional climax to the Blake–Avon rivalry that had coursed through Series A and B. When seen as a motivator for Avon both leading his rebel companions against the Federation in Blake's absence and searching for the missing hero himself in "Terminal" and "Blake," the respective final episodes of Series C and D, these words had catalyzed Avon's journey to struggle with his still-developing troubled heroic identity.

In other ways, Darrow's summation of the lack of consistent heroic direction in *Blake's 7*'s two final two seasons is correct. Perhaps the theme of these two seasons is to blur the line even further than before on the show between heroism and villainy, most especially in regard to Avon, who repeatedly stumbles in his attempt to fill the leadership gap left by Blake's disappearance. As an example, in the Series C episode "Rumours of Death," Avon investigates the death of his lover, Anna Grant, only to discover that she never died since she was, in truth, a Federation spy who had been assigned to arrest him and any of his criminal associates. During the course of this dark adventure, Avon comes across Servalan, who is chained to a wall in her presidential palace on Earth. He wishes to set her free in exchange for information concerning Anna. When Avon's compatriot, Tarrant, however, points out that Servalan may have let herself be captured and chained up in her own palace by a few dozen guerrilla fighters, this exchange is prompted between her and Avon:

> AVON: Is that it? Have you finally lost your nerve? Have you murdered your way to the wall of an underground room?
> SERVALAN: It's an old wall, Avon. It waits. I hope you don't die before you reach it.

While the wall to which Servalan refers could be a physical one in which a murderous person such as herself is chained up for her crimes, it also refers to the metaphorical wall of guilt to which one cannot escape in recognition of his or her killing of others. Avon, who ends up shooting Anna at the end of the episode to prevent her from stabbing him, begins his journey to this wall. More importantly, Servalan's words take on a prophetic import in regard to "Blake," the show's final episode, as Blake, who has been killed by Avon, lies at his feet, soon joined in death by Dayna, Vila, Soolin, and Tarrant, as they are subsequently shot by Federation soldiers. With the episode's closing moment, Avon, surrounded on all sides by the soldiers, stands astride Blake's corpse, raises his gun to attack them, and enigmatically smiles, arguably, in recognition that, in his own way, he has at last reached Servalan's metaphorical wall of death and regret.

While Series C would present Avon's crew on the run from the Federation, which is given the consistent face of Servalan, who covets the Liberator and Orac, it is not until "Terminal" when a potential heroic quest—finding Blake—is offered to viewers. As the wounded and bearded

Blake presented in that episode is proven to be a deceptive illusion on Servalan's part, the reality of its conclusion—Avon's crew marooned on the artificial planetoid of Terminal with the Liberator destroyed—presents a downbeat, unheroic counterpoint to Series B's upbeat "Star One" cliffhanger. The following final series of *Blake's 7* would continue with a grouping of episodes where Avon's crew would fight against the Federation with a new ship, the Scorpio, but it is not until the show's penultimate episode, "Warlord," where Avon tries—and fails—to organize a confederation of worlds against the Federation that a concrete story arc emerges. While one can argue that Avon attempts this ambitious feat in imitation of Blake, one can equally say that he seeks out allies in order to help ensure his own survival against the overwhelming enemy that is the Federation.

With the series finale, "Blake," moreover, Avon once again embraces a quest to reunite with Blake, claiming to his crewmates that the man will represent an inspirational figurehead for their rebellion. By the episode's end, however, the Scorpio has crashed on Gauda Prime, and Avon has shot Blake in a tragic misunderstanding due to the fact he thought his former leader had betrayed him in his guise as a bounty hunter (which, in reality, was part of a scheme to find and recruit new resistance members). Moreover, since Vila, Dayna, Tarrant, and Soolin have seemingly been shot and killed by Federation soldiers in the episode's climax, *Blake's 7*'s fans were left with a problematically shocking and downbeat conclusion to their beloved show.

In regard to "Blake's" conclusion, scholar John Kenneth Muir argues, "Avon crossed the line into insanity. So paranoid was he, so angry at the thought of betrayal, that he murdered Blake without hearing him out. In the final moments.... Avon realized what he had become ... and smiled. The joke was on him. If he had trusted a little more, shown a little more of Blake's idealism, the resistance, the crew and Avon would have survived" (133). Muir's interpretation of Avon's final actions in "Blake," of course, reveals an aca-fan reading of the episode, as his obvious knowledge of the series and the character of Avon proffers his personal version of Series D's mythological narrative—Avon descending into madness. Other viewers or fans could easily pose the argument that Avon bravely smiling in the face of potential death as he raises his gun functions as the final defiant act of a survivor. For this aca-fan writer—and many other viewers—a more flexible answer may be that Avon in "Blake" represents a postmodern distillation of an existential character since he can embrace either heroic or villainous traits at any moment, therefore delivering a process of self-discovery apparent to both encoders (the writers and performers of *Blake's*

7) and decoders (viewers and fan fiction writers) alike. As a result, the dualistic hero/antihero embodied by Avon is a rather problematic and exhilarating figure for everybody because he represents the uncertain unknowability inherent in all human beings as his very identity forms a fluidic essence that can be overwritten in any given catalytic life situation.

For Neil and Sue Perryman, who run a *Blake's 7* viewing blog, *Adventures with the Wife and Blake*, a sense of play accompanies their conversation concerning the final moments of "Blake" and the closing credits' diegetic sounds of blaster fire being exchanged:

> SUE: They could have brought it back if they really wanted to.... [T]hose shots we heard could have been the guards firing at the ceiling.
> NEIL: And why would they do that?
> SUE: To put the shits up Avon.
> NEIL: I'm guessing that Avon shot a few guards while they were pranking him. Yes?
> SUE: A couple. Yes. Look, does it matter? They could have used stun guns. We didn't see any blood.

Sue and Neil's conversation, interestingly, represents the tongue-in-cheek reciprocal power dynamics occurring in their blog, where Neil, an old-school *Blake's 7* fan who possesses a three-decade-long knowledge of the series, exposes his wife, a non-fan, to the show for her fresh viewer perspective. In short, the charm—and marketable elements—of this *Kickstarter*-funded blog[12] lies in the complementary give-and-take of Neil's exclusive fan perspective of *Blake's 7* and Sue's inexperienced "newbie" reactions. In this instance, Neil views the ending of "Blake" as a definitive conclusion to the series, in which Avon most likely died in a firefight with the Federation soldiers. His opinion—cemented by the fact that another season of *Blake's 7* never rectified this ending—has been shared by many viewers of the series. Conversely, Sue's reaction, unencumbered by the passage of time, along with her playfully crude language, serves as an outside-fandom viewer analysis that reminds even the most die-hard *Blake's 7* fan that the show nonetheless is just another fictitious work in which death, an ever-malleable component of the literary form, can be undone.

Post-Gauda Prime Narratives: Encoders and Decoders Continuing the *Blake's 7* Saga

Like *Star Trek* fandom of the 1970s, who told new stories of Captain Kirk, Spock and the rest of the Enterprise crew in the fallow years between the show's cancellation in 1969 and its revival as a movie series in 1979,[13] *Blake's 7* writers and fans, via the medium of the "post–Gauda Prime" story[14] have continued to tell their own versions of what happened to the Scorpio crew, particularly Avon, after their apparent demise in 1981's "Blake." Pertinent to understanding this process is Henry Jenkins's declaration, "Organized fandom is, perhaps first and foremost, an institution of theory and criticism, a semistructured space where competing interpretations and evaluations of common texts are proposed, debated, and negotiated and where readers speculate about the nature of the mass media and their own relationship to it" (86). As an application of Jenkins's comments, this section examines how fans create, celebrate, or criticize professional, semiprofessional, and fan-generated post–Gauda Prime stories.

In 1984, Target Books published the first "official"[15] continuation of the *Blake's 7* saga, *Afterlife*, written by Tony Attwood. Avon, for undisclosed reasons, had survived "Blake's" climatic shoot-out on Gauda Prime while Vila is revealed to have lived because he faked being shot. The two survivors, along with Orac, are joined by a new antiheroic character, Korell, and they go on an adventure that ultimately presents the demise of Servalan and the introduction of Tor, Avon's sister, who is part of a revolution that is on the verge of toppling the Federation. For many *Blake's 7* fans, however, *Afterlife* has been viewed as an unsuccessful, overly complicated, muddled continuation of the show's storyline. Alternatively, Jason P. Juneau, a fan writer well aware of what he calls the "almost universal rejection by fans" of the novel, points out,

> *Afterlife* really focuses on Avon as a conspirator, problem solver, and field technician.... His dialogue is a bit strange at times and over the top, e.g., "I will not be defeated again," but after having viewed the 4th series, this did not seem too out of place. Campy portrayals I could forgive because this was by and large the Avon I liked, secretive, determined, not some emotional cripple who could not face his feelings, but a man with an agenda.

Juneau's observation that Attwood's characterization of Avon in *Afterlife* more or less is in synch with how the character was written in *Blake's 7* Series D is versed in the accepted discourse of *Blake's 7* fandom, as they decode Avon's dialogue and motivations according to his ever-changing encoding in the four respective seasons of the show. He also accepts the more controversially pragmatic version of Avon as written by Robert Holmes in "Orbit": "This Avon could dump Vila out of an airlock, or keep him around. It would simply depend on how useful Vila was at the moment." Nevertheless, while Avon has been rather cutthroat in his desire to stay alive throughout the four seasons of *Blake's 7*, he still simultaneously functions as a hero.

Attwood himself highlights Avon's inconsistent motivations on the show via the character of Korell in *Afterlife*, as she asks Avon at a latter point in the novel, "What does Kerr Avon do with credit? He is already the antihero of a whole Galaxy. He could command any sum just to lend his name to a revolution attempt at any place in the Milky Way. Or to solve some irritating little computer problem even on an Inner World. Avon could drive forever on Terminal up and down the Galaxy, just as he could on *Liberator* after Blake disappeared" (187–88). In a meta way, Attwood has underscored the logical inconsistencies of a character purportedly encoded to represent rationality and heroism. Yes, Avon is on the surface a character who will do whatever it takes to survive. But it is this antiheroic mindset that has made him more of a dynamic character than the righteous, messianic Blake to *Blake's 7* writers and fans alike.

Regarding Avon's motivations, the acquisition of wealth was indeed his original motivating factor before meeting Blake. Series C and D, however, presented a new, conflicted Avon: a man who weighed his overriding need for survival against his newfound desire to make a heroic difference against the ultimate enemy of freedom: the Federation. The episode "Blake," however, complicated this more altruistic iteration of Avon, as, to many fans, he appeared as the cold-blooded murderer of Blake. For other fans, his act of killing Blake was borne out of a misunderstanding created by the rebel leader himself, whose mental state may have matched his face's physical scarring. Moreover, for fans who preferred the latter two seasons of *Blake's 7* to the first two, Avon's killing of Blake serves the symbolic purpose of allowing him to finally destroy the man whose name and memory overshadowed any of his own heroic efforts.

For fans more interested in the psychoanalytical (or slash) dimensions of Avon's killing of Blake, the act represents a narrative jumping point for a realization of these desires. In fan writer Zenia's post–Gauda Prime short story "Gauda Prime: A Fairytale," the author composes an immediate follow-up scene to Avon standing astride Blake's body in the closing moments of "Blake":

> There was a moment in the silence when Avon allowed himself to relax. No pain. No fear. He dropped down to cover Blake's body with his own, ignoring the warm stickiness of blood. Sentiment breeds weakness, but Blake's eyes were staring upward, heartbreakingly empty. Avon tangled his fingers in Blake's curls. They were dusty and soft. He had wondered from time to time but had never allowed his curiosity to be satisfied. But now he could, as much as he wished to.

Zenia has indeed composed a surreal, fantasy-influenced piece by presenting a scenario in which Avon has somehow avoided the Federation soldiers' gunshots, shifted into another reality, or receded into his personal intimate thoughts. The fan author, moreover, adds an erotic quality to Blake's corpse by writing about the "warm stickiness of [his] blood." And, of course, the writer subscribes to the homoerotic standards of Blake–Avon hurt-comfort[16] slash in having Avon now tenderly touch Blake after brutally murdering him. Fan fantasy, in terms of Avon finally coming to terms with his repressed feelings for Blake, is likewise realized, adding a warmer resolution to the Blake–Avon conflict. In other words, with this decoding situation, Zenia not only channels fan sexual fantasies for *Blake's 7*'s two leading men but also resists and reencodes the ending to the series, thereby enacting her agency as a fan writer.

Other imaginative *Blake's 7* fans have realized their fantasies for a post–Gauda Prime story by creating new characters and placing themselves in their own video productions. In 1994, a group of fans filmed their own follow-up narrative to "Blake": *Blake's Legend*. Initially working around the televised narrative of "Blake," this video production offers a new crew of rebels traveling aboard a ship close in appearance to the Liberator: the Icarus, which the group found on Space World, from which Blake's appropriated sister ship had originated.[17] Like the original *Blake's 7* heroic characters, these fan-actors are dressed in retro-futuristic garb that could have reasonably been worn onscreen by the original cast. Moreover, they have built replicas of the Liberator's teleport bracelets and guns, an effort which shows their preference for *Blake's 7*'s heroic adventures being realized aboard this ornate ship rather than the more unsophisticated Scorpio freighter. However, due to obvious budgetary limitations, the production does not recreate the Liberator's main cavernous set but instead features the characters interacting in a set that combines elements from the teleport room and one *Blake's 7* character who had been housed in the main Liberator set—Zen. Moreover, they even hired actor Peter Tuddenham to once again voice the character, adding a sense of authenticity to their unauthorized production.

As for *Blake's Legend*'s narrative, it tells of rebel leader Lusk's desire to join Blake in his rebellious crusade against the Federation. Appropriating footage from the final shootout in "Blake" into this opening storyline, episode one intercuts the Icarus crew's mission with the catastrophic events on Gauda Prime. Remarkably, when Lusk considers teleporting down to the planet, he makes this remark to Esa, his female crewmate, who wishes to take on the dangerous task in place of him: "You make a habit of taking my risks for me. I can't let you." However, Esa replies, "I'm faster. You know that." Thus, in direct contrast to *Blake's 7*'s Series A and B scenario, where Jenna and Cally would often stay aboard the Liberator while their male counterparts would teleport down to a given planet, Esa embodies the leading active heroic role in the first part of this fan spin-off.

In the second episode of *Blake's Legend*, two visions of empowered female sexuality are also featured. In one scene, Federation officer Shontalle makes the following remark to her superior officer, Commander Veneer, in regard to the cadets he is training: "I do hope you haven't worn them all out. I might like to take one home later." Obviously channeling Servalan's predatory erotic traits as displayed in Series A to D of *Blake's 7*, this fan-created character celebrates and underscores the refreshingly open sexual freedom evinced by Pearce's original performance, one that would traditionally be essayed by such SF characters as *Star Trek*'s Captain Kirk or *Star Wars*' Han Solo. In other words, officer-class characters such as Shontalle and Servalan can openly enact their sexual agency when they are imbued with the traditional masculine characteristics of power and command. In the other sequence, set on the planet Ellif Major, Jector, one of Lusk's compatriots, uses her body in order to gesture to a Federation soldier to follow her for a hinted sexual rendezvous. Once he is close to her, however, she knocks him out to help facilitate her group's intended raid on a Federation installation housed in a mountain.[18] Dualistically, Jector's act could either be viewed as an empowering moment in which a heroic female character employs her sexuality as a weapon, or as a reminder that rebel women in *Blake's 7* proper, such as Jenna, Cally, Dayna, and Soolin, often function as a form of attractive "eye-candy" for male viewers.

When viewing the fan act of creating *Blake's Legend*, which was, according to TaftKirk Productions, created through the participation of over seventy people, one needs to weigh its significance in relationship to *Blake's 7* as a marketable brand. Neither sanctioned by the BBC nor B7 Enterprises, who holds the legal rights to the *Blake's 7* license, *Blake's Legend* exemplifies the most altruistic motives of a gift economy. In his book *The Gift: Creativity and the Artist in the Modern World*, Lewis Hyde writes, "It is the cardinal difference between gift and commodity exchange that a gift establishes a feeling-bond between two people, while the sale of a commodity leaves no necessary connection" (72). In relating Hyde's thoughts to *Blake's Legend*, one can argue that its very collaborative act of creation, shared between the actors, writers, director, costume, sets, props and CGI artists, is representative of a "feeling bond" in which a well-organized group of *Blake's 7* fans celebrated their shared adoration of the defunct series and contributed to extending its narrative in the wake of a television corporation such as the BBC failing to accomplish this task.

On the note of this anti-corporate appropriation of *Blake's 7*'s universe, one can again refer to Hyde, who points out,

> There are many connections between anarchist theory and gift exchange as an economy—both assume that man is generous, or at least cooperative, "in nature"; both shun centralized power; both are best fitted to small groups and loose federations; both rely on contracts of the heart over codified contract, and so on. But, above all, it seems correct to speak of the gift as anarchist property because both anarchism and gift exchange share the assumption that it is not when a part of the self is inhibited and restrained, but when a part of the self is given away, that community appears [120].

Although one can pose a cynical counterargument that *Blake's Legend* is serving BBC/B7 Enterprises' corporate interests by working as an unpaid media marker of the show's existence, which could potentially attract new fans (i.e., consumers) to the *Blake's 7* brand and its ancillary merchandise, this production's existence as a fan work that bravely develops its own characters nearly negates this position. Ironically, while this group of fans can appropriate the Liberator's design, Zen, and footage from "Blake," thus "shun[ning] the centralized power" that is the BBC, neither that corporation nor B7 Enterprises can utilize the Icarus, which is a streamlined CGI redesign of the Liberator, or such characters as Lusk, Esa, or Shontalle in any of its video, audio, or book narratives. *Blake's Legend*, in other words, works as a non-profit gift that doubles as anarchist property because it eschews any notion of a sole artist or corporation profiting from its creation. Instead, *Blake's Legend* has worked toward uniting a portion of *Blake's 7*'s fandom and continues to promote the online survival or proliferation of this somewhat dormant community through its newfound existence on *YouTube*, where viewers can continue to express their critique and appreciation of this unique work through message boards.

Continuing with the discussion of how females function in a post–Gauda Prime *Blake's 7* universe, one can explore how Servalan, who noticeably did not appear in "Blake," is portrayed by different encoders and decoders. In *Afterlife*, Attwood depicts her as still scheming against Avon in order to gain possession of Orac. However, the author also presents her demise at the hands of Korell as she first shot a "laser ray [that] missed Servalan's heart but took her clean in the stomach" (193) and soon after "sent two blasts into Servalan and watched coldly as the former President of the Federation and one time Supreme Commander of its Armed Forces stopped moving and lay motionless on the floor" (195). Although Korell claims to have killed Servalan as revenge for a professional grievance against her, the uncomfortable truth remains that a male author has employed a female character to carry out a sadistic death he has penned for a once-powerful and indomitable *Blake's 7* female villain.

In 2013, Paul Darrow's *Lucifer*, the first part of a trilogy of post–Gauda Prime *Blake's 7* novels, features an aging Avon and presents an older Servalan as focused on wresting Orac from him yet ultimately dying at the hands of a female protagonist, Magda, who kills the still-powerful woman in order to stop her from shooting Avon in the book's climax. As Servalan dies, Darrow writes, "she scratched the surface of the earth and began to crawl towards Avon, all the time moaning in agony. A crossbow bolt protruded from her lower spine. Servalan looked up at him with pleading eyes that, even as she did so, began to dim, as if she did not care to glimpse what lay on the other side of death. She tried to smile. Instead, she pitched forward and lay still (199).

Although this passage retains the sadomasochistic overtones of Avon and Servalan's onscreen *Blake's 7* relationship,[19] it also conveys a sadistic rape-like tone as the aging woman moans, crawls, and looks at her longtime enemy with pleading eyes before dying at his feet. Once more, Avon, as he did at the end of "Blake," stands victorious over someone he viewed as a threat. But his stance is not particularly a triumphant one as he did not deliver the killing blow this time. When one considers that Darrow has presented an older Avon as cunning, sprightly, and murderous as his televised counterpart of thirty years earlier throughout the novel, his refusal to have his fictitious counterpart deliver a well-justified killing blow to his archnemesis comes off as a rather curious choice. In theory, perhaps Darrow is admitting that Avon again is incapable of finishing off Servalan, whom the character reluctantly admires, and/or fears that fans would criticize him too harshly for having Avon become the killer of both her and Blake.

On a simple note in regard to Attwood and Darrow's conflicting depictions of Servalan's demise, one could likewise say that, in both writing situations, the authors have continued to develop the theme of her trying to gain control of Orac, a box that possesses a male voice yet, arguably, offers female overtones in a vaginal/psychoanalytical sense. These writers are also cautious in avoiding accusations of misogyny by having females, not Avon, who at times hit women and/or shot them[20] in *Blake's 7*, being the ones who kill Servalan. Then again, the very act of these male authors finding it necessary to ensure that Servalan receives her "just desserts" through a prolonged death while the similarly murderous, antiheroic Avon lives, brings up the possibility of their patriarchal preferences in the encoding of their respective post–Gauda Prime narratives.

In both *Afterlife* and *Lucifer*'s narratives, furthermore, and in *The Logic of Empire*, an unauthorized fan audio production, no explanation has been provided for Avon's survival post–"Blake." When one considers that the diegetic sounds of the episode's closing credits relay a single laser bolt being fired (probably from Avon's gun) followed by several more shots (most likely from the Federation soldiers' weapons) before the *Blake's 7* theme music plays, the need for an explanation or follow-up to this unseen action is reasonably a paramount concern for some fans. Fortunately, to some degree, *The Logic of Empire* cowriter Alan Stevens offers his rationale for why he does not provide a reason for Avon's survival at the end of "Blake":

> The explanation as to how Avon survived the shoot-out on Gauda Prime is not an important strand of the plot and is meant to be obscure. The idea of a character coming back from the dead is a powerful one and quite a number of films (*High Plains Drifter*, *Point Blank*, *The Crow*, *Halloween*) and television programs (*Doctor Who*, *Edge of Darkness*, *Pennies from Heaven*, *Babylon 5*, *Buffy the Vampire Slayer*) have used it to great effect. Very rarely is any explanation given as to how these characters overcame death, and if there is, it's usually meaningless ["Alan Stevens' Comments"].

Occupying a nebulous space between fan fiction and a proper place in *Blake's 7* spin-off narratives, *The Logic of Empire* perhaps represents the finest example of encoding/decoding/encoding I can offer in this book. For the encoding end of this formulation, the forty-five minute audio production involves the participation of *Blake's 7* performers Paul Darrow, Jacqueline Pearce, Peter Tuddenham, and Gareth Thomas vocally performing the characters they essayed on television: Avon, Servalan, Orac, and Blake.[21] Simultaneously, on the decoding end of this quotient, Stevens and David Tulley, two fan writers, scripted this production, which does not contain the official *Blake's 7* branding as it had not been officially endorsed by the BBC.

During an interview with Alan Stevens and Alistair Lock, Jacqueline Pearce, who did not appear in "Blake" as Servalan, offers her cautiously optimistic vision of her character's future: "She's still alive, she's become a legend. Immortal. So they did me a favour without meaning to. However at the time I was very distressed. I'd taken it very personally. I'm a bit older now. Once it was over I let her go. If ever we did it again then I'd have to think about that." Remarkably, Pearce would be given the chance seven years later to participate in the continuation of Servalan's tale with her co-interviewer, Alan Stevens, when he co-wrote *The Logic of Empire*. Unlike Attwood and Darrow's termination of Servalan in *Afterlife* and *Lucifer*, *The Logic of Empire* not only encodes her as a powerful enemy who successfully lays a trap for Avon but as one who lives to rule over the Federation by the audio narrative's ending as well.

The plot of the tale initially revolves around a tired, older Avon joining together with an old lover, Elise, and a few criminals, Lydon and Kelso, to rob the Federation. Unexpectedly, the story reveals that Avon is, in actuality, heading into a trap engineered by Servalan via psychostrategist techniques, in which one's actions are predicted and realized by setting a specific sequence of events in motion. Regarding her scheme, Servalan gloats, "Avon is now no more than an actor stumbling through his farewell performance." While this comment foreshadows *The Logic of Empire*'s conclusion, it also functions on a metafictional level as one can draw parallels between the manipulated actor–Avon and the actor Paul Darrow, who, at the time of recording this audio adventure, could well have been delivering his final performance as the cynical, antihero. In a favorable review concerning *The Logic of Empire*'s continuation of Avon and Servalan's conflict, fan reviewer Joe Escobar remarks,

> Stevens conveys the character of Avon flawlessly. His reactions to the idiotic plans to steal gold from a Federation installation remind the listener of his acerbic retorts to Vila and the rest of his compatriots. The plot, as is usual for a *Blake's Seven* story, is convoluted. Avon and Servalan are playing a high stakes chess match. Just when you think you have everything figured out, you are thrown another curve.

Through this review, Escobar points out one of the paradoxes of classic *Blake's 7*—its often convoluted plotting, which can be viewed by fandom as one of the show's charming strengths or deplorable weaknesses. At the same time, he praises how *The Logic of Empire* engages fan-listeners in terms of guessing its outcome but, like televised *Blake's 7* itself on occasion, surprisingly resists being entirely predictable through its tangential plotting.

After Avon has been captured, Servalan, who is once more president of the Federation, informs him that he is going to somehow help her maintain her power. On this enigmatic note, they share this exchange:

> SERVALAN: The destruction of Earth was ... regrettable.
> AVON: But at least you have power again.
> SERVALAN: Oh yes, and you are going to help me keep it. Without enemies, the Federation will not survive. And these days, there are so very few of the enemy left.
> AVON: So you have to invent them?
> SERVALAN: Something like that. Goodbye, Avon. We won't meet again.

In the closing part of *The Logic of Empire*, Servalan's scheme is revealed: Avon, now living in a Gauda Prime city dome[22] and referred to by the name Blake, is approached by a member of the resistance who wishes for him to rejoin their cause. Echoing Roj Blake's introductory dialogue in "The Way Back," the amnesiac Avon-Blake's words inform the listener that the *Blake's 7* saga has come full circle, with Avon taking the place of Blake by literally embodying the fallen rebel leader by beginning his heroic journey anew.[23] Moreover, this development lends Avon's final exchange with Servalan a doubled meaning. On a textual level, it continues *Blake's 7*'s core conflict of presenting the so-called heroically masculine Blake leading a rebellion against the Federation, which is, for a second time, given a face with Servalan's powerful feminine villainy. On a symbolic level, Servalan's parting words that she will not meet Avon again ring true since he has become Blake in all aspects except for his physical appearance. At the same time, the fact that Avon-Blake retains Avon's voice reminds *The Logic of Empire*'s listeners that, perhaps, he will eventually regain his former identity and confront Servalan, thereby potentially encoding a self-identity heroic quest for the doubly amnesic character. On this production's intriguing final plot twist, Escobar writes, "The ironic ending is far more satisfying and yet just as bleak as the non-resolution of 'Blake.'" Appropriately, for Escobar and other *The Logic of Empire* listeners and fans, this audio production pleasingly continues the *Blake's 7* narrative past "Blake" but does not bring the story to a definitive conclusion. Arguably, to do so would be tantamount to giving an unwanted gift to fans, one they could not reciprocate by continuing Stevens and Tulley's post–Gauda Prime narrative situation for Avon.

Blake's Junction 7—A Rest Stop or Final Resting Place?

Colloquially defining an old SF show as "cheesy" or "old school" may form one of the necessary audience reception steps that eventually leads to its rehabilitation in the form of a contemporary reboot. For example, part of fandom's process of classifying a show such as *Blake's 7* as "classic" television involves mutually praising the virtues of the series and highlighting its flaws. In other words, fans' collective memories of *Blake's 7*, as channeled by the Continuum of Nostalgic Continuity, both preserve and mock their source media text. One can also point out that the fans' ability not to take a sometimes solemnly encoded SF television program too *seriously* represents a sincere, playful act of decoding *Blake's 7*. This truth was not lost on B7 Enterprises when they chose to produce a fifteen-minute *Blake's 7* parody film—*Blake's Junction 7* in 2005. As a result, in an encoding move that embraces the postmodern elements of parody and pastiche, this short film equally celebrates and destabilizes many elements present in the original BBC series.

In a manner unlike the several opening title credits to the classic *Blake's 7* series—and more like the introductory narrative crawls to the *Star Wars* movies—*Blake's Junction 7* begins with the following computer text being typed across the screen in a somber way:

> It is a time of great change...
> The known galaxies have been enslaved by a merciless and corrupt woman and her army of all-powerful stormtroopers...
> Pursued across the stars by these dark forces are a group of seven rebels, who, despite the loss of their original leader, Blake, continue to fight a brave war of survival...
> This is the saga of...
> *Blake's Junction 7.*

If viewers of this parody were unfamiliar with *Blake's 7*, this opening text's narrative encoding would create the idea that the short film they are about to watch will present a serious struggle for freedom occurring between a heroic group who are implied to be struggling to recover from the loss of their patriarchal leader and an evil, dominant woman who commands faceless stormtroopers. In short, for fans of *Star Wars*, which has a significantly larger fandom than *Blake's 7*'s cult following, Servalan is being textually reimagined as a Darth-Vader-like indomitable villain, not as the deadly yet camp version of the character as played by Jacqueline Pearce. In addition, by centering this opening text on Servalan and the missing Blake, the parody articulates the major loose story arc threads of Series C and D, as the Avon-led crew frequently encounter Servalan, who is pursuing them, and attempt to act as effective freedom fighters without the leadership of the charismatic Blake.

For several seconds, moreover, the dramatic mood is sustained as *Blake's Junction 7* opens with a shot of Avon emerging from a night fog and speaking into his wrist communicator to inform his teammates that they have arrived somewhere. Although another actor, Mark Heap, is playing the part as originated by Paul Darrow, he is accurately mimicking his predecessor's deadpan performance style. In other words, he is playing a straightforward version of Avon, who is operating in a parodic narrative. Ostensibly, this opening sequence could begin any given episode of *Blake's 7* that was filmed on location in an English forest or quarry. However, to the accompaniment of dramatic orchestra music, the camera pans back to reveal a long shot of a contemporary British highway rest stop. As ridiculous as this contemporary setting may appear to some fans of *Blake's*

7, director Ben Gregor's choice to utilize its everyday, commonplace environment echoes the decision of the show's original producers to film episodes in such everyday locales as British corporate buildings or refineries of the latter 1970s.

Viewers then learn that Avon and his group, instead of having teleported to the planet's surface from aboard either the Liberator or Scorpio starships, travel in an everyday station wagon to which is attached an RV. Also present in this opening sequence are the classic *Blake's 7* characters of Gan, Jenna, Cally, and Dayna, who are dressed in costumes that could have authentically been worn by the original actors playing their roles. Since Gan and Jenna never interacted onscreen with Dayna as the two had respectively died in "Pressure Point" and were written out of the series in "Aftermath," viewers of this parody unfamiliar with *Blake's 7* have been presented with what could be regarded by long-term fans of the show as a continuity error. Then again, *Blake's Junction 7* is not concerned with enacting a religious devotion to the series' continuity as it works as an affectionate parody to the original show. Put another way, the production's CNC reimagining of the classic series pairs up its various characters in the ultimate act of professional-quality yet fan-fiction-like filmmaking, where memory and nostalgia comingle to eschew the all-too strict trappings of any fan-generated obsession with "proper" *Blake's 7* continuity. If it were attempting to serve as a proper adaptation—or continuation—of the original series, or even as a "continuity implant" that could fit somewhere in the Series C or D components of *Blake's 7*'s televised narrative, *Blake's Junction 7* would then arguably function as just another piece of spin-off media that could fit snugly within its expanded universe timeline.

Like *The Five(ish) Doctors Reboot*, which will be produced eight years later, this parody employs comedy to celebrate and rewrite the myth of *Blake's 7*, and it strives to be something new rather than act as a recycled tribute to the master text that is the series proper. Concerning this laudable mindset toward originality, Linda Hutcheon points out, "An adaptation is not vampiric: it does not draw the life-blood from its source and leave it dying or dead, nor is it paler than the adapted work. It may, on the contrary, keep that prior work alive, giving it an afterlife it would never have had otherwise" (176). In regard to the "afterlife" that *Blake's Junction 7* lends the legacy of *Blake's 7*, on a simple level, it reminds the greater television public that the show, which at that point had been off the air for nearly twenty-four years, had existed. For the first type of the parody film's viewers—those familiar with *Blake's 7*—the production will function as a nostalgic reminder of a show they watched when they were younger. For the second variety—those uninitiated with *Blake's 7* or its cult fandom—*Blake's Junction 7* potentially works as an introduction to its intergalactic anti-totalitarian government saga. It is this group that is probably more important to a proper revival of the brand as they are, most likely, younger and better attuned to social media than their older counterparts. In short, for *Blake's 7* to survive as a brand, the show will need a strong presence of online supporters—its core fandom—to serve as free advertising for a reimagination of the series through their proliferation of episodic reviews, character analyses, cosplay, fan art, fiction, and general face-to-face and/or online conversation. However, since a reboot of the show is still stuck in an indeterminate media state—or "development hell"—if one wishes to employ a Hollywood term—this conjecturing remains academic.

If anything, *Blake's Junction 7* adds a new subtext to *Blake's 7*'s original narrative by including actors Martin Freeman and Mackenzie Crook, who had achieved success playing comedic rivals Tim Canterbury and Gareth Keenan in the BBC-produced original series of *The Office*, which aired in the early 2000s. In addition, the parody's cast includes comedians Mark Heap and Johnny Vegas, who are quite familiar to British (and some international) audiences in 2005 and the present decade. With the inclusion of these actors, *Blake's Junction 7* is lent a contemporary edge as it adds their comic sensibilities to the master text of *Blake's 7* in a manner that celebrates, preserves, and points out the still-existing potentiality of the series and its characters. One can also assert that the involvement of director Ben Gregor and many of the actors involved in this production serves as a crucial example of decoders becoming the new millennium comedic encoders—or reinterpreters—of *Blake's 7* since they had grown up watching and adoring the classic series on television.

Regarding this note, the parody that is *Blake's Junction 7*, while not canonical, is nonetheless, as a form of adaptation, no less relevant to the ongoing saga of *Blake's 7* than its televised episodes. Hutcheon argues, "We retell—and show again and interact anew with—stories over and over; in the process, they change with each repetition, and yet they are recognizably the same. What they are not is necessarily inferior or second-rate—or they would not have survived. Temporal precedence does not mean anything more than temporal priority" (177). Nearly ten years on, *Blake's Junction 7*, as it presents the story of an Avon-led group of rebels struggling to go on without their original leader, although comically set at a rest stop, indeed retells *Blake's 7*'s loose quest story arcs for Series C and D but still has a temporal relevance in employing the comedic art form of snarky satire to achieve its storytelling goals of offering a shortened version of a typical fifty minute episode of the show. In other words, the temporal precedence of telling a *Blake's 7* narrative in a timeframe close to an hour has been reinvented by *Blake's Junction 7* to be told in a shorter form more akin to the compressed storytelling of a humorous sitcom, which generally tells its stories in a span of twenty-two to twenty-five minutes.[24]

Like *Blake's 7* proper, however, Vila remains a complainer who irritates his teammates. He even functions as longtime *Blake's 7* fandom's mouthpiece in this exchange with Avon that expresses his feelings of loss for the missing Blake:

> VILA: My back is killing me. Avon, why can't I ever go in the front? Blake would let me go in the front. He always lets me go in the front.
> AVON: Vila, just stop going on about it, all right? I know it's difficult, but he's gone, okay. Blake's gone. Just help me with Orac, will you?

Vila's childlike need to sit in the front of the station wagon since Blake allowed him to do so also echoes and parodies the dynamic of Series A and B, where his former leader often served as his protector against Avon's manipulations. Once Blake had disappeared in Series C, Vila became more of an easily duped character[25] in relation to Avon and Tarrant, who debuted in the third season of the show. Characteristically, Avon has logically dismissed Blake's departure from their itinerant crew as an accepted given. However, for fans of the original *Blake's 7*, Avon insisting that Vila put his unresolved feelings for Blake aside and help him carry Orac reminds them he regards the weaker man as his servant—or cannon fodder. For fans familiar with the Series D episode "Orbit," moreover, their innocuous exchange can project a darker overtone since Avon nearly killed Vila in that episode in order to preserve his own life.

As for Avon and company's sojourn itself, the script presents a nod to the character of Gan with his parodic counterpart. While working on a crossword puzzle inside the rest stop, Gan asks Avon, "How do you spell inhibitor?" which references the *Blake's 7* plot device of him having an inhibitor device in his brain that blocks him from committing aggressive acts against people. Orac, the genius translucent computer box, is also present in *Blake's Junction 7*. However, an additional complicated postmodern layer has been encoded by the facts that the Orac prop resembles its original design and Peter Tuddenham, who had voiced the genius computer in *Blake's 7*, is once again lending his vocal talents to the cantankerous character in this production. At the same time, a sense of play is occurring as Orac, who never consumed organic matter in *Blake's 7*, drinks brown ale from a straw. The comedy continues as Federation soldiers show up in the production to the accompaniment of ominous music as they travel in a big-rig truck rather than a pursuit ship. Instead of serving as a credible threat to Avon's group, however, Servalan and her soldiers are revealed to be lost in a scene set at another stop before they reach the rest stop where Avon's crew is relaxing. Furthermore, when they finally encounter their enemies, Cally and Dayna, who are playing first-person shooting video games in the rest stop's arcade, they dumbly glance at them without recognizing the Federation outlaws. Humorously, however, onlooker Vila's frightened expression[26] cleverly tells the viewer that he is well aware of the threat the soldiers pose.

Concerning dryly humorous moments like this one, fan reviewer Parsley the Lion writes, "What this film really made me think was 'why only 15 minutes?' I don't think the comedy of the service station is heading beyond its rightful place in this film, but what about a fully-fledged *Blake's 7* film or TV series?... This film proves that *Blake's 7* could easily come out of the audio book and into production, and new techniques could make the whole thing stunning." While Parsley the Lion views *Blake's Junction 7* as a work underlining the potential inherent in reviving the classic series, another fan reviewer, wildw, does not believe that the short film even serves as a proper tribute to the original show:

> Besides the costumes and props, which are excellent, there's very little that's very "Blake's 7" about it. For an homage to a show loved for its dialog and characters, the script is really lacking—the characters don't interact or have dialog anything like those they're emulating, and there's pretty much zero plot. I got to the end feeling "is that it?" They could've done something so much better with a 15 minute short like this, considering the effort gone to, if only the writers and cast had taken some interest in the subject matter.

For wildw, the short parody film's more lateral take on the characters, which shows them casually interacting in a mundane rest stop setting rather than a hazardous alien planet or a dangerous space station (settings that were commonplace in *Blake's 7*) does not authentically satisfy his viewer expectations. Admittedly, *Blake's Junction 7* purposely misses an opportunity to have Avon and company directly confront Servalan and her Federation soldiers, but their comedic encoding point is to show how inept the Federation can be when apprehending this group of rebels. In short, like *Blake's 7* proper, this short film comments on the fact that neither the freedom fighters nor their enemies can achieve a lasting victory over the other, since, to accomplish this goal would end their respective heroic or villainous quests—and, by turn, the reboot potential of the show itself.[27]

In some ways, affectionately parodying the master text that is a classic BBC SF television show may be part and parcel of the process that leads to the show's eventual revival. For example, during *Doctor Who*'s "Wilderness Years," when the series was mostly off the air for nearly sixteen years (1989–2005), two notable productions nostalgically celebrated the show and simultaneously mocked it. The first, "Dimensions in Time," a two-part 3D special produced for *Children in Need* in 1993, ostensibly reunited viewers with Doctors Three to Seven and their companions in a mashup adventure combining them with the cast of the BBC soap opera *East-Enders*. The finished result, although produced for charitable purposes, was received by fans as representing a rather cheap, poorly written production that emphasized to the greater viewing public the budgetary and narrative shortcomings *Classic Who* occasionally evinced at times in its history. In other words, to fandom, "Dimensions in Time" looked as if it were unwittingly mocking its source text, which made the special look like a comedic wake rather than a practical means of celebrating its thirtieth anniversary. Likewise, *Blake's Junction 7*, with its convenience shop setting and station wagon substituting for the crew's spacecraft, while offering a comedic look at the master text, *Blake's 7*, also reminds the viewer that the original series proper's sets had been produced on a relatively modest BBC budget. In this case, like the greater viewing public's perception of "Dimensions in Time" in 1993, those who have watched *Blake's Junction 7* since 2005 may see it as a sarcastic media grave marker of a pathetic, cheaply-produced BBC SF show.

Perhaps, then, the second *Doctor Who* comedic special, "Doctor Who and the Curse of Fatal Death," which was produced by the BBC in 1999 for their Red Nose Day charity telethon, more positively points toward *Blake's 7*'s future by showing how a well-produced parody can somewhat pave the path of a nostalgic audience's positive reception of a BBC SF show's reboot. Written by Steven Moffat, who has been writing for *NüWho* since its beginning and served as its second showrunner, "Doctor Who and the Curse of Fatal Death" features a Doctor, played by Rowan Atkinson, who is married to his younger female companion. Considering that *NüWho* would depict the Tenth Doctor romancing companion Rose Tyler and the Eleventh marrying River Song, the special's comedic sexualized inversion of *Classic Who*'s Doctor-companion dynamic feels less unlikely in retrospect. Furthermore, the special concludes with the Doctor fatally wounded and rapidly regenerating into new forms as played by Richard E. Grant, Hugh Grant, Jim Broadbent, and Joanna Lumley. As the Doctor becomes a woman with the final humorous regeneration in "Doctor Who and the Curse of Fatal Death," this female version of the Time Lord offers sexual innuendo when looking at her sonic screwdriver and continues her relationship with her companion in a new lesbian context.

While the audience and *Classic Who* fandom were amused by this ending, *NüWho*, with Series Eight's "Dark Water," would make its conclusion a dramatic reality as the penultimate episode of that season reveals that Missy, the Twelfth Doctor's nemesis in the tale, is, in actuality, a female incarnation of his longtime male enemy, the Master. In comparison, as stated, *Blake's Junction 7* turns Servalan, a female character, into a masculine-looking female, or, depending on one's reading of Crook's performance, a man in drag. Like Pearce, Crook performs an imposing Servalan, whose cold, commanding, thinly-veiled-anger demeanor can easily disconcert her male underlings.

This dynamic is repeated in a parodic sense via a scene presented at a highway rest stop as Travis, once more Servalan's senior underling in this production, and her soldiers watch her reactions to them being lost on the British highway. Later at the rest stop where Avon and his comrades are hanging out, Crook's Servalan, dressed in an elegant white gown and a light black-feather topped cloak, walks around the arcade, languidly playing a crane-grab game and then aggressively engaging in a sit-down driver game while her soldiers watch over her. In some ways, the simple leisure games Servalan is playing could present a comedic micro-version of the various villainous machinations that she precipitated across four seasons of *Blake's 7*. But, again, similarly on display to *Blake's Junction 7* viewers is Crook's unsmiling, ethereal imitation of Servalan's layered, obscure femininity. Crucially, Judith Butler's thoughts on the true nature of gender construction can help to decipher Crook's complicated performance as Servalan:

> The notion of gender parody ... does not assume that there is an original which such parodic identities imitate. Indeed, the parody is *of* the very notion of an original; just as the psychoanalytical notion of gender identification is constituted by a fantasy of a fantasy, the transfiguration of an Other who is always already a "figure" in that double sense, so gender parody reveals that the original identity after which gender fashions itself is an imitation without an origin [188].

With Butler's fluidic gender formation in place, one can argue that Crook's affected interpretation of Jacqueline Pearce's measured, poised performance on *Blake's 7* as a feminine yet predatory Federation Supreme Commander is a copy of another actor's copy of a female-gendered villainous role that has no original identity. In other words, Pearce's essaying of the role of Servalan, a strong-willed woman who, depending on the given situation, appears feminine or androgynous, does not possess a precedent or origin as her role in SF television forms a uniquely gendered interpretation of the deadly female villain. Thus, Crook's "fantasy of a fantasy" drag performance as Servalan, like Pearce's essaying of the role, offers yet another new expression of this fascinating character, who reminds viewers that any notion of a gendered identity, fictitious or real, is always in the process of being socially constructed.

Blake's Junction 7's contemporary queering of classic *Blake's 7* continues with Avon encountering Blake in the rest stop's men's bathroom. As Blake comes out of a stall, the two former comrades simply bump into each other, but Avon, unlike his original counterpart in "Terminal," is not too pleased with being reunited with his former leader. In contrast, Blake, who is enthusiastic to see Avon, says, "Look, we should maybe get together some time," to which Avon flatly replies, "Yeah." At this moment, fans of *Blake's 7* do not witness the two characters discussing their shared struggle against the Federation or any bits of reference to the master television text their performances are parodying, particularly the catastrophic ending of "Blake." Instead, the scene initially alludes to the slash Blake/Avon fiction that was a popular subgenre for elements of American *Blake's 7* fandom in the mid–1980s.[28] Visually, this allusion has been created by the two having their ambiguous exchange in a men's bathroom, a popular historical meeting place for discreet homosexual liaisons, which underscores the subtext of their dialogue. However, the direct intention of the scene is finally relayed to viewers with Blake's final imploring piece of dialogue to Avon: "God, this is so weird. So are you seeing anyone right now?" In response, Avon dismisses his former friend (and potential lover) with a smug, "Blake..." hinting that any chance of them resuming their former relationship is nonexistent. Interestingly, Avon's one-word naming of Blake inverts the pair's final exchange in "Blake," as Blake, who has just been fatally shot twice by Avon due to a tragic misunderstanding, moans his former comrade's name before collapsing dead at his feet.

Unlike "Blake," where all of the series regulars are most likely killed in a shootout with Federation soldiers on Gauda Prime, *Blake's Junction 7*, an oblique post–Gauda Prime narrative, ends on an appropriately postmodern note. After Avon's crew are all aboard their station wagon—with Vila at last victoriously sitting in the front seat—the short film switches to a shot of four rest stop camera monitors focused on the rebels' vehicle. Instead of merely driving away, the station wagon warps into another dimension—presumably the futuristic totalitarian world of classic *Blake's 7*. More importantly, in a symbolic sense, this playful, optimistic ending serves as a whimsical counterpoint to the dry humor of the parody, where CNC representations of the characters, who had interacted in a mundane rest stop environment, return to their proper, other SF universe, which continues to energize fan affection and hope for an extended, legitimate return of *Blake's 7* to television airwaves.

* * *

In contrast to the franchises of *Star Trek* and *Doctor Who*, which have both experienced extended periods of media dormancy, *Blake's 7* remains in a limbo state. Granted, Big Finish[29] has been producing officially licensed spin-off audios and books that both create original tales with the aging members of the classic cast[30] that fit amongst the narrative interstices of Series A to D. At the same time, the majority of these tales are caught in a CNC vortex as they cater to fans' sentimental feelings toward the original series, so their potential influence in helping to jump-start a reinvigoration of *Blake's 7* fandom is rather limited. If anything, on a more optimistic note, Big Finish's audio productions remind contemporary SF fans who are discovering older BBC shows that *Blake's 7* existed and may still hold a mythological resonance if the show were properly rebooted.

As a closing thought that anticipates this book's conclusion, perhaps it is the fact that *Blake's 7*'s fan base has had over three decades to collectively cement what it defines as the classic tropes of the show which may consequently disrupt any potential encodings of a reboot. In the last few years, a Syfy and then an Xbox Live service produced *Blake's 7* reboot has been announced to the media, but, so far, this attempt at reimaging the show has not been officially commissioned. Fans, however, are naturally skeptical of this reimaging of the show since it is not being produced by the BBC, who had successfully reintroduced *Doctor Who* to a contemporary audience in 2005. In theory, some fans may argue that a reboot of the show should redefine the messianic Blake's ongoing quest to topple the malevolent Federation while others could argue that the antiheroic Avon should be given, as in the original show, equal importance to his narrative rival. Also pertinent to this discussion should be the question of how "retro" the show should appear in a meta context that both celebrates and updates the original series. For instance, how close in appearance should the Liberator appear to its original 1978 Roger Murray-Leach design? Will the new series' costumes once more feature fetish leather and flamboyant fabrics? And should its villains, perhaps new versions of Servalan and Travis, as with the performances delivered for them by their original actors, project a sadistic androgyny or hint of queerness? Or would a new version of *Blake's 7*, in order to appear more contemporary, be better off in presenting direct representations of bisexual or gay characters?

Ultimately, while hardcore SF television fans only represent a portion of the potential consumer base that would subscribe to a cable or digital-channel produced *Blake's 7*, it is their powerful decoding media productions—found in the form of blogs, art, videos, and tweets, and *Facebook* postings—that could positively or adversely affect the success of this theoretical new start for this distinctively gendered heroic quest.

Chapter Four

What a Smegging Quest! The Journey of Red Dwarf *and Its Fandom*

Out of the four BBC SF series modules that this book has been exploring, *Red Dwarf*, created by Rob Grant and Doug Naylor, most likely represents the best articulation of postmodern television storytelling. A self-aware, heroic comedy-drama quest set three million years in the future, *Red Dwarf* is a show that celebrates the fact that it often does not take itself too seriously or even adhere to its own continuity.[1] More importantly, the show's dynamic characterization for its four leads—Dave Lister, Arnold Rimmer, Cat, and Kryten—and two semi-regular characters—Holly and Kristine Kochanski—demonstrates that the series' encoding is enthusiastically open to change and development. Perhaps it is the encoded hybrid nature of *Red Dwarf*—as it amalgamates the television standards of sitcom and ongoing SF series storytelling—that has allowed the show's writers and producers to create an ongoing heroic quest narrative that repeatedly challenges viewers' expectations.

When its SF and comedy elements formed a successful combination in *Red Dwarf*'s initial six seasons, which aired from 1988 to 1993, the show achieved media and viewer acclaim. However, when the series' brand changed direction too dramatically, *Red Dwarf* fans were quite vocal in their displeasure. This situation most noticeably occurred in the wake of Series VII's transmission in early 1997, when Naylor chose to drop the studio audience, place more of an emphasis on dramatic storytelling, and replace the temporarily departing Chris Barrie, who plays Rimmer, with a parallel-universe version of Kochanski. At the same time, it is precisely the producers' willingness to experiment with the series' formula and its characters that has, in many ways, assured its legacy and continued vibrant dialogue with fans as the show approaches the production of its eleventh series nearly three decades after BBC Two's 1988 transmission of *Red Dwarf I*. As a critical result, this chapter discusses the truly synergistic role of *Red Dwarf*'s encoders and decoders in shaping its ongoing gendered heroic quest.

One easily arguable view concerning the encoded gendering of *Red Dwarf*'s leading males in the show's first two seasons—Lister, Rimmer, Cat, and Holly—is that it presents men operating in a distant future universe free of any female influence. While this situation places Lister and his posthuman companions in a situation where they cannot depend on or blame a female character for their problems, it also serves to highlight their masculine flaws. Simultaneously, this act of spotlighting their masculine traits reposits the show's leads, Lister and Rimmer, in a homosocial domestic situation in which a masculine-feminine divide still manifests itself. For example, Lister serves as the more "manly" character out of the two, as he likes spectator sports,[2] fancies himself a potential rock star through his dismal guitar skills, and prides himself on his slovenly lifestyle. In contrast, Rimmer is more decidedly feminine, as he maintains a neat appearance and living space and is obsessed with giving the robotic Skutters domestic duties to maintain the internal appearance of the ship. He could also be viewed as Lister's nagging "wife" in the sense that he is constantly berating his bunkmate for his career and personal shortcomings, primarily within their bedroom.

Cat himself is likewise gendered in a more feminine manner as he is myopically concerned with his appearance, wearing shiny suits and flamboyantly colorful fabrics, which would more likely be employed for female fashion in the late 1980s. At the same time, his need to mate with a female lends him a hypersexuality that is not equally present in Lister, whose romantic desires are focused on the long-dead Kochanski, and Rimmer, who possesses a near juvenile perspective on sex. As for Holly, although he displays an attraction to Hilly, his female counterpart in the episode "Parallel Universe," his senile traits and constant joking are easily transferable to the second female Holly, who adopts Hilly's facial features and personality. With this fact, one can argue that Holly's masculine gendering is subject to change as he does not display a corporeally complete male body.

When placing Grant and Naylor's decision to focus on an all-male cast for *Red Dwarf*'s first two series within the greater context of 1988, when women have proven to represent a significant portion of the transatlantic workforce and have been featured as leading and supporting characters in television and cinema, one must wonder why this masculine grouping would prove to be popular with the show's casual viewers and fandom. Additionally, when one considers that contemporary *Doctor Who* had been focusing on presenting a strong female character in the form of the streetwise teenaged Ace and even *Blake's 7* had presented a progressive woman villain with Servalan around a decade earlier, this choice takes on even more of a troubling shading. Although an answer to this question cannot be generated in an absolute manner, for many of the show's fans (and this aca-fan researcher) *Red Dwarf*'s depiction of its male heroes offers a refreshingly frank look at flawed masculine heroes who are not afraid to reveal their shortcomings to one another. For example, over the course of *Red Dwarf I* and *II*, Lister conveys his yearnings for love and true human companionship while Rimmer gradually admits his career failings and troubled relationship with his father.

In regard to *Red Dwarf*'s fandom, remarkably, the show did not start to become a BBC Two hit until the airing of its second series in the fall of 1988, six months after the transmission of *Red Dwarf I*. In terms of fan support for the first six seasons of the show, it was quite positive, as fandom and conventions grew in size. However, once cowriter Rob Grant split with Doug Naylor, and the latter radically changed the format of the show with *Red Dwarf VII*, which eliminated the show's traditional live studio audience and introduced a polished female character to the cast, the fans became divided. Then, *Red Dwarf VIII* (1999), in many fans' eyes, added too many resurrected characters to the mix of a last-man's survival narrative/quest, while the three-part *Red Dwarf: Back to Earth* (2009), for some of them, may have been overly long in running time[3] too self-referential, and significantly lacking in regard to utilizing a live participatory audience. *Red Dwarf X*, however, which aired in 2012, was well received by fandom, mostly because the series returns to the show's roots of four guys surviving in deep outer space while joking and having eccentric adventures in front of a live studio audience.

During the airing of any of these series, fan conventions have nevertheless been consistently held in England, and fan fiction, videos, and art have been produced. But, since the show did not air new episodes for over a decade, and the film Naylor repeatedly tried to produce failed to secure proper funding, some fans have become a bit cynical at times. Furthermore, in terms of size, while *Red Dwarf*'s fan culture is significantly smaller than *Doctor Who*'s global fandom, which will be discussed in chapter six, they do, like this larger social grouping, represent a convention-based and online community that is passionately supportive of the show when it sticks to its storytelling roots and critical of its encoding choices when substantial narrative or gender-based deviations occur.

A Show in Search of Its Identity: *Red Dwarf I* and *II*

For *Red Dwarf*'s original run of eight seasons, the show was intermittently on the air from 1988 to 1999,[4] yielding a fifty-two episode count, the number the series' producers saw as making it marketable for a year's worth of weekly syndication airings for overseas markets. After the production ended on these episodes, Doug Naylor planned on writing and producing a *Red Dwarf* movie, which, as planned, would have introduced the brand to a wider international cinematic audience. Despite the fact that the problematic, long-term development of this film eventually ended in failure,[5] and the show would not return for new episodes on the digital channel Dave until 2009, a near complete encoding cycle of *Red Dwarf* as both a heroically gendered quest and a television production is provided by the series for its audience.

With *Red Dwarf I*'s first episode, "The End," Lister emerges as an unlikely hero. Finding himself the last surviving human[6] aboard the Jupiter Mining Corporation ship the Red Dwarf after Holly, the ship's mainframe computer, has awakened him from three million years in stasis,[7] Lister thus has initiated his televised heroic adventure. Moreover, the setting of deep space, which contains no other humans and is filled with evolved creatures,[8] viruses, and the unknown becomes the Campbellian *"region of supernatural wonder"* (30) for the awakened Lister. On this note of the heroic quest, Joseph Campbell writes, "For those who have not refused the call, the first encounter of the hero-journey is with a protective figure (often a little old crone or old man) who provides the adventurer with amulets against the dragon forces he is about to pass" (69). In Lister's case, his protective figure is Holly, who acts as a wise man/guide/senile patriarchal figure. Though not strictly alive in an organic sense, Holly, in the latter time period presented in "The End," is now over three million years old, male, and "little" in the sense that only his head can be seen on viewing screens and movable equipment aboard the ship. As for the "amulet" that he gives to the adventurer Lister, one can argue that this object is laterally realized by Holly resurrecting his dead bunkmate Rimmer in order to give the last human being company. Consequently, the incorporeal Rimmer virtually functions as the SF equivalent of a ghost while Cat, who is descended from Lister's pregnant feline, Frankenstein, fulfills the part of the animal-man creature companion a hero meets along the adventure-journey's path that populates many mythologies. Of course, with these companions (and the audience) as his witnesses, Lister needs to announce his quest before he can begin to properly maneuver through his new world. Thus, like *Blake's 7*'s first episode, "The Way Back," in which the disgraced, framed titular character announces his decision to return to Earth, Lister similarly needs to vocalize his reset life's goals when he exclaims, "Holly, plot a course for Fiji.[9] Look out, Earth—the slime's coming home!"

In regard to *Red Dwarf II*'s presentation of gendered heroism, the series' most fantastic development occurs in "Parallel Universe," when the crew meets their alternate reality counterparts. Although Lister, Rimmer, and Holly's opposites are female, the fastidious Cat's analogue is revealed to be a filthy male canine-humanoid character named Dog. Rimmer, however, is repeatedly shocked by his female equivalent, Arlene, making sexual passes at him. As for Lister, he ends up having inebriated and unprotected sex with his parallel universe counterpart, Deb, yet he is the one who ends up being impregnated because he is subject to the biological laws of her universe, where the man bears the child.[10] While Lister's role as father/mother to his two children may offer a progressive view on cultural attitudes toward childbearing, online fan reviewer RomanatorX claims,

> Arnold Rimmer is probably as unlikeable as he gets in the show thus far, with his complete and utter disregard toward women. The alternate Rimmer manages to be even MORE unlikeable [than] Rimmer is (especially when she declares that she hopes Dave gets pregnant), which shows how far the characters can go. Deb also comes off as quite unlikeable when she tries to defend herself after being grilled by Dave. Since the two characters are supposed to be opposite sex clones of the male Dwarfers,[11] it makes the episode quite disturbing.

RomanatorX's belief that the alternate female Rimmer and Lister present disturbing versions of *Red Dwarf*'s leading men brings up a problematic point. On the one hand, one can argue that it takes these women's reverse sexist behavior to reflect (equally, to the audience and the characters themselves) Rimmer's deplorable attitude toward females and Lister's carefree, party-centric mindset. With this approach, irony and satire combine to empower these female analogues of the Dwarfers. On the other hand, Grant and Naylor's simple use of these female characters to embody Lister and Rimmer's flawed masculine characteristics may actually function in an antifeminist manner. In this sense, these female characters' disagreeable traits present a dark representation of women on *Red Dwarf*. Bearing in mind that females have already been marginalized on the show throughout its first two seasons, one can also maintain that Grant and Naylor's decision to employ the other Rimmer and Lister as negative, not positive, counterparts to the regular cast members represents a missed encoding opportunity for the writers.

In other words, "Parallel Universe" could have perhaps benefited from presenting female versions of Rimmer and Lister who could have encoded hard-working, mature counter-representations of career women in the future, which would have, in turn, served as an accurate SF extrapolation of the transatlantic working women of the latter 1980s. At the very least, Hilly offers a positive alternative female characterization to Holly, which is more or less genderless in the eyes of the fans to the extent that her face could acceptably replace his for *Red Dwarf III–V*. Nevertheless, the encoding of an educated, career-oriented regular female cast member character does not occur on the show until *Red Dwarf VII*, with the introduction of the alternative universe version of Kristine Kochanski. Unfortunately, decoder-resistance to this encoding of the second Kochanski, as I will discuss later in this chapter, leaves the lingering impression that a majority of fandom prefers their Dwarfers to only be flawed and foolhardy male characters.

Red Dwarf: A Refinement of *Classic Who* and *Blake's 7*?

Addressing the argument as to why *Red Dwarf*, whose first episode, "The End," which premiered on BBC Two on February 15, 1988, found itself on the rise as a BBC SF brand while *Doctor Who*, the television corporation's long-running property airing on BBC One and entering its penultimate season in September of that year, was heading toward cancellation[12] is a complex process. The easy answer, of course, would be to say that one show provided a refreshingly new viewing experience that presented fallible, apathetic heroes for the viewing audience whereas the other was possibly recycling a tired, old formula of a mysterious, patriarchal man traveling the totality of time and space and constantly defeating his foes.[13] A more complicated answer stemming from this thought would be to argue that, in the latter 1980s, serious BBC SF had run its course. Case in point, *Doctor Who* had already presented seven different incarnations of its titular hero, and it had accumulated twenty-four years of narratives, whose characters and plots presented an often intimidating aggregate of fan-centric knowledge. In other words, the brand was publically perceived, especially during the John Nathan-Turner years, as a show weighed down by its rich-yet-complicated backstory. Correspondingly, *Blake's 7* earlier in the decade had already presented more mature and sexualized storytelling than *Doctor Who*, offering both storylines that younger audiences members could enjoy and sexual innuendo and situations that older viewers could pick up on and appreciate. As a consequence, when *Red Dwarf* had reached the BBC Two airwaves, it presented a combination of the best of *Doctor Who* and *Blake's 7* encoding choices: the former's approach to colorful storytelling and playful narrative and the latter's presentation of troubled heroes and its frank attitude toward sexuality.

The success of the relatively low-budgeted *Red Dwarf*, on an economic note, in opposition to *Doctor Who*, which, in 1988 and 1989, had a higher BBC budget and eight more episodes[14] than its fellow SF show, must also be discussed. In *Doctor Who*'s case, since the show had already experienced unfair comparisons to the significantly larger budgeted *Star Wars* movies and *Buck Rogers* in the early 1980s, and *Star Trek: The Next Generation* in the latter part of the decade, the series was always being written off by certain fans/anti-fans and sectors of the media as the "show with the wobbly sets" and the "rubber monsters." *Red Dwarf*, however, which would employ the same BBC special effects unit as *Doctor Who*, seemed to flourish with these arguably limited production resources for one major reason: it is a sitcom, a television format which often requires less exotic settings or rapid-location scene shifts than what is conveyed in typical action-adventure shows.

One of the standard elements of a sitcom is to utilize standing sets as a cost-cutting measure in contrast to more expensive television productions that are either filmed on location or require the building of different sets for each episode. While 1980s *Doctor Who* would use one standing set, the TARDIS control room and the police box shell exterior prop, the show, due to the nature of its space-and-time traveling format, needed to constantly shift locales, hence requiring sets, that, depending on the budget, designers, and lighting, would either succeed or fail in the viewers' eyes. As for location shooting, the show often, to the perennial joking of fans, used English quarry pits to double as alien planets. In contrast to *Doctor Who*, *Red Dwarf*, as mentioned, could set the majority of its first series' stories in the interior of the Red Dwarf mining ship, most effectively in the bunkroom shared by Lister and Rimmer and in the vessel's control room. Put another way, the scenario of the show—the last surviving human existing in a massive mining spaceship alongside the ship's computer, a sentient hologram, and a creature descended from cats—works best in a consistent setting as Lister is forced to coexist with them for the sake of mutual survival. Like *Doctor Who*, the show features characters who are traveling across the cosmos, but, unlike its SF progenitor, whose narratives may falter if certain scenes go on for too long in the

TARDIS interior,[15] *Red Dwarf* can repeatedly—and successfully—sustain many of its episodes' tales in a single setting.

On the note of how audiences respond to *Red Dwarf*'s standing set format, the argument can also be made that viewers who are accustomed to the format of sitcoms are more receptive to its lower-budgeted format in comparison to *Doctor Who* fans, who, most likely, watch other SF television and cinematic productions. In other words, *Red Dwarf*, which straddles the encoding line between SF adventure and situational comedy, when it connects to an audience appreciative of its latter aspects, thrives on a visual and storytelling viewer-geared vocabulary attuned to the comfort of watching beloved characters interact in settings that are familiar and can be seen as extensions of one's home. To better explain this thought, one can reason that the featured domestic spaces of the Red Dwarf ship, since they contain bedrooms and eating and recreational areas, are, despite some "futuristic" design work, still recognizable as living areas. Accordingly, viewers can identify with the domestic, or situational comedy, as performed by the show's cast members in these settings. Moreover, when, for example, Lister and Rimmer initiate any of their numerous petty arguments in their shared quarters or either one of them sulks in an existential moment of self-pity, the audience can empathize with their emotions because they too experience such moments in the setting of their own homes.

In considering Rimmer, Lister, Cat, and Holly's characteristics as flawed masculine heroes in *Red Dwarf I* and *II*, one can look to *Blake's 7* as setting the tone for these refreshingly original encoding choices. Throughout *Blake's 7*'s four seasons, Vila Restal is often portrayed as a cowardly and sometimes inebriated character. In comparison, Arnold Rimmer, a self-admitted coward, always wishes to ensure the continuation of his consciousness, even though he is living an incorporeal, digital afterlife existence as a hologram. Furthermore, like Vila, both he and Lister can be seen drinking to the point where they embarrass themselves and/or make wrong choices. For instance, *Red Dwarf II*'s third episode, "Thanks for the Memory," presents an intoxicated Rimmer confessing to Lister that he has only slept with one woman during his mortal life while the season finale, "Parallel Universe," shows Lister becoming pregnant after having a night of alcohol-fueled sex with his alternate reality female counterpart. Although Cat would later be encoded as a more heroic character in the following seasons of *Red Dwarf*, for the first few, he would prove to be, like the common household cat, a narcissistic figure, one who is reluctant to help his fellow shipmates. Perhaps his gradual heroic evolution makes him best comparable to *Blake's 7*'s Avon, who likewise did not choose to become a hero but transformed into one over the course of Series A and B. Equally, for Cat and Avon, these characters become more heroic on both a practical level as a means of surviving, and, on a more altruistic one, as a result of respectively interacting with Lister and Rimmer and Blake's rebel crew. Overall, in *Red Dwarf*, as well as *Blake's 7*, the majority of the characters have to learn how to be less selfish in order to protect one other and to achieve their respective quests.

Kryten, a Female Holly and the Studio Audience: *Red Dwarf III–VII*'s Variable Elements

With the arrival of *Red Dwarf III* on BBC Two in November 1989, cosmetic, cast, and narrative changes further altered the series. The sets are more colorful, brighter, and flashier, and all of the cast, not just Cat, are now stylishly dressed. The permanent addition of the android Kryten to the cast displaces the Lister-Rimmer domestic dynamic that hitherto formed the crux of the series, but this choice also opens new plot doors for Grant and Naylor, who are now focused upon writing adventurous group dynamics. Furthermore, Holly has become a woman since the ship's computer has decided to adopt the appearance of Hilly, "his" female counterpart from "Parallel Universe," which somewhat undermines the "boys only" nature of the show. However, scholar Elyce Rae Helford argues,

> Though by necessity divorced from biological sex, this computerised sex change still gives viewers a new perspective on this formerly stereotypical "male" character. The "female" Holly, when compared with her male predecessor, manifests traits identifiable as stereotypically feminine (primarily an accentuated naïve stupidity, which began with the original Holly, but becomes exaggerated with the appearance of the feminine personality) [24–25].

Helford's analysis of the second Holly's role is correct in that the first version of the character could act as a fellow male toward the crew in addition to satisfying his role as their protector while the female iteration of the character predominantly functions as a protective "mother" who watches over her adventurous "children." She does, however, share a moment of camaraderie with the Dwarfers when she attends Kryten's "farewell" party in "The Last Day." Conversely, Holly acts in a distinctly clichéd, "feminine" manner when she faints after meeting the "manly" Ace Rimmer in the *Red Dwarf IV* episode "Dimension Jump."

Helford continues, "[Holly] is also generally desexualised and seems to have little effect on the masculinities of the series' male characters. (That her part is also much smaller than that of the first Holly may signify the tension in maintaining the feminine character within the generally masculine play of the series)" (25). In regard to Helford's opinion that Holly has been desexualized, Hattie Hayridge, who played the role, writes in her memoir, *Random Abstract Memory*, "The 'senile bald old git' Holly was now younger, blonde and female. Apart from her appearance, Holly was somehow neuter but, in her own way, still the senile bald old git" (207). Concerning Hayridge's interpretation of the second Holly, one could conclude that the actress views the character as being neuter, regardless of the sex of his/her performer.

Although Helford has also observed that the second Holly receives noticeably less screen time and involvement in the show's plotlines than her male predecessor, the *Red Dwarf IV* episode "White Hole" places a strong focus on the character. In this story, Kryten's experimental attempt to reverse the computer senility affecting Holly's programming and restore her natural IQ of six thousand actually results in this number being doubled. With her hair slicked back in an attractive, businesswoman manner and her personality reflecting a newfound confidence brought on by these changes, this version of Holly offers a more feminist-oriented iteration of her character. Moreover, she works as a sympathetic character in the eyes of the audience as she wishes to preserve her life since Kryten's experiment has left her with only 3.45 minutes of run-time. At the same time, while the crew are working in a heroic manner by both initially trying to restore Holly's intelligence and attempting to save her life later in the episode, they do not demonstrate any reaction to her changed appearance as a female.

The Dwarfers' non-reaction is continued in *Red Dwarf V's* "Demons and Angels" as the Low[16] version of Holly exudes a cruel sexuality as her blonde hair and lips are now colored a Goth-like black while she delivers her lines with a dominatrix-like intonation, but none of the members of the equally corrupted version of the crew flirt or comment on her appearance. From these two examples, one may agree with Helford's observation that the female Holly has been desexualized in the eyes of the male crew. Simultaneously, unlike the male iteration of Holly, this version of the ship's computer has been occasionally granted attractive features, consequently gendering her as a comely cybernetic female hero.

In regard to the *Red Dwarf* fan community's reaction to the second Holly, Hattie Hayridge's faithful interpretation of the role (as originated by Norman Lovett) has consistently been embraced and supported by them over the years at conventions and via online blogs and reviews. Like

Lovett, Hayridge encodes Holly as a self-deprecating, fun-loving computer, who enjoys joking with the rest of the Red Dwarf crew. By comparing this positive mass viewer decoding of the second Holly to the notable fan resistance that accompanied Chloë Annett's initial performance for the sophisticated parallel-universe version of Kristine Kochanski in *Red Dwarf VII*, one can conclude that fandom is more receptive to leading female heroic characters who operate on the same intellectual (i.e., lowbrow) level as the rest of the male Dwarfers, not standing apart from them in a class-based manner that is imbued with elitism.

Character development continues in BBC Two's *Red Dwarf V*, which debuted in February 1992, albeit not as closely as in former seasons, perhaps due to Grant and Naylor's "conscious decision to change their approach to the narrative: the balance between comedy and science fiction was tipped somewhat towards the latter" (Howarth and Lyons 100).[17] Most notably, the final episode of this series, "Back to Reality," which presents the crew awakening to the Despair Squid's false reality of the "Red Dwarf Total Immersion Video Game," restates Lister's heroic quest. Within this false reality, Andy, a game attendant, tells Lister the goal of the "Red Dwarf" game: "You're separated [from Kochanski] to begin with. Then basically it's a love story across time, space, death and reality." For viewers, this meta fantasy-fueled analysis of Lister's situation sums up his journey so far and, arguably, foreshadows the miraculous plot developments found in *Red Dwarf VII* and *VIII*.

Red Dwarf VI, which began airing in October 1992 on BBC Two, presents a radical departure for the show as the crew, sans Holly, embark on a survival "quest within the quest" as they travel through space in the small ship Starbug facing constant danger from various threats while searching for supplies and the missing Red Dwarf. Grant and Naylor's "desire to make life more of a survival challenge" for the Dwarfers hereby reencodes them as a unit that achieves a level of camaraderie[18] previously unseen on the show (Howarth and Lyons 117). The writers also mock the decoder-fans of the show with the episode "Emohawk: Polymorph II." During this story, Rimmer, freed of his bitterness by the emotion-stealing emohawk,[19] is temporarily transformed into the heroic Ace Rimmer. In regard to Cat, who has likewise been attacked by the emohawk and robbed of his "cool," which thus changes him into his nerdy, unattractive alter ego, Duane Dibbley, "Ace" remarks, "He's looking so geeky, I don't think he could even get into a science fiction convention." While this comment seemingly mocks *Red Dwarf* fandom, in actuality, it acknowledges the decoders' existence and continual support of the show.

Airing a little over three years after *Red Dwarf VI* in January 1997, *Red Dwarf VII* continues the narrative of the Dwarfers searching for their missing ship, but it differs greatly in narrative tone from the prior series, for Rob Grant had ended his longtime writing partnership with Doug Naylor. The show, now solely in the hands of Naylor and several cowriters, shifts in its dramatic emphasis to comedy-drama, harkening back to the rather serious tone of *Red Dwarf I*. Furthermore, the heroic evolution of Rimmer's characters reaches an apex in "Stoke Me a Clipper," when he is called upon by a dying Ace Rimmer to take up his mantle as a hero. Upon assuming the guise of Ace, Rimmer is surprised by the fact that Lister does not reveal his secret to Cat and Kryten. Additionally, when the last human and the hologram view the former Ace's light bee[20] coffin joining the millions of other Ace Rimmer coffins, Rimmer comments, "All those Aces!" and Lister adds, "They all did it. They all became Ace and passed on their flame. Are you really going to be the one to break the chain?" In this scene, Lister's words both convince Rimmer to become Ace and, on an encoding level, remind longtime *Red Dwarf* viewers that beneath all the comedic bickering in which the two men repeatedly engage, Lister has gained a full level of respect for Rimmer as a comrade, and, in return, he has served as a successful heroic role model for his friend.

The void created by Rimmer's departure is filled by the addition of Kristine Kochanski to the Dwarfer crew in the episode "Ouroboros." Although she is a parallel universe variant of Lister's ex-girlfriend, the character virtually fulfills his romantic quest to be somehow reunited with her. Unlike the second Holly, whose feminine nature rarely surfaced, Kochanski functions as a disruptive female force since her intelligence and confidence, along with her taste in culture, preference for fine living, and her disregard for any male chauvinism, place her at odds with her crewmates. Essentially, then, her encoding fulfills Rimmer's role as the show's antagonistic character. Furthermore, the conflict occurring between her and the crew, particularly in regard to Kryten, echoes the Lister-Rimmer domestic squabbling that was a trademark feature of *Red Dwarf*'s early seasons. Her skills and competence as a navigation officer, however, add a sense of professionalism[21] to the crew that had been previously absent.

Regarding its production features, *Red Dwarf VII* was recorded on specially treated video tape, giving the glossy appearance of film to the episodes. Moreover, the series was filmed without a live studio audience. This absence signifies a leaning towards drama, for the traditional function of the live studio audience is to hone the actors' comedic performances.

Although online reviewer Dave Foster praises *Red Dwarf VII*'s production values, which include closed sets and better lighting for the episodes, he argues, "The negatives arrive in the form of reduced comic timing, with the actors and most shockingly the director and editor literally waiting for an audience reaction between readings, when there is no reaction to be had (other than canned laughter added in post). This ultimately leaves many scenes overplayed for laughs, with too many obvious pauses and not enough snap to the actors' rhythm."

In Foster's opinion, the lack of participation of a studio audience removes a vital component that was present in a given episodic recording during the previous six seasons of the show: the interactive performative relationship occurring between live viewer and actors. Regarding this thought, Foster continues, "On a secondary level, there is also no audience interaction, something which not only affects the actors' performances, but in the case of a series like *Red Dwarf*, leaves the comedy purely in the hands of the writers, as opposed to the instant reaction a live audience offers and would reflect on later scripts and script revisions." With this argument, Foster has added a third, unseen component to a *Red Dwarf* production: the writer. While the actors and audience are spatially positioned in proximity to one another during a particular studio recording for the first six seasons of the show, the writers, Grant and Naylor, have been separated from the live performance by time in the fact that they generally wrote the scripts for the series well in advance of their filming. Their knowledge of audience behavioral responses to specific scripted lines for the characters naturally informs the encoding of their writing. Moreover, if a scene does not elicit the expected level of audience laughter, then the actors can adjust their performances once—or twice—more.

For a finer understanding of the decoder-studio-audience end of a *Red Dwarf* episodic recording, one can refer to media scholar Mark Duffett, who writes,

> Perhaps the primary pleasure that unites fans with performances is simply *enjoyment through engagement*. This enjoyment is more than a passive process of consumption or reception. It involves the fan being active in suspending disbelief, making meaning and participating. There is a sense here in which *performance sets the tone* and fans, making meanings as they go, *engage in various adaptive forms of counter-performance* [178–79].

Duffett's thoughts on fans enjoying an object of affection through engagement definitely applies to *Red Dwarf*'s studio audience, who, in most cases, are true fans of the show.[22] Instead of simply *passively* watching the pre-recorded serials at home, they are *actively* reacting to the actors' live performances for the majority of the scenes[23] comprising an individual episodic narrative. These fans are also willingly—and playfully—suspending their disbelief in that, while they are watching the actors perform on an open set, they need to imagine them interacting on a ship that is the size of a city and traveling deep space three million years in the future. Besides, they must view such *Red Dwarf* actors as Chris Barrie, Danny John-Jules, and Robert Llewellyn respectively essaying the fantastical roles of an incorporeal hologram, a feline humanoid and a synthetic butler, not as performers wearing makeup and outlandish costumes. Without this active reception of *Red Dwarf*'s central concept, which demands a certain acceptance of the show possessing its own internal logic—or realism—despite being a situational comedy, the actors' dialogue and humorous moments would fail to entertain the audience.

In comparison to other live audience groups such as rock fans, however, *Red Dwarf*'s participatory studio audience stands apart. Duffett continues, "At live music events, ... counter-performances are visibly and audibly expressed in ways that can include delightedly screaming, heckling, calling for attention, singing along and applauding. Such events are usually a summation of each fan's ongoing engagement with media products that reflect previous performances" (179). While *Red Dwarf* audience members have most likely consumed the media product that is the series and its ancillary merchandise (e.g., videos and/or DVDs of past episodes, tee shirts, and toys), their mode of participation does not involve "heckling" or "calling for attention," as their expected (and somewhat controlled) counter-performance is to laugh at the actors' words and actions. Numbering in the low hundreds versus the typical thousands of fans found at a larger rock concert, a *Red Dwarf* audience, which is situated in a more intimate, polite studio setting best comparable to a live theatrical performance, does not participate in an environment that more readily promotes rambunctious, rebellious behavior.[24] Moreover, a *Red Dwarf* episode recording, unlike a rock concert, which is performed at multiple locations and often repeats a variation of a band's play list, is a unique collaborative artistic creation. In both situations, nonetheless, the frenetic, contagious fan excitement generated by a live performance oftentimes inspires the actors or musicians to offer the best possible vision of their respective talents at that moment. In fact, Robert Llewellyn, who plays the android Kryten, admits in his autobiography, *The Man in the Rubber Mask*, that, while he and his *Red Dwarf* costars enjoy performing before a live audience, it is more expensive than a closed-set recording, highly technical, and "Everything is condensed and faster, [and] the pressure to get the show done in under two hours is enormous" (308–9). Additionally, Doug

Naylor comments upon how the *Red Dwarf* cast members benefit from a given live audience recording: "When they hear the laughter from the audience, they know, 'Oh, that was funny,' and they can milk situations because it's like constantly getting feedback of 'Yeah, that's really funny!' and equally, 'No, that's really boring'" ("Tank"). Consequently, in the situation of a *Red Dwarf* episodic recording, the stress the encoder-performers-technicians experience before a decoder-fan-audience, who wish to be entertained by their beloved actors, creates a catalyst for achieving a successful live comedy production filled with reciprocal energetic performances.

This is not to say, however, in regard to a *Red Dwarf* studio performance, that a sense of playful antagonism does not inform this synergistic exchange of live acting and audience reception as Llewellyn likewise makes this claim regarding the live *Red Dwarf* audience: "[T]hey love it when we smeg up, they are almost willing us to fail. The Smeg Ups and Smeg Outs[25] have been hugely popular and we've produced bucket loads of them over the years" (304). Though one can argue that the *Red Dwarf* audience may passively be sabotaging the actors' performances by wishing them to fail in terms of flubbed lines or missed cues, even their potential collective act of "willing the [actors] to fail" is all part of the reciprocal performance process that not only gives the actors the impetus to deliver their best enactments of their lines but also, if they do botch a scene, a collection of blooper reels that today[26] serve as DVD extras.

According to Llewellyn, *Red Dwarf* audience fans have also exhibited a strong sense of loyalty to the actors and writer-producer Doug Naylor by not going online and disseminating spoilers of untelevised plot points from a live recording. Before the cast began performing "Trojan," the first episode of *Red Dwarf X*, Llewellyn writes,

> [Naylor] made a short speech pleading with the audience not to post spoilers on *Twitter* and *Facebook*. He explained about the battle we'd been through to get a live audience and if the web were to be flooded with spoilers we'd never convince broadcasters to let us do it again. I am very pleased to report that all the wonderful audiences who attended the recordings were incredibly honorable and posted not a smeg stain of spoilerdom [309].

In a media age in which instant photos and tweets can threaten to spoil any given live location filming of a scene from an SF show such as *NüWho*, the fact that *Red Dwarf* fans adhered to their collective implied promise not to reveal any exclusive knowledge they had concerning the recording of the "Trojan" episode is rather significant in terms of positing this group of decoders as being respectful of their encoder counterparts' wishes. Simultaneously, one could argue that the intimate fan knowledge that they possess motivates this select viewing group to identify more with the encoder-writer-production-crew-performers with whom they creatively collaborated in the recording of "Trojan" as the decoder-live-audience than with the rest of *Red Dwarf* fandom, who would not see the episode until several months later, when it aired on Dave.

Lister and Cat: Race via the Complementary Lenses of *Homo Sapiens* and *Felis Sapiens*[27]

In comparison to *Blake's 7* and *Doctor Who*, namely *NüWho*, the function of race in *Red Dwarf* needs to be addressed. Remarkably, for a British SF television show airing in 1988,[28] the series feature a pair of black actors playing two of the three leads, Craig Charles as Lister and Danny John-Jules as Cat. Nine years earlier, *Blake's 7*'s producers had cast Josette Simon as Dayna Mellanby, as part of Avon's crew in Series C and D. Although she had started out on the show as a strong character, vowing revenge against Servalan, who had murdered her father, Dayna gradually (and debatably) lost her agency as a heroic figure of *lex talionis*.[29] A similar weakened black character also initially manifests in *NüWho* in the form of semi-companion Mickey Smith, Rose Tyler's boyfriend, whose cowardly attributes prevent him from traveling with the Ninth Doctor. While Mickey does gain a utilitarian purpose in the Ninth's, and later, Tenth Doctor's eyes when his computer skills assist the Time Lord in his heroic adventures, it is not until this companion stays behind on a parallel Earth to replace his fallen alternative self, Ricky,[30] that the character truly embraces a hero's lifestyle. In this sense, then, does Mickey's heroic encoding echo Lister and Cat's somewhat similar journeys in *Red Dwarf*.

One can also mention Tenth Doctor companion Martha Jones, a medical doctoral student who poignantly pines after the Time Lord throughout Series Three of *NüWho*. Like Lister, whose problematic love for both the long-dead and parallel universe versions of Kristine Kochanski[31] informs his heroic journey throughout *Red Dwarf*'s ten seasons, Martha presents a black character who pines away for an inaccessible and/or hurtful white love interest. Indeed, while one could view the potentiality of a mixed-race romance as a form of progressive encoding in either *Red Dwarf* or *NüWho*, the fact that the British black characters are relatively unsuccessful in their romantic quests inevitably weakens them in their respective audiences' eyes, thus inviting criticism that their producers may unwittingly be claiming these characters are undeserving of a white character's love. At the same time, Martha proves to be a stronger black character than Lister due to the fact that she stops pursuing the Doctor at the end of Series Three, temporarily ending her journeys with him, while Lister vows in *Red Dwarf: Back to Earth* to resume his quest to find Kochanski, who has left him because of his offscreen depressive behavior that occurred between *Red Dwarf VIII* and that story.

The question of whether or not Lister and Cat offer negative racial depictions in *Red Dwarf* must likewise be posed. In terms of England's population in the latter 1980s, being black British would definitely place one in a minority category. Despite this fact, Grant and Naylor's choosing two black actors (Craig Charles and Danny John-Jules) to balance out two white ones (Chris Barrie and Norman Lovett) in *Red Dwarf I* and *II* offers a progressive televised representation of race for a then-contemporary Great Britain. Significantly, however, neither Lister nor Cat has been encoded as educated or as a member of some sort of futuristic middle class. Orphaned as a baby and growing up as a member of Liverpool's working class in a future England,[32] Lister easily works as an analogue for a lower-class young British black man living in the latter 1980s. At the same time, he holds the same rank of Second Technician on the Red Dwarf mining ship as Rimmer, who was raised in boarding schools as a member of a futuristic upper-white British class. Since he often holds his own during witty arguments with his snobbish bunkmate, Lister's self-taught intelligence represents a counterbalance to any of Rimmer's culturally-ingrained notions that one's class or level of formal education inherently guarantees one's social superiority to members of the lower class. As a positive result, Dave Lister embodies an intelligent, sensitive representation of a latter 1980s British black male.

In Cat's case, the fact that he is descended from felines potentially sets him apart from any human-orientated social-class stratification. Then again, his obsession with clothing, his meticulous appearance, and his desire to seduce females arguably make him the equivalent of a lower-class womanizing British black male. Elyce Rae Helford, however, reads Cat as a skewed representation of the black American pop-singer or stereotyped male: "His shouts and dance movements parody James Brown, while his feminised narcissism brings Prince to mind. Specifically, he enacts a comic version of media myths of the lazy and oversexed black American male" (23). Working against this potential cultural stereotype is Cat's appearance in a dream sequence occurring at the beginning of the final *Red Dwarf II* episode, "Parallel Universe," where he performs a song-and-dance number, "Tongue Tied," while Lister and Rimmer serve as his backup singer/dancers. In this instance, one could contend that Cat also works as an analogue of a late 1980s British pop singer. Since successful pop-music performers' art often helps them to transcend traditional demarcations of race and class for a popular music audience, in this dream situation Cat thus functions as the equivalent of an upwardly mobile British black male.

For the *Red Dwarf IV* episode "Dimension Jump," Lister and Cat are given two middle-class counterparts in Ace Rimmer's parallel universe: Spanners and the Padré. Spanners represents an alternate version of Lister, who is a flight engineer in the Space Corps and had married Kochanski, with whom he has two twin sons, Jim and Bexley. As for the Padré, although he does not work as a direct parallel universe equivalent to Cat, he strongly resembles him. On the decision to present middle-class representations of Cat and Lister in "Dimension Jump," the episode's cowriter, Rob Grant, comments,

> I remember there was a furore ... about who the other characters would play in Ace's dimension. Originally, we'd written Danny as a really slobby cleaner, which we thought was funny—but then there was a big argument about positive, black role models, which I found infuriating. I mean, *Red Dwarf* does have two black characters in it, and we never make a mention of it, and I think that's the way it should be. We didn't hire them for their colour, and we don't make any play of it at all—so it annoyed me, really, that we had this thing about negative role models when we felt we'd been presenting positive role models for so long [qtd. in Howarth and Lyons 97].

This situation surrounding the draft script of "Dimension Jump" reveals sensitive race encoding concerns about Cat's alternate reality counterpart's portrayal in the episode. Although Grant claims that Craig Charles and Danny John-Jules's race should not affect how he and Naylor write their characters, the reality is that their skin color indeed demands a scrutinized level of encoding and decoding expectations. In the following season of *Red Dwarf*, moreover, with "Back to Reality," Grant and Naylor would present yet another alternate version of Cat—Duane Dibbley, a buck-toothed, fashion-challenged nerd. While this antithesis of Cat's character would prove to be a hallucination triggered by his and his fellow Dwarfers' exposure to the alien Despair Squid's ink, it reveals the writers acknowledging that the character's excessive vanity has presented an obstacle for his heroic evolution.

Heterosexist or Queer-Friendly? *Red Dwarf* and Sexuality

For a show primarily featuring male actors in its cast, *Red Dwarf* does not fail in addressing queer issues. Unfortunately, the series often takes a heterosexist stance on homosexuality. For example, the *Red Dwarf III* episode "Polymorph" presents Rimmer walking in upon the spectacle of Kryten apparently sodomizing Lister, who is spasmodically undulating upon his back on the floor of their shared quarters. In reality, the android has been frantically attempting to remove a Polymorph (a dangerous shape-shifting mutant) who is masquerading as a pair of Lister's boxer shorts. On the one hand, this scene presents a typical sitcom moment of "misunderstanding," in which one character's lack of knowledge of a previous given scene creates a comedic situation for the live (and at-home) audience, who possess a prior, or complete, knowledge of the event. From that perspective, the show entertains its audience, who is accustomed to—and expects—risqué humorous performances from the *Red Dwarf* cast. In contrast to *Classic Who* and *Blake's 7*, *Red Dwarf* importantly takes a more direct approach to sexuality that is both sophisticated and crude, thereby working as a reflection of a then-contemporary 1989 BBC Two audience's viewing desires. This sequence, on the other hand, elicits laughter by ridiculing queer sexuality. Equally, considering that a conservative British government headed by Prime Minister Margaret Thatcher, who famously promoted anti-homosexual legislation, was in power during the airing of this episode, one can contend that cowriters Rob Grant and Doug Naylor had scripted a sexualized scene reflecting popularly accepted negative views on homosexuality.

However, with the *Red Dwarf V* episode "Demons and Angels," Grant and Naylor present the spectacle of an alternate Rimmer dressed in sadistically-styled drag. In this tale, the crew and ship are split into two versions of themselves as a result of Kryten experimenting with a triplicator.[33] On the one ship, the Highs represent peace-loving versions of Lister, Rimmer, Cat, Kryten, and Holly who offer the distillation of their best qualities. Conversely, on the other ship, the Lows embody the Dwarfers' worst features, as they are duplicitous and murderous. In particular, Rimmer offers the most dramatic makeover of the traditionally sniveling character, as he channels a Dr.-Frank-N.-Furter-like[34] transvestite sexuality, albeit one more sadistic than his cinematic forbearer. Dressed in sparkly boots, thigh-high fishnet pantyhose, a short skirt, a low-cut leather top, and wearing a spiked choker collar, leather jacket, and a large feather boa, this version of Rimmer embodies a gender-bending punk-rock mindset. Moreover, his sadistic streak is realized through the "H"[35] symbol on his forehead being tilted at a forty-five degree angle, approximating the appearance of the Nazi swastika. His sadomasochistic personality is further exemplified when he tells Lister, "I'm going to lash you to within an inch of your life, and then I'm going to have you," before knocking him out with a crack of his holo-whip. Viewed within the context of *Red Dwarf*'s ongoing episodic depiction of the Lister-Rimmer conflict, this moment works on two levels: as a reversal of their power dynamics, which gives Rimmer the upper hand, and as a quasi-rape scene as Rimmer employs his phallic-like whip to render Lister helpless and then unconscious.

With the online fan fiction piece "Nadir," RoseCathy offers a sado-masochistic interpretation of the Low Lister and Rimmer's relationship as she writes about the hologram torturing his bunkmate with his holo-whip:

> The bluish tail grazed Lister's cheek. The feeling was little more than a tickle, but he still shivered and his breath still caught—and it came again, and again, and he threw his head back and let ecstasy take him—
> "Look at me."
> The holo-whip snapped loudly across his disobedient face.
> "I said *look at me.*"
> *No.* The last traces of consideration in the strokes were replaced by brutality. Lister laughed in sheer delight.

Fascinatingly, while RoseCathy is offering a queer rewriting of the Low Lister and Rimmer's relationship, which has not been clearly delineated in "Demons and Angels," she is likewise providing a sexualized metaphor for the regular version of the couple's personal dynamics. Replacing their cutting comedic barbs is an exchange and negotiation of power as the transvestite Rimmer enjoys inflicting pain on Lister while his "victim" takes pleasure in both resisting his torturer's commands to look at him and accepting the repeated lashes of the holo-whip across his face. Like the regular Lister, this corrupted version of the character clearly encourages and relishes his dead bunkmate's physical attacks that metaphorically replace his verbal insults upon his person and which, in turn, grant a form of sadistic pleasure to the hologram.

On an encoding level, in response to the Low version of Rimmer in "Demons and Angels," actor Chris Barrie says, "Everything about that costume was just incredibly unpleasant, and maybe it was that way to make me feel very unpleasant, cause everything I had to say was pretty unpleasant" ("Heavy Science"). Interestingly, Barrie's words reveal the creative encoding tensions occurring between him and the writers, Grant and Naylor, and the costume designer, Howard Burden,[36] in this episode, as the "unpleasant" feeling produced by the situation energized his sadistically sexualized interpretation of the role. For online fan reviewer, The_AG, however, Grant and Naylor's vision of the Low Rimmer differs from the one he or she envisioned for his or her favorite character on *Red Dwarf*:

"I think that there is more to Rimmer [than] the sexual being he is. There is also the need to be an officer. And to me that is more about him [than] the sexual part. I think they were going for what they felt was funnier rather than what the character was really about. Which was sad, because it threw me out of the episode." In The_AG's view, Grant and Naylor's writing of a sexualized version of Rimmer does not represent an accurate distillation of the character's darker impulses, which this reviewer believes should have been focused on representing his desire to become an officer on Red Dwarf. In other words, for this fan, a more dramatic reworking of Rimmer's character is more important than the writers achieving a humorous vision of the hologram, which is closer in tone to *Red Dwarf V*'s overall comedy-adventure theme. In addition, The_AG argues, "I would have loved this episode if they would have just looked at the characters a little more in depth. Rimmer's was not the only one I would have changed. I would also have changed Lister ... [who] should have been the dominatrix, not Rimmer!" Perceiving Lister to be the more masculine and dominant heroic figure of *Red Dwarf*, The_AG would rather see him have power over what he or she views as the more feminized, submissive character of Rimmer. If one demarcates *Red Dwarf* as a domestic comedy in which two bunkmates stuck in deep space embody homosocial roles, with the living, organic Lister being the more dominant figure to his whiny, submissive incorporeal counterpart, Rimmer, then The_AG's criticism of "Demons and Angels'" presentation of the show's leads as Lows contains more than an element of truth and an innate understanding of the series' central characterizations.

Perhaps the best realization of certain *Red Dwarf* fans' fantasies regarding a Lister-Rimmer romance can be found in cowriters Kim Fuller and Doug Naylor's encoding of the Series VII episode "Blue." While missing Rimmer, who had departed the Starbug crew in order to take up the heroic mantle of Ace Rimmer in "Stoke Me a Clipper," Lister experiences a dream in which his hologrammatic bunkmate returns. During the course of their conversation, they discuss new Starbug crew member Kristine Kochanski, which leads to Rimmer asking if she is more attractive than him, to which Lister replies, "Don't be daft. She couldn't hold a candle to you, man." The characters next mutually confess how they miss one another, culminating in them embracing in an openmouthed kiss. While *Nü Who* would present its lead character, the Ninth Doctor, allowing the omnisexual Captain Jack to gently kiss him on the lips in the 2005 episode "The Parting of the Ways," the only other place (before or after the airing of "Blue") where fan fantasies of two SF television heroic male lead costars could be realized would be in the medium of fan fiction, particularly, slash. In other words, cowriters Fuller and Naylor have both played to some *Red Dwarf* fans' desires for a queer coupling of Lister and Rimmer and generated LGBTQ-friendly broadcast material that sets the show one step ahead of the more family-friendly *Classic Who* or the overtly heteronormative yet queer-subtext-promoting *Blake's 7*.

Regarding his mental preparation for performing this scene, Craig Charles, who plays Lister, jokingly comments, "I don't know if I was looking forward to it; I slightly was looking forward to it, and I was slightly scared of doing that scene as well" ("Back from"). On the surface, Charles' comments reveal his dualistic excited anticipation and moderate fear of kissing his male costar, Chris Barrie. On a deeper, more psychological level, however, his words perhaps underline the tensions facing an actor who wants to perform a sexually progressive scene to a projected broadcast viewing audience[37] who may be repulsed by the sight of two men kissing, even if the moment has been encoded within the context of a dream sequence.

In one fan fiction short story titled "Blue Christmas," writer gt52 imagines a sequel of sorts to "Blue," in which Rimmer takes a break from his newly adopted Ace Rimmer persona and visits the Dwarfers aboard Starbug around Christmastime. Viewing Lister's homoerotic dream in that episode as revealing the last male human's true feelings for Rimmer, gt52 writes a lighthearted, soft-erotic piece, which is categorized as "fluff" in slash fiction writing circles. After having Lister and Rimmer consummate their mutual attraction with a passionate kiss and discussing their desire for one another, gt52 has the two queered characters engaging in the "cute" action of changing into pajamas, so they can cuddle together in bed:

> "What should I wear?" Rimmer asked.
> "Whatever you want. I'm still in me Christmas pajamas," said Lister, gesturing down to his candy cane pants and red shirt.
> "I guess that works," said Rimmer, pulling up the control panel on his watch and generating his own pair of hard-light holographic Christmas pajamas.
> Sexy," chuckled Lister.
> "Shut up, you gimboid. Whose bed are we using?"
> "Bottom bunk's easier," shrugged Lister.

In an authentic manner, gt52 retains Lister and Rimmer's combative relationship but adds a romantic undercurrent to their interaction in this passage, where changing into pajamas functions as a metaphor for two traditionally antagonistic characters shifting into a softer emotional mood with one another. When compared with the dark S/M atmosphere Rose-Cathy crafts via her queered reading of the Low versions of the pair seen in "Demons and Angels" with her piece "Nadir," gt52's story creates a more sympathetic example of slash fan writing. At the same time, "Nadir" and "Blue Christmas" creatively complement each other's narratives, offering two diverse fan interpretations of Lister and Rimmer's complex relationship on *Red Dwarf*. As a positive upshot, dualistic homoerotic fantasies of the characters' gendered and sexual identities have been realized, disseminated, and supported by certain members of the *Red Dwarf* online fan fiction writing community.

Red Dwarf VIII: Lister as a Last-Man-No-More?

Debuting in February 1999 on BBC Two, *Red Dwarf VIII*, which saw the show return to being a comedy-adventure, conceivably serves as the "ultimate" vision of the series as it amalgamates successful elements from previous seasons and offers a culmination of long-running themes. Case in point, the entire Red Dwarf crew who were present in the show's first episode, "The End," have been resurrected by the nanobots, and the extended cast of Lister, Rimmer, Cat, Kryten, Kochanski and the first male Holly are all together onscreen. Moreover, the show once again prominently features the type of comedy-adventure encoded in the writing of *Red Dwarf II–VI*.

On a decoding note, *Red Dwarf VIII* contains the return of the live studio audience, indicating a renewed emphasis on performative comedy. For example, a comedic situation ensues in "Back in the Red: Parts One–Three" when the Dwarfers attempt to escape prosecution from the nanobot-resurrected Red Dwarf crew for "stealing" Starbug.[38] With the five remaining episodes of this series, they subsequently experience prison life aboard the ship and join the Canaries, a prisoner commando squad. This return to comedic-adventures completes the crew's journey from the darkness of being separated from Red Dwarf in Series VI and VII. In a roundabout way, moreover, Lister's initial rescuing of and kindness towards Kryten has benefited the last new survivors of humanity aboard Red Dwarf because the android's rebellious nanobots resurrected them. Since the hero who is Lister has returned *"from [his] mysterious adventure with the power to bestow boons on his fellow man"* (Campbell 30), he and his crewmates have arguably completed their journey of "separation–initiation–return." However, the fact that Lister has been reunited with Kochanski and the Red Dwarf crew does not deter him from his desire to complete his quest, since, in the episode "Cassandra," he asks the Cassandra prophecy computer, "[Do] we ever get back to Earth? Has the human race survived?" On a mythological note, then, Lister's spoken desire to reach Earth and be reunited with his species demonstrate that the ancient literary need of the hero to return to his homeland remains valid in this encoded television journey.

As for the parallel-universe version of Kochanski, she more or less becomes a full-fledged heroic member of the Dwarfer crew in *Red Dwarf VIII*, joining their escape attempt in "Back in the Red: Part Three," going on Canary missions with them, and playing on their inmate basketball team in "Pete: Part One." Unfortunately, from a sexual viewpoint, she now also functions as an object of lust for both the show's characters and viewers alike. As an example, she wildly kisses Lister in a Red Dwarf elevator when he contracts the lust virus in "Back in the Red: Part Two." Later, in "Cassandra," a gleeful Rimmer cannot wait to make love to her when he thinks that the Cassandra computer has predicted the act. Most egregiously, "Krytie TV" shows the male inmates gaining pleasure from the videos of her and fellow female prisoners showering, and "Only the Good..." triggers audience laughter from Kryten unwittingly "celebrating" her period.

In contrast, the Kochanski of *Red Dwarf VII* had been encoded as an intelligent, empowered woman, not as the sexualized object of *Red Dwarf VIII*, whose feminine presence fuels sexist humor. This division of Kochanski as hero/sex object reflects a troubling encoding mindset, in that women appearing on television can be as heroic as men yet still be subjected to the lascivious gaze of male audience members. Perhaps Naylor's intent for modifying Kochanski's characterization in Series VIII may have been to both "soften" her character and appeal to a male audience. In fact, regarding his decision to earlier cast Chloë Annett as an alternate universe version of Kochanski in *Red Dwarf VII*, Naylor writes, "The movie people I'd spoken to had made it pretty clear a 'gorgeous actress' was essential if we were to raise sufficient funds to make the film and retain the British cast. I thought the idea of making the film with an all-star American cast was pointless. I wanted to retain the gang, and this was the one sweetener I had to throw the way of the movie moguls" (14). If one explores Naylor's choice of words in reference to Annett's casting, then his description of her as an attractive "sweetener" he had to throw in the direction of what appears to be male movie moguls to retain the *Red Dwarf* "gang," also men, definitely adds weight to the argument that Kochanski primarily works as a beleaguered sexual object in Series VIII.

At the same time, perhaps the function of Kristine Kochanski's character since *Red Dwarf I* has been to represent Lister's (and the audience's) fantasy lover. Online writer Genevieve Koski and others claim that Scottish performer Clare Grogan's version of Kochanski "had been written as little more than a lust object for Lister." They add, "A few years into the show, however, the writers decided it was a tad unseemly for their hero to essentially engage in holographically aided masturbation fantasies with a woman who'd been dead for millennia, and decided to retcon Kochanski's characters so that she'd once been Lister's actual girlfriend." While these writers are correct in humorously assuming that Grogan's version of Kochanski represents an object of sexual desire for Lister, they miss the fact that her iteration of the character likewise embodies a romantic ideal for the last surviving human. Put another way, for Grant and Naylor, Lister's dualistic feelings of love and lust for Kochanski initially served the greater narrative purpose of encoding him as a realistic hero who yearns for the satisfaction of his heterosexual urges and a fulfillment of his emotional needs for a mate and children.

Koski and her cowriters continue, "This led to a welcome expansion of [Kochanski's] personality and an improvement in her screen time (eventually, an alternate-universe version of [the character] joined the *Red Dwarf*'s crew), but unfortunately, she was replaced by Chloë Annett, an inferior actress whose supermodel looks didn't mesh well with the Everyman-ish Lister." Again, Koski and company place an emphasis upon Kochanski's physicality in relationship to Lister. Although these writers' assessment of Annett's acting skills is subject to debate (and may be echoed by members of *Red Dwarf* fandom who did not enjoy her performance), their comment regarding her attractive appearance reveals a superficial indictment of the woman. In this case, one can argue that Koski and others' fan appreciation and understanding of *Red Dwarf* and the character of Kochanski has been subsumed to the demands of crafting a snarky, brief, and superficial article for a profit-generating Web site, *A.V. Club*. In other words, by writing a short, scathing article, "The Darrin[39] Effect: 20 jarring cases of recast roles," which considers subpar interpretations of beloved television characters, the writers may have attracted potential new viewers to *Red Dwarf* while also providing an all-too brief, biased critique of a complex, problematic character, Kochanski, who nevertheless offers the much-needed addition of a heroic female presence to the show's cast.

The Dwarfers: Posthuman Manifestations of the Present and Future

At this point, a discussion of *Red Dwarf*'s projected organic and cyber-

Four. What a Smegging Quest! The Journey of Red Dwarf 133

netic representations of a future posthuman condition is quite vital for theorizing why the characters have successfully connected with a television audience. For Lister, the last human, one can easily argue that his unambitious, slovenly, relaxed personality serves as a common encoding reference point for the audience. This is not to say that *Red Dwarf* fans—or SF television fans in general—are underachievers or unintellectual. Instead, Lister represents a fallible and likeable character, and, if anything, these are human traits with which most people can identify. Unlike *Doctor Who*'s main character, who is a multitalented, incredibly brave genius, Lister often stumbles through his deep-space adventures, sometimes benefiting from his street-smart intelligence, while, on other occasions, being rescued by his shipmates.

For *Red Dwarf I–VI*, his only humanoid companion is Cat, who gradually progresses from a wild, free, vain, self-centered character into a relatively domestic, fully functioning member of the Dwarfer crew, who fights alongside his shipmates and utilizes his natural alacritous feline skills to pilot Starbug in latter series. Although he greatly resembles *homo sapiens*—baring his prominent fangs—his self-absorbed, sociopathic obsession with his looks and wardrobe—often to the annoyance of his shipmates—both emphasizes his biological and cultural status as a member of the species *felis sapiens*. Simultaneously, for *Red Dwarf* viewers, Cat's overexaggeratedly performing the human characteristic of narcissism, his unfulfilled virginal need to have sex with a female, and his continual resistance to group bonding within a confined social situation, encode him as another reference point for viewer identification.

On the cybernetic end of the Dwarfer crew, viewers have Holly, Rimmer, and Kryten, who, in various ways, incorporate human characteristics. For a better understanding of their dualistic organic-machine situation, one can turn to Donna Haraway, who, in "A Cyborg Manifesto," writes, "Our best machines are made of sunshine; they are all light and clean because they are nothing but signals, electromagnetic waves, a section of a spectrum, and these machines are eminently portable, mobile.... People are nowhere near so fluid, being both material and opaque. Cyborgs are ether, quintessence" (153). In the case of Holly, whose floating head can ubiquitously appear throughout the Red Dwarf ship on viewscreens and movable computer contraptions, the "eminently potable, mobile" part of Haraway's thoughts is quite applicable. Moreover, despite his occasional computer senility,[40] Holly's wise decision to give Lister a form of human companionship in the form of the hologram who is Rimmer and his tension-relieving comedic quips also demonstrate the "ether [and] quintessence" of his ability to represent the best elements of humanity to the benefit of the last human.

Arnold Rimmer, in his incorporeal state, offers another manifestation of Haraway's conception of ethereal cyborgs, but, when one applies the idea of this irate character being "made of sunshine" and "all light and clean," the conceit only truly applies to his clean-cut physical appearance. Indeed, this post-life reconstruction of Rimmer's organic being preserves the man's flawed traits, which include his lack of social graces and self-loathing. On a gendered note, he embodies masculine traits in that he believes his upper-class, prep-school breeding entitles him to the privilege of being an officer, a "man of honor," like his father and three brothers. However, his organic self's sole sexual relationship with a woman[41] and his excessive cowardice demarcate him as an unsuccessful alpha male. In other words, going against Haraway's utopian conception of a genderless, quintessential representation of the human condition via bodiless cyborgs, Rimmer, through Grant and Naylor's playful masculine authorship, exposes all of the flaws inherent in latter twentieth-century cultural conceptions of male heroism. Nonetheless, these writers' encoding of this troubled hero has resonated with *Red Dwarf* audiences as they have created a sympathetic character, one whose personal growth over *Red Dwarf*'s ten seasons complements Lister's ongoing heroic quest.

Perhaps the most problematic—and complicated—example of a post-human cyborg on *Red Dwarf* may be found in the form of the android Kryten. Although he possesses elements of organic tissue in his brain,[42] the majority of his form is an exaggerated, distorted approximation of the human body, visibly positing him as a mechanical servant. Ironically, his Caucasian-like skin tone underscores his symbolic role as an Othered, subaltern servant in relation to the privileged twenty-third century humans who had possessed the capital to purchase and subsequently command him to engage in unpaid domestic labor. However, in regard to racial implications for latter twentieth-century viewers, the fact that Lister, a black British man, successfully works toward breaking Kryten's subservient programming over the course of *Red Dwarf II–VII* emphasizes their shared status as outer-space minorities who need to resist the oppressive economic and cultural forces wielded by a future humanity engaged in the imperialistic pursuit of establishing a galactic empire. As a result, *Red Dwarf* viewers witness the personal evolution of characters, who, like the rebellious Doctor before them, who fled his apathetic Time Lord society, and Roj Blake's reformed criminal crew, who struggle against the totalitarian Federation, serve as sympathetic representations of anti-establishment heroes.

Kryten also embodies an intersection point in regard to his gender. While the *Red Dwarf IV* episode "Camille" presents him functioning in a heteronormative manner as he romances the pleasure GELF[43] after whom the episode had been named in a gentleman-like, masculine manner, he conversely offers a queered vision of himself to his fellow Dwarfers in *Red Dwarf VII*'s "Tikka to Ride." In the first half of this episode, Kryten's primary head has been replaced by one of his spare heads, and his guilt chip has been overridden by Lister, who wishes for the reluctant android to help him use the time drive[44] to travel to Earth in the past, so he can restock his destroyed curry and lager supplies. As a result, when he is serving dinner to the crew, the now-morally-corrupted android uses one of his phallic-like groinal attachments to stir their drinks. With this action, the droid has basically wielded his cybernetic penis to sexually shock and harass his Starbug crewmates in a homoerotic manner.

The theme of Kryten's attachable—or missing—penis denoting his hermaphroditic sexuality is further developed in the following season with the second installment of the two-part story "Pete." Earlier in the series, Kryten had been assigned to live in a female cellblock room[45] with Kristine Kochanski since his lack of male robotic genitalia had caused him to be classified as a female. Furthermore, in the episode "Krytie TV," while Kryten is on a Canary mission with his fellow prisoners, Kill Crazy and Cat, they ask him to smuggle a camera into the women's shower and film them, prompting this exchange:

> KRYTEN: Are you asking me to betray the people I live with? To ignore their humanity and reduce them to mindless sex objects merely there for your moronic titillation?
> CAT: Yes, please.
> KRYTEN: If you'll excuse me, I forgot who I was for a moment.
> KILL CRAZY: What are you doing?
> KRYTEN: I'm a woman and proud of it. If you'll excuse me, I'll be with my fellow sisters—doing it for ourselves.

Significantly, Kryten, despite having the external facsimile appearance of a male, now self-identifies as a woman, most likely offering SF television's first transgendered cyborg. Applicable to this thought is Donna Haraway's argument that "The cyborg is a creature in a post-gender world; it has no truck with bisexuality, pre-oedipal symbiosis, unalienated labour or other seductions to organic wholeness through a final appropriation of all the power of the parts into a higher unity" (150). For Kryten, his exploration of his neutered programming and mechanical reality work toward him achieving a "higher unity" of his post-gender identity. Therefore, in regard to his personal heroic journey, he has experienced an odyssey of self-discovery, learning how to choose his gender despite his neutered status. Sadly, this progressive encoding of his character is later diminished in "Krytie TV," when his fellow inmates manage to reprogram him to film the female prisoners showering and subsequently exploit the video of their appropriated naked bodies for public viewing consumption and profit.

Despite this narrative setback, Kryten continues his personal quest to define his cyborg sexuality in "Pete: Part Two." Wishing to explore his masculinity, he builds a sentient cybernetic penis he names "Archie." After he fails to capture the elusive mobile device in the prison quarters he shares with Kochanski, she comically quips that he now is "like all men" because he has "absolutely no control over [his] penis." While Naylor has employed sexual humor to delineate Kryten's gender confusion, his literal attempts at addressing his lack of a phallus reveal his all-too-human and feminized penis envy. Working against potential audience expectations, however, Kryten's decision to build himself a penis does not result in him acting more "manly" or even masculine. At the same time, his misplaced attempt to bond with Kochanski in *Red Dwarf VIII*'s finale, "Only the Good...," by posting a banner reading "Have a Fantastic Period" and offering her a gift-wrapped tampon as a present reveal Naylor's uninspired dependence on hackneyed sexist humor in order to elicit laughter from his live studio audience.

Continuing an Endless Quest: *Red Dwarf* in the Wake of a Failed Cinematic Offering

In the several years since the airing of *Red Dwarf VIII*, Doug Naylor repeatedly tried to raise funds for an independent production of a film that would both resolve the cliffhanger ending of "Only the Good..." and potentially depict the Dwarfers finally returning to Earth. In a 2005 interview with Leah Holmes, Naylor commented on the situation: "It's not so much in 'development Hell!' right now as it is in 'finding money Hell!' The script's all beautiful; it's just the money! I'm constantly meeting with people who say they've got the money, they'll get the money, they're about to get the money, who then turn out not to be telling the entire total truth. The film world seems to be riddled with people like that" (87).

Naylor's comments on the funding issues surrounding his attempts to mount an independent film production of *Red Dwarf* reveal the problems encountered by a creative encoder who lacks corporate support. Without the BBC's financial backing (or commissioning a ninth season of the show), *Red Dwarf* had thus become a brand that was considered to be past its television prime. Naylor, however, in touch with the *Red Dwarf* fan base through conventions and online communication, and aware of the significantly high video (and later, DVD) sales for *Red Dwarf I–VIII*, reasonably believed that the show represented a still-viable brand. In other words, his awareness of decoder creative and financial support of his co-creator-owned SF brand had given him the confidence to argue he had a stable foundation for bringing the property to the next level: an independent film production. However, as Naylor states, he was given the runaround on ensuring stable financial backing for the projected film. This fact, moreover, was constantly shared online with *Red Dwarf* fans, which shows Naylor's honest form of communication with his decoder-supporters, but which also opens the frustrating situation up to playful fan criticism.

When the *Red Dwarf* production office opened up a competition for fan-produced films celebrating (or playfully mocking) the series, one of the entries that Naylor chose as a distinguished winning entry indeed satirizes his repeated attempts to find backer funding for the long-delayed film. Directed by fan Ian Symes, the short production, "The Movie: Yeah, No, Yeah, No," in one scene presents "Doug Naylor" as sitting before four male Hollywood executives[46] who want big-name actors such as Hugh Grant, Patrick Stewart, and J-Lo to respectively play the parts of Lister, Holly, and Kochanski. They also offer new titles for the film as they find the name *Red Dwarf* to be politically incorrect since it could potentially offend dwarves. Their replacement title ideas then include the following pitches: "Red Vertically-Challenged Person," "Like *Star Trek*, Only Funny," and "Bleeding Hell!—It's a Spaceship!" Consequently, this sequence works on a dual level of parodic resistance. One, it satirizes the often embarrassing manner in which Hollywood film producers usurp a brand by "Americanizing" a proposed movie project with A-list actors and terrible titles. Secondly, the scene sympathizes with Naylor's tireless attempts to sell *Red Dwarf* to skeptical investors while humorously presenting him dealing with a hypothetically untenable situation, as the real-life writer-producer likewise was intent on retaining his original British cast and creative ideas for the film.

Ultimately, the fact that Naylor not only offered a competition for *Red Dwarf* fans to create their own versions of the show but hosted a mock awards ceremony[47] as well shows his healthy and productive relationship with the series' decoders. Unlike producer John Nathan-Turner, whose early 1980s relationship with *Doctor Who* fans turned into a media-fueled acrimonious situation during the latter part of that decade, Naylor, to date, has remained on good terms with his fan base. It is this somewhat synergistic dynamic, between an encoder who has embraced an auteur role by writing, directing, and producing *Red Dwarf: Back to Earth* and *Red Dwarf X* and his decoder-viewers, that has enabled Naylor to create new seasons of the series that are supported economically and critically by the fans.

On the subject of *Red Dwarf: Back to Earth*, a three-part special[48] that aired on the digital channel Dave from April 10 to 12, 2009, this continuation of the show's televised saga demonstrates the resilience of the franchise despite a lack of BBC support. Due to the economic necessity of utilizing blue screen and CGI technology and the desire to shoot on location, *Back to Earth*, however, features neither a live studio audience's interaction nor a post-production recorded viewer laugh track. In terms of its narrative, the Dwarfer crew are back, with the exception of Kochanski, who is apparently dead (yet, in reality, has left them due to Lister's lingering depression), and Holly, who has been disabled by water flooding since Lister left a bath running for nine years. After they seemingly fight and destroy a giant squid who had invaded the ship's water tank, they are joined by a new female hologram, Red Dwarf's science officer, Katerina Bartikovsky. Wishing to ensure that Lister repopulates the human race, Katerina manages to open a portal to another dimension, where he can potentially find a mate.

In actuality, the plan goes awry as the last human and company are sucked into the portal and, via television screens in a London department store, arrive on Earth in the year 2009. But this version of Earth is not located in Lister's reality, but our own. In a postmodern manner, the Dwarfers subsequently find themselves in a reality where *Red Dwarf*, as in the viewers' world, is a long-running SF show that is being revived in a television production titled "Red Dwarf: Back to Earth." As the crew next travel through the mall on an escalator, they find themselves pointed out and laughed at by people who most likely believe them to be fans cosplaying the *Red Dwarf* cast. Then, the Dwarfers realize they are characters in a TV show once they find a mock-up version of the forthcoming DVD for "Back to Earth," which (as with the packaging for the actual DVD for the story) includes a back cover synopsis of their adventure so far and the upcoming plot for the episode: "Knowing they will die in the final episode, the Dwarfers, in best *Blade Runner* tradition, attempt to track down their creators to plead for more life. First the crew attempts to track down the actors who play them in the series, and their metaphysical odyssey begins...." As a paradoxical result, Lister reading these words functions on two levels as it both provides a plot summary and serves as an example of product placement. Within the meta-narrative of this episode, this DVD plot synopsis establishes the newly self-aware characters' postmodern quest to find the writer of their masculine-heroic adventures. From an economic standpoint, however, Naylor's act of writing into the episode the product that will eventually become the DVD of *Red Dwarf: Back to Earth*, while a clever plot point and visual gag, also works as a promotional tool to the viewers who watched the original airing of the episodes on Dave in April 2009.

With his online review of this three-part story, Richard Mann points out the self-promotional overtones of this tale: "Overall, *Red Dwarf: Back to Earth* is a demonstration piece. It self-promotes almost in every scene, showing merchandise, DVDs and *SFX* magazines with 'Red Dwarf' emblazoned on them ... [that] merely shout out to the TV channels: 'We're back ... we're as popular as ever, and we want this franchise to continue!' For my part, I am with them. *Red Dwarf* should return." While Mann correctly summarizes *Back to Earth*'s function as both a capitalistic and sincere promotion of the long-dormant franchise, one can likewise point out how the three-part production briefly recreates its brand to a parodic degree. In the director's cut, a scene is restored in which Rimmer and Lister comically discuss the last man's unwittingly misusing a bathroom hand dryer in the children's furniture section of a department store. As a result, the sight of Rimmer and Lister sitting at a small children's table with a bunk bed behind them, which contains red bed sheets and a guitar attached to its top bunk, visually and playfully parallels the pair's Red Dwarf bunkroom scene from the first part of the story. Potentially, for viewers new to the series, the encoding of this scene could work to introduce them to these rather outlandish characters via a familiar, real-world setting.

Later in *Back to Earth*, the Dwarfers visit a comic book store called They Walk Among Us!, reminding viewers that such a place serves as a locus for purchasing *Red Dwarf* paraphernalia. In addition, the store's clerk, Noddy, coincidentally, is a *Red Dwarf* fan, thus working as a direct fan-viewer surrogate. Consequently, even if this scene fails to promote the show's ancillary merchandise to the audience, it does work as an esoteric means of acknowledging a common gathering place for certain members of the *Red Dwarf* fan base. After this scene, the crew drive around in a fan-customized, compact car version of their travel craft, Starbug. Via this visual presentation of the Dwarfers driving around a British town in this whimsical vehicle, *Red Dwarf*'s typical outer space travel scenes have been temporarily reimagined as a buddy-buddy road trip sequence—the type that can be seen in many non–SF television shows and movies.

Intertextuality is similarly applied to the encoding of *Back to Earth* as Lister meets "Craig Charles" on the *Coronation Street*[49] set and then ironically laments, "I'm so glad I'm not him. The guy's a wreck and pretends to be somebody else all day. That's no way to make a living. Smeghead!" Afterwards, the remainder of the episode becomes a *Blade Runner* parody with scenes reminiscent of director Ridley's Scott's 1982 dystopian SF film, as the Dwarfers meet up with their fictitious creator,[50] and crash through several panes of glass[51] while being shot in a dream sequence. Moreover, in *Back to Earth*'s climax, which resembles *Blade Runner*'s studio-enforced original cut, Lister travels in a car to the countryside with a dream version of Kochanski, who visually resembles the replicant Rachael in Scott's film. Perhaps one means of interpreting this complicated visual satire of *Blade Runner* would be to conclude that Doug Naylor views *Red Dwarf* as resembling Scott's film because they both present sympathetic posthuman characters searching for identity and meaning and have amassed impressive cult fan followings.

As a parodic work, *Red Dwarf: Back to Earth* also resembles Peter Davison's production, *The Five(ish) Doctors Reboot*, and B7 Enterprises' short film, *Blake's Junction 7*. In a similar manner to the former 1980s Doctors, Peter Davison, Colin Baker, and Sylvester McCoy, trying to find their way into the *NüWho* fiftieth anniversary celebration, "The Day of the Doctor," the Dwarfers are attempting to find their "real world" writer-creator in order to demand that he write more episodes in which they can have new adventures, or simply put, live. While the two meta-fictional approaches differ in the fact that the *Classic Who* actors are parodying their real-life selves and the *Red Dwarf* actors are remaining in character, the end result is that both postmodern satires are commenting upon the viability of their characters/actors as brands. Moreover, both *Back to Earth* and *The Five(ish) Doctors Reboot* cater to their decoders by both declaring and implying that their fans adore them and will probably emotionally and economically support any new televised product featuring their respective actors.

When compared to *Blake's Junction 7*, however, *Back to Earth* both complements and departs from that earlier meta-tinged production. On the one hand, both works employ contemporary Earth settings to reintroduce old and new viewers to their respective future-based SF concepts and ongoing heroic narratives. In other words, ostensibly, the mall scenes contained in *Back to Earth* depict the Dwarfers struggling to understand twenty-first century consumer culture, and the rest-stop location of *Blake's Junction 7* portrays Avon's rebel crew interacting in a mundane setting, but they are visible reminders that such fantasy-based shows are simply futuristic allegories for real-world situations. As Lister and company strive to find their identities in a large London mall, and Blake's former crew continues to function as a unit at a rest stop despite the loss of their leader, viewers are entertained by extraordinary characters interacting in familiar settings in which they themselves may struggle with similar personal challenges. Equally, then, *Back to Earth* and *Blake's Junction 7* have been encoded to connect with their audiences in the shared hope that their fan-decoders will assist in their respective creative attempts to revive their brands.

However, *Back to Earth* possessed more of a chance of achieving media success than *Blake's Junction 7* as it employed its original actors while the latter work relied on well-known comedy actors to recreate the classic *Blake's 7* cast's roles. In addition, Naylor's production aired on Dave nine years after *Red Dwarf VIII*, and he had stayed in close contact with his loyal fan base. In comparison, *Blake's Junction 7*, which did not air on any television channel, was produced twenty-four years after the final episode of *Blake's 7* aired in 1981, and its once large and organized fandom had been diminished over the years. By comparing these facts, one can surmise that, in order for a dormant SF television brand to achieve a successful media revival, encoders may be required to include the following elements in their individual productions: the original cast, a true continuation of its heroic quest, and a synergistic relationship with its decoders.

While *Back to Earth*'s title suggests that Lister and company will return to his and Rimmer's home planet twenty-one years since he made that promise to do so in "The End," the ultimate result is quite misleading as their adventures on Earth are revealed to be a shared hallucination generated by the Dwarfers' exposure to a female Despair Squid's toxin earlier in the story.[52] Granted, the crew have interacted in a present-day setting, which, in a postmodern manner, brings the characters back to an iteration of Earth. Their situation, unfortunately, does not deliver on the story's potential titular promise of revealing the fate of the planet three million years in the future. On his encoding choice of temporarily deceiving the *Back to Earth* audience into believing that the events depicted in the previous fifty-two episodes of *Red Dwarf* did not actually occur since the characters were simply fictitious, Naylor comments,

> Many people think a really good way to create good stories is to look at what's the worse possible thing that can happen to your character. And I looked at it in a slightly different way; I looked at it from the point of view of "What's the worse possible thing that could happen to my audience?" And it seemed to me that the worst possible thing that could happen to my audience was somehow what they'd seen wasn't real ["Making of *Back*"].

Regardless of the positive or negative results of Naylor's intention to play with his audience's emotions, one reading of his decision of bringing the Dwarfers into the past that is contemporary London circa 2009 could be to suppose that Lister's quest of searching for home and happiness is shared by the viewers and thereby satisfied in a postmodern reflective way that yields a form of catharsis in the sense that both the characters and their audience have briefly shared the same reality space.

But perhaps this reading is too optimistic as Naylor encodes an ending to *Back to Earth* that offers a dark postmodern twist to the story when the Dwarfers share this conversation back aboard their mining ship home:

> CAT: What's going to happen to everybody in the reality we left? The guys all watching us on TV.
> KRYTEN: Well, they'll continue to exist as a consequence of us creating them in our hallucination, sir. It's quantum mechanics. Every decision that's made creates a new universe, as do all dreams and hallucinations. It's multiverse 101.
> RIMMER: But those sad suckers will live out the rest of their lives convinced they're the real ones and we're characters from a TV show.
> LISTER: And you know if you told them the truth, you know what they'd probably do?
> RIMMER: Laugh.
> LISTER: Yeah. (They all laugh.) They probably would.

Even though *Red Dwarf* traditionally offers its viewers a fantastical, futuristic escape from the reality of their lives, Naylor's fourth-wall-breaking writing in this scene has inverted and destabilized the power structure in which television characters' existences are subject to the all-seeing gaze of an audience who enjoys sympathizing with and/or laughing at their serious and comical adventures. In fact, maybe it is fittingly ironic that Arnold Rimmer, who has been subject to the twin ridiculing forces of his fellow *Red Dwarf* characters and his external television audience, is the one to write off the latter group as "sad suckers." With this moment, Naylor turns a self-reflective existential mirror back upon his decoder-fans. Of course, many of *Back to Earth*'s audience members will easily accept the writer's characteristically playful mocking of their existence. However, there remains the unseen gray area of the viewers who may be disconcerted by this closing scene. While their forum for critiquing *Back to Earth* exists in the multimedia platforms of the Internet, telephone, and portable texting devices, it is interesting to note that the dismissive laughter the "truly realistic" characters of Rimmer and Lister suspect they may have triggered in their unseen viewers upon being told that the Dwarfers are indeed the creators of their fourth-wall reality has been lamentably muted by the lack of any live studio audience's humorous response.

A more optimistic counter-response to this criticism of *Back to Earth*'s complex ending would be to say that Lister and Rimmer's closing exchange equally represents a call for action directed toward *Red Dwarf*'s viewers. Put another way, with a clever postmodern flourish, these two longtime, odd-couple bunkmates are asking their viewers to be more cognizant of their roles as consumer-viewers who may be simply—and passively— amused by *Red Dwarf: Back to Earth* as a work of fleeting television comedy. When viewed from this direction, Lister and Rimmer's dialogue works toward counteracting *Back to Earth*'s earlier obvious action of self-promoting itself as a television and merchandise brand. More importantly, their conversation invites the *Red Dwarf* audience, which includes both old fans and new viewers, to stop being couch potatoes and embrace their own inherent agency as an audience of independent thinkers who can formulate coherent counterarguments to the smug postmodern pronouncements of self-awareness proffered by these fictitious Dwarfer constructs.

In October 2012, *Red Dwarf* returned to air on Dave once again, branding itself as the tenth season of the show[53] and returning to the series' traditional format of six episodes. Moreover, due to a budgetary situation,[54] the show could only afford one day of location filming, leaving the production to be predominantly filmed in the studio. Thus, like *Red Dwarf I*, which contained no location filming, the series returned to its roots of telling a sitcom-based SF narrative in enclosed spaces. At the same time, like *Back to Earth*[55] (and the initial six seasons of the show), it problematically limits the appearances of females on the series. For instance, the opening episode, "Trojan," presents a female character, Sim Crawford, as murderously bent on destroying Lister since he is a member of her hated enemy, the human race. Another villainous female is rendered in "Fathers & Suns," with Prix, Red Dwarf's new beautiful but deadly mainframe computer, who applies predictive logic and bureaucratic rules that result in her endangering Lister and his crewmates. Finally, in "Entangled," the crew come across Professor Edgington, a surviving human female who had been placed in stasis. Unfortunately, by the end of the episode, she is sucked out of an airlock on Red Dwarf as a result of her natural ability to get things wrong.[56] With these three examples, female guest stars are consequently encoded as villainous, deadly, and foolish. As with Naylor's reworking of Kochanski as an object of lust in *Red Dwarf VIII*, these stereotypical representations of women on the series, while generating a significant level of live audience laughter, come at the cost of ignoring the more egalitarian heroic balance of the sexes as seen in *Red Dwarf VII*.

Despite its failure in depicting positive women, *Red Dwarf X* continues Lister's development as a flawed yet sympathetic example of a masculine hero by having him struggle with aging and his paradoxical roles of being both his father and son in "Fathers & Suns." The episode "Dear Dave," additionally, delineates him dealing with the potential of—and failed outcome—that he had impregnated a former girlfriend and hence generated an impressive family line three million years earlier. This theme of patriarchal desires and inadequacies is shared by Rimmer, who measures his mortal and post-life career against the hologrammatic version of his priggish older brother, Howard, in "Trojan." However, Howard ultimately reveals to his sibling that he, like Arnold, had not achieved the rank of an officer, but is only a lowly ship repairman.

With *Red Dwarf X*'s concluding episode, "The Beginning," the last episode of the series to date, Rimmer is further relieved of his childhood emotional baggage by the revelation that his cold, insulting father is not his biological one, leading him to find the inner confidence to mastermind a successful defensive strategy against four Simulant death ships that are attacking him and his crewmates, who have been fleeing their adversaries in the travel craft Blue Midget. After accomplishing this heroic goal, the hologram proudly tells[57] Kryten to set their ship on a return course for Red Dwarf, adding, "The Slime's coming home!" As a narrative-bookend inversion of the same words Lister spoke twenty-four years earlier in *Red Dwarf*'s first episode, "The End," Rimmer's heroic promise symbolically repositions the mining ship Red Dwarf as the Dwarfers' home, not the near-mythical, futuristic Earth. More significantly, although *Red Dwarf XI* and *XII* will respectively be airing on Dave in 2016 and 2017, this episode presently provides a form of narrative closure to the show's ongoing quest narrative.

In response to Rimmer's heroic evolution in "The Beginning," online fan reviewer jedsocrazy writes, "Having Rimmer declare 'The Slime's coming home!' brought back a lot of memories and reminded me of what makes this show awesome. It's fantastic to see Rimmer grow as a character, and I'm interested to see if this change continues into series eleven." For this fan, Rimmer's masculine heroic evolution is basically on par with the narrative journey of *Red Dwarf*'s apparent lead, Lister. Agreeing with jedsocrazy, one can likewise argue that Rimmer's journey across *Red Dwarf*'s ten seasons has ultimately been more fulfilling for viewers than his bunkmate's. In other words, while Lister has endured various traumas in his episodic adventures, Rimmer represents the true underdog of the show since he is neurotic, unlikeable, and, most importantly, dead. As a result, his posthuman, post-life journey leads him to falling in love with a fellow hologram in *Red Dwarf V*'s episode "Holoship" and embracing the heroic mantle of Ace Rimmer in *Red Dwarf VII*'s "Stoke Me a Clipper." His resurrected human counterpart also kicks Death in the groin at the cliffhanger conclusion of *Red Dwarf VIII*'s "Only the Good..."[58] demonstrating how resilient the character has become at his core. Although the Arnold Rimmer who skillfully outmaneuvers the attacking Simulant ships in "The Beginning" could be either the original hologrammatic version of the character or a cybernetic recreation of the resurrected human iteration introduced in *Red Dwarf VIII*, the bottom line is that the final episode of the show to date presents a culmination of his journey from coward to hero.

* * *

As this work anticipates discussing the encoding and decoding of gendered heroism in another BBC SF television show, *Torchwood*, one must ask how *Red Dwarf* foreshadows that series. Even though *Red Dwarf: Back to Earth* aired in 2009, the same year as the five-part *Torchwood: Children of Earth*, the former had been caught in a state of development limbo for a decade, during which the latter show had aired its first series of episodes in the autumn of 2006. For a show with an ensemble cast, *Red Dwarf*, as shown, has been predominately focused on presenting masculine visions of gendered heroism. When it comes to its female characters, the second Holly and the parallel universe Kristine Kochanski, their character development and heroic narratives are often subverted to support the primary stories of the male Dwarfers. While part of this focus has been initiated by Rob Grant and Doug Naylor in order to present sympathetic, flawed aspects of male heroism, their efforts also satisfy many fans' expectations for a quintessential *Red Dwarf* featuring the adventures of the four central male characters, Lister, Rimmer, Cat, and Kryten.[59] In a way, then, the female Dwarfers' secondary status to their male counterparts continues the precedent set by *Blake's 7*, in which the female rebels, Jenna, Cally, Dayna, and Soolin, are often overshadowed by the strong masculine heroism embodied by Blake and Avon, and to a lesser extent, Vila, Gan, and Tarrant. In comparison, *Torchwood*'s first two seasons, as I will discuss in the next chapter, offers a better balance than *Red Dwarf* between its male and female characters, which helps the series to reflect the expectations and desires of its diverse fandom.

If *Red Dwarf* fails to offer a lasting progressive vision of a well-balanced portrait of gendered heroism reflecting both sexes, then perhaps the show's legacy rests with its outrageous sexual humor and situations, which vocalize *Blake's 7*'s veiled sexual innuendo and sets the television stage for the entrance of *Torchwood*'s Captain Jack Harkness, whose omnisexual lifestyle and frank onscreen discussion of sexuality has both shocked and endeared him to viewers and fans. More importantly, *Red Dwarf* must be given proper credit for providing a postmodern comedic vision of the televised gendered heroic quest throughout the majority of the 1990s, when a successful BBC SF series was absent from its two channels. Arguably, without *Red Dwarf* reminding audiences and BBC managers and producers that an SF program could still present relevant characterizations and situations, would a new series of *Doctor Who* have been commissioned in 2003, laying the path for its spin-off, *Torchwood*? Although this question is mainly conjectural, the fact remains that *Nü Who* echoes *Red Dwarf*'s theme of featuring the heroic adventures of a species' last man in its sensitive encoding of the PTSD-suffering, Time-War survivor, the Ninth Doctor, and both shows, either consciously or otherwise, have reflected and refined *Red Dwarf*'s playful application of the SF tropes of time travel, body horror, and posthuman lifestyles.

Chapter Five

Everything's Constantly Changing: Sex and Death on Torchwood

For the producer-actor-encoders and the fan-decoders comprising the two media ends of the BBC SF show *Torchwood*, their relationship, like the ever-changing show itself, can be quite intense and incendiary. From the series' opening episode, "Everything Changes," to "The Blood Line," the finale of the controversy-generating BBC/Starz fourth series coproduction, *Miracle Day*, *Torchwood* has not failed to both excite and anger its large transatlantic fan base. Two of the show's narrative components—sex and death—arguably ignite the catalyst for vocal fan support and resistance. Taking the darker themes found in *Blake's 7* several thematic steps farther, *Torchwood* has repeatedly told its viewers that its characters are bisexual and can die. As a result, this chapter will discuss how the show's twin tropes of sex and mortality inform how *Torchwood* fans identify with or rebel against the series' ever-evolving depictions of gendered heroism.

When Russell T Davies was developing the idea of *Torchwood*, he wanted to create a post-watershed BBC SF series that could serve as a British cousin to such American genre television shows as *Buffy the Vampire Slayer* and *Angel* (Rawson-Jones).[1] Both series, indeed, are successful in that they present realistic, flawed characters, initially antiheroes, who serve as viewer surrogates for fans witnessing their struggles to overcome personal flaws and redeem themselves as true heroes. British SF TV is likewise replete with examples of imperfect heroes. As this book has shown, *Doctor Who*'s encoding of William Hartnell's First Doctor presents an alien outsider who must learn to put aside his instinct for self-preservation to selflessly aid humanity and alien species across the totality of time and space. On a similar trajectory is *Red Dwarf*'s underachieving Dave Lister, who associates with a motley crew as he tries to return to Earth three million years in the future. Perhaps the best iteration of the damaged hero, however, is found in the sociopathic Kerr Avon of *Blake's 7*, as he repeatedly struggles between the extremes of remaining loyal to his quest to defeat the fascist Federation and to a person equally dear to his heart—himself. In all of the above examples of BBC SF television, however, men embody the heroic leading roles while the females are often relegated to a secondary, supporting role status. While *Torchwood* somewhat reverses this patriarchal course with Gwen Cooper, who is featured in all four seasons of the show, other female characters such as Toshiko Sato and Esther Drummond, as this chapter will discuss, function as self-sacrificing heroes whose actions occur in the shadow of the leading male's greater acts of heroism.

Davies and his writing staff, however, have upped the ante on the sexual politics in the four series of *Torchwood* to date by offering viewers male characters who are not instantly likeable in the form of Captain Jack Harkness, Dr. Owen Harper, Ianto Jones, Rhys Williams, Captain John, and Rex Matheson. Unlike *NüWho*, from which it is anagrammatically and spiritually derived, *Torchwood* thus repeatedly promotes the theme that its heroically reluctant male leads must pass through an extended filtering process in the viewers' eyes before they can be perceived as being selfless protagonists. In other words, Captain Jack and company continue the BBC SF television trope of the antihero who must learn how to become heroic.

The question, moreover, of how *Torchwood*'s portrayal of sexuality works in conjunction with its depictions of heroism is a complicated one. In comparison with *Doctor Who*, *Blake's 7*, and *Red Dwarf*, *Torchwood*, by far, shows the most graphic rendering of sex. While no frontal nudity or bare buttocks are displayed by any of its lead characters, viewers witness Jack and Ianto engaged in the act of making love in the Series Two episode "Adrift." Although the camera shoots the two characters nude from the waist up and groping at one another as Gwen stumbles upon them in the Hub hothouse, no suggestion of penetration is relayed to viewers. However, "Day One," *Torchwood*'s second episode, depicts a character, Carys, who is possessed by an alien entity that is addicted to human orgasmic energy while she is copulating with a man in the bathroom of a Cardiff bar. Although no nudity is shown, the two characters erotically move and loudly grunt to portray the act of having sex upon the bathroom counter before the man is incinerated by alien energy upon achieving his orgasm.

Being a pre-watershed BBC show, neither *Classic* nor *NüWho* has explicitly depicted its lead characters (or guest stars) having sex. However, playful allusions to the Ninth Doctor engaging in this intimate biological act are proffered in Series One's "The Doctor Dances" while the Eleventh Doctor's married companions, Amy Pond and Rory Williams, have clearly conceived their child, Melody, offscreen while traveling with the Time Lord. *Blake's 7*, as discussed in chapter three, contains a great deal of sexual innuendo, yet only one episode, "Sand," contains the hint that two of the show's leading characters, Servalan and Tarrant, have made love.[2] Taking *Blake's 7*'s approach to sexuality to the next level of comedic humor and awkward situations, *Red Dwarf*, in the episode "Holoship," depicts Rimmer and fellow hologram Nirvanah Crane laying in her bed after their lovemaking, but, on a whole, the series often talks about sex but seldom shows it onscreen.

Since *Torchwood* takes a more adult approach to sexuality by being aimed at an older post-watershed BBC Three and Two audience for its first two series, the argument can be put forth that mature viewers need their heroes to be sexual. This mindset can be based upon a desire to watch a show that feels "realistic," as adult characters, like their viewers, get involved in relationships or romantic affairs and have sex. However, for heterosexual males looking for a solid viewer surrogate with Captain Jack, their desires will mostly remain unsatisfied. At the same time, for gay, bisexual, and straight allies, *Torchwood*'s depiction of Jack, Owen, Ianto, and Tosh's shared bisexual (or, in Gwen's case, bi-curious) identities offers them a show that progressively encodes the sexuality of these characters.

Bisexuality, Rape and Race: *Torchwood*'s Encoding of Problematic Issues

Before *Torchwood* premiered on BBC Three with "Everything Changes" on October 22, 2006, the character of Captain Jack Harkness, as played by John Barrowman, had been introduced in the *NüWho* Series One episode "The Empty Child." In this story, Jack reveals that he is a former member of the Time Agency, which operates out of the fifty-first century. However, he had left its ranks to pursue his own selfish objectives—an act that is definitely unheroic. Perhaps then it is only appropriate that the rebellious Ninth Doctor is the one who sets a higher heroic standard for Jack. After all, this is the same Doctor who has become a better Time Lord as a result of the humanizing influences of his numerous companions over the years, so it is fitting that he passes his heroic mindset onto Jack. Thus, in his five-episode character arc spanning "The Empty Child" to "The

Parting of the Ways,"³ Captain Jack successfully metamorphoses from a charming rogue Time Agent into a selfless hero. Moreover, the most revealing line of his dramatic transformation occurs in "The Parting of the Ways" when Jack, about to embark on defending the Game Station from the attacking Daleks, tells the Doctor, "Wish I'd never met you, Doctor. I was much better off as a coward." Then, Jack kisses the Doctor, an act which can be interpreted as a sign of the Time Lord's bisexuality or as a simple indication that he is sensitive to LGBTQ issues. Regarding this scene, John Barrowman, in his autobiography, *Anything Goes!*, writes,

> Russell [T Davies] had made it clear to me that Jack's character would be unlike any other in the classic *Doctor Who* series. As a result, the subtle sexual chemistry among all three characters—the Doctor, Rose and Jack—was always in play. Contrary to the tabloids' fixation, though, the relationships were by no means driven by desire. When the Doctor and Jack kiss goodbye in "The Parting of the Ways," ... for example, the kiss is full of fondness and respect, and absolutely no tongue [18].

Although Barrowman accurately points out Davies's unique encoding of Jack as an omnisexual character on *NüWho*, when he is spun off into *Torchwood* as a leading man, his bisexual nature has been noticeably downplayed to focus on his gay relationship with Ianto Jones during the first three series of the show. Moreover, a Series One episode, "Captain Jack Harkness," presents Jack temporarily stranded in the Cardiff of 1941 and romancing the man whose name he appropriated from historical records, the real Captain Jack Harkness, an American fighter pilot who will die battling the Germans. Three seasons later, in *Miracle Day*, the episode "Rendition" shows Jack having a graphically depicted one-night stand with a man he meets in a bar, and a flashback-heavy episode, "Immortal Sins," tells the poignant story of his relationship with Angelo Colasanto, an Italian immigrant, in 1927 New York City.

Regarding Jack's sexuality, Davies commented in 2006, "Without making it political or dull, this is going to be a very bisexual programme. I want to knock down the barriers, so we can't define which of the characters is gay. We need to start mixing things up, rather than thinking, 'This is a gay character, and he'll only ever go off with men'" (Martin 40). While the aforementioned examples point to the possibility that Jack has, in fact, ended up as an exclusively gay character on *Torchwood*, he is, at times, encoded to reflect his more heterosexual side. For instance, he kisses the alien-possessed Carys in "Day One" and Martha Jones in "A Day in the Death" and flirts with women in various episodes. Nonetheless, Jack has not been depicted as seriously romancing any females in all four seasons of the show.⁴

Five. Everything's Constantly Changing: Torchwood

As for how the rest of the Series One *Torchwood* cast relates to Davies's promises for fluidic interpretations of sexuality, only Ianto consistently fulfills this goal. Although Gwen is depicted as also kissing Carys in "Day One," she thereafter engages in hetero relationships with her fiancée, Rhys, and has a brief affair with Owen.[5] The gendered encoding of Tosh and Owen in "Everything Changes" is likewise subject to scrutiny. In three cross-edited scenes, the two characters, along with Torchwood team member Suzie Costello, are enjoying the fruits of some top-secret pieces of alien laboratory that were supposed to remain in the Hub. While Suzie tests out the temporary life-restoring properties of the Resurrection Glove, Owen uses a powerful aphrodisiac hormone spray to seduce a woman and her boyfriend while Tosh spends a private night at home utilizing what appears to be a text-translator device that scans in books and immediately digitizes their content. With these two scenes, Tosh is thus encoded as a reliable, bookish British Asian woman, one whose appropriation of alien tech is rather innocuous. Arguably, she may also be fulfilling a television and cinematic stereotype of the marginalized, Othered Asian character who excels in math and science but, in contrast to the white characters, is rather asexual and undesirable. In comparison to Tosh, Owen, a white British male, has been more or less encoded as a date rapist. Upon being immediately rejected by a beautiful blonde woman in a Cardiff bar, Owen remarks, "Look, I got to be up early. I got a hell of a day tomorrow, and I really can't be bothered with all the chat." He then sprays himself with alien pheromones, adding, "So do you want a drink or what?" After suddenly kissing him, the woman responds, "Bloody hell-fire! You're coming home with me, you are. Right now." For the *Torchwood* viewer, the inevitable result is that Owen, who is purportedly part of a team of heroes, has been encoded as a villainous rapist. On her blog, *Torchwood* fan (and *Doctor Who* novelist) Kate Orman asserts,

> In "Everything Changes," Owen uses an alien spray to make a woman, then a man, want to have sex with him. It's clear from the episode that neither of them wanted to have sex with him before he used the spray. We're not told how the spray works, but the Web site describes it as making the user "irresistible." If that's so, then it takes away the other person's ability to say "no"—which means that using the spray to have sex is rape.

Agreeing with Orman's assessment of Owen's actions in "Everything Changes," one can add that although the woman is neither unconscious nor exhibits slurred speech—which would be the normal symptoms of a date-rape drug—her decision-making capability, her agency or free will, has been morally compromised by Owen's purloined spray. Conversely, one could argue that the couple, with their inhibitions drastically lowered, went on to experience a night of sexual experimentation and bliss. The somber fact remains, nonetheless, that the couple entered into a sexual tryst that they otherwise would have avoided if not for the overpowering effects of the pheromone. More importantly, it is the moral gray area formed by the application of this alien pheromone spray that makes Owen sexually irresistible to his victim, and which therefore places the onus of guilt upon him as the woman and man he exposes to its powerful effects behave in a manner akin to not only intoxication but borderline brainwashing as well. Consequently, Owen is undeniably guilty of rape.

Returning to Ianto's initial heterosexual encoding, in the episode "Cyberwoman," he is depicted as desperately trying to save his girlfriend, Lisa Hallett, who has been partially cybernized. During Lisa's first appearance in the episode, she is presented as being as unconscious and strapped into a Cyber conversion unit. However, a fetishistic sexuality has been created by the fact that her midsection and thighs are mostly bare, with a metal circle drawing attention to her navel[6] and a metallic, lower bikini-like section covering up her genitalia. In addition, her breasts have been augmented by a large metal chest plate that retains and accentuates their feminine shape. This last detail is an especially curious one, as the two previous *Nü Who* Series Two Cybermen stories[7] had established that these parallel–Earth cyborgs' metal exterior were neuter, or generically masculine in appearance.[8]

As much as Lisa's cyborg body has been fetishized by *Torchwood*'s production team, the color of her skin—black—also brings up the problematic issue of why Ianto keeps her a secret from his teammates. The easy response is that Ianto behaves in this manner since he does not want his colleagues to destroy her, but the unsettling fact remains that he is keeping a female body of color hidden in the basement of the Hub. Moreover, the now-cybernetic Lisa wishes to carry out her programming of "upgrading" the entire human race, so they can become Cybermen. At the same time, she is willing to discard her own black body, as seen in this exchange with Ianto in the Hub basement:

> IANTO: Lisa, please. I brought you here to heal you, so we can be together.
> LISA: Together. Yes. Transplant my brain into your body. The two of us together. Fused. We'll be one complete person. Isn't that what love is?
> IANTO: No.
> LISA: Then we are not compatible.

On a positive note, Lisa's offer of combining her feminine brain, which contains the unique mind and memories of a black woman, with Ianto's masculine white body may offer a utopian possibility of a love relationship in which race and gender lines can be blurred in an amalgamated new form. Equally, this concept of a female brain controlling a male body relates to Donna Haraway's thoughts concerning possible futuristic control strategies in "A Cyborg Manifesto":

> Control strategies will be formulated in terms of rates, costs of constraints, degrees of freedom. Human beings, like any other component or subsystem, must be localized in a system architecture whose basic modes of operation are probabilistic, statistical. No objects, spaces, or bodies are sacred in themselves; any component can be interfaced with any other if the proper standard, the proper code, can be constructed for processing signals in a common language [163].

Arguing that Lisa's cybernetic concept of love via an interchangeable female-male body is similar to Haraway's theoretical recipe for humans achieving a common language poses an endless debate as it involves the two universal ideals of love and language. At the very least, both this *Torchwood* character and Haraway have reduced bodies to a series of organic building blocks that eschews cultural and biological divisions of race, sex, and gender. This concept of collective bodies in relation to the show's position on gendered heroism likewise skews the lines demarcating Lisa as a villainous component of the Cybermen collective race and Ianto as the emotionally conflicted hero.

Curiously, later in "Cyberwoman," after Lisa's cybernetic body has been mortally wounded by the Torchwood team's pet pterodactyl, she transplants her brain into the appropriated body of a young, white pizza delivery woman. However, her offer to Ianto for them to continue their love affair and together work toward "upgrading" the human race is cut short by Jack, Gwen, and Owen shooting her down with a hail of bullets. On the surface, the heroic Torchwood team has protected the entire human race from being potentially cybernized. Yet the fact that these three Caucasian characters have also destroyed the brain of a black female who has commandeered a white woman's body presents the show taking a questionable position on race. Additionally, as with Mickey Smith unsuccessfully pursuing ex-girlfriend Rose Tyler in *NüWho* and Dave Lister constantly chasing the elusive Kristine Kochanski across time and space in *Red Dwarf,* Lisa's inability to resume her love affair with Ianto posits *Torchwood* as continuing a troubling theme of black characters who are featured in BBC SF shows failing to achieve lasting romantic relationships with their white objects of affection.

Representations of Female Sexuality on *Torchwood*

"Cyberwoman" can also be viewed as a problematic episode of *Torchwood* since the story leaves Tosh as the odd-person-out in its twin couplings of Owen-Gwen and Jack-Ianto. While Lisa is trying to cybernize the Torchwood team members, Owen and Gwen hide in a mortuary slab. During this time, Gwen remarks that she can feel Owen's erect penis through his pants. Nonetheless, they still manage to kiss, an action precipitated by the ostensible need to mask their breathing from Lisa. Juxtaposed with this scene, intriguingly, is the homoerotic spectacle of Jack granting the unconscious Ianto the "kiss of life" via mouth-to-mouth resuscitation. With both of these scenes, the impression that *Torchwood* is comprised of a group of individuals who work and "play" together is encoded to the audience. At the same time, Tosh, a representation of a minority Asian-English woman, has been marginalized by these two exclusionary couplings.

This fact is complexly continued in "Greeks Bearing Gifts" during a few scenes where Tosh possesses the ability to read Gwen and Owen's minds thanks to a telepathy-granting necklace given to her by Mary, a mysterious alien who is wearing a human form. Earlier in the episode, Tosh had been gently ridiculed by Gwen and Owen while they flirted with each other in the Hub, which intensified the perception that she has not only been passively rejected by Owen but is also being mocked by the suggestion that they are secret lovers. However, when she dons the necklace, she assumes the role of a voyeur as she walks around the Hub and telepathically "hears" Gwen's intimate thoughts concerning Owen's scent still lingering on her body after a morning sexual rendezvous in his car. Tosh likewise hears Owen sizing up her viability as a potential sexual partner and him thinking about Gwen's tongue running across his teeth and how this mental image is sexually arousing him. As a result, Tosh is once more marginalized as a desirable sexual person and, instead, encoded as a lonely woman who unhappily watches others enjoy intimate relationships.

Fortunately, "Greeks Bearing Gifts" manages to likewise work as Toshiko's wake-up call from heteronormativity as she engages in a lesbian affair with Mary. In an interview with Carole Gordon, Naoko Mori, who plays Tosh, points out the sensitive encoding of this queer relationship: "Mary was like a really good friend, an ally, someone she can talk to ... and if anything the sexual thing came as an afterthought. She didn't even realize it was happening." Regrettably, by the end of the episode, Mary is revealed to be villainous and consequently disposed of by Captain Jack in the Hub. With this development, Tosh's sensitive lesbian romance with Mary, unlike Owen and Gwen's illicit affair, which spans several episodes in Series One, is brought to an abrupt, all-too convenient conclusion.

In the following season of *Torchwood*, which aired on both BBC Two and Three from January to April 2008, the episode "Adam" presents Tosh experiencing a problematic heterosexual love affair with the titular alien. In other words, the fact that Adam has both implanted memories in Tosh that she has experienced a love affair with him and is currently having sex with her (as one scene in the episode that is set in her bedroom implies) can either be interpreted as a manifestation of the fantasy-romance she always wanted with a man or as a form of rape. This situation is a result of Adam manipulating the Torchwood team into believing he has been their close colleague and friend for the last few years, when, in reality, he has been part of their lives for two days at the cost of affecting another part of their memories. Clearly, Tosh is the only one who emotionally benefits from this scenario as Owen has become an overly sensitive geek, Gwen loses her memories of Rhys, Jack is tormented by a long-repressed traumatic child memory of losing his brother Gray during an alien invasion of the Boeshane Peninsula, and Ianto later suffers from an Adam-implanted false memory of killing several women. Regarding "Adam," online fan writer Philip Sandifer claims the episode "is about a malevolent character ... [who] rapes Tosh and revels in his cruelty to Ianto." On this note, Sandifer likewise declares,

> So we have Owen and Tosh's roles in their relationship flipped, with Owen becoming the shy one and Tosh becoming the confident and sexually active one. (There are, as ever, frustrations here. There's at least a fleeting line that makes clear that Adam's memory-wiping Tosh so that he's her lover is rape, but an inexplicable failure of anyone to treat this as though it's one of the worst things Adam does in the episode. Of course, nobody is that bothered by what he does to Ianto either, but as ever, there's an infuriating willingness to treat rape as less real when it uses sci-fi conceits.)

Sandifer is indeed correct in asserting that *Torchwood*'s questionable presentation of rape in this episode glosses over the longtime ramifications of such a physical abuse of another's body, even if one's memories have been modified to render the victim as acceptable to the sexual violation.

However, "Adam," as Sandifer points out, nonetheless empowers Tosh as a sexually active character in contrast to the episode's temporarily emasculated version of Owen. On a physical level, Tosh and Owen have basically exchanged their typical characteristics since she walks and talks with a newfound confidence while he seems to slouch and lacks his former cynical tone and instead speaks in a soft, hesitant manner.[9] During one early scene in "Adam," Tosh and Owen share a beer in the Hub conference room while having this conversation:

TOSH: Adam and I have been together for one year today.
OWEN: Right, right.
TOSH: A whole year. My stomach still flicks when he touches me. I've never known anything like it. The two of us, we just fit. Do you know what I mean?

OWEN: Um, not sure I do, no.
TOSH: Don't worry. You'll meet the right girl one day.

As Tosh stresses that last line with a condescending pat on Owen's arm, the impression that she has achieved a romantic victory over her former unrequited object of affection is relayed to the audience. This inverted power dynamic, furthermore, has been relayed to *Torchwood* viewers by Tosh's decision to sit on a table above Owen, who is sitting in a chair in front of her, thereby making him appear tiny in comparison. Via intercut middle and close-up shots positioned from a low camera angle, which emphasize her bare legs being situated at Owen's eyelevel and her low-cut top from his POV, Tosh visually towers over the emotionally castrated man. Unfortunately, by the end of the episode, Tosh and her teammates' memories of the last forty-eight hours have been erased by amnesia pills since they needed to obliterate all mental aspects of Adam in order to send him back to the Void[10] from whence he came. Consequently, Owen is restored to his former sarcastic self, the one who no longer yearns after Tosh, who, in return, once again hopelessly loves him. Although the audience has theoretically received pleasure from witnessing Tosh become a content, confident woman and Owen reasonably suffer from her rejection of him in "Adam," Tosh ultimately remains a flawed character who is once more weakened by her attraction to an equally faulty man.

For a show offering a few sexual pairings of its core cast, particularly a queer coupling of Jack and Ianto, *Torchwood* veers away from presenting a lesbian romance between Gwen and Toshiko. Though one could make the argument that placing these female characters in a romantic situation would be clichéd, sexist, or forced, especially when considering that the two arguably do not possess any onscreen sexual chemistry, the fact remains that portions of the *Torchwood* fan fiction community who are actively interested in producing and reading slash writing productions fantasize about the scenario of Gwen and Tosh being lovers. With one particular story, "The Appliance of Science," fan writer ionlylurkhere imagines Tosh and Gwen as initiating a sexual relationship. Set between the end of *Torchwood* Series One and the beginning of Series Two, the story works as a loose sequel to the Toshiko-as-lesbian theme developed in "Greeks Bearing Gifts." In fact, during the story, when the two are watching the film *Dangerous Liaisons* in Tosh's apartment, Gwen remarks to her coworker that Michelle Pfeiffer is gorgeous, prompting Tosh to ruminate, "Oh, here we go.... This was the real reason she'd kept quiet at work about being into girls until the business with Mary had dragged it all rather painfully out into the open. She wasn't in the least bit ashamed, but the conversations with straight girls turned bi-curious after a few drops of booze were deeply, deeply tedious." Gwen, however, soon reveals to Tosh that she has indulged in previous sexual encounters with women. Unlike the televised *Torchwood*, then, in which the episode "Day One" depicted Gwen kissing Carys, "The Appliance of Science" reimagines her as an experienced bisexual character. As Gwen's seduction of Tosh continues in the story, this exchange occurs between them:

> "You're bloody gorgeous, Tosh. I've fancied you ever since we first met. You're definitely the most fuckable member of the team."
> Tosh's eyes widened involuntarily. "Really?"
> "Oh, yeah. I mean, Owen's got that, you know, raw masculinity—" Tosh nodded, then worried she was seeming too enthusiastic "—and Jack's Jack, and Ianto—well, it's weird to even think about it, he's so into Jack, and I secretly think he'd be a bit ... you know, stern. But you're well sexy. I love your bum."
> Tosh leaned over gently and kissed her on the cheek, then whispered in her ear, "Stop talking now."
> "OK."

With this passage, ionlylurkhere demonstrates his or her fan understanding of *Torchwood*'s masculine gendering of Owen, Jack, and Ianto, especially in regard to Owen's overt presentation of his sexuality, which led to him successfully seducing Gwen in Series One. At the same time, the fan writer lends a sense of sexual agency to Gwen as she becomes the seducer in this passage, creating an atmosphere in which Tosh feels comfortable taking the first physical step toward a sexual union with her coworker via a kiss on her cheek. From this perspective, ionlylurkhere's tale illuminates a missed opportunity for the encoding of *Torchwood*'s first few seasons, one in which two complex leading female characters could present a dynamic lesbian relationship to the show's sexually diverse viewership.

Tosh: *Torchwood*'s Finest Example of a Hero?

On the subject of Tosh's role as a hero, she represents a positive vision of a female member of the Torchwood organization. As an example, Tosh comes into her own in a telling scene in "Combat." After she and Jack release a captive Weevil and watch the men whom they have been following attack and abduct the creature, the shaken Toshiko asks Jack, "Just so I know where we stand: we would never deliberately put a human being through that, but Weevils are fair game? Is that right?" Jack's subsequent sad reply of "We need to follow them" barely covers his dubious decision to endanger the Weevil. From the encoding of this scene, moreover, one can qualify the fundamental difference between Tosh and Jack. Whereas Toshiko would never directly endanger a lifeform regardless of its savage nature, Jack would do the opposite in order to serve the greater good. One could, of course, attribute this division of choice according to gender lines, saying that the masculine Jack is pragmatically aggressive in order to solve a case while the feminine Toshiko is compassionately protective of all life, but the simple answer is that Jack's moral code obviously does not subscribe to a traditional hero's handbook for such values.

While Tosh ultimately remains true to the Torchwood team, she is constantly weakened by her love for Owen as he repeatedly rejects her and sleeps with other women. By the time he finally reciprocates her feelings when he tentatively agrees to go on a date with her in "Reset," at the end of the episode, he has been ironically killed by a vengeful Dr. Aaron Copley as a result of helping to shut down the morally dubious man's experimental medical facility, The Pharm. While Owen is brought back to life in the following story, "Dead Man Walking," via Jack's use of the second Resurrection Glove, his body, though it is not decaying, is dead in all clinical terms, and so he is unable to consummate his budding relationship with Tosh on any physical level. Subsequently, when Tosh comes to Owen's flat to spend time with him in the next episode, "A Day in the Death," he darkly tells her why he believes she has chosen to visit him: "For some reason, you want me. You know, I don't know why, but you always have, always looking at me, watching me screw all those other women, your heart breaking. And now it's different, because I'm safe now, aren't I? And it's all cozy, and it's romantic, and isn't it beautiful, you know." In many ways, Owen expresses various *Torchwood* fans' feelings of anger and confusion as to why Tosh, an intelligent and compassionate woman, would be attracted to this man who is constantly dismissive of her emotions for him. With this viewpoint, Owen's rhetoric reflects the thoughts of a sadistic white man who enjoys mentally abusing his more sensitive Asian female coworker. At the same time, it shows a man who has been emasculated by the death of his body and thus tortured by the state of his post-life impotence.

After Tosh asks Owen what is wrong with him during this emotional outburst, he exclaims, "I'm broken, Tosh! I don't work. I got no heartbeat, no feelings, no tears! I have got nothing to give you! I ... do you understand that? Maybe that's what you want. Maybe you want somebody who is as screwed up as you! Who's twisted and screwed up like you are! Well, you want to see broken? Do you want to see broken, Tosh?" To her protests, he then breaks the pinky finger on his left hand in order to demonstrate to her that his undead body no longer possesses the sensory ability to process pain. Although this moment ostensibly holds no overt sexual meaning, to a Freudian psychoanalytical degree, the grotesque spectacle of Owen breaking his irreparable pinky finger serves as a masochistic form of self-castration. More importantly, since Owen has argued that Tosh is as "twisted and screwed up" as he is, his act of symbolically castrating himself doubly serves the metonymic purpose of sadistically and irrevocably "breaking" her unrequited affection for him.

This researcher's psychoanalytical aca-fan readings aside, online message board fan writers such as shawnlunn2002 view this Owen-Tosh scene in a more direct light:

> [W]hile I love Toshiko to bits, her insecurities must ring as a red flag for a bloke like Owen. Even when she came round to see him, all Toshiko did was make pointless small talk because she couldn't really face up to what she was thinking.... If it hadn't been for his current predicament, I would've hated him for those remarks. That being said, Toshiko needs to grow a spine because it doesn't look like Owen is ever going to see her the way she wants him to. Perhaps Martha [Jones] could give her advice on how to get over an unrequited crush.

Even though the argument can be made that Tosh has been encoded as a weak, pining character for the majority of the stories featuring her in *Torchwood* Series One and Two, shawnlunn2002 reads her insecurities as offering a realistic portrayal of a troubled, lonely woman. In that sense, Toshiko has been encoded to serve a positive purpose as the example she provides of a professional woman involved in an emotionally abusive friendship with a colleague could serve as a reminder to female (and male) *Torchwood* viewers that such negative connections with others should be well avoided in their own lives.

Regardless of Owen's sexist and deplorable treatment of her throughout the first few seasons of *Torchwood*, Tosh's unwavering loyalty to this man is most strikingly shown in the final episode of Series Two, "Exit Wounds." Placing her own dying agony aside after being fatally shot in the stomach by Gray, Jack's mentally unstable brother, Tosh consoles Owen when he hovers on the edge of his final death, undoubtedly defining her as a fallen hero. In reaction to Tosh's death, online fan reviewer fairyd123 comments,

> [H]er death was really quite shocking. I was expecting the bullet, but the sight of Tosh in agony dragging herself down the stairs leaving a massive trail of blood behind her so that she can save the city absolutely devastated me. And Naoko's acting in that sequence where she tells Owen that he's breaking her heart was extraordinary. She may not have been my favorite character, but she got a fitting end.

In fairyd123's viewpoint, Tosh's heroic death satisfyingly brings her story to an end on *Torchwood*. Ultimately, in assessing whether or not Tosh embodies a strong or weak character, one is more inclined to argue that she is a problematic representation of a marginalized Asian woman who endures an honorable death that worryingly enough concludes the process of gradually silencing and diminishing her agency as a female hero.

Owen and Jack's Masculine Heroic Journey of Repeated Deaths

By far, the most significant example of a Torchwood male team member bettering himself is Owen. Granted, he is a troubled character who commits date rape in "Everything Changes," but subsequent episodes of the show encode him as a more sympathetic hero. Later in Series One, Owen claims that he is upset after his newest lover, Diane Holmes, decides to leave him in order to explore the space-time rift in "Out of Time," but the truth is that she was a temporary romantic interest who could barely divert him from his deeper-rooted pain and rage. Consequently, after Owen enters into a cage fight with a Weevil in "Combat" and admits that the dangerous match made him feel a sense of peace for a few seconds, one can begin to question his love of self. In a later Series Two episode, "Fragments," a flashback scene depicts Owen physically attacking Jack in the graveyard where Owen's fiancée Katie has been buried. Although it is understandable that Owen is lashing out at Jack since he somewhat believes the man could have saved Katie from being killed by a parasitic alien tumor that was harboring in her head, using violence as his means of emotional expression is not a healthy choice. Then again, if one goes back to Owen's childhood, as recounted by the character in "Adam," one learns that his mother was verbally (and potentially physically) abusive to him.

What truly encodes Owen in a sympathetic light as a flawed male *Torchwood* hero, however, is his death at the end of "Reset." Upon his reanimation via the second Resurrection Glove into a state of living death, Owen truly becomes a sympathetic character. A telling episode depicting this transformation is "A Day in the Death," in which Owen peacefully sits on a rooftop with a suicidal woman, Maggie, and gradually talks her out of jumping off the building. Death, without a doubt, has given the cynical Owen a fuller appreciation of life. Coupled with Jack, who is practically an expert when it comes to being resurrected, Owen serves as a self-help text for how a post-life existence can help an antihero to become more authentically heroic.

Aside from the unsettling, evil, and downright bizarre threats Jack and Owen have fought during their time with Torchwood, their most challenging adversary is death itself. For Jack, dying is a pain to which he is repeatedly subjected. As for Owen, death is more final in that his body cannot feel any sensory input, meaning he cannot enjoy food, sleep, or the comfort of another's touch. Although these characters prove they can continue living after their initial deaths, their resolve is truly tested in "Exit Wounds," where they respectively complete the Campbellian heroic journey of "separation–initiation–return" (30).

At the beginning of "Exit Wounds," Jack is dealing with the return of his brother Gray, who is obsessed with revenging himself upon Jack since he blames his older sibling for abandoning him to unseen vicious aliens years earlier. Later in the episode, when Gray, via Captain John, transports Jack to 27 AD Cardiff and buries him in the ground, Jack does not resist. In fact, he accepts his fate and endures the agony of continuous death and resurrection until the Torchwood team of 1901 finds him and places him in cryogenic storage within the Hub's morgue so that he can revive in the twenty-first century. Upon discovering his brother-nemesis alive inside the Hub in that time zone, Gray is shocked to hear Jack forgive him, obviously believing that the only one who wields the power of absolution is himself. Jack, consequently, completes his rite of passage that began with his "separation" from the rest of humanity, which occurred when he became immortal; continued with his "initiation," which was how he dealt with the agony that was his repeated deaths in the Cardiff earth for nearly two millennia; and concludes with his "return," through which he brings his message of absolution to Gray. On a greater, transatlantic communal scale, Jack arguably delivers the message to viewers that absolute forgiveness is a virtue that a masculine hero must embrace in order to be complete.

As for Owen, who, unlike Jack, is not too experienced with dying, which is his "separation," and post-life experiences, which form his "initiation," one finds a man who exposes his antiheroic traits as he faces his fate of final dissolution, or his "return," after he has been trapped in a nuclear failsafe lockdown in the Turnmill Nuclear Power Station's control room. Instead of reacting with dignity to Toshiko's grim prognosis of his situation regarding the radioactive waste that will vent into his area, Owen rails, "Not like this! I'm not doing it! Get me out of here, Tosh! Get me out of here! I died once! I'm not doing it again!" Gradually, under Toshiko's calming influence, he recovers his composure, soon gently reassuring her, "It's all right. Really, Tosh—it's all right."

In celebration of this scene, fairyd123 writes, "I really liked that when it came to it Owen wasn't happy about dying. That he was frightened and that he raged at it just as we all would. And when Tosh calmed him down his acceptance of his fate was heartbreaking. Never has a screen fading to white been such a powerful image." As Owen achieves his "return" by accepting his looming decomposition-by-radiation death, he finally shines as an absolute hero, not because he is perfect, but since he is finally trying to be strong in the face of his inevitable death. As a result, *Torchwood*, a show ostensibly about a team of flawed heroes repeatedly saving Cardiff from a myriad of alien threats, potentially reveals itself to be encoded as a televised guide for one improving oneself, regardless of whether or not one self classifies as a hero, villain, or antihero.

Fifty-First Century Bisexuality: Captain Jack's Blueprint for a Utopian Society?

In countries such as Great Britain and the United States, the primary and secondary markets for the broadcasting of *Torchwood* for all four of its seasons, both conservative and liberal media, governmental, and cultural forces continually struggle to define moral standards and the parameters of what demarcates human rights. Obviously, *Torchwood*, which was developed by an openly gay man, Russell T Davies, and which features a pansexual character, Captain Jack, is going to take a more liberal stance than the majority of television shows airing on both sides of the Atlantic Ocean in promoting LGBTQ issues. In fact, Jack's flirtatious sexual mission statement of being open to relationships with both men and women is what lends an entertainingly unpredictable air to the character, and which, by extension, makes him an intriguing focal point for *Torchwood*'s transatlantic audience. For bisexual viewers, Jack then perhaps becomes their reassuring viewer surrogate as he equally flirts with women and men in such episodes as *Torchwood*'s "Everything Changes" and *NüWho*'s "The Doctor Dances." Since society is composed of a multitude of genders, and, as a whole, is constantly culturally evolving, is its ideal, utopian form a world where everyone is bisexual? In this theoretical model, there perhaps would be no categorization of sexual division in terms of straight/gay or such personal identification as male/female/transgendered since everyone would be open-minded to the concept of having a relationship with everybody, regardless of one's identity. As a result, with the premise of Russell T Davies's and Steven Moffat's futuristic fifty-first century Earth, a utopian civilization exists that offers endless permutations of love and sex.

However, does the fact that Captain Jack actor John Barrowman, an openly gay man who initially embodies a bisexual character rather than a strictly gay man, unwittingly encode a cultural message to the *Torchwood* audience that bisexuality is a preferable (or superior) sexual identity to homosexuality? One online fan writer, Quizzical Pussy, offers these thoughts on *Torchwood*'s depiction of bisexuality:

> Is a future that has eradicated our current diversity of sexual identities indeed a more mature one? Many portrayals of our species' distant future, most notably those playing with utopian themes and their deconstruction, involve humanity moving forward—or being forced into—homogeneity. But wouldn't true evolution and social progress involve social pressure to embrace increasingly different otherness?

Quizzical Pussy's question, which is directed as a critique of *Torchwood*'s thematic presentation of bisexuality (or pansexuality) can be similarly leveled against two other televised BBC futuristic narratives, *Blake's 7* and *Red Dwarf*. While the former presents veiled or arguable examples of queerness via the villainous characters of Servalan and Travis, the latter, with the exception of the sensationalistic dream sequence Lister-Rimmer kiss in the episode "Blue" more or less erases the future existence of any queer sexuality from its episodes. In this context, Jack and company's embracing or dabbling in a bisexual lifestyle on *Torchwood* seems innovatively groundbreaking in terms of the show's encoding of gendered heroism. However, on this note, Quizzical Pussy continues, "Of course, the 51st Century is not portrayed [on *Nü Who* and *Torchwood*] as the pinnacle of human evolution by any means, but with their 30,000 years on us, the message is right there: one day we will be beyond such petty things as sexual orientation, which is clearly a cultural construct because deep down we're all omnisexual, obviously."

If one considers Quizzical Pussy's indictment of Jack's fifty-first century sexuality as a normalizing force, one can then connect it with Michael Warner's thoughts on how society attempts to homogenize its citizens as he argues that the goal of such mass media publications as *Newsweek* is to promote the idea that "It is normal to be normal" (69). Warner continues, "The kind of consciousness one has of the world in mass culture, in other words, has a tendency to normalize us; that is, to make us aspire to be normal, to make us adjust our perceptions of ourselves and others, so that we fit within the common range" (69–70). Earlier in his work *The Trouble with Normal*, Warner writes about the hierarchies found in gay culture, a result of their bargaining with dominant society for a "debased pseudo-dignity, the kind that is awarded as a bribe for disavowing the indignity of sex and the double indignity of a politics around sex" (65–

66). Put another way, the gay couples who are homonormative in the sense that their lifestyles are most comparable to the domesticated, mainstream lives of their hetero counterparts are better accepted by dominant society than those existing on the margins of queer culture. Warner then defines these "others" as

> the queers who have sex in public toilets, who don't "come out" as happily gay, the sex workers, the lesbians who are too vocal about a taste for dildos or S/M, the boys who flaunt it as pansies or as leathermen, the androgynes, the trannies or transgendered whose gender deviance makes them unassimilable to the menu of sexual orientations, the clones in the so-called gay ghetto, the fist-fuckers and popper-snorters, the ones who actually like pornography [66].

While *Torchwood* is a unique SF show that innovatively presents gay, lesbian, and bisexual characters throughout its four series, it does not offer representations of the marginalized members of LGBTQ culture as defined by Warner in this incendiary passage. The pointing out of this fact is not to devalue *Torchwood*'s significance as a queer-friendly media text but to contextualize the show in relation to Warner's underrepresented members of gay culture. In short, Jack and Ianto may proffer a more socially acceptable vision of a gay couple in that their somewhat private lovemaking is not enacted inside a public toilet or a gay club. More importantly, throughout their televised relationship in Series Two of *Torchwood* and *Children of Earth*, the slim possibility exists that they could end their tender love affair and respectively begin hetero couplings with women. After all, such episodes as "Cyberwoman" and the back storyline of *Children of Earth* show them having serious relationships with women.

Jack, John and Ianto: A Queer Love Triangle

With the episode "Kiss Kiss, Bang Bang," Captain John Hart, a sociopathic yet charismatic killer, played by *Buffy the Vampire Slayer* and *Angel* alum James Marsters, heralds the more upbeat, action-oriented encoding vibe of the show's sophomore season. John, while ostensibly villainous, is a substantially complex character, which allows him to skirt the edges of being categorized as an antihero. In his very first scene, he rescues a man who is being attacked by another on a rooftop. Nevertheless, in the midst of this heroic act, he gleefully hurls the attacker off the building to his death, thus displaying his sadistic tendencies.

John next enters a Cardiff bar and pulls out his two holstered guns to frighten off its patrons in order to attract Jack's attention. When Jack and John subsequently finally behold one another after many years apart, facing each across the empty bar, the latter opens his hip gun holsters as if he is going to draw his weapons on his former partner. But Jack's action is quickly revealed to be a form of symbolic phallic foreplay as they walk up to one another and begin passionately kissing. However, the scene immediately takes on an S/M-toned hue as John punches Jack in the face, and his smiling victim retaliates. As the two proceed to punch and kick each other, consequently wrecking the bar, the non-diegetic pop-rock single "Song 2," by Blur, forms the soundtrack to their fight, lightheartedly encoding the sequence with the impression that the two men are experiencing an entwined feeling of pain and pleasure. In other words, par for the course of the S/M lifestyle, both former lovers are willingly (and simultaneously) embodying the roles of a sadist and masochist. The sequence then ends with the two captains drawing their weapons upon one another in a moment of phallic stalemate.

Viewers soon learn that John's decision to travel to the past is twofold: to retrieve three valuable canisters with Torchwood's unwitting assistance and to attempt to win Jack back as his partner-in-crime and lover. To further complicate matters, John and Jack's past relationship is revealed to be substantially more personal when John reminds the omnisexual Jack they were once virtually married, with John playing the feminine role of "wife" while they were trapped together in a two-week time loop that amounted to five years' time. John, thus, already a vigilante and rogue, also assumes the mantle of the bitter spouse who wants some sort of revenge against his former masculine "husband."

Clearly, Captain Jack and John's public S/M fight-kiss scene in "Kiss Kiss, Bang Bang" straddles a more controversial line in presenting a rougher vision of queer sex to the BBC Two viewing public. In contrast, Jack and Ianto's gay copulating in "Adrift" is both private and public. In regard to this second coupling, these two characters are well-dressed, polite, and culturally sophisticated. To the external public of their fictive world, mostly set in Cardiff, they could pass, like many males in Western society, as either straight or gay men. But the fact remains that they have been encoded as bisexual characters. In regard to the type of private space Jack and Ianto utilize for their lovemaking in the Hub hothouse, Leo Bersani, in *Homos*, argues,

> Our culture tells us to think of sex as the ultimate privacy, as that intimate knowledge of the other on which the familial cell is built. Enjoy the rapture that will never be made public, that will also (though this is not said) keep you safely, docilely out of the public realm, that will make you content to allow others to make history while you perfect the oval of a merely copulative or familial intimacy [165–66].

For Jack and Ianto, their lovemaking in the Hub hothouse functions as a private act which is "merely copulative" in that their shared biology as males will not lead to reproduction. At the same time, while they are not copulating in a public setting, the hothouse is "public" in the fact that its translucent windows enclose a space that is both intimate and open to display to the rest of the Torchwood team members. But when one considers the fact that this scene has been broadcast to millions of viewers, their queer lovemaking definitely satisfies the criteria for representing a public display of an alternate sexuality.

Torchwood fan writers are especially interested in the Jack and Ianto pairing, which they affectionately refer to as "Janto," but they are likewise interested in the coupling of Jack and John. Naturally, some slash fan fiction productions fantasize about all three bisexual men making love in a *ménage à trois* fashion. In one such short story, "I Love a Man in a Uniform," by a fan writing under the screen name tardisjournal, Captains Jack and John are presented in the form of their younger selves, who are in their early twenties and still working for the Time Agency. Additionally, they are in pursuit of a criminal mastermind, one Ianto Jones, a time-traveling thief from the twenty-first century who has been attempting to interfere with Earth's history during such eras as Victorian London and 1920s America. Although this story has been categorized as an alternate universe (AU) tale in the summary preceding the piece for the obvious reason that it conflicts with the continuity of the series proper as Ianto has never been presented as a time-traveling criminal, either in the first three seasons of *Torchwood* or via flashbacks, the synopsis ends with a final question, "AU—or is it?" With this enigmatic question, tardisjournal thus invites his or her readers to take this extrapolation of an alternate-reality vision of *Torchwood*'s continuity, which involves a slash threesome situation occurring amongst the Time Agents Jack and John and their prisoner Ianto, and potentially craft their own explanations for how it could fit in with the official continuity of the show.

After capturing Ianto in the tale, the two place him in an interrogation cell, but their questions soon take on a darker S/M-tinged sexualized meaning as John repeatedly slaps Ianto's face, and Jack smacks the captured man's buttocks. At one point in the story, however, Jack offers Ianto a choice to either agree to or reject an offer for him to engage in a full-on sexual encounter with his captors:

> "We're still taking you in. That hasn't changed. But you get to choose when. Either we go in five minutes, or whatever you need to pull yourself together and get dressed, or...."

"Or?"

Jack grinned in a toothy manner that no one had yet told him resembled a shark's, but someday would. "Or we go in an hour, or whatever it takes for the three of us to get off in a mutually satisfactory way."

Jones met his eyes then, and answered Jack's grin with a smile of his own.

"I pick Door Number Two."

"I hoped you'd say that."

"Me too," John chimed in.

Although the preceding sections of "I Love a Man in a Uniform" could conceivably have presented a vision of a rape-like fantasy involving these three bisexual *Torchwood* characters to a reader uninitiated with the sexual intricacies of slash writing, this sequence tastefully reflects that, within S/M culture, a form of consent is often required before sexual contact can continue between participants. Regarding this note, Leo Bersani offers his thoughts on S/M's inherent power dynamics: "S/M, far from dissociating itself from a fascistic master-slave relation, actually confirms an identity between that relation and its own practices. It removes masters and slaves from economic and racial superstructures, thus confirming the eroticism of the master-slave configuration" (89). In this utopian vision of S/M, Bersani provides a model of pleasure exchanges, not true pain, taking place between the master and slave. Within the context of tardisjournal's story, Jack and John hence function as Time Agent "masters" and Ianto as their prisoner "slave," but the erotically rougher sex taking place amongst them remains consensual.

Heteronormative society, unfortunately, from an outsider perspective, usually views any S/M situation, particularly a homosexual iteration of one, as projecting a lopsided power dynamic in which the master simply inflicts pain upon his slave. On this note, Bersani continues, "It is of course true that, outside such extreme situations as police- or terrorist-sponsored scenarios of torture, this configuration is, in the modern world, seldom visible in the archaic form of face-to-face relations of command and violation" (89). Fortunately, with tardisjournal's sexual-fantasy-influenced conception of a Jack-John-Ianto S/M grouping, Bersani's understandable fear of this unique form of sexuality being misinterpreted as one of "command and violation" by the greater uninformed heteronormative society is allayed via the safe-zone formed by the *Torchwood* fan fiction writing community. Ultimately, when one also considers *Torchwood* has been broadcast to both heteronormative and LGBTQ viewers, an argument could be made that the show and its resultant diverse online fan fiction productions work toward presenting a more positive interpretation of this alternate queer lifestyle choice.

Defining Feminine Cosplay: Captain Jaq Harkness, a Kinging Master and Camp Captains

In terms of *Torchwood*'s convention-based fan culture, Captain Jack and Captain John have proven to be popular cosplay subject matter for both male and female fans. When it comes to the latter's interpretations of Jack and John, which is also known as femme cosplay, one fan Web site, *FemmeLords*, run by two *NüWho/Torchwood* aficionados, shows fellow fans how to affordably purchase material for making their own female-modified version of Captain Jack's costume. Calling her version of Jack, Captain Jacqueline (Jaq) Harkness, one of the site's writers, explains why she is drawn to John Barrowman's character: "Captain Jack Harkness. I can't begin to describe Jack Harkness, other than he's Captain Jack. He's fun, he's flirty, he's open and free, and he's loyal and caring.... And his outfits are relatively uncomplicated, but quite obviously and recognizably *Jack Harkness*." For Jaq Harkness, Jack's positive characteristics and costume offer a means of fan identification, which she has chosen to personally decode and customize by incorporating her own feminine identity. In terms of her modification of Jack's outfit as worn in *NüWho* Series Three's final three episodes, "Utopia," "The Sound of Drums," and "Last of the Time Lords," Jaq Harkness adds female boots,[11] and, in terms of figuring out her hairstyle, she writes that she is "debating between 1940s pin curls or basic 21st century straightened." Moreover, her makeup may either be "1940s glam or basic clean/fresh," which shows her decision to place her own feminine mark upon Captain Jack's masculine appearance.

For other female *Torchwood* fans who cosplay Captain Jack and Captain John, they choose to retain these characters' male appearance in their fan interpretations of their costumes. In this situation, Judith Halberstam's thoughts on the critical possibilities of examining drag kings are especially applicable: "Drag King culture, I believe, constitutes ... a counterpublic space where white and heteronormative masculinities can be contested, and where minority masculinities can be produced, validated, fleshed out, and celebrated" (128). Via the lens of my aca-fan interest and participation in *Doctor Who* and *Torchwood* fandom, I would like to now recount an experience I had where I firsthand witnessed femme cosplay overlapping with the performative qualities of kinging.

While serving as a guest at Gallifrey One's 2008 fan-organized and funded *Doctor Who* convention that was held in Los Angeles, I entered the costume contest dressed as John Simm's Master. While on stage, I struck an intense "masculine" pose that the Master had given off in the show. In other words, to fandom's applause, I was parodying his masculine anger with my own male body, which, at the time, somewhat resembled Simm's. Later that evening, I met another cosplaying Master, a young lesbian from Florida whose slender frame and short-cropped hair allowed her to serve as another, perhaps more authentic Master than mine in that her focused body language and forceful personality projected the dramatic aspects of Simm's performance, which, at times, could also border on the campy absurd. When I remarked to her that we both were wearing a black suit as the Master had worn in "The Sound of Drums" and "Last of the Time Lords," she curtly responded that my outfit was just a store-bought suit while hers, meticulously embracing the DIY aspects of cosplaying, had been hand sewn—a truth she emphasized by opening her jacket to expose a red lining exact in hue and material to the Master's. Years later, I am still mulling over the symbolism of this moment, especially in regard to the exposed red lining of that uber-fan's magnificent jacket, wondering if the color represented her masked female body, her proud lesbian identity, or the burning undercurrent of female masculinity she was manifesting to the world. To be honest, at the time, I also had not been conversant in Halberstam's definition of the term "Lesbian Masculinity,"[12] but now that I am, I can better articulate my encounter with this memorable drag-king Master.

On this note, I also witnessed my Master-twin interacting in character with two other kinging lesbian femme cosplayers, *Torchwood* fans, who were dressed as Captain Jack and his lover, Captain John, wearing Jack's trademark trench coat and Jack's high boots and Sergeant-Pepper-like jacket. Writing about writer-actor Mike Myers's performance as Austin Powers, Halberstam points out, "Austin's clothing, his fashion photography career, and his overall camp affect suggests that his imperfect masculinity owes much to gay male models of manhood; but his nonphallic, emphatically prosthetic, and endearingly cloddish attentions to women make his sexual identity look butch or kingly rather than 'faggy'" (143–144). Much of this commentary on the character of Austin Powers may be extended to John Barrowman's over-the-top interpretation of Captain Jack, as he makes tongue-in-cheek advances towards both men and women in *Doctor Who* and engages in S/M-like acrobatics before sharing a passionate kiss with his former partner and lover Captain John in "Kiss Kiss, Bang Bang." Returning to the two kinging cosplayers, I see a nexus for a variety of gender inversions: as masculine lesbians in this moment, they were parodying Barrowman's and James Marsters's camp performances as Captains Jack and John, who provide a parody of hypermasculinity and affect. In short, the complex play of gender on display with the kinging Captains Jack and John represents a microcosm of the widespread masculine parody that occurs across the spectrum of SF, fantasy, and comic-book fandoms.

Torchwood: Children of Earth: An Obliteration of the Show's Bisexual Values?

Cementing *Torchwood*'s continuing success as a BBC SF series, its third season, bearing the subtitle *Children of Earth*, transatlantically aired on the corporation's flagship channel, BBC One, and on the North American cable channel, BBC America, as a five-part event on July 6–10, 2009. In the wake of Tosh and Owen's deaths in the previous series, *Children of Earth* does not take the obvious narrative path and simply replace them with two new characters. Instead, the Hub is destroyed in the first episode, "Day One," leaving Torchwood as a rogue team that must survive in the more metropolitan setting of London. With this encoding choice, the show's producers tell viewers that the series is no longer confined to the rather provincial setting of Cardiff and its Welsh countryside but is playing for higher—and more sensationalistic—stakes in Great Britain's capital. Moreover, the Torchwood team now faces a global threat in the form of the 456,[13] aliens who are demanding that humanity surrender ten percent of its children in order to avoid destruction.

On this note, one can argue that the *Children of Earth* encoders' choice to play on viewers' fears of their children being endangered by an external alien threat, which one could read as a metaphor for Middle-East terrorism or nuclear-armed rival countries such as North Korea or Russia, represents a reinforcement of the familial anxieties surrounding a reproductive lifestyle. In short, since children are a motivating force for the transatlantic acceptance of a nine-to-five lifestyle in which the rearing and education of one's offspring is usually synched to one's workday, *Children of Earth*, in a classical horror sense, is conveying a universal fear of losing one's offspring to a more mainstream viewership than *Torchwood*'s core bisexual/gay/queer fan community. This argument is put forth not to dismiss the parental anxieties of LGBTQ couples who watch the show but to suggest that such a fear is more proportionately shared by the heteronormative members of the show's transatlantic audience. At the same time, Jack's decision to sacrifice his grandson to defeat the 456 in *Children of Earth*'s final episode, "Day Five"—as I will discuss in this section—provides a troubling representation of *Torchwood*'s leading bisexual hero.

In *Children of Earth*, another black woman, Lois Habiba, joins the Torchwood team, albeit on a loose espionage basis as she spies on the Prime Minister's inner cabinet of the British government via eye camera lens supplied to her by Gwen. She thus functions as the "eyes" and revolutionary voice box of the team as she eventually announces to the cabinet in "Day Four" that Torchwood has clandestinely recorded their decision to sacrifice the "lowest-achieving ten percent" of Great Britain's children to the 456 and that her team will release this evidence to the people if the government proceeds with their controversial plan. Like Martha Jones, who featured in three episodes[14] during Series Two, Lois adds a black presence to the cast, but her role is rather limited as she does not become a regular character on the series. Additionally, unlike Martha Jones[15] or the rest of the *Torchwood* cast to date at this point, she is not presented as flirting or having sex with anyone. However, Lois is briefly encoded in a sexualized manner during *Children of Earth*'s third episode, "Day Three," when she falsely intimates to her supervisor, Bridget Spears, that she is having an affair with the Home Office Permanent Secretary John Frobisher in order to gain access to his negotiations with the 456 representative in Thames House, so she can record the event with her eye camera lens.

"Day One" likewise reveals that Jack has a daughter, Alice Carter, who, because of her father's immortality,[16] looks older than he does, which motivates her to tell her son, Steven, that his grandfather is his uncle. In fact, Alice explains to Jack why she wishes for him to keep his distance from her and Steven: "I just can't stand it, Dad. I look older than you do, and it's never going to stop. I get older and older, and you stay the same. One day you're going to be standing at my funeral, looking just like did when you were standing at Mom's. No wonder she was so furious. You make us feel old." Arguably, for Alice and her mother, Jack's eternally young body is monstrous to them, especially in regard to the fact that it never ages within the temporal confines and intergenerational structuring of the heteronormative, reproductive lifestyle to which they subscribe. Thus, since Jack cannot physically embody the traditional aged appearance of a grandparent, he is relegated to an artificial, marginalized status as Steven's distant fake uncle. Regarding this arrangement of estrangement, Jack and Alice discuss the possibility of him revealing his true relationship to Steven while he is still a child:

> JACK: I could make the most of it while he's still young. Take him out, buy him stuff. Me-and-him sort of thing.
> ALICE: You mean today?
> JACK: While I'm here, may as well.
> ALICE: Oh, you bastard. Something happens to kids, and you want to spend time

with him on the same day. You are not experimenting on that boy, Dad. Not ever. That's why I want you to stay away—because you're dangerous.

Since "Day Five" will depict Jack sacrificing Steven in order to defeat the 456, this scene takes on a darker foreshadowing for the encoding of his character in *Children of Earth*. It similarly others Jack as an immortal man who should be feared, particularly in considering that his non-heteronormative lifestyle involves him fighting and defeating alien threats to the planet at any cost. Consequently, in Alice's view, these dangerous life choices preempt Jack from participating in the nine-to-five rearing of her child.

In a similar fashion to Alice's othering of Jack's slowly aging, undying corpus, Ianto's sister, Rhiannon Davies, in the same episode, performs an act of sexually marginalizing her brother, whom she had thought was exclusively heterosexual. While they are having tea in her home, Rhiannon tells Ianto that her friend Susan had seen him and Jack at a "posh" Cardiff French restaurant sharing an "intimate" dinner with a man who is "gorgeous like a film star, like an escort." She then insensitively asks him, "Have you gone bender?" Although she next tells Ianto that one of her daughter's friends has two moms in an attempt to demonstrate that she is sympathetic to gay sexuality, her insistently inquisitive need to have her brother confess that he is gay continues to permeate their conversation. On this note, Eve Kosofsky Sedgwick, in the *Epistemology of the Closet*, argues, "Even at an individual level, there are remarkably few of even the most openly gay people who are not deliberately in the closet with someone personally or economically or institutionally important to them" (67–68). Although Ianto had chosen to keep his relationship with Jack in the closet from his sister, he finally surrenders to her probing[17] by saying (in reference to his lover), "He is really handsome," eliciting a satisfied, excited response from her. Then, he makes this troubling remark concerning his relationship with Jack: "It's weird. It's just different. It's not men. It's just him. It's only him. And I don't even know where it is really, so ... so I'm not broadcasting it."

In K. Tempest Bradford's online article "Invisible Bisexuality in *Torchwood*," the critic argues that the series is guilty of performing a form of bisexual erasure via main characters whose "sexual encounters with both men and women ... [are] often brief and easily dismissed." In regard to Ianto, Bradford critiques *Children of Earth* for presenting this scene in which he rationalizes his bisexuality to his sister. For Bradford, Ianto's delimiting of his bisexuality as a one-off attraction to Jack creates the impression to *Torchwood* viewers that the character is not truly bisexual in the sense that he would naturally be attracted to both men and woman at all times.

While Ianto's conversation with Rhiannon in "Day One" encodes a questionable position on bisexuality for *Torchwood*, his death during the conclusion of *Children of Earth*'s penultimate episode, "Day Four," definitely upset and enraged viewers of the show. As much as "Day One's" destruction of the fan-beloved Hub, which doubled as Jack and Ianto's "closet," upset audience members, this development brought their criticisms to another level of online opposition to the encoders' story choices. In the episode, Jack and Ianto find their way to the 456 ambassador's chambers in Thames House and demand that he leave Earth and its children alone. However, in defiance of their terms, the alien releases a deadly virus in Thames House that kills all of the people trapped within its walls when the building goes on emergency lockdown. Included in this number of victims is Ianto, who dies in Jack's arms. Critiquing this traumatic plot development, Bradford also argues, "Ironically, this event may be the final proof that [Ianto] is indeed bisexual. After all, he dies for the purpose of giving a more important character angst and heart-rending development, a role all too often assigned to the character who belongs to the most marginalized group. Jack is the target of the angst-making, so it can't be him. And Gwen is the heteronormative standard-bearer. So Ianto it must be."

From a plotting perspective, "Day Four" writer John Fay, along with *Children of Earth* co-plotters Russell T Davies and James Moran, killed off Ianto as they believed the storyline demanded such a death in order to show how far the 456 would go to achieve their goals and to elicit feelings of pathos in the audience when they witness Jack and Ianto's tender, still-evolving relationship coming to a tragic end. Reacting to Ianto's death in "Day Four," one online fan reviewer, Mark Oshiro, admits,

> I wanted some *deus ex machina* to save Ianto Jones. I didn't care how illogical it was or how out-of-character it may have seemed. I did not want that man to die. But this is a story about all hope being lost, of risks being taken and the ramifications that come with them. I can't imagine a more depressing way to die than begging the man you love to not forget you. That's what Ianto died thinking about.

In contrast to Bradford's belief that Ianto's death completes a form of bisexual erasure on *Torchwood*, Oshiro simply views Fay, Davies, and Moran's storytelling choice as a means of poignantly upping *Children of Earth*'s dramatic ante. For other, more upset, viewers of "Day Four," they resisted this development by protesting Ianto's death via social media, blogs, and message boards, often demanding that his character be resurrected in a then-potential fourth season of the show. On the one hand, this vocal form of *Children of Earth*'s passionate decoders pushing back in criticism of Ianto's heroic death against its encoders had satisfied Fay and his co-plotters' intention to provoke a sincere emotional response from their audience. On the other hand, it also triggered negative responses from fans, particularly when some of them went online, disconcertingly criticizing and threatening Moran on his blog.[18]

In regard to fan fiction, stories have inevitably been composed that imagine Ianto somehow being resurrected. As an example, one short story, "Not easy to get rid of," composed by fan writer HayamaRei, presents Ianto being miraculously given new life via the Cardiff Rift, into which he was pulled following his death in "Day Four." After reuniting with Jack sixty-two years in the future, the two share this moment:

> "I thought I had lost you. Forever," Jack whispered, and his eyes were full with tears.
> Ianto couldn't help but smile. "I'm sorry, sir. I'm not easy to get rid of."
> "Good." Jack returned the smile before locking their lips in a desperate kiss that said what Jack didn't get the chance [to] say out loud. "I love you, too."

With this scene, HayamaRei channels certain *Children of Earth* decoders' needs to see Jack and Ianto reunited as lovers. As a means of catharsis, this fan writer's ending undoes the tragic conclusion to the couple's love affair as depicted in "Day Four." More significantly, by setting this reunion of these two lovers six decades in the future, HayamaRei imagines a distant—and, for now—untouchable decoder-generated fictive terrain through which his fantasy-influenced continuation of the Janto pairing can exist free from any post–*Children of Earth* televised stories, where Ianto remains permanently dead and always separated from Jack.

Captain Jack and Oswald Danes as Death-Drive Motivated Characters: Reproductive Futurism and the Sinthomosexual in *Torchwood*

In his work *No Future: Queer Theory and the Death Drive*, Lee Edelman provides a provocative definition and application of the term *sinthomosexual*, which opens up a fresh analysis of the male villain's function in literature and cinema. In turn, this term can be equally applied to both Captain Jack during the climax of *Children of Earth*, "Day Five" and to *Miracle Day*'s child-killer character, Oswald Danes. Commenting on heteronormative society's monopoly on reproductive futurism, Edelman writes,

> [W]hile lesbians and gay men by the thousands work for the right to marry, to serve in the military, to adopt and raise children of their own, the political right, refusing to acknowledge these comrades in reproductive futurism, counters their efforts by inviting us to kneel at the shrine of the sacred Child: the Child who might witness lewd or inappropriate intimate behavior; the Child who might find information about dangerous "lifestyles" on the Internet[19] [20–21].

For Edelman, queer culture's enjoyment of liberty is "eclipsed" by the Child who "terroristically holds us all in check and determines that political discourse conform to the logic of a narrative wherein history unfolds as the future envisioned for a Child who must never grow up" (21).

Standing in opposition to this Child is Edelman's formulation of "sinthomosexuality," which,

> denying the appeal of [Lacanian] fantasy, refusing the promise of futurity that mends each tear, however mean, in reality's dress with threads of meaning (attached as they are to the eye-catching lure we might see as the sequins of sequence, which dazzle our vision by producing the constant illusion of consequence) offers us fantasy turned inside out, the seams of its costume exposing reality's seamlessness in mere seeming, the fraying knots that hold each sequin in place now usurping that place [35].

In other words, the sinthomosexual must stand up for himself in society in order to represent the jouissance-driven urges of the queer death drive, a manifestation of Lacanian fantasy that resists a heterosexist political application of the Real through reproductive futurism.[20]

In the case of presenting Jack as a sinthomosexual, one could initially object by pointing out that he logically sacrifices one child's life, Steven's, to prevent the 456 from taking and subsequently torturing ten percent of Earth's children, who number in the tens of millions. However, Jack had already been posited as a sinthomosexual earlier in *Children of Earth* during the conclusion of "Day One." In a scene set in the Hub, Gwen scans her hand on a piece of purloined alien technology to ascertain that Clem MacDonald's[21] earlier comment that she is pregnant is indeed correct. As Jack is congratulating her upon this news, he places his hand upon hers, and the machinery detects that Jack has had a bomb placed within his stomach when he was captured and operated on by Agent Johnson.[22] Of course, Gwen and Ianto escape the Hub before it is destroyed by the detonation of the powerful explosive residing inside of Jack, but the lingering image remains that Gwen, a mortal woman, is pregnant with life, while Jack, the immortal man, is pregnant with death. With this sole image, it may require somewhat of an intellectual stretch to classify Jack as a sinthomosexual according to Edelman's application of the term. However, when one regards the image of him incorporating mortal death in his immortal bowels and combines it with the fact that he gave up eleven children to the

456 in 1965 and then later surrendered the life of his grandson to defeat them in 2009, one can reasonably argue that he truly serves as a powerful representation of death in *Children of Earth*.

At the same time, going against Edelman's formulation that the sinthomosexual promotes the queer death drive's jouissance-driven urges in opposition to reproductive futurism, one can posit that Jack both undermines this representation by preserving a heteronormative (or otherwise) future for the ten percent of the Earth's children who would have been abducted by the 456. Nevertheless, when it comes to the original English children handed over to the 456 and Steven, Jack has indeed assured that they will not participate in human society's commitment to reproductive futurism. Moreover, for those eleven children whose lives have been unnaturally expanded by the 456 since they have been enslaved in a form of living death for forty-four years, neither Jack nor the invader-aliens have given them the jouissance release of death. Steven, correspondingly, has been freed of his potential life-long commitment to reproductive futurism, but whether or not he has been given the jouissance of oblivion via his forced heroic death is naturally subject to individual debate.

From this perspective, Jack, at the cost of one child's life, is preserving the tenets of reproductive futurism for countless families. At the same time, Steven works as a televised representation of the sacred Child, who ironically never ages, which offers a symbolic contrast to the literally eternal Jack. Russell T Davies, however, does not satisfy certain *Children of Earth* audience members' desire to see Steven remain safe and protected by the man who most likely should assure his grandson's survival—the heroic Captain Jack Harkness, who has saved the Earth on numerous occasion in *Torchwood* and *NüWho*. Paradoxically, then, in "Day Five," Jack embodies both the masculine heroic paradigm by protecting millions of Earth's children and the sinthomosexual model by killing one. On his character Captain Jack's decision to sacrifice Steven, John Barrowman, in an interview with Charlie Jane Anders, argues,

> He didn't *murder* a child. He *sacrificed* the child's life in order to save the human race. Jack has always said that he will do whatever it takes to save mankind. The way I look at it, he did the thing that nobody else would do. Because if somebody were to ask you to sacrifice a child or a family member, you wouldn't have done it. You'd have let the world go to pot. Jack took the responsibility on, and unfortunately his grandson paid the price.

In analyzing Barrowman's words, it is interesting to note that he defines Jack's heroism according to the fact that he possesses the ability to commit actions that no one else could manage in order to protect humanity. Typically, this sort of mindset would apply to any SF, fantasy, or comic-book hero. Nevertheless, in many of those heroic situations, a child is saved from the precipice of death, particularly someone who is biologically related to the masculine hero. In other words, the extraordinary hero rarely—if ever—pragmatically sacrifices a family member to achieve a victory over one's enemy.

Jack, however, is not the only Death-Drive-focused individual featured in *Children of Earth* as this troubling role is shared by the elite members of the British government. In short, using privileged upper-class adults' treatment of at-risk lower-class children as its focusing theme, *Children of Earth* delivers a scathing critique of the English class system. When the Prime Minister and his inner cabinet, along with an American representative in the form of General Austin Pierce, choose to sacrifice the children of England's lower class to the 456 in the latter episodes of *Children of Earth*, they make a utilitarian governmental decision based on who will potentially be the most productive members of a future English society. In short, those children who will, in a statistical sense, grow up to be teachers, medics, and businesspeople, not unemployed welfare recipients or criminals, are judged to be the most worthy of survival. For the remaining ten percent, they are written off as fodder for the 456, who, in "Day Five," reveal themselves to be alien drug addicts who need the "hit" that their purloined human children provide for them.[23]

Though the 456 vastly extend the lives of these children, as seen in "Day Three," these tortured youth have been bound to these aliens in a state of constant misery. Moreover, this violation may not technically be sexual in nature, but, since it renders a feeling of exquisite pleasure to the 456 ambassador, the overall effect demonstrates that these aliens have committed a form of physical and mental rape upon these slowly aging children. Like Jack, whose life has been extended by an external force,[24] their bodies have been *queered* in the sense that they will not age with the rest of human society. Caught in a monstrous, near-undead state, their enslaved forms, which are tethered to their 456 masters, have been castrated in regard to their ability to age, reproduce, or function as members of English human society. Therefore, in a disquieting form of collaboration, occurring in both 1965 and 2009, the English government and the 456 have equally agreed to commit an act that not only has/will remove undesirable members of the English populace from the reproduction pool but will form a near-eternal imprisonment and punishment of their unwanted bodies as well.

Two years later, with *Miracle Day*, Jack is laterally given an opportunity to redeem himself as a sinthomosexual. In this coproduction, which transatlantically aired on the American Starz cable network and BBC One from July to August in 2011, Russell T Davies and his writing team present a scenario in which death has been rendered obsolete as no one can die, due to the "Miracle," a simultaneous mysterious event that makes everyone on Earth immortal. Ironically, the Miracle has now also turned Jack mortal. During the episode "Dead of Night," while Jack is involved with a joint Torchwood-CIA investigation to stop the Miracle, he confronts Oswald Danes, a man whose execution by lethal injection for the torture and murder of twelve-year-old Susie Cabina failed because of the Miracle's moratorium on death. In Oswald's hotel room, Jack enters into an argument with the man, who represents a darker version of himself:

> JACK: I saw you on television saying you feel forgiven for taking the life of a child. That's a lie! I know that's a lie.
> OSWALD: How do you know that, Jack, with such certainty?
> JACK: Tell the truth! The murder of Susie Cabina—you don't feel sorry at all.

In response to Jack's accusation, Oswald goes on to reveal his reasoning for sadistically torturing Susie. After he claims that he felt Susie's life leave through him, he tells Jack, "You know that feeling. I think you do, and I relive it every single night because that was the best moment of my life." In response, Jack says, "Now I understand. You do know this cause you're searching for one thing. One simple thing: execution." After Jack makes this pronouncement, the two share a sigh and a smile, revealing a moment of empathy that is being experienced between two tortured child killers. Whether or not Jack himself wants to die at well for killing his grandson, Steven, in "Day Five" of *Children of Earth*, however, is not clearly stated in this scene or throughout any of *Miracle Day*'s episodes. Granted, his act was committed out of the practical need to save the millions of children about to be taken by the 456 while Oswald's murder of Susie was perpetrated from a selfish desire to feel powerful. Regardless of their philosophical differences for taking the life of a child, both Jack and Oswald share a reciprocity in functioning as sinthomosexuals via their actions.

Regarding the resolution of Jack and Oswald's shared need to find peace (or absolution) for their individual crimes by committing themselves to the jouissance-filled urges of the death drive, the climax episode of *Miracle Day*, "The Blood Line," somewhat delivers on this desire. In this episode, Jack and Oswald confront a senior Families member, the Mother, at the excavated Shanghai location of the Blessing[25] as she is about to blow up any access to it, which will preserve the Miracle, meaning humanity will not be able to reclaim its mortality. Jack, however, along with CIA-ally Rex Matheson, who is positioned on the opposite pole of the Earth in Buenos Aires, thwart the Families' intention by having the Blessing suck up Jack's mortal blood, which is effectively spread to humanity, once more giving them the ability to die. After this act is achieved, Oswald, who is wired with explosives, grabs the Mother and blows them both up when he destroys the Shanghai entrance to the Blessing.

Whether or not Jack helps to actually redeem Oswald by giving the man the opportunity to kill himself in "The Blood Line" depends on each *Miracle Day* viewer's (or decoder's) reaction. As an example, one unnamed online reviewer posting on the Joss Whedon fan Web site *Whedonopolis*, states,

> In this finale, Danes is turned into Torchwood's own suicide bomber who martyrs himself in order to give Jack and Gwen the chance to escape after they had reversed the Miracle. This is not the kind of character that I want as a tragic hero. He was built up as an unrepentantly evil man, and even when his soul is reflected back at him by the Blessing, he shrugs off the sudden weight of guilt like it's no big deal.

In agreeing with this fan reviewer's position, one can consider Oswald's final line before he dies, when, in reference to his belief that he is heading to hell, where "all the little girls" go, he exclaims, "Susie, keep running! I'm coming to get you!" As a result, the image of him as an unrepentant sinthomosexual who wishes to continue experiencing the pleasure of his death-drive jouissance-laden impulses at the price of eternally tormenting his child victim has been uncomfortably relayed to the audience. In this sense, Oswald's death, unlike Owen or Ianto's in the previous two seasons of the show, fails to provide another satisfactory example of a masculine *Torchwood* antihero redeeming himself.

Jack vs. Rex: *Miracle Day*'s Dueling Sexualities

With CIA agent Rex Matheson's introduction in the first episode of *Miracle Day*, "The New World," the character is encoded as a cynical, skeptical (i.e., typical) American action hero. Moreover, after he is fatally impaled in the chest by a metal rod that came loose from a car in front of him on the highway, Rex discovers he cannot die thanks to the Miracle. Thus, in a similar manner to Owen in Series Two of *Torchwood*, he is experiencing a post-life existence. Unlike Owen, his body still retains all of its biological functions despite his unhealing chest wound. Moreover, Rex is African-American, which grants *Torchwood* its first regular-cast black character. Unlike the softer characterization given to Martha Jones in Series Two, Rex projects a harder edge that expresses his reluctance to work with a top-secret British team, Torchwood, and reinforces his loner mindset. He also adds a new dynamic to the series as he represents a heroic rival—or foil—to Jack. Determined to break the mystery of the now-defunct Torchwood, Rex, interestingly, is the first male character on the show (notwithstanding Rhys, who is not a team member) to not be encoded as a bisexual heroic character. Perhaps, then, the show is demarcating British representations of sexualized heroism as open-mindedly bisexual, while conversely presenting a twenty-first-century American hero as stolidly (and boringly) heterosexual. In other words, as much as Captain Jack's opening voiceover narration for *Torchwood* Series One and Two contains the line, "The twenty-first century is when everything changes," *Miracle Day*'s encoding of Rex shows that, in terms of the series' interpretation of a male American action hero, the status quo of heteronormativity remains.

In the second episode of *Miracle Day*, "Rendition," for example, the audience is directly told that Rex is a straight—and potentially homophobic—male. As he is riding in a plane while escorting his prisoners, Jack and Gwen, back to America for questioning in regard to Torchwood's connection to the Miracle, he makes a heterosexist assumption about the sexual identity of the male airplane attendant, Danny, who is attempting to find painkillers for him in this scene:

> DANNY: Sorry, all I could find was an aspirin. It was in the copilot's pocket. I gave it a quick spritz to take the lint off.
> REX: It's, uh, Danny, right?
> DANNY: Yeah.
> REX: Now, listen, I'm not gay, but, uh, I'll let you feel me up if you go get me a vodka.
> DANNY: Oh, I'm not gay either.
> REX: All right, then. Well, (points to Lyn, who is sitting behind him) I'll let you feel her up if it'll get me a vodka.

Rex's conversation with Danny not only mocks the man's potential homosexuality by offering a disingenuous offer for a sexual groping but likewise displays his sexist attitude toward his CIA colleague and former lover, Lyn Peterfield, as he reduces her Asian body to a commodity that he believes he can possibly exchange for the exchange of alcohol. The scene is also problematic because both Rex and Gwen (as she later tells Danny that his tie denotes him as a gay man) function in the same manner as Ianto's sister, Rhiannon, in "Day One" of *Children of Earth*, when she insisted on outing her brother from his gay closet. In other words, both Rex and Gwen firmly represent markers of heteronormative culture in *Miracle Day*, ones who feel obligated to point out their supposed queer counterparts.

Eve Kosofsky Sedgwick's thoughts regarding a heterosexual individual's hold over a gay person are likewise applicable to Rex and Gwen's self-perceived shared "understanding" of Danny's denied—and unrevealed—closeted homosexuality: "[T]he position of those who think they *know something about one that one may not know oneself* is an excited and empowered one—whether what they think one doesn't know is that one somehow *is* homosexual, or merely that one's supposed secret is known to them" (80). Although Danny's "true" sexuality is ultimately not revealed in this episode, a third invisible individual has become—for better or worse—indirectly encoded via Rex and Gwen's production and sharing of secret knowledge concerning the male steward's denied sexual identity: the hetero or LGBTQ *Miracle Day* viewer.

When one takes into consideration the idea that Davies and his *Miracle Day* writing team, composed of both British and American writers, were encoding a version of *Torchwood* that would not only potentially entertain the show's fan base but a new Starz-generated North American audience as well, this scene takes on an even greater significance. Ultimately, however, the diverse audience members of "Rendition" can decode this sequence as either reflecting a fair-minded assessment of Danny's repressed queer self or as a biased and myopically heterosexist censure of a possible gay man who has chosen to remain in the closet.

Despite Jack's omnisexual encoding in *NüWho* and Russell T Davies's 2006 proclamation that the original BBC Three incarnation of *Torchwood* would present characters whose sexuality is fluidic and somewhat ambiguous, the third episode of *Miracle Day*, "Dead of Night," is encoded to establish a distinct divide between Jack's now-apparently sole gay desires and Rex's heterosexual needs. During the episode, Jack is immediately hit on by a bartender, Brad, at a Los Angeles night club, and the two, in their next scene together, are seen as making out in the bartender's apartment. Consequently, this scene can initially be interpreted as depicting two members of gay culture as haphazardly engaging in sex without taking any precautions. However, while Brad is already naked, Jack is still mostly clothed as this exchange occurs between them:

JACK: Do you have protection?
BRAD: What for? Can't die now. Don't need nothing in between.
JACK: That's not how it works anymore. A lifetime of regret just got even longer—that's all.
BRAD: Fine. You're calling the shots.
JACK: Yes. Yes, I am.

On the one hand, this scene offers a positive depiction of Jack as a leading hero who is a responsible gay man, and who, in especial recognition of his newly mortal status, is concerned with sensibly avoiding contracting HIV/AIDS. Concerning this scene, Emily Asher-Perrin, a professional online reviewer, argues, "Jack advocates safe sex. Sure, it's a brief exchange in a long episode, but there is something uncommonly impressive about even mentioning this on television. While the premise actually makes the concern legitimate ... the bottom line is that it was addressed onscreen, something that is practically never done unless dramatic irony is employed later." Asher-Perrin has correctly underscored the importance of "Dead of Night's" progressive encoding of Jack's conversation with Brad. On the other hand, this moment heavy-handedly preaches a safe-gay-sex message to the audience. More importantly, the fact that Rex is not encoded as discussing wearing a condom with Dr. Vera Juarez before his sex scene with her reinforces the view that Jack's conversation with Brad is concerned with relaying to the audience the impression that he is a trustworthy, sexually conscientious gay hero.

However, the scene immediately shows that Jack indeed is "calling the shots" in this sexual rendezvous when he kisses Brad and pushes his head down to his crotch area for oral pleasuring. At the same time, subsequent scenes of their lovemaking, which are intercut with scenes of Rex having sex with Vera, depict Jack being the "top" as he penetrates Brad, and then becoming the "bottom" as he receives the man's member in his anus. Before Rex and Vera's lovemaking, however, when he tells her that he needs her to provide medicine and care for him as she applies a fresh bandage to his unhealing chest wound, this exchange of reciprocal power dynamic occurs:

> VERA: I'm just taking your word for it that you're not a traitor.
> REX: Oh, yeah? But, you know, you've already given me drugs, taken me into your home, and you know we both have the power to make a case against one another.
> VERA: Nice.
> REX: Yeah.
> VERA: So what you're saying is, that's what our relationship comes down to—blackmail.
> REX: Huh. Well, when you put it that way, it's kinda hot.

Like Gwen and Tosh at times during Series One and Two of *Torchwood*, and, in a similar fashion to Esther during this season of the show, Vera is assuming the role of the female caregiver for a leading male hero. Conversely, she enacts a form of power over Rex as she possesses the ability to withhold her valuable medical knowledge and drugs from him and could turn him in to the CIA. She also, unlike Esther, who is Rex's loyal colleague and quietly in love with the man, holds sexual capital in his eyes since her subsequent weak protest to him that she is exhausted leads to them having sex. Thus, like Owen Harper, who rejected Tosh and slept with various women throughout *Torchwood*'s first two series, Rex only appears to romance females who can match his aggressive, equitable-power-predicated form of heterosexuality.[26]

Curiously, Vera meets a tragic end in the fifth episode of *Miracle Day*, "The Categories of Life," as she is incinerated before Rex's eyes in an overflow camp burning unit as he reluctantly films her demise in order to capture evidence that the American government is burning people's bodies instead of medically treating them. As a result, like Tosh's excruciating death in the conclusion of "Exit Wounds," a heroic female member of the *Torchwood* cast has been killed off in order to elicit feelings of pity from the audience. At the same time, Rex, like Jack, is encoded as a survivor, one whose existence as a male hero can continue. In a similar troubling fashion, when Esther dies in the climax episode of *Miracle Day*, "The Blood Line," as she has been fatally shot by a Family representative just before Rex and Jack restore all of humanity to a mortal existence, her subsequent death echoes Tosh's and Vera's. In all three scenarios, women[27] have selflessly died in order to ensure that the male heroes, Owen and Rex, achieve their respective heroic goals.

Considering Rex's hypermasculinity and humorously stated heterosexist beliefs, much can be theoretically made of the fact he, like Jack, is rendered immortal in "The Blood Line." Ending on a cliffhanger note, the episode shows Rex reviving from being fatally shot and then watching the wound heal, causing him to exclaim to a surprised Jack, "You, World War II,[28] what the hell did you do to me!?" On a literal level, Jack has not turned Rex into an omnisexual like himself, but he has inadvertently contributed to the queering of his CIA-ally's body as the man now stands apart from the rest of humanity via his newfound immortality. It is also telling that the means to this fantastical modification of Rex's body and life force is achieved via a blood transfusion, which conjures problematic allusions to a heterosexual male contracting HIV/AIDs from a gay or bisexual man. Since Rex had chosen to have Esther help him to exchange his blood for Jack's in "The Blood Line," the true burden of the man's transformation rests upon him, but the uncomfortable insinuation remains that Jack's immortal blood is cursed or tainted, rendering his formerly "normal" human body "different" and "apart"—in other words, *queered*. In short, Rex can no longer naturally exist according to the rhythms of society's nine-to-five, child-rearing, heteronormative lifestyle, as it is geared toward the regimentally timed evolution of one's mortal life from youth, to early adulthood, middle age, old age, and death.

Moreover, by the conclusion of *Miracle Day*, Rex and Jack still have not comfortably—or satisfyingly—bonded onscreen. For one online reviewer, JeromeWetzelTV, however, Rex's transformation into an immortal man represents a positive plot development for *Torchwood*: "It's a welcome new story, with plenty to explore in future *Torchwood* installments. It also makes Rex very important for upcoming adventures, and permanently changes the dynamic for the Torchwood crew. For these reasons, and the fact that [Mekhi] Phifer[29] makes Rex extremely intriguing, it is a welcome change for the current run to end with." Taking JeromeWetzelTV's views into consideration, which are shared by a portion of *Torchwood* fans, one can argue that, theoretically, although the foundation has been set by Davies and his transatlantic *Miracle Day* writing team for a buddy-buddy pairing of a gruff African-American action hero and a more flamboyant white counterpart, a follow-up fifth *Torchwood* season, to date, has not been greenlit as either a co-funded BBC/Starz series or as a sole BBC production.

* * *

When evaluating *Torchwood*'s four-season meteoric rise, which is demonstrated by the show first being broadcast on BBC Three in the fall of 2006, airing on BBC Two and One in 2008 and summer 2009, and finishing as a BBC/Starz coproduction in 2011, one must finish this chapter with a crucial question: Was it worth it? From a media perspective, this unprecedented movement of a mature-viewer encoded BBC television series from its humble roots on the corporation's third channel to a lavish co-production on an American cable station certainly solidifies *Torchwood*'s importance in the history of transatlantic SF television series. Furthermore, in considering the encoders' financial stakes in these productions, the answer to the question is obvious as series creator Russell T Davies and the BBC itself reaped lucrative financial rewards via *Torchwood* DVD sales and such ancillary merchandise as books, magazines, and audio CDs.

Paradoxically, from the viewpoint of the encoder-viewers, or to be more specific, *Torchwood*'s devout fan base, the severe cast and format changes the show embraced in order to evolve and stimulate media attention were some of its most egregious alienating features. Although Owen started out as a problematic character in Series One, the following season's depiction of his post-life heroic redemption and final death endeared him to viewers. Equally, when the long-suffering, ever-patient Toshiko heroically faced her death in "Exit Wounds," fans began their long-term mourning for her departure from the show. Yet it was the death of Ianto in "Day

Four" of *Children of Earth* that motivated a number of fans who had enjoyed the character's romance with Jack to express their frustration online in a manner that was damaging to their relationship with encoder-writer James Moran.

Returning to the show's dual themes of sex and death, it seems *Torchwood* connects best with its fan base when the series satisfies Davies's original intention of featuring characters who embrace a bisexual lifestyle. As these sexually and emotionally diverse characters, Owen, Tosh, and Ianto, are killed off, *Torchwood* fans have expressed feelings of collective sadness and rage, which Davies and his writing colleagues had naturally expected and intended to occur. Arguably, this media-enabled outpouring of emotions, which are cathartic in that they allow the fans to express raw and/or repressed feeling, are definitely preferable to fandom's feelings of ennui and disappointment with *Miracle Day*, as the show became more Americanized in tone and setting and their former audience-surrogate bisexual characters were nonexistent. While *Torchwood*'s future as a continuing television narrative is undetermined at present, a strong feeling exists amongst online fandom that, in order for the show to continue in a successful manner, the series should return to its fundamental Cardiff roots and earlier emphasis on character-based and pansexual storytelling. From a Darwinian Hollywood perspective, this mindset may seem creatively and economically suicidal, but, after all, *Torchwood*, like *Doctor Who*, *Blake's 7*, and *Red Dwarf*, will most likely find the future means for success via its cult SF core audience—the fans.

Chapter Six

NüWho's Quest to Stay Relevant with Its Fans

With the eighth series of *Doctor Who* since its 2005 rebirth, the show encodes an older, patriarchal Doctor, yet simultaneously presents the character questioning and shaping his heroic identity in relation to his still-evolving twelfth persona.[1] While the Doctor embarks on this season-long personal quest, his troubled ethics clash with companion Clara Oswald, who herself is struggling to balance her various roles as a school teacher, girlfriend to her colleague, Danny Pink, and a space-time-traveling hero. Concerning Danny, a PTSD survivor, this character, along with Coal Hill School student Courtney Woods, presents some thought-provoking commentary on the black SF hero. Standing in opposition to the Doctor, Clara, and Danny is the villainous Missy the first female regeneration of the Time Lord's longtime nemesis, the Master. As a result, the themes of patriarchy, race, and sexual identity intermix and collide during this series of *NüWho* when presenting gendered heroic and villainous quests, which, in turn, fuel audience support and resistance.

NüWho Series Eight: The Show's Densest Manifestation of EDE to Date?

As a foundation to my discussion relating to the encoding of these characters and fan reactions to them, I would like to discuss *NüWho* fandom, particularly in relation to the encoding of Series Eight's opening credits title sequence.[2] Concerning the encoders behind the production of *NüWho*, one of their most interesting biographical aspects is that many of them were fans of *Classic Who*, adding weight to the theory that encoding/decoding/encoding (EDE) represents a prevalent feature of the twenty-first century series. Russell T Davies, Steven Moffat's showrunner predecessor, was a childhood fan of the show, as was Tenth Doctor David Tennant. Furthermore, Moffat himself has frequently mentioned to the media that he grew up loving the show, so it is interesting to note this fact when analyzing his casting of Peter Capaldi for the role of the Twelfth Doctor. Like Moffat, Capaldi is not only in his mid-fifties, but he is a former active participatory culture member of the show as well, since he was a devoted teenage viewer who started his own *Doctor Who* fan club and had a letter published in the *Radio Times* when he was fifteen. One can also cite the fact that many of the Series Eight writers—Phil Ford, Mark Gatiss, Gareth Roberts, and Frank Cottrell-Boyce[3]—all professional television and/or film writers, were once young fans of *Classic Who*. This fact thereby adds further weight to the argument that EDE continues to have a considerable effect upon the production of *NüWho*.

With the case of the aforementioned examples, however, these acting and writing professionals had proven themselves in their given careers before becoming affiliated with *NüWho*. Very seldom, then—for *Doctor Who*—or any other televised SF production, does a decoder-fan—or novice/unproven artist—make the leap to being an encoder-professional.[4] In the late summer of 2014, however, the media and *Doctor Who* fan press circulated the story of Billy Hanshaw, a professional graphics designer, whose *YouTube* fan-generated *NüWho* credits sequence had become the basis for the Series Eight official title sequence. Moreover, since social media was a crucial factor in ensuring that Hanshaw made the leap from a fan who appropriated *NüWho* design elements to an official contributor to the show, one can apply Henry Jenkins, Sam Ford, and Joshua Green's concept of "spreadability," which "refers to the technical resources that make it easier to circulate some kinds of content than others, the economic structures that support or restrict circulation, the attributes of a media text that might appeal to a community's motivation for sharing material, and the social networks that link people through the exchange of meaningful bytes" (4).

In breaking down these three scholars' thoughts on spreadability in relationship to Billy Hanshaw's fan-generated title sequence, an interesting cross section of encoding/decoding cascading across several media platforms occurs. Regarding the technical resources Hanshaw utilized in order to create his vision of how the then-future Series Eight opening credits should appear, he relied on various software, including Cinema 4D, After Effects, Photoshop, and Illustrator. Additionally, with the aid of the economic structure which is *YouTube*, a social media Web site that possesses the technological capacity to host countless user-generated (or bottom-up) videos, Hanshaw was able to upload his work for online global public consumption. As a result, *Doctor Who* fans could access his video and comment upon its attributes via its message board. In terms of Hanshaw providing a "media text that might appeal to [the *Doctor Who* fan] community's motivation for sharing material," dozens of fan-generated *NüWho* title sequences have been uploaded to *YouTube* over the years, many of them, like his, offering a vision of a future title sequence for the show. However, Hanshaw's title sequence was the first of its kind to attract the attention of current *NüWho* showrunner Steven Moffat, who wished to offer a visual departure from the opening sequences the show had been featuring in the last several years.

In regard to fans supporting and promoting Hanshaw's creation through their interaction on the *YouTube* message boards positioned beneath his video and contacting the BBC offices via email in order to draw attention to the video, one can ask a crucial question: What demographics of *NüWho* fandom do they represent? Obviously, anyone who watches *Doctor Who* needs to have access to a television or computer in order to view the show's episodes. However, in regard to participating in online fandom, one needs to possess a certain amount of technological skills, not to mention a certain level of literacy and writing in order to effectively communicate with others involved who are geographically spread across the globe. This communication can occur through a simple tweet, a message board posting, or, on a more involved level, through regularly maintaining a blog dedicated to the show. While Jean Burgess and Joshua Green assert that *YouTube* is "a potential site of cosmopolitan cultural citizenship"[5] they also state that "access to all the layers of possible participation is limited to a particular segment of the population—those with the motivations, technological competencies, and site-specific cultural capital sufficient to participate at all levels of engagement the network affords" (81).

Burgess and Green's thoughts in this instance are building upon what Henry Jenkins terms a "participation gap" in *Convergence Culture*. While discussing the digital divide that characterizes different cultural groups' access to the Internet and social media, Jenkins writes,

> [W]e need to confront the cultural factors that diminish the likelihood that different groups will participate. Race, class, language differences amplify these inequalities in opportunities for participation. One reason we see early adopters is not only that some groups feel more confidence in engaging with new technologies but also that some groups seem more comfortable going public with their views about culture [269].

Jenkins's thoughts regarding the cultural factors that influence the degree of one's online participation via social media can be applicable not only to *NüWho* fandom but to all of the other modules that have been under discussion in this book. In other words, for one to actively and comfortably participate in many of the discussion boards or fan fiction transatlantic Web sites pertaining to *Doctor Who*, *Blake's 7*, *Red Dwarf*, and *Torchwood* fan cultures, which, in many situations, demand more than a basic command of the English language, as many of the posters seem to possess average (or above) writing skills, one should probably be modestly educated and well read. What these unofficial prerequisites amount to is that they potentially (or inadvertently) exclude nonnative English speakers. Granted, these fans who have access to a computer and an Internet connection could still "lurk" on social media via reading message boards and blogs, but their voices are often muted by their inability to actively participate. At the same time, in the case of *NüWho* global fan culture, fan groups have been proliferating in such countries as South Korea, Brazil, and Mexico,[6] where fans interact online or meet in person to discuss the show or enjoy cosplaying their favorite characters.

Case in point, the BBC-produced special, "*Doctor Who*: Earth Conquest—The World Tour," which aired on BBC America, shows Peter Capaldi, Jenna Coleman, and Steven Moffat embarking on a global world tour in the summer of 2014 in order to promote the new Twelfth Doctor and the then-upcoming Series Eight. Amongst the countries they visited were South Korea, Australia, Brazil, and Mexico. Notably, many of the South Korean fans are successfully cosplaying the Eleventh Doctor and other characters from the series but are also struggling to speak the English language. Of course, some fans demonstrate a more proficient knowledge of English than other fans featured in the video, but the overall impression created is that these fans' knowledge of the language may still require study and conversational practice.

In understanding the geographical extent of *NüWho*'s global fandom, one should also consider economically impoverished third world countries, where, due to a lack of a strong technological infrastructure, one's access to a computer or the Internet is limited or nonexistent. In this case, *Doctor Who* does not reach all of its possible global audience, thereby excluding these potential viewers and fans from participating online or via social gatherings. As a result, on a global level, a form of cultural, technological, and language-based social stratification demarcates those individuals who possess the most creative/disruptive and/or inspiring/incendiary voices when it comes to *NüWho* and other SF/fantasy fandoms.

As an example, although Hanshaw has been promoted by the *Doctor*

Who and greater media as an ordinary fan who has achieved his dream of contributing to the show, his technological training and expertise posits him as anything but the average fan. In fact, the designer himself has made this statement in an interview with Connor Johnston concerning his fan title sequence:

> It was designed as a portfolio piece—even though it's a bit rough round the edges. It was created in downtime and spare time. Corporate presentations and TV spots often don't allow you to craft something like this, so if you don't go ahead and create personal work, you'll never be able to show what you can do. Sites like *YouTube* are a great platform for creative expression. There's a massive audience out there, and if you can tap into something which is already huge in terms of followers, then you stand a chance of getting noticed.

From an economic standpoint, the time and labor Hanshaw devoted to designing his title sequence was not motivated by an altruistic fan "gift economy" as promoted by Lewis Hyde.[7] Instead, he had appropriated the BBC corporate brand's *Doctor Who* logo, TARDIS police box copyright, and Gallifreyan symbol in order to put together a portfolio piece that could generate business for himself. Moreover, in regard to the participatory level of Hanshaw's *Doctor Who* fandom, he comments, "People expect me to be one of those SUPER fans. Don't get me wrong—the show has a huge place in my heart. It's something I loved watching as I grew up. Tom Baker was my favorite." With this statement, Hanshaw subtly distances himself from *NüWho* fans by limiting his fandom to the now distant time of the *Classic Who* episodes that aired in the latter 1970s and featured Tom Baker's Fourth Doctor. In this sense, Hanshaw safely qualifies himself as an adult modern graphic artist professional who possesses a fond nostalgic fan-memory and adoration for the show.

As a result, one could contend that Hanshaw's knowledge of *NüWho*'s substantial global fan audience, which repeatedly demonstrates its impressive numbers via their continuous participation on social media sites, has allowed him to manipulate this audience into promoting his financially motivated "portfolio" piece to the BBC, arguably one of his targeted potential television corporate clients. In other words, while Hanshaw has monetarily profited from contributing to the finished official *NüWho* Series Eight title sequence, the fans who promoted his efforts via social media and directly to the BBC have received no financial compensation for their collective efforts. On a more positive note, one could say that the reward they receive is the shared knowledge—or mass-conviction—that "one of their own" has been given the chance to shape a piece of the show. At the very least, this mindset could lead other creative fan-decoders to make the successful transition to serving as encoders of *NüWho* in the form of actors, writers, designers, or other members of the series' production team. If the history of the encoding of *Classic* and *NüWho* offers an indicator of the show's future iterations, in that many of its actors, writers, directors, designers, and producers confess to being childhood or adult fans of the series, then the theory that today's *NüWho* decoders are its future encoders will indeed be proven true.

Despite Hanshaw limiting the timeframe of his *Doctor Who* fandom to his childhood, one can still classify his credit sequence as an example of encoding/decoding/encoding. Working from his childhood and adult perceptions of *Classic* and *NüWho*'s various encoded opening credits sequences, Hanshaw created a title sequence that added an element he thought needed to be featured in the opening credits: a clock. Put another way, Hanshaw decoded the classic and modern *Doctor Who* sequences as lacking an obvious visual metaphor—a clock and its mechanical components—to signify to the show's viewers its central thesis—time travel. Now that Hanshaw's graphic design efforts have been utilized by BBC designers to produce the finished televised work that is the Series Eight title sequence, he has officially become one of the show's encoders, which effectively completes the EDE cycle for him. Consequently, his onscreen work is now itself subject to fan decoding. On this note, Hanshaw remarks, "I've heard the comment that the use of clockwork is wrong because it is too 'human' a way to represent time travel. My answer to that is that as far as I'm aware, humans make up the entirety of the viewing audience, and so will immediately understand the analogy. After all, a title sequence is meant to reflect the show's core themes." Ironically, with this explanation, Hanshaw is responding to fan-decoder critiques of his title sequence with an encoder-imbued rationalization that his clockwork design represents their human experience as audience viewing members. Perhaps future *Doctor Who* title sequences that are likewise designed by former decoders of the show will encode a design work that serves as a counter-response to Hanshaw's 2014 title sequence. Thus, this current manifestation of EDE can be perpetuated via upcoming iterations of the show's opening credits.

The Twelfth Doctor's Face: Too Old for *NüWho*?

In "Deep Breath," the opening story of Series Eight that features Peter Capaldi's full debut as the Twelfth Doctor, the character, as per every new incarnation of the long-living Time Lord, experiences post-regeneration trauma as he settles into his transformed body and mind. Unlike his previous incarnation, the Eleventh Doctor, who appeared to look like a human being in his late twenties/early thirties, the Twelfth Doctor resembles a man in his mid-fifties—a point which is not lost upon his distraught companion, school teacher Clara Oswald. For example, as she is sitting at the convalescing Doctor's bedside in Madame Vastra's home, located in Victorian-era England, Clara comments to Jenny, the Silurian Vastra's human lover and wife, "Why did he get that face? Why's it got lines on it? It's brand new. How can his head be all gray? He only just got it." Serving as the voice for the "Deep Breath" viewers who may be troubled by the Twelfth Doctor's older appearance, Clara thus functions as a means of addressing their concerns and anxieties regarding his age.[8] Her conversation with Jenny, however, takes on a deeper meaning in the exchange that follows her complaints about the Twelfth Doctor's face:

> JENNY: It's still him, ma'am. You saw him change.
> CLARA: I know. I do. I ... I know that.
> JENNY: Good.
> CLARA: It's just...
> JENNY: What?
> CLARA: Nothing. If ... if Vastra changed, if ... if she was different, if she wasn't the person that you liked?
> JENNY: I don't like her, ma'am. I love her. And as to different, well, she's a lizard.

With this conversation, Clara and Jenny present diametrically opposed views on love, which can be divided according to a heteronormative/queer divide. For Clara, the Eleventh Doctor she "liked" was around twelve hundred years old when she traveled with him, but he appeared to be only a few years older than her. Together, the two of them flirted, yet never romantically nor physically consummated their feelings for one another. Nonetheless, these feelings could be categorized as heteronormative, at least from Clara's perspective, since her original Doctor looked as if he could theoretically marry and have children with her. In short, Clara feels as if her attraction to the younger-looking Eleventh Doctor was legitimated by his appearance while his older-appearing successor does not satisfy her desire to potentially be with a mate who is her own age in an external sense. Consequently, the Twelfth Doctor, in Clara's heteronormative mindset, is "different" from his predecessor due to the fact that he does not present an agreeable younger appearance that is theoretically conducive to sex and potential childrearing.[9] In contrast to Clara, Jenny doubly queers her lover, Madame Vastra, by playfully defining her "difference" in saying that the woman is a lizard. Nonetheless, Jenny, unlike Clara, accepts and celebrates her lover's reptilian appearance and shared queer sexuality.

Later in the episode, Clara encounters the Doctor in the TARDIS, which he has slightly remodeled to include bookshelves, a leather chair, and a darker lighting scheme, objects which one could argue reflect his more mature appearance in a phenomenological sense. Fully recovered from his regeneration, he ominously walks down the TARDIS control room steps, somberly announcing to her, "I'm the Doctor. I've lived for over two thousand years, and not all of them were good. I've made many mistakes, and it's about time I did something about that." In terms of this new incarnation of the Doctor announcing his title to his companion, he is adhering to one of the show's tropes, as both *Classic* and *NüWho*'s newly regenerated Doctors have affirmed their identity to his companions. From an encoding perspective, moreover, this scene is written to reassure the audience that, although this character possesses a new face and body, he is, at the core, the same Doctor whom they have watched for years on television, either in the form of one or several of the actors who have performed the role.

Returning to the Twelfth Doctor's speech to Clara, his need to confess that he has a dark past for which he needs to rectify his actions continues the theme of *NüWho*'s post–Time War Doctors sharing a common troubled history, which adds a layer of complexity to the character. However, the Doctor immediately adds, "Clara, I'm not your boyfriend." After she replies, "I never thought you were," the Doctor responds, "I never said it was your mistake." In some ways, this scene, written by showrunner Steven Moffat, could be seen as his means to returning to *Classic Who*'s platonic Doctor-companion dynamic. It could also be viewed as Moffat's positive attempt to mollify the quite vocal portion of fandom who did approve of the Eleventh Doctor's flirtatious relationship with Clara in Series Seven, as they found it inappropriate for a well-experienced, then-1,200 years old Time Lord to be wooing a somewhat naïve twenty-five-year-old human female.

In addition to refining the Doctor and Clara's relationship during "Deep Breath," Moffat includes a cameo appearance from the Eleventh Doctor, who is calling Clara from Trenzalore shortly before his regeneration into his twelfth persona at the end of "The Time of the Doctor." After the Twelfth Doctor has set the new parameters of his friendship with Clara, she receives a call from the Eleventh Doctor, who, upon hearing the Twelfth Doctor's older voice in the background, initiates this exchange with the future version of his companion:

> ELEVENTH DOCTOR: He sounds old. Please tell me I didn't get old. Anything but old! I was young. Oh! Is he gray?

CLARA: Yes.
ELEVENTH DOCTOR: Clara, please, hey? For me? Help him. Go on. And don't be afraid. Goodbye, Clara. Miss ya.

As much as the scene has been encoded to work as a cathartic means for Clara to deal with the fact that the Twelfth Doctor cannot return to looking like his former younger self, it is also Moffat's direct means of reassuring *NüWho*'s global audience that the new Doctor, despite looking noticeably older than his recent tenth and eleventh incarnations, is still the same character at the core.

In reaction to this scene, fans appear to be divided. While certain fans were surprised and emotionally moved by the Eleventh Doctor's unexpected appearance in "Deep Breath," other fans viewed the Eleventh Doctor-Clara scene as Moffat's heavy-handed way of spelling out to the *NüWho* audience that it is acceptable for the Time Lord to currently look like an older man. For example, in reaction to the Eleventh Doctor's cameo in the episode, fan reviewer Eris Walsh writes, "I rolled my eyes and sighed with derision when he popped up on the screen. That was completely unnecessary. Smith's Doctor needed to be brought back one last time to explain to Clara that she needs to accept his new regeneration? Really? Moffat has written such a weak character that he couldn't even find a way to have her come to that on her own?"

Walsh brings up an interesting point in observing that Clara requires the voice of the Eleventh Doctor to convince her that his successor embodies an acceptable regeneration of his persona. From this perspective, one could argue that the patriarchal presence—or telephonic specter—of this past Doctor works as Moffat's way of taking away Clara's agency to independently recognize the Twelfth Doctor's inherent worth as a friend to her. Walsh also laments, "That scene, to me, pulled down an otherwise entertaining episode a notch and left a very bad taste in my mouth. It turned an episode that was supposed to be the exciting, long-awaited introduction to Capaldi's Doctor into yet another far-fetched, overly dramatic farewell to Matt Smith." With these words, Walsh positions himself as a *NüWho* fan who desires to see the show move narratively forward in establishing the Twelfth Doctor as the series' leading man rather than offering one last surprise nod to the former incumbent in the role. If one were to agree with Walsh's assessment of Smith's appearance in "Deep Breath," one could add the thought that Moffat is perhaps misreading *NüWho* fans' affection for Matt Smith. In other words, the showrunner may be subscribing to the more inertia-ridden properties of the Continuum of Nostalgic Continuity by attempting to address, heal, and win over the members of *NüWho* fandom who possess a sentimental attachment to the now-departed Eleventh Doctor by convincing them through the mouthpiece of the dying Time Lord that the Twelfth Doctor is a worthy successor to his heroic mantle.

Though the Twelfth Doctor and Clara have been strictly encoded as friends by Moffat and his fellow Series Eight writers, this platonic situation, as always, does not stop *Doctor Who* fans from creating their own alternative sexual fantasies for the Time Lord and his companions via fictitious productions. In one comedic story, "The Blue Pill," fan writer xXdreameaterXx concocts a comedic scenario in which the Doctor is suffering from a headache and accidently takes Viagra in Clara's flat. This scenario occurs after the Time Lord mishears his companion's directions for how he can find the alien headache medicine they had picked up at a space market[10] in her blue medicine box as her telling him to take the blue pill—hence Viagra. On an immediate, witty level, xXdreameaterXx's play on words—"blue medicine box" and "blue pill"—work as metonymic extensions of the blue police box exterior of the Doctor's TARDIS. Taken to a more sexualized level, the police box then serves as a symbolic extension of the Time Lord's phallus.

But there is also the greater narrative import of the Viagra in the story. Although Peter Capaldi is at the ideal age to take the sexual-performance-enhancing medication, the Doctor himself embodies an alien whose physiology differs from humans in many unexplained ways. In other words, just because the Doctor appears to be an older human male,[11] this does not mean to say that he would require the aid of any medication in order to sustain a penile erection, especially when it has been established in both *Classic* and *NüWho* that Time Lords can live for hundreds of years in just one body. For xXdreameaterXx, however, the Twelfth Doctor's physical appearance posits him as an older male who would need the assistance of Viagra to satisfactorily please Clara in a sexual manner. In fact, once the Doctor is feeling the full effects of the blue pill, xXdreameaterXx writes about how this fantasy scenario affects Clara:

> The sight of the aroused Time Lord stirred something rather unexpected inside her. It wasn't like she had never considered it before; she had just always assumed that he was some sort of asexual being who wasn't remotely interested in sex, especially not with her. But what if he was? Clara knew that even Viagra couldn't just magically make you want something or someone, so he must have at least considered it.

In xXdreameaterXx's opinion, the Twelfth Doctor's older appearance does not preclude Clara from being attracted to him, despite the fact that no televised evidence from Series Eight can support this claim. The writer likewise creates a scenario in which the Viagra does not exist as the only catalyst for the Doctor's attraction to Clara, hinting that his romantic/sexual feelings for her are preexisting in his two hearts. This possibility, however, is feasible in reference to Series Eight in that one could argue that the Twelfth Doctor's jealousy of Danny and his continual need for Clara's companionship is indicative of a greater, deeper unspoken love for his companion.

Once Clara starts touching the Doctor in "The Blue Pill," he resists but then quickly succumbs to her physical advances and kisses her: xXdreameaterXx writes,

> The Doctor picked her up and effortlessly lifted her to sit on the table when Clara suddenly broke the kiss, gasping for air.
> "Gosh, how long has it been for you?" she asked breathlessly.
> "Centuries," he replied before cupping her face in his hands and kissing her again. Clara parted her legs to wrap them around him, pulling him closer to herself, her hands trying to remove his jumper.

Mirroring the episode "Listen," in which one of its closing scenes depicts Clara kissing her new paramour, Danny, "The Blue Pill" thus reimagines the Doctor as her virile romantic love interest, thus lending him, in xXdreameaterXx's view, a necessary sexual agency in regard to his relationship with his companion. The passage similarly utilizes the Twelfth Doctor's older face to represent that he is two thousand years old and has not had sex in hundreds of years. More importantly, for longtime fans reading this piece who hold the impression that the Doctor has not enjoyed sexual intercourse since the beginning of the show in 1963, this scene and the ending of "The Blue Pill," where the Time Lord subsequently penetrates Clara, could function as a cathartic manifestation of their desires to witness him feeling such bodily pleasure.

A Time Lord's Clock Strikes Twelve: A Fortification or Subversion of the Show's Patriarchal Values?

Like the various antiheroes presented in this work, the Twelfth Doctor, during the entirety of Series Eight of *NüWho*, must learn how to be a heroic character. This journey is immediately encoded with the climax of "Deep Breath," which presents the Half-Face Man, the Time Lord's sympathetic nemesis in the episode, meeting his end after he has either fallen off the side of a small restaurant that he and the Doctor were standing in while floating above Victorian London in a giant balloon made of human skin or possibly has been pushed off the structure by the Doctor himself. Regarding this complex encoding of the Twelfth Doctor, fan reviewer Jon Meek points out,

> One of the notable things about "Deep Breath" that has always stayed with me is a sense that this new Doctor is a little bit dangerous. Most telling of all was the moment where he watched the Half-Face Man fall to his death at the end of the episode. For a moment, his eyes flicker, and then they snap wide open, and he looks right down the camera at you. The question he is asking is: What do you think? Did he jump, or did I push him? The look is startling and utterly inscrutable.

Meek's observation that the Doctor's intense, direct stare at the camera is filmed to engage the viewer illuminates the postmodern encoding of this scene. In other words, the moment is showing the Doctor's enigmatic antiheroic nature, not telling the answer to whether or not he has committed murder to save Clara and his friends, Madame Vastra, Jenny, and Strax,[12] from the Half-Face Man and his fellow sentient, semi-organic automatons who were attacking them in the bowels of a building below him.

In comparison to *Blake's 7* titular character, Roj Blake, who, due to a Federation-induced amnesia, cannot remember his heroic past at the beginning of "The Way Back," the Twelfth Doctor must rediscover what makes him a hero. For instance, as Blake assumes his heroic mantle as a resistance leader over the course of *Blake's 7*'s first two seasons, he increasingly struggles with the utilitarianism of sacrificing the lives of others in order to successfully achieve his goals. This inner and outer conflict culminates in the Series B finale, "Star One." In this episode, Blake's crew initially questions his decision to blow up Star One, the communications hub for the entire system of worlds under Federation control. While this action could potentially cripple the Federation's intergalactic infrastructure, it will, most likely, come at the cost of thousands of innocent civilian lives as planets' weather control systems and other technological-related variables will be adversely affected. Blake, however, pragmatically rationalizes that such a cost is worth the greater good of defeating the despotic Federation.

Correspondingly, the Twelfth Doctor makes a similar controversial pragmatic decision during the episode "Into the Dalek," which depicts the Time Lord, Clara, and a group of soldiers who are fighting in the Dalek Wars of the thirty-first century being miniaturized in order to explore the interior of a Dalek since it has been uncharacteristically demonstrating human-like emotions. During their expedition inside the Dalek, the cybernetic creature's autonomic antibodies start attacking them, finally surrounding Ross, one of the soldiers. In response, before Ross is killed, the Doctor tosses him a tracking device to swallow, well aware the man is going to die, but not warning him about this fact. On a pragmatic level, this action helps the group to continue to survive inside the Dalek as it leads them to the alien's recycling center. Yet, on a problematically moralistic level, the Doctor manipulated the man into carrying out his bidding by giving him the false hope that the device would somehow help him to survive the antibodies poised to attack him.

Earlier in the episode, moreover, Clara once again functions as the Time Lord's moral barometer as she sits down next to him upon the steps of the TARDIS control room, and he humbly says, "Clara, be my pal and tell me.... Am I a good man?" In response, she claims, "I ... don't know." Evidently, Clara is fulfilling her role as viewer surrogate by voicing her doubts concerning this rather darker version of the show's leading Time Lord's questionable embodiment of his predecessor's more overt heroic qualities. When one factors in the possibility of the Doctor representing a patriarchal hero in this situation, however, one could either argue that he himself is questioning—or deconstructing—this vision of heroism through confiding in Clara or that he has once more exerted his patriarchal hold over her by marginalizing her as his female sidekick, one whose job is to simply witness and comment on his morally ambiguous behavior.

The Doctor also behaves in an antiheroic manner during "Mummy on the Orient Express," in which he and Clara find themselves facing a mummy that kills people in sixty-six seconds while they are traveling aboard a faithful spaceship recreation of the Orient Express. At one point in the story, the Doctor and a group of experts whose expertise can potentially lead them to capturing the mummy are being held hostage in a research car by the ship's computer, Gus. As they are trying to figure out who will be the mummy's next victim, since the creature preys on people who have medical or psychological disorders, the ship's commanding officer, Captain Quell, has this private conversation with the Doctor:

> Captain Quell: When you said I'd lost the stomach for a fight, I wasn't wounded in battle as such, but my unit was bombed. I was the sole survivor. Not a scratch on me. But post-traumatic stress.... Nightmares. I still can't sleep without pills.
> The Doctor: Which means that you are probably next, which is good to know.
> Captain Quell: Well, not for me.
> The Doctor: Well, of course not for you, because you're going to die. But I mean for us, from a research point of view.
> Captain Quell: You know, for a Doctor, your bedside manner leaves—

His words cut short by the appearance of the mummy, Captain Quell then experiences his final sixty-six seconds of life, but his observations of the approaching creature allow the Doctor and the scientists know that it is not a hologram and can teleport. Afterward, from analyzing Captain Quell's corpse, the Doctor and Perkins, the train's conductor, also learn that the creature, whom they have concluded is a soldier using ancient tech, takes his victims out of phase for sixty-six seconds in order to drain all of their cellular energy. While the Doctor eventually employs this information to stop the mummy-soldier, the question remains as to the morality of his treatment of Captain Quell before his death. Even though one can agree that the Time Lord is being logically blunt with the man regarding his inevitable demise at the hands of the soldier, one can likewise argue that his words toward the man are imbued with a mocking, callous attitude—not the usual characteristic of an altruistic hero.

Concerning this problematic scene, fan reviewer Dorf Johnson writes,

> Whereas Eleven or Ten would have comforted the man in his final 66-seconds, Twelve utilizes the man to learn new information about the creature. Although this comes across as heartless and cruel, it is in fact simply more realistic. There was no way for the Doctor to save the man, so why not use him to save the lives of every other person on board? The Doctor in his twelfth incarnation no longer desires to be seen as the hero by those around him. He is okay with Clara thinking of him as cruel and cowardly if he knows that he is doing the right thing and ultimately saving more lives.

Johnson brings up an interesting point in contending that the Twelfth Doctor rationally exploits the head of security's final sixty-six seconds of life whereas his former two incarnations would have applied a compassionate approach. One could also demarcate this difference along the lines of an older Doctor encoding a more world-weary heroism versus the youthful optimism and kindness evinced by his predecessors. Since Clara now has basically become the younger viewer's voice of compassion for the show by way of contrast to her older mentor-companion, an additional distinction could be proffered to the argument that the two characters epitomize a gender binary of feminine empathy/masculine pragmatism.

In contrast to the potentially patriarchal Twelfth Doctor questioning and/or denying the worth of his heroism, he defines his masculine heroic self through a meta, intertextual encounter with Robin Hood in Series Eight's third episode, "The Robot of Sherwood," which offers a lighter, more playful depiction of the Time Lord. Trying to prove to Clara that Robin Hood, one of her beloved heroes, is not real, the Doctor brings her to Sherwood Forest during the medieval England era in the year 1190, only to immediately discover that Robin of Locksley does indeed exist. Robin, however, since he is a thief, wants to claim the TARDIS as his own, thus provoking the Doctor to defend his time machine by using a spoon in order to duel his younger sword-wielding opponent.

Like Clara in "Deep Breath," "The Robot of Sherwood" directly works toward underscoring the Doctor's older appearance through the character of the younger, dashing Robin, who makes several jokes about the Time Lord's age, which include calling him a "bony rascal," a "gray old man," and a "desiccated man-crone." But the episode is more notable for presenting the Doctor frequently questioning Robin's legitimacy as a living person. However, even after discovering that Robin is not a robot, the Doctor, in one of the episode's final scenes, expresses his lingering doubts as to Robin's very existence. In response, Robin attempts to remind the Doctor that, like him, he was a "man born into wealth and privilege," but eventually rejected that lifestyle in order to help others. During this speech, Robin also subtly references the Doctor's origin story of stealing a TARDIS to "[f]ly among the stars, fighting the good fight," a revelation that makes the Doctor upset at the fact that Clara had revealed his secrets to the man. Nonetheless, this exchange next occurs between the two:

> ROBIN: You are her hero, I think.
> THE DOCTOR: I'm not a hero.
> ROBIN: Well, neither am I. But if we both keep pretending to be. Ha-ha! Perhaps others will be heroes in our name. Perhaps we will both be stories. And may those stories never end.

With this fanciful, postmodern exchange, two iconic masculine British characters both discuss their heroic worth and reaffirm to the *NüWho* viewing audience that they are fictitious constructs. In contrast to the ending of *Red Dwarf: Back to Earth*, where Lister and Rimmer sarcastically relegate their silent viewers to a fictitious status, the Doctor and Robin optimistically appear to be more comfortable with accepting the fact that they embody an ever-growing set of heroic stories, which may inspire heroism in their readers—or viewers.

In addition, despite the Doctor's proclamation to Robin that he is not a hero, he eventually reverses his position on the matter by the final episode of Series Eight, "Death in Heaven," when he declares his heroic worth via this candid speech to Clara, Missy, and Danny in a London graveyard: "I am not a good man. And I'm not a bad man. I am not a hero. I'm definitely not a president. And, no, I'm not an officer. You know what I am? I am an idiot, with a box and a screwdriver, passing through, helping out, learning." With this part of his monologue, the Doctor thereby realizes Robin's definition of him as an individual who is ever involved in the process of living his ongoing narrative to deny or define his (anti)heroic value.

Although the Twelfth Doctor remains pompous and callous at times during Series Eight, he is predominantly encoded as a looser, more relaxed figure throughout the following season. Perhaps to a somewhat embarrassing degree, his newfound love of playing the guitar, wearing (Second-Doctor-like) baggy pants and sonic shades, and exuberantly expressing his emotions to Clara and others encode him as more playful and accessible hero, one written and performed more in the vein of his tenth and eleventh incarnations. Simultaneously, regarding how he realizes Joseph Campbell's heroic monomyth, he ultimately refuses its final ramifications when he refuses to stay with his people, the Gallifreyans, in the concluding Series Nine episode, "Hell Bent." Campbell writes,

> When the hero-quest has been accomplished, through penetration to the source, or through the grace of some male or female, human or animal, personification, the adventurer still must return with his life-transmuting trophy. The full round, the norm of the monomyth, requires that the hero shall now begin the labor of bringing the runes of wisdom, the Golden Fleece, or his sleeping princess, back into the kingdom of humanity, where the boon may redound to the renewing of the community, the nation, the planet, or the ten thousand worlds [193].

Admittedly, the Doctor and all of his former incarnations managed to save Gallifrey in "The Day of the Doctor," the show's fiftieth anniversary celebration, by giving them the "life-transmuting trophy" that is his centuries of accumulated knowledge for how to send them to a pocket dimension where they can safely escape the Daleks' deadly barrage of their planet. By way of contrast, the Twelfth Doctor, in terms of "bringing the runes of wisdom" back to his own people in "Hell Bent," rejects this responsibility.

To better explain, after the Doctor deposes Lord President Rassilon in the episode, the Time Lords believe that he can protect them from their various enemies. However, by abusing his rights as acting Lord President to use an extraction chamber in order to pull Clara out of time before her final heartbeat (which occurred in the previous episode, "Face the Raven"), the Doctor once again rejects his people's plea to lead them and thereby renews his ongoing status as an outsider to Gallifreyan society. On a further encoding level, however, the Doctor, as an alien hero who channels modern older white human male masculinity, cathartically reminds his audience, "the [viewing] kingdom of humanity," that he fights for their fictionalized world by attempting (yet poignantly failing) to find a way to restore his (and, by extension, *their*) "sleeping princess," Clara, to complete life. By the end of "Hell Bent," although he has lost most of his memories of Clara, which can be seen as a mixed blessing, the Doctor has been renewed in many of the audience's eyes as he steps into his TARDIS, finds another phallic representation of his power in the form of a new sonic screwdriver, which is bestowed upon him by the maternal time machine, and dematerializes his vessel as he heads off onto further adventures in time and space.

NüWho 2014–15: A Cyclical Recycling or Reworking of *Classic Who* Themes?

While Series Eight's encoding of the Twelfth Doctor as a significantly older, more irascible incarnation of the heroic Time Lord, reaffirms the show's 1963 roots of presenting an initially unlikeable leading man via the First Doctor, do Coal Hill School teachers Clara Oswald and Danny Pink and their student, Courtney Woods, likewise represent modern analogues of the First Doctor's traveling companions, Barbara Wright, Ian Chesterton, and Susan Foreman? For a theoretical perspective on this question, one can turn to the first serious academic analysis of the long-running BBC SF series: media scholars John Tulloch and Manuel Alvarado's *Doctor Who: The Unfolding Text*,[13] which was published in 1983, the year marking *Doctor Who*'s twentieth anniversary. Within this work, the authors assert that *Classic Who*'s nineteenth season, John Nathan-Turner's second as producer, "re-introduced the 1963 element of Doctor and companions who don't always 'get on with one another,' but—very consciously—for 'character' rather than 'bitchy' reasons" (217). In this passage, the two scholars are referring to William Hartnell's First Doctor, who was encoded as a reluctant hero (or antihero) in the show's first episode, "An Unearthly Child," and who experienced a tense early relationship with Coal Hill School teachers Ian Chesterton and Barbara Wright. Tulloch and Alvarado continue, "Nathan-Turner's new female companions Tegan and Nyssa were a contrasting pair, taking the programme back to its roots when it had two female companions back in 1963. Tegan (like Barbara) was a professional woman, was older than the other female companion, and was 'of her year' (Tegan's 1981/Barbara 1963)" (217).

Significantly, with the transatlantic airing of *NüWho*'s eighth season from August to November 2014 on BBC One and BBC America, showrunner Steven Moffat consciously encoded the opening episodes of the Twelfth Doctor's era to cyclically echo elements that were present in the series' very first season, which aired from November 1963 to September 1964. Like Barbara, companion Clara Oswald similarly now works as a teacher at Coal Hill School. Admittedly, while Barbara often stands her ground against the Doctor, particularly in "The Aztecs," when she tries to ignore his warning that she cannot "rewrite history—not one line," as she tries to put an end to the Aztec's religious practice of human sacrifice, she gradually warms up to this curmudgeonly, mysterious man. Moreover, in various ways, Barbara serves as a surrogate mother figure to her former Coal Hill School student, the Doctor's granddaughter, Susan. Clara, by way of contrast, persistently challenges the Twelfth Doctor's questionable moral code. In a similar fashion to Barbara, however, she wishes to preserve her role as a teacher. Fortunately for Clara, the Twelfth Doctor demonstrates a finer mastery of his somewhat erratic TARDIS than his first incarnation since he can return her to her proper time zone in order to facilitate her desire to regularly teach her English classes and maintain a romantic relationship with Danny.

Comparatively, in Australian air stewardess Tegan Jovanka's case, from her debut in the Fourth Doctor's final tale, "Logopolis" (1981), until her exit from the series in the 1984 Fifth Doctor story "Resurrection of the Daleks," her acerbic characterization only mildly softens as she regularly argues with the Time Lord. Unlike Barbara, who is keen to be returned to a mid–1960s London so she can resume her career as a history teacher, once Tegan makes it back to her own time period in the season nineteen finale, "Time-Flight," she discovers she had been fired from her job. However, since she no longer wishes to be an air stewardess and misses traveling in time and space with the Doctor and Nyssa, she returns as a regular companion in the season twenty opening story, "Arc of Infinity." In comparison to fellow companion, Nyssa, who hails from the planet Traken, and is a good five years younger than her, Tegan functions as a sister-like figure to her alien friend. Furthermore, when comparing her to Clara, one can see that the encoding of this companion's more acerbic personality serves as a blueprint for the Twelfth-Doctor era version of Miss Oswald. In other words, while the "Impossible Girl"[14] iteration of the character who viewers witnessed during the latter episodes of the Eleventh Doctor era had been independent and cautiously flirtatious with the Time Lord, the older Clara of Series Eight, like Tegan before her, often argues with the Doctor. This encoding, in turn, adds a sense of friction occurring between a Doctor and his companion that has been rarely seen in the show since its revival in 2005.

Their Doctor-companion conflict, however, reaches a dramatic crescendo in the episode "Kill the Moon." After traveling to the Moon of 2049 with Clara and Courtney, the Doctor ultimately forces the two, along with Captain Lundvik,[15] to make a choice to either bombard the Moon and the giant embryonic creature inside of it by using the nuclear warheads aimed at its core or to allow the living being to hatch, which forms an ethical dilemma that both reinforces and challenges the assumption that the Time Lord embodies a patriarchal hero. On the one hand, as the lone male in the situation, he possesses patriarchal power in the form of his future knowledge about the Moon and through his immediate technological means to safely dematerialize away from the situation via the TARDIS. On the other hand, one which is more metaphorical (or allegorical) in nature, the Doctor's choice to remove himself from the quotient of what amounts to a "pro-choice" or "pro-life" decision posits him as a progressive, anti-patriarchal character. Regardless, Clara views the Doctor's position as condescending to both herself and humanity, which is demonstrated when they have this exchange concerning his earlier actions inside the TARDIS near the end of the episode after she has decided to let the creature live and successfully hatch from its Moon-egg:

> CLARA: Do you know what? It was ... it was cheap. It was pathetic. No, no, no. It was patronizing. That was you patting us on the back, saying, "You're big enough to go to the shops by yourself now. Go on, toddle along."
> THE DOCTOR: No, that was me allowing you to make a choice about your own future. That was me respecting you.
> CLARA: Oh, my God, really? Was it? Yeah, well, respected is not how I feel.

Despite the Doctor's rationalization of his actions toward Clara as being respectful, her response reveals that she feels as if she has been patronized and marginalized not only as his assistant, who is forced to carry out his plans, but as a member of an inferior, childlike species as well. In addition, though the two are not discussing a broken romantic relationship with one another, their argument reveals that, for Clara, her intimate emotional and trust-layered connection with the Time Lord has been damaged.

A few episodes later, however, "Flatline" offers the intriguing scenario of Clara temporarily assuming the show's heroic lead role while the Doctor is stuck inside the TARDIS, which has been reduced to the size of an object that can fit inside the school teacher's purse. To further emphasize the Doctor's lack of heroic agency, this episode depicts one scene in which he is forced to give her two objects that assist him during his adventures: his psychic paper and sonic screwdriver. Clara subsequently utilizes these objects to convince a group of community workers who have been painting over murals found on some Bristol tunnel walls that she is the only one capable of leading them to safety from the Boneless, two-dimensional aliens who are trying to kill them. Privately, however, she shares this conversation with the Doctor:

> CLARA: I just hope I can keep them all alive.
> THE DOCTOR: Ha. Welcome to my world. So what's next, "Dr. Clara"?

CLARA: Lie to them.
THE DOCTOR: What?
CLARA: Lie to them. Give them hope. Tell them they're all going to be fine. Isn't that what you would do?

In response, the Doctor admits that Clara's strategy does allow him to give people hope when he employs it during his own adventures. While the legitimacy of employing a lie to save others can be debated philosophically to no definitive conclusion, the fact remains that Clara is now becoming more empathetic to this older Doctor's darker heroic code.

Additionally, at the end of the episode, she tells the Doctor that Danny is accepting of her decision to continue traveling with him despite the contrary being true. Regarding her actions, Tom and Lorenzo, two bloggers, write,

> Clara's starting to see the bigger picture and how it's affecting her. The Doctor wasn't even bothered to find out she'd been lying to him. If anything, it was part of the lesson he was trying to teach her about what it means to be him. Rule One: The Doctor Lies. And now she's as good at it as he ever was. But if she's starting to understand and accept the whys of the Doctor, does it mean she should accept the influence he has on her? It's one thing to lie to people in danger in order to save as many as you can. It's another thing to lie to your boyfriend about what you're doing when he's not around.

If Clara is becoming more powerful and effectively brave by learning to act like the Doctor, then does this mean she is aspiring to a masculine heroic paradigm, one which demands that one lies to one's lovers? Working from this scenario, one could conclude that Clara has assimilated the Doctor's more questionable heroic (or antiheroic) traits, which occur when he lies and accepts the sacrifice of the lives of others as a practical means to achieve a victory, in order to become a more successful female hero. Conversely, one could argue that these rather unsavory traits undermine Clara's heroic value as the female companion who questions his ethics and thereby serves as a viewer surrogate counterpoint of identification.

In contrast to these two viewpoints, one could make the more progressive argument that Clara's act of subscribing to the utilitarian tenants of the well-traveled heroic Time Lord supersedes any binary demarcations of gender. Furthermore, in her relationship with Danny, she exerts herself as the more dominant mate, denying him the opportunity to curtail her adventures with the Doctor. In this case, Series Eight has laid the encoding foundation for future *Doctor Who* episodes that may continue to blur the line between the show's traditional formula of a troubled heroic male Doctor and his moralistic female companion who wishes to marry a dependable man, perhaps leading to stories in which these boundaries will be blurred and interchanged between future gendered and characterized iterations of this traveling duo.

Although this chapter's discussion has been focused upon Clara's encoding in Series Eight, one must bring up the end of her story arc on *NüWho* in Series Nine's "Face the Raven" and "Hell Bent." In the former episode, she recklessly sacrifices her life to save her friend Rigsy[16] from a Quantum Shade that takes her life instead. Ironically, she did not have to die as the immortal Ashildr, who made a deal with the Quantum Shade, could have broken its chronolock on Rigsy. Sarah Dollard, the writer of the episode, however, was illustrating the culmination of Clara's Series Nine story arc, which involved the theme of her becoming like a version of the Doctor, albeit a more reckless and ultimately mortal version.

With "Hell Bent," however, Steven Moffat somewhat reverses this heroically sacrificial discourse by presenting a Clara who has been extracted out of time by the Doctor, courtesy of Gallifreyan technology, from a moment between her final heartbeats. Essentially immortal, but also strangely unalive since she possesses no heartbeat or pulse, this version of Clara, along with her "companion" Ashildr, now travels the universe in an appropriated TARDIS. Thus, in a manner similar to the First Doctor at the beginning of "An Unearthly Child," they are on the run from his people, all the while traveling the totality of time and space performing heroic deeds. Remarkably, moreover, they represent a completely feminized iteration of travelers and time machine—a progressive encoding step on Moffat's part, one that may signal future versions of *Doctor Who*.

In addition to one comparing Clara to Barbara and Tegan, the parallels existing between Coal Hill School students Susan Foreman and fifteen-year-old Courtney Woods can be examined. Returning to Tulloch and Alvarado, they write that Susan and Nyssa were added to *Classic Who* so that children viewers could identify with them (217). They also point out, "Nyssa and Susan were 'SF' companions, marked by special powers. Just as Susan's telepathy and extra-sensory perception enabled her mind to become sensitised by psychic energy in 'The Sensorites' (1964), so too Nyssa could act as a medium between the Doctor and the [X]eraphin in 'Time-Flight' (1982) because her special sensory perception was catalysed by psychic energy" (217–18). Although Courtney does not serve as a regular companion for the Twelfth Doctor, she does assist him in "The Caretaker" and travels to the future Earth and Moon with him and Clara in "Kill the Moon." From this perspective, she functions in a semi-companion capacity. In stark contrast to Susan and Nyssa, however, she does not possess any telepathic or psychic abilities, nor does she demonstrate a genius-level intellect in regard to science or mathematics.

Commenting on Courtney's characterization in "Kill the Moon," an unnamed online reviewer posting on his or her fan blog *TARDIS Archives*, writes, "[S]he is a realistic character; she doesn't immediately accept things that a normal person wouldn't in real life, ... she screams when she sees a dead body, and she does the most realistic thing I can think [of]; when finding herself being attacked by creatures on the moon, she says she wants to go back; she almost lost her life, and like most 15 year olds, she would want to be safe again" ("Kill"). Quite ordinary in many ways, Courtney has been encoded by Moffat and his writing collaborators as a street-level black British teenager.[17] Much like the Seventh Doctor's companion Ace, Courtney represents an opinionated, anti-authoritarian London youth, one whose energy level and honesty is valued by the Doctor. At the same time, if a longtime *Doctor Who* viewer is indeed expected by Moffat and company to regard Courtney as a character who parallels Susan, one can reasonably wonder why she has not yet become a regular traveling companion for the Doctor.

Danny Pink: A Martyred Heroic Alternative to the Doctor?

When one compares Danny Pink to Ian Chesterton, one can agree that, in their own ways, they function as the Doctor's muscle. The difference in either of these characters fulfilling this relatively vital role for season one of *Classic Who* and the eighth series of *NüWho* rests on how they exist in proximity to the headstrong Time Lord. With Ian, he has no choice but to travel with the First Doctor and live in the TARDIS until he and Barbara finally make it back to their own time and space—mid–1960s London. Danny, conversely, even when given the opportunity to take a trip in the TARDIS at the end of "The Caretaker," politely refuses the Doctor's offer. Unlike Ian, he can retain his social identity and subsequent capital as a popular Coal Hill School teacher and is not forced to repeatedly take part in the Doctor's adventures via the role of a reluctant male sidekick. Ian, however, during the course of his journey with the First Doctor, often engages in more physical adventures than his older traveling companion. For example, in "The Aztecs," he fights and defeats Ixta, an Aztec warrior, and, in "The Romans," he holds his own in a forced sword fight with Delos, his fellow Roman slave.

On an encoding level, the character, played by William Russell, was written to engage in the type of visceral-inducing fisticuffs in which neither William Hartnell nor his character could realistically take part. By way of comparison, Danny also displays a caliber of extraordinary physicality not regularly evinced so far in the show by Peter Capaldi.[18] In other words, while the Twelfth Doctor has dynamically dueled Robin Hood above a forest river with only a spoon in "The Robot of Sherwood," Danny, in "The Caretaker," distracts the Skovox Blitzer, a killing machine from an unnamed future war, when he performs an Olympic-level flip over the automaton's head, so the Doctor, in turn, can defeat it. Nevertheless, in terms of both Danny and Ian's respective fates on *Classic* and *NüWho*, the latter is allowed to resume his existence as a school teacher, along with Barbara, at the end of the 1965 serial "The Chase." The former, conversely, loses his mortal life in "Dark Water," when he is accidently struck by a car while crossing the street as he is talking to Clara, who had distracted him by professing her love to him. Then, later, in "Death in Heaven," Danny experiences a second death as he sacrifices his posthuman body as a still autonomous Cyberman in order to destroy Missy's Cybermen-producing rain clouds.

One can correspondingly compare Danny to Ninth and Tenth Doctor semi-companion Mickey Smith in order to demonstrate how these two black British characters are both in love with white women, Clara and Rose Tyler, who prefer traveling with the itinerant Time Lord rather than committing themselves completely to their relationships with these men. When it comes to their individual heroic journeys, however, Danny, a veteran soldier, is already ready-built as a hero whereas Mickey is initially depicted as a coward in *NüWho*'s opening episode, "Rose"—one who is terrified of even traveling with the Doctor in the TARDIS. Although he evolves into a hero in Series Two, Mickey is written out of the series as he remains behind on a parallel Earth to take care of his grandmother.[19] In this case, Mickey, like Danny, is encoded as a caregiver who places the demands of his conscience over his desire to romp around all of time and space. Put another way, both Danny and Mickey represent moralistic yet domesticated characters. At the same time, unlike Mickey, who wishes to assimilate himself according to the Doctor's criteria for a selfless hero, Danny does not feel the need to heroically prove himself by transgressing the confines of his time, 2014, and his space, London, or more precisely, Coal Hill School.

When Danny meets the Doctor in "The Caretaker," however, even his ordinary status as a mathematics teacher is not accepted by the Time Lord, who has temporarily assumed the guise of Coal Hill School's caretaker during the episode. In one scene, the Doctor is working on an electrical box when Adrian, a teacher at the school, introduces Danny to him, saying that he is a former sergeant, which somehow leads the Doctor to assume that the man simply teaches physical education. Danny then corrects the Doctor's mistake, telling the Time Lord he is a mathematics teacher, which leads them into this conversation:

> THE DOCTOR: How does that work? What if the kids have questions?
> DANNY: About what?
> THE DOCTOR: Maths.
> DANNY: I answer them. I'm a maths teacher.

At this point, the Doctor probably should just accept the veracity of Danny's statement. However, since the Twelfth Doctor has been constantly encoded this season as a single-minded character whose myopic mindset leads him to missing the obvious, he responds to Danny's answer in this manner:

> THE DOCTOR: But he said you were a soldier.
> DANNY: Yeah. I was a soldier. Now I'm a maths teacher.
> THE DOCTOR: But what about all the PE?
> DANNY: I don't teach PE. I'm not a PE teacher.
> THE DOCTOR: Sorry, that seems very unlikely.

Shortly afterwards, the Doctor still tells Danny to get to his PE class, saying, "[Y]ou'd better run along, sergeant. That ball isn't going to kick itself? Is it?" and Danny reminds him that he is a mathematics teacher. The Doctor claims, "Nope, sorry. No, I can't retain that. I've tried. It's just not going in." Although one can claim that the Doctor is behaving like an absent-minded genius, most fans who are aware of the Time Lord's vast memory and intelligence would decode this scene as emblematic of the his twelfth incarnation's insensitive nature, which could potentially be viewed as racist. In *Doctor Who Magazine*, "The Caretaker" reviewer Graham Kibble-White brings up this sensitive issue:

> Am I the only one who felt uncomfortable with the Time Lord failing to comprehend that Danny Pink could possibly teach maths? The gag is, because of Danny's military background, the Doctor presumes he's only good for PE. That's a reductive enough joke as it is, but the appearance is even worse. Here's an educated white man telling an educated black man, "That ball isn't going to kick itself." Please, no [67–68].

Kibble-White, a *Doctor Who* fan turned professional reviewer, brings up an interesting point regarding the racial encoding of "The Caretaker." Although Series Eight encodes Danny as a younger, educated, talented mathematics teacher, it perplexingly presents an older-appearing white

Doctor who cannot understand that this black British man could possibly teach mathematics. Even though one of the running themes of this series is that the Doctor does not feel comfortable around soldiers, when one considers that both *Classic* and *NüWho* have often depicted its main character as a man who demonstrates a genius intellect and a sensitivity to all races, human or alien, this mindset is doubly problematic.

At the same time, in trying to comprehend the Doctor's trouble with understanding Danny's capability as a mathematics teacher, one can bring up a similar scene occurring in the *Classic Who* story "Mawdryn Undead." During part two of the tale, after the Fifth Doctor has been reunited with his old UNIT colleague, the retired Brigadier Alistair Gordon Lethbridge-Stewart, he is surprised to learn that the former soldier is now teaching mathematics at a boy's preparatory school. In response, the Brigadier quips, "Oh, I know how many beans make five, Doctor. You don't have to be a Time Lord to cope with A-level maths." However, the Doctor accepts this explanation without further questioning his friend's qualifications for teaching the subject.

In comparing the Fifth Doctor's earned respect for the Brigadier as a mathematics teacher to the Twelfth's disdain for Danny holding the same educational role, perhaps this distinction could be qualified by arguing that the Time Lord discriminates against Danny's qualifications as a teacher due to his social class. On this note, Rick Aragon, a fan blogger, points out,

> [Danny's] basically an orphan with few if any prospects. If the set-up in the UK is the same as in the States, the military provides a way for lower-to-lower-middle-class men and women to advance in society and get an education. Certainly in the U.S. joining the armed services provides structure in people's lives, a chance to go outside their hometowns, and after their tour, a way to get an education and other benefits. The military, therefore, appears to be a way for Danny to get away from the boys home and get the tools to be a math teacher.

Interestingly, Aragon is applying his American vision of an upwardly mobile classed social system via military service to its British counterpart. If one factors Danny's race into this equation, the many complex historical and cultural differences occurring between the United States and England will obviously manifest concerning black citizens joining respective branches of either nation's military forces. However, despite these differences, one can agree that both nations indeed offer socially disadvantaged citizens a positive opportunity to overcome their economic situations by receiving a government-funded education after serving in the military. Regrettably, the Twelfth Doctor seems to be ignorant of this fact as he repeatedly cannot accept Danny's role as a mathematics teacher. From a decoding perspective, this character flaw could be viewed as a projection of encoding perspectives on the British military establishment that are shared by the Series Eight writers.

With the episode "In the Forest of the Night," moreover, Danny is encoded as a reliable, heroic protector of his eighth year gifted students, who have been separated from their homes and families due to the inexplicable fact that a forest has grown up over London (and around the world) virtually overnight. At one point in the episode, Clara tells the Doctor that he should leave Earth in his TARDIS to save himself in case the growing trees have malevolent intentions for humanity, which thereby prompts this exchange:

> THE DOCTOR: We're all going. We're taking the kids.
> CLARA: Taking them where? What are you going to do with them? Leave them on an asteroid? Find a space academy for the gifted and talented? They just want their mum and dads, and they're never gonna stop wanting them.
> THE DOCTOR: I can save you and Danny.
> CLARA: Danny Pink will never leave those kids so long as he is breathing.

Freed from the normal constraints of time and space thanks to his TARDIS and his itinerant life style, the Doctor does not have to subject himself to any societal, or, in the case of this episode, environmental woes affecting humanity. Likewise, he possesses the power to bestow this survival escape-clause "gift" upon Clara, Danny, and the Coal Hill School children. However, as his conversation with Clara demonstrates, the Doctor's survivalist value system is meaningless to children who are accustomed to the heteronormative rearing and protection granted to them by their parents. Danny, consequently, functions as their surrogate parent in this situation, and it is this protective mindset that ensures Clara's attraction to him. As a result, she chooses Danny as a representative of heteronormative values—and as a potential mate for child rearing—over the Doctor, who subscribes to a queered version of time.

While some *NüWho* fans enjoy Clara's romance with Danny, others decode the relationship as rather forced and insincere. On this note, in a fan review of "In the Forest of the Night," Undie Girl asserts, "They still seem to be pushing this strange love triangle angle between the Doctor, Clara and Danny Pink, but I'm just trying to ignore that." Undie Girl is correct in summarizing the emotional dynamics occurring amongst the Doctor, Clara, and Danny as a "strange love triangle" since the Time Lord and his companion share a deeply platonic relationship—or "mental affair"—while Clara simultaneously experiences a romantic and physical connection with Danny. Undie Girl continues,

> Danny Pink is still terribly disappointing, particularly the way that his time as a soldier seems to be his only defining characteristic. His answer for everything is

that he was a soldier once and now he knows things that Clara doesn't, which makes him come across as condescending. It seems to suggest that he is more mature than Clara because he has moved beyond the desire for adventure, and it's making me wonder what the hell she sees in him.

For Undie Girl, Danny is not heeding the heroic call to action that she feels is necessary in defining a male companion/love interest in *NüWho*. Although Danny ultimately never travels with the Doctor in the TARDIS during Series Eight, he does achieve a sense of heroic redemption in the season's two-part finale, "Dark Water" and "Death in Heaven." Offering a stark contrast to the sinthomosexual antiheroes presented in chapter five, *Torchwood*'s Captain Jack Harkness and convicted child murderer Oswald Danes, Danny Pink exemplifies a hero who truly redeems himself for causing the death of a child. Regarding this character development for Danny, in a "Dark Water" flashback sequence set in Afghanistan when the man was serving as a soldier, viewers learn that he killed a young boy when he stormed into a potential insurgent's home, shooting first before looking at its occupants. In the present, after he had been accidently killed when crossing a street while talking to Clara, Danny finds himself in the Nethersphere, an afterlife which appears to be a modern city whose architecture wraps around in many dimensions. During his time in the Nethersphere, he is reunited with the boy whom he killed, and the child is naturally uncomfortable around his killer. However, in the following episode, "Death in Heaven," when Danny is presented with the option of returning to Earth with his body restored, he instead gives this opportunity to the boy, telling Clara he is sorry and that she needs to help reunite the resurrected child with his family in Afghanistan.

Though Danny's sacrifice is quite heroic, his death also separates him from another domesticated BBC SF television hero—*Torchwood*'s Rhys Williams. While the two characters respectively experience storylines in which their lovers, Gwen and Clara, lead more dangerous lifestyles with Captain Jack and the Doctor, Rhys, unlike Danny, gets to live and marry his woman. Like Martha Jones, whose passion for the Tenth Doctor is never consummated as he rejects her attraction to him, and, in a similar fashion to *Red Dwarf*'s Dave Lister, who is repeatedly separated from Kristine Kochanski, Danny is denied romantic happiness. As a result, Danny Pink has joined the increasingly troubled ranks of the BBC black SF hero who fails to find lasting emotional satisfaction or companionship with his or her white love interest.

More importantly, while Missy's resurrected-humans-as-Cybermen obviously shroud all indicators of race as the formerly human body is encased in a sexless, metallic shell that is identical to all of the other cyborgs, questions remain as to whether or not "Dark Water" attempts to act as an erasure of Danny's black skin. Case in point: within the Nethersphere, where Danny's consciousness awakens after he dies, Seb, a white bureaucrat[20] ostensibly working for the 3W Institute, reunites him with the boy he killed in Afghanistan years earlier when he was a soldier. Though Seb is attempting to use both this situation and Danny's grief at being unable to touch Clara in the physical plane to persuade the former soldier to delete his emotions, so he no longer has to feel any pain, in reality, his true intention is to have the man willingly submit to the process of having his mind "upgraded" to the emotionless state necessary for Missy's army of Cybermen. Moreover, while the hundreds of deceased minds who had accepted Seb's offer most likely have originated from multiple races, no one other than Danny has been depicted onscreen in the episode as accepting this deal to purge one's emotions. This fact thus can create the televised impression in "Dark Water" that an imperialistic white individual, Seb, working under another white woman, Missy, is attempting to cybernetically colonize darker skinned bodies—Danny and the Afghanistan boy.

By the following episode, "Death in Heaven," Danny has rejected Seb's offer, but he still later wants Clara to turn on his emotion inhibitor after he has awoken in his new Cyberman body. Even after the Doctor carries out Danny's wish for the pragmatic purpose of linking him into the Cybermen hive mind, so he can learn about Missy's plan for them, Danny does not act like an emotionless automaton as he protects Clara instead of harming her. His heroic choice could lead to the assessment that one of the ostensibly uplifting themes encoded in "Dark Water" and "Death in Heaven" is that "love conquers all," even when an individual such as Danny has been transformed into a potential cybernetic killing machine. The more troubling undertone of this romantic sentiment, however, may be that a black body has been sacrificed to ensure the Doctor's more optimistic sentiments concerning humanity. Unlike fellow black British *NüWho* character, Mickey Smith, who is seen as having married Martha Jones in the conclusion of the Tenth Doctor's final episode, "The End of the Time: Part Two," Danny is definitely not given a happily-ever-after ending with Clara. Even more problematic is the fact that Danny was trying to put his military past behind him, yet one of his final actions in what remains of his organic body is to function as a de facto sergeant once again as he commands his fellow undead Cybermen army to fly into and destroy Missy's deadly rain clouds, which are positioned across Earth's upper atmosphere as part of her plan to convert all of humanity into Cybermen.

In other words, Danny does not achieve his victory over the enemy by cleverly applying any of his mathematical skills—as frequently exemplified by many incarnations of the Doctor or such past *Classic Who* companions as Zoe, Romana, Adric, or Nyssa—but by falling back upon his regimented military training in order to bark orders to subordinate soldiers as he tells the undead Cybermen, "Attention! This is not a good day! This is Earth's darkest hour! And look at you miserable lot! We are the fallen, but today we shall rise! The army of the dead will save the land of the living! This is not the order of a general, nor the whim of a lunatic. This is a promise—the promise of a soldier!" In reaction to this scene, one can view Danny's death as a resurrected Cyberman from dual directions. On a positive note, he has both retained his humanity by resisting Missy's programming and protected his species by halting their mass cybernization. However, when Danny's situation is viewed more critically, one can assert that, in his cybernetic post-life existence, he has been marginalized in his reduction by both Missy and the Doctor to the role of a soldier. In other words, it is neither Danny's education nor his mathematical knowledge that assures his saving of the entire world, but his regimented ability to act like a commanding army sergeant in order to lead his fellow converted Cybermen to explode in the Earth's upper atmosphere.

The Malevolent Missy: A Soul Mate for the Doctor?

When she first appears at the end of "Deep Breath," Missy, who will not reveal herself to be the Master until Series Eight's penultimate episode, "Dark Water," is dressed in a Mary Poppins–like Victorian outfit. She tells the Half-Face Man, whose soul she has pulled into the Nethersphere, that the Doctor is her "boyfriend" and that he loves her. Additionally, she comments, "I do like his new accent ... think I might keep it," in reference to the Twelfth Doctor's (i.e., Capaldi's) Scottish accent. Thus, in both a binaried gendering and via a shared accent, the formerly male Master now complements the Doctor in a romantic, though not necessarily heteronormative, sense. Commenting upon her interpretation of Missy, actress Michelle Gomez believes, "[T]he dynamic has changed hugely, just for the fact that the Master was once a man, and now ... what you've got is a sort of suggestion—or a question—of, what has been their history? Was there a romance there?"(17). She likewise asks, "What do they mean to each other? Who is she to him? The audience's imagination is encouraged to go with that" (17).

Gomez's conception of the Doctor and the Master potentially having a romantic affair in the past brings up an interesting point. Although even the Twelfth Doctor refers to Missy and himself as once being friends when they were "boys" in "Death in Heaven," one could add a deeper, more sexual reading to their relationship in light of Missy's attraction to her old friend.

At the same time, can one reasonably label their theoretical romance as strictly homosexual? This form of demarcation, after all, is perhaps best applicable to human society and its incessant need to label people according to their sexual orientations. However, Gallifreyans, as revealed in the *NüWho* Series Six episode, "The Doctor's Wife," possess the ability to switch gender when they regenerate. Equally, while one could claim that Missy either provides a transsexual version of the male Master or has initiated a form of drag by regenerating into a female form, these terms may ultimately prove to be too limiting when it comes to understanding such a complex character.

Simultaneously, one cannot simply classify Missy as a queered character. In a comparable manner to *Blake's 7*'s Servalan as encoded by Jacqueline Pearce, Gomez's female incarnation of the Master encodes a form of gender performance á la Judith Butler as well as the usage of drag as encoded by male actor Mackenzie Crook's interpretation of Servalan in *Blake's Junction 7*. By taking the latter example into consideration, one can assert that Missy is still in the process of learning to embody feminine characteristics. At the same time, Crook is playing a female character in *Blake's Junction 7*, and, in no point during that parody, do any of the other characters state or hint that Servalan is, in fact, a man in drag. Missy, conversely, embodies a female version of a character who had been a man for all of her previous incarnations in both *Classic* and *NüWho*. Her femininity, as a consequence, is much more complicated, as biologically she is now a woman, but, psychologically, she retains all of her memories of being born male and living as a man for the majority of her centuries-long existence. The concept of drag, nonetheless, can offer some insight into the process of identity-shaping Missy is practicing via her appearances in Series Eight. During her captivity aboard Boat One, UNIT's presidential airplane, in "Death in Heaven," Missy shares this dark exchange with Osgood, a UNIT scientist:

> MISSY: I'm going to kill you in a minute. I'm not even kidding. You're going to be as dead as a fish on a slab any second now, all floppy and making smells. But don't tell the boys. This is our secret girl plan.
> OSGOOD: Why would you bother killing me? I'm not even important.
> MISSY: Oh, silly! Why does one pop a balloon? Because you're pretty. You should have a bit more confidence in yourself.

In order to demonstrate to Osgood that her hands are indeed free of the handcuffs, Missy takes out her lipstick and applies some to her lips as she points out that the handcuffs in Osgood's pocket were the ones formerly shackling her. At this moment, Missy's action with the lipstick is encoded with both a sinister comedic meaning and a form of gender parody. However, within the next few moments of the scene, she carries out her promise to kill Osgood, vaporizing her with her handheld multipurpose device. On the encoding of this scene, Moffat claims it was designed to make fans truly comprehend the depths of Missy's evil, but, on a decoding level, it actually ended up angering female viewers who had been identifying with the fan-surrogate character.[21] Nonetheless, the scene does remind viewers that Missy, despite her status as the Master regendered as a woman, feels no solidarity with any of the other female characters. This fact, furthermore, is ironically signaled to Osgood when Missy both claims to her that they are sharing a "secret girl plan" (which, in actuality, is the twisted Time Lord's intention to murder the UNIT scientist) and when she tells the young woman she is pretty and to have more confidence in a self that she plans on cruelly, and immediately, destroying. Accordingly, Missy's dialogue parodies and malignantly subverts the type of intimate conversations Moffat may believe women have with one another when they are not in the company of a man.

In *Bodies that Matter*, Butler shares these thoughts concerning gender performativity and drag, which one can extend to Missy:

> How, if at all, is the notion of discursive resignification linked to the notion of gender parody or impersonation? First, what is meant by understanding gender as an impersonation? Does this mean that one puts on a mask or persona, that there is a "one" who precedes that "putting on," who is something other than its gender from the start? Or does this miming, this impersonation precede and form the "one," operating as its formative precondition rather than its dispensable artifice? [230].

By applying Butler's theories on gender as an impersonation to Missy, one can argue that this female regeneration of the Master now forms the "one" from which her new persona enacts her ongoing gender performance. In other words, via her new body, Missy's heterosexual desire for the Doctor and her miming of feminine characteristics work as a formative precondition that overwrites and shades her past feelings for the heroic Time Lord, which, in her male form, the Master, may have just been platonic, not romantic and/or sexual in nature. Furthermore, in an equal manner to Missy's past incarnations as the Master, her present incarnation is yet another mask or persona that reflects and shapes her ongoing, evolving televised gender performance on *Doctor Who*.

One fan-generated reading of the Doctor-Missy dynamic can be found in Legs Nose Robinson's *YouTube* video "Hey Missy." In "Dark Water," while being physically restrained by UNIT on Boat One, Missy playfully sings a few lyrics from Toni Basil's 1982 pop hit, "Mickey." Even though Basil's original song, which is actually an adaptation of the 1979 song "Kitty,"[22] expresses admiration for a man, Mickey, with the catchy hook, "Oh, Mickey, you're so fine. You're so fine, you blow my mind," the song likewise states the narrator-singer's frustration with Mickey, who flirts with the woman but never takes her home for the night, despite his promises. While Basil's version of the song is about a female longing for an unattainable man, Legs Nose Robinson's fan video rewrites the hook lyrics to read, "Oh, Missy, you're so fine. You're so fine, you blew our minds. Hey, Missy!" in reference to Michelle Gomez's performance as the female Master. The song also reverses the romantic power dynamics of Basil's "Mickey" since the singer, although still a female, is telling Missy that she will not be able to successfully seduce the Doctor. For instance, Legs Nose Robinson sings,

> Oh, Missy,
> what a pity
> you don't understand
> you're messin' with the Doctor,
> not playin' with your friend.

With these lyrics, Legs Nose Robinson demonstrates a fan-knowledge of the long-term Master-Doctor dynamic, since the two were childhood friends and attended the Gallifreyan Time Lord Academy together, but, at one point, became mortal enemies.

Nonetheless, as demonstrated in the *Classic Who* story "Colony in Space," when the Master offers the Third Doctor the opportunity to rule the universe with him via the Doomsday Weapon, and, in the *NüWho* episode "The End of Time: Part Two," as the so-called villain sacrifices himself to send the Time Lords back into the Time War so that the Tenth Doctor can escape their grasp, the Master, at times, tries to reignite their former friendship. However, in Missy's female incarnation of the Master, this former apparently platonic desire has become complicated with her newfound romantic feelings for the Doctor. On this note, in another part of "Hey Missy," Legs Nose Robinson, in reference to Missy's actions in "Death in Heaven" of giving the Doctor an army of Cybermen to do with as he pleases, sings,

> Oh, Missy,
> what a pity
> you don't seem to see

he doesn't want an army.
He just wants you to leave.

Like "Death in Heaven," in which the Doctor is not only shocked by Missy's conflicted attempt to both kill and love him but wishes for her to simply leave him alone, Legs Nose Robinson's lyrics add a playful, pop-music shading to the Time Lord's outright rejection of his female nemesis' emotionally motivated gift of cyborg warriors.

For an alternate, more romanticized fan decoding of the Doctor-Missy coupling, one can refer to the short story "Locked in Orbit," in which author yonderdarling presents the Twelfth Doctor and Missy as a married couple, who, though enemies, recognize their oppositional roles as hero and villain. The story itself flashes back to their early days on Gallifrey before they answered to the monikers "Doctor" and "Master" and to various moments spanning their past and future regenerations. During one moment in the narrative, the Doctor encounters Missy in the remnants of the Nesputian palace after she has destroyed their species simply because she hated them: "She stands, takes two steps, and kisses him, because there's no one else left alive on this planet, and they're the only two who'll ever know, and he tastes like saltwater and smoke and feels like reluctance. He stands and lets her, and when she finishes, to his credit, he only takes one stuttering step back." In a similar fashion to the Twelfth Doctor's encoding in "Dark Water," when he resists Missy's kissing of him inside the 3W Institute building (in actuality, the interior of St. Paul's Cathedral), he once more feels a bit of revulsion when receiving her kiss. However, yonderdarling also decodes the Doctor's actions in "Dark Water" as a form of reluctant performance for Clara, who had witnessed the kiss. Alone with Missy in the alternate reality of this fan fiction piece, this vision of the Doctor can come to terms with his conflicted feelings for his archenemy.

[Y]onderdarling continues her tale with the Doctor and Missy sharing this conversation:

"I wish you wouldn't do this."
"I know."
"I don't like being touched."
"I know." She kisses him again, watches the discomfort growing on his features, tension radiating through his body. "I know. But I'm the last. It's my right."

Although both in this passage and in several episodes of Series Eight ("Deep Breath," "Dark Water," and "Death in Heaven"), the Doctor vocalizes his disdain for being hugged and/or kissed, the underlying motivation for this viewpoint could be to say that the Time Lord fears physical intimacy.

But, as yonderdarling discusses in this piece, the Doctor's personal feelings may not count when one considers that, in the absence of Gallifrey ever returning to normal space at this point in time, he and Missy represent the last opposite members of their race. As a result, the biological imperatives of his species' survival may have posited the Doctor as not only an itinerant hero but a reproductive one as well. Put another way, Missy may represent a firm counterpoint to the Doctor. In another passage found in "Locked in Orbit," yonderdarling defines the two characters via a reflection on their masculine/heroic and feminine/villainous divide: "Noninterference is (was) the way of the Time Lords, and so they chose interference. Exploration and interaction, domination and mastery of all. Intense love and intense control. She and the Doctor were defined in opposition to Time Lords, and she is defined as the Doctor's darker binary." While this passage could be written off as yonderdarling's decoded fan-fantasy influenced poetic perception of the Doctor-Missy onscreen relationship, her words could very well serve as an articulation of Steven Moffat's unconscious (or otherwise) intention to rewrite the Master as a twisted romantic interest for the Doctor in the form of Missy.

Conversely, in an apparent response to fan fantasies or criticisms[23] regarding a Doctor-Missy romance, Moffat addresses—or, in some ways, preempts—the issue with the Series Nine opening episode, "The Magician's Apprentice." While Clara is meeting with Missy in an open-air café, surrounded by UNIT soldiers who have their guns poised on the villainous Time Lord, they share these words concerning the missing Doctor:

> CLARA: He's not your friend. You keep trying to kill him.
> MISSY: He keeps trying to kill me. It's sort of our texting. We've been at it for ages.
> CLARA: Mmm, must be love.
> MISSY: Oh, don't be disgusting. We're Time Lords, not animals. Try, nano-brain, to rise above the reproductive frenzy of your noisy little food chain and contemplate friendship. A friendship older than your civilization and infinitely more complex.

Through this exchange, Moffat is reinforcing his encoding of a more traditional Doctor-Master relationship, where the two, like the Third Doctor-Master "frenemy" dynamic that occurs during the Jon Pertwee era of *Classic Who*, are engaged in an ongoing game of wits and on-off again alliances. At the same time, one can conclude this chapter with the lingering thought that perhaps Moffat is trying to destabilize *NüWho* fans lasciviously decoding the ostensibly heterosexually heroic Time Lord and his problematic regendered archnemesis as potentially engaging in a romance that could certainly be imbued with a queer subtext. Paradoxically, then, Missy may be the character encoded in Series Eight and Nine who has proven to be the most dynamic yet difficult in regard to showing the possibilities of a Time Lord embracing fluidic gender roles. In short, for *NüWho* fans and scholars alike, she is the character to watch for a televised foreshadowing of the show's future take on its traditionally male heroic lead.

Conclusion: Encoders and Decoders Shaping the Destinies of Four Cult SF TV Sagas

Throughout my analysis of *Doctor Who*, *Blake's 7*, *Red Dwarf*, and *Torchwood* in this book, one constant has been present—time. In an encoded narrative sense, all of these shows deal with this paradoxically literal and philosophical concept to some extent. With *Doctor Who*, the show presents the ultimate treatise on time in its fifty-three-year-old, ongoing televised tale of a virtually immortal alien who performs heroic deeds via traversing the temporal bounds of all known (and elsewhere) space and multiple dimensions. In *Blake's 7*'s case, a dark future for this planet and its potential intergalactic government has been envisioned with the concept of the totalitarian Federation. Yet time affords hope for Blake and his freedom-fighting compatriots as their valiant efforts remind viewers that it is never too late—either "now" or in the future—to stand up against corrupt governments. A good three million years onward from *Blake's 7*'s timeline, *Red Dwarf* and its posthuman representations of flawed male characters equally cultivate the theme that heroism can still occur in the future—even when virtually all of humanity has become extinct. Then there exists *Torchwood*, which is ostensibly set in the present but, like *Doctor Who*, encodes a masculine hero—Captain Jack Harkness—who is from the future yet has lived in the past many times, bending the temporal confines of reality as he perpetually seeks to refine his heroic identity.

Time is also ever present in an always-evolving decoding sense as the four fan cultures discussed in this work continue to build upon their DIY cultural productions that celebrate, criticize, and recreate their televised objects of affection. They are, more importantly, quite powerful to the extent that their views contributed to the cancellation of *Classic Who* and led Doug Naylor to continually adjust his formula for *Red Dwarf* until he finally reencoded a show that was close in tone to the original few seasons of the series. In this conclusion, I will likewise discuss how fan arguments are currently shaping *NüWho* and could contribute to how potential future series of *Torchwood* are encoded. On the one hand, the near future comprising the next few years of BBC SF shows can be reasonably extrapolated from current media events. On the other hand, the act of attempting to predict how these shows will evolve or flounder in ten—or even five—years, especially in relation to their respective fandoms' expectations and demands for conservative or innovative variables of gendered heroism, is purely academic. Ironically, then, time becomes pure theory—just as speculative as the possible futures projected by *Doctor Who*, *Blake's 7* and *Red Dwarf*.

Unlike *Blake's 7*, *Torchwood*, or *NüWho*, perhaps *Red Dwarf* is the one show presented in this book that has the least chance of reinventing its masculine heroic quest. As proven by the show's history, *Red Dwarf* fans are resistant to the series adding regular humanoid cast members to the Dwarfer crew. Furthermore, with the critical and financial success of *Red Dwarf X*, which has led to Dave commissioning both an eleventh and twelfth series of the long-running show, the audience has confirmed that they will overwhelmingly support a version of the series that preserves its original encoding roots, in which all-male heroes travel in deep space and occasionally encounter female characters. While one could imagine a future reboot of the series that, like the *Red Dwarf* episode "Parallel Universe," regenders the Dwarfers as females, this possibility is purely hypothetical as neither the media nor the show's fans have vocally called for such a progressive reinterpretation of the show. However, instead of viewing *Red Dwarf* fandom's desire for Naylor and the show's cast to respectively write and perform storylines that preserve a patriarchal mindset of men in space, one can view this shared desire as presenting the more positive features circulating in the Continuum of Nostalgic Continuity. In other words, yes, this fandom demands a show that presents four representations of masculinity to share bumbling adventures in space, but they are also fiercely supportive of the continuation of Dave Lister's last-human quest to find Earth. As chapter four's discussion has demonstrated, the flawed masculinities encoded in the show—and heartily decoded by its fans—offer a more identifiable form of heroism than the more macho forms of the SF hero that are found in North American cinema and television.

At the same time, *Red Dwarf*, in regard to encoding a black British male heroic lead is literally decades ahead of *Doctor Who* doing likewise in terms of casting a nonwhite actor in the titular role. Equally, the lack of a considerable social media outcry for a minority actor to play the Doctor could very well represent a BBC SF viewing audience that is satisfyingly accustomed to seeing Dave Lister as a leading hero. In the *Star Trek* universe, moreover, Commander (later Captain) Benjamin Sisko of the spin-off series *Star Trek: Deep Space Nine* (1993–98) has similarly provided a strong leading black actor in a prominent heroic SF role. Perhaps, then, the examples of Dave Lister and Benjamin Sisko, who are still relatively recent encodings of heroic leads, remain in the SF audience's consciousness when they are searching for more innovative embodiments of the Doctor.

Torchwood's Captain Jack can likewise be added to the list of progressive alternative encoding options for the Doctor with his omnisexual lifestyle. However, as much as fans celebrate Jack's modern vision of human sexuality, they often wish to see the character having televised adventures in his default setting—Cardiff. In one *Torchwood* fan fiction piece set post–*Miracle Day* titled "*Torchwood* Series 5—Operation Cardiff Cleanup," online fan writer MissSarahG1 expresses her (or his) fantasy to see the show return to its Cardiff setting, as its heroes fight against alien threats emanating from the Rift. In addition to presenting the Hub as being rebuilt in a similar manner to how it looked before it was destroyed in "Day One" of *Children of Earth*, the author offers her dream lineup for a renewed Torchwood team: Captain Jack, Gwen, Rex, Martha Jones, and Mickey Smith. With this interesting fan encoding of a potential Series Five cast, MissSarahG1 presents a Torchwood team that would contain three black characters, Rex, Martha, and Mickey, in relationship to two Caucasian actors, Jack and Gwen. Thus, like *Red Dwarf*, her version of *Torchwood* would present a near-equal division of white and black characters. She also officially makes Rex a member of the Torchwood team, not just a CIA ally, which he was encoded to be in *Miracle Day*. Building upon Rex's skepticism as displayed in that BBC/Starz series, MissSarahG1has Rex functioning as the reader surrogate in her piece, as he asks Mickey and Martha about such extraordinary subject matter as the Rift and Torchwood's origins in 1879 as an organization formed by Queen Victoria to protect England from alien threats. Through this fan-decoding of Rex in a Cardiff-centric imagining of a fifth season of *Torchwood*, the character becomes assimilated into the British model of the series in opposition to Jack and Gwen's situation in *Miracle Day*, which mostly set the show in America, with an emphasis on CIA-conspiracy intrigue rather than a presentation of any investigations into alien activities beginning in the Hub.

As optimistic as MissSarahG1's fan-fantasy scenario tonally reads toward restoring *Torchwood* to its early encoding roots, it also reveals a subscription to the Continuum of Nostalgic Continuity. Realistically, judging from Russell T Davies's direction for the series—in that he constantly has made changes to its cast, setting, and plot direction, the possibility of a future *Torchwood* series returning to its Cardiff roots seems quite unlikely at this point. However, if a fifth season of *Torchwood* brings the show in a direction that further distances itself from the direction of Captain Jack and Gwen serving as representatives of the Torchwood Institute who fight alien threats, fans may continue to be dissatisfied and express this displeasure *en masse* via online communication. In theory, would this form of group dissatisfaction lead to the show's final cancellation or to Davies or other future *Torchwood* producers ultimately resetting the show back to its basic formula of Captain Jack's team of adventurers fighting threats emanating from the Cardiff Rift via their rebuilt Hub headquarters?

While the producers of *Torchwood* still retain the strong possibility of continuing the show's televised narrative since its lead, Captain Jack, provides a troubled yet intriguing fan-beloved masculine heroic lead, *Blake's 7* potential future producers are encumbered by the historical encoding of its two problematic leads, Roj Blake and Kerr Avon. Thus, considering the original *Blake's 7* as representing a failed masculine heroic quest could be another reason for why attempted narrative continuations or reboots of this dystopian SF show may have been unsuccessful. In other words, audiences want to root for heroes who ultimately save the day—their families—the universe—whatever requires "saving" in any quest mythology. As an example, when *Classic Who* originally went off the BBC airwaves in 1989 with the third and final part of "Survival," the Doctor and Ace walked off happily triumphant from their adventure fighting the Master and the Cheetah People. This image resonated in both viewers and future *NüWho* writers' heads, leaving the impression that this time-traveling heroic quest still had a lot of narrative mileage left in its future storytelling. On a darker note, *Blake's 7*'s final episode, "Blake," left viewers distraught by the image of the show's titular hero lying dead at the feet of his killer—and former comrade—Avon. Naturally, the post–Gauda Prime prospect of attempting to continue Avon's narrative through either a resolution of "Blake's" cliffhanger ending, in which he was surrounded by Federation troops, or as a new series, where he could join forces with younger freedom fighters, is problematic as both scenarios must somewhat work toward redeeming this character in a heroic sense.

Any potential rumored reboot of *Blake's 7*—whether it is produced by the BBC, Syfy, or the Xbox Live service[1]—likewise has to deal with not only the specter of a failed heroic quest but also a missing hero—Blake— who was notably absent for the majority of two seasons' worth of episodes for the classic series.[2] More problematically, since December 21, 1981, when "Blake" aired, fans have been left with the impression that Blake was both mentally and physically scarred[3] even before Avon killed him. Granted, any new iteration of the show would begin anew Blake's quest to topple the malevolent Federation without the character disappearing from the show if it is fortunate enough to be renewed for several seasons, which could bring it to match or exceed the original *Blake's 7*'s fifty-two episode count. However, would fans or viewers who are aware of the classic series' trajectory for Blake expect (or desire) a reboot to encode the character in a manner that always puts him on the edge of sanity due to the stress of embodying an increasingly messianic hero?[4] As a potential answer to this question, one could cite the AMC survival horror series, *The Walking Dead*, which is an adaptation of the popular Image comic series. In both the comic and TV show, lead character Rick Grimes, a police officer before the onset of the zombie apocalypse, gradually loses his sanity. Thus, if contemporary SF/horror viewers are intrigued and accustomed to witnessing their masculine heroes struggle with or succumb to mental issues, then perhaps it is not too far of a stretch to theorize that a reimagined *Blake's 7*, like its progenitor series, could encode a psychologically-fragile lead.

At present, the official teaser blurb for the proposed rebooted *Blake's 7* on FreemantleMedia's Web site reads: "The year is 2136. Blake wakes up on one side of the bed. He reaches for the other side. There's nobody there. As reality sets in, this handsome ex-soldier sits up and looks at a photo of his wife Rachel. Beautiful. Deceased" ("FreemantleMedia International"). Immediately, this introductory scenario diverges from the premise of the single Blake who was presented in the classic series' opening episode, "The Way Back," adding a clear-cut heterosexual encoding to this widowed version of the character. Although whether or not this new iteration of the hero is likewise initially amnesiac as was his predecessor is unclear in this synopsis blurb, he does obviously share the original Blake's misfortune to be a framed hero as the blurb also reveals, "*Blake's 7* tells the story of seven criminals—6 guilty and 1 innocent." Additionally, the blurb continues that this group is "on their way to life on a prison colony in space" and that they "together wrestle freedom from imprisonment ... and acquire an alien ship which gives them a second chance at life and become the most unlikely heroes of their time." With this encoding setup, Blake again will most likely function as a resistance leader whose example will inspire his criminal colleagues to embrace a more heroic lifestyle. The phrase "of their time," however, is rather ambiguous at that point, for not enough information has been provided by the blurb to establish the exact nature of the probable dystopian future of 2163.

In addition to this official blurb synopsis, three production paintings have been released online depicting renderings of the new Liberator, with an exterior depiction of the ship and an interior shot of its corridor, and of Trafalgar Square, London, which is filled with futuristic buildings and flooded.[5] Fans, however, while they appreciate the future London painting, seem resistant to the more industrialized, thicker, dirtier version of the Liberator. Although this projected vision for the ship retains the classic *Blake's 7* design elements for the Liberator, it possesses neither its more streamlined look nor its luxurious interior. On this note, Matt, a discussion board participant on the *Nerdist* Web site, writes, "[T]he Liberator does look like something we've seen before (a lot). It is supposed to be alien in design; it's supposed to be sleek; it's supposed to be something that is so far advanced it leaves everything that the Federation has in its wake. I know the image is concept art, but it misses those very points in its design. Make it pristine, make it clean, make it everything that the other ships in the show are not." In Matt's view, the designs for the new Liberator should build upon designer Roger Murray-Leach's vision for the original version of the ship, presenting alien technology that is far in advance of any future human effort. However, responding to Matt's views, Leon Clarance, one of the backers for the intended reboot of *Blake's 7*, points out, "Re[garding] the Liberator, you may think it ungainly, but compared to the spaceships of our near future, it is still a near-fantastical machine. You haven't even seen what it can do yet.... Believe me, it's still unbeatable, unchaseable, unmatchable...." Without an actual produced and broadcast version of Clarance's shared vision for this new Liberator and its adversarial Federation ships, however, it is not yet possible to assess the accuracy of his promise to Matt.

Nonetheless, one can speculate that the vision of the future that Clarance and his associates have been planning for a *Blake's 7* reboot may be heading in the direction of presenting a dystopian London, where there is economic and environmental unrest, a darker vision that is perhaps complemented by gritty, antiquated ship technology. More importantly, in the absence of a new *Blake's 7* series, one can only theorize if Matt's somewhat Continuum-of-Nostalgic-Continuity-filled expectations for a

Liberator design that replicates that which is shown in classic *Blake's 7* is the right design ethos that would please long-term and projected viewers and fans of the potential series or, conversely, if Clarance's strong beliefs in the darker redesign of the ship will prove to supply the necessary encoding elements for a financially and critically successful relaunch of the show.

On the subject of a reboot encoding Blake's gendered heroism, one may also present the intriguing possibility of reimagining (or regendering) Blake as a woman. Case in point, the 2003 Syfy miniseries reboot of *Battlestar Galactica* regendered fighter pilot Lieutenant Starbuck, who was a man in the original 1978 NBC series, as a woman. As a result, this choice, mostly due to the strong writing for the character and Katee Sackhoff's performance, proved to be successful with fans and critics. For other strong examples of a female SF hero, one can point to lead characters Katniss Everdeen and Beatrice "Tris" Prior, respectively featured in *The Hunger Games* and *Divergent* book and film trilogies. In both of these instances, female heroes, like Blake, struggle against corrupt governments. A strong female fan following of readers and viewers naturally identify with Katniss and Tris and support these brands through blogs, fan fiction, art, tribute videos, and reviews. Perhaps, then, an extension of this vocal fan demographic would similarly support a female version of Roj Blake. Equally, online fan resistance to a regendering of Blake could preemptively prove critically and economically disastrous for a *Blake's 7* reboot.

Although a new iteration of *Blake's 7* will most likely choose not to create a female lead, a future series of *NüWho* may very well offer a realization of this intriguing idea. With Series Eight of *NüWho*, the show has undoubtedly caught up with the fan zeitgeist in presenting Missy as a female incarnation of the Master, which, in some ways, can be viewed as a preliminary step toward the show introducing a female Doctor. In fact, Steven Moffat, via an interview with Chris E. Hayner, has made this remark regarding his encoding steps toward setting the narrative stage for a female iteration of the show's lead character: "[C]onsciously part of my approach to *Doctor Who* is not just implanting the continuity that it can happen—which is demonstrated with the Master turning into Missy—but also to have female characters who get a bit Doctor-y." With the creation of River Song, whose time-crossed meetings with the Tenth, Eleventh, and Twelfth Doctors have demonstrated her progression from a troubled girl to a heroic woman, and through the encoding of Clara, who learned to be as morally complex as the Twelfth Doctor, Moffat has indeed added "Doctor-y" elements to *NüWho*'s supporting female characters.

At the same time, his decision to experiment with changing the sex of a Time Lord through one of the series' staple male villains may be perceived as a form of the showrunner playing it safe since the character, as far back as the John Nathan-Turner era of the 1980s, had already possessed a queer aura around him. Moreover, by regendering the sex of the Master, Moffat may be deflecting the rising demands from the media and sections of *Doctor Who* fandom for a sex change geared toward the Doctor himself. In an interview with Tom Spilsbury, however, Moffat comments, "I've been attacked for being so socially progressive that I *need* to change the Doctor's gender.... And for being so right-wing that I *refuse* to change the Doctor's gender!" Paradoxically, Moffat has thus found himself in a no-win situation as a twenty-first century *NüWho* showrunner in that, as much as he is pleasing certain vocal members of fandom, he is likewise angering or disappointing others. As a result, this powerful producer-writer encoder finds himself in a dialogue with fandom through which he rather proportionately experiences support and resistance.

Regarding the possibility of regenerating the Twelfth or a future incarnation of the Doctor into a woman, Moffat also argues,

> I want the most conservative, reactionary, traditionalist *Doctor Who* fan to come with it. Because if we lost half the audience, the show would go off the air! There's still a sizeable number of people who are extremely sceptical of the idea. That's fair. Not as many as there used to be, but there's a lot of people who say, "I don't like that idea." So if and when such a thing happened, *all* those people have to be saying, "Why didn't I know that would be brilliant?' Get that *wrong* ... and it's finished!"

From his position as the steward of the *NüWho* brand, Moffat is understandably protecting the series. Although he is not discussing his relationship with the BBC's upper management or Board of Governors regarding the possibility of regendering the Doctor as a woman, one must likewise attempt to sympathetically consider the basic fact that he also needs to protect his job. In other words, if Moffat (or future showrunner Chris Chibnall) were to introduce a Thirteenth Doctor who is a woman and this choice resulted in mass fan criticism and/or adversely affected the show's overall ratings, he could lose his job as showrunner. Furthermore, this theoretically controversial encoding decision could affect his professional standing within the BBC and his career as a television and film writer. When viewed within the greater context of encoders and decoders, the latter group wield more power than Moffat to imagine the possibility of a female Doctor. Put another way, while fans possess the freedom to fail, as none of their potential art, fiction, musical, or video interpretations of a regendered Doctor need to be limited in regard to plot, length, time, or BBC managerial/branding constraints, Moffat is saddled with all of these complicated restrictions whenever he writes and produces *NüWho* episodes.

On a more objective scale, if a future version of the lead Time Lord were a woman, and the series suffered from significantly low ratings and severe critical fan backlash, then *NüWho*'s successful decade-plus run would most likely come to an end, and the series would be cancelled. As a historical precedence, mid–1980s *Doctor Who* slowly and inexorably traveled down the road to its final cancellation in 1989 beginning with the casting of Colin Baker as the Sixth Doctor, which generated criticism from both BBC Controller Michael Grade and large sections of fandom. If history were in any way to repeat itself with both negative internal BBC corporate dissatisfaction and external online fan criticism directed toward a female-lead version of *Doctor Who,* then the idea that corporate managers and fans will only accept a version of the series that promotes a trustworthy masculine heroic vision of the Time Lord will truly be reinforced. However, in many ways, the show will thus prove to be "dead" in a sense as it will have demonstrated its absolute limits in terms of representing a progressively regendered vision of the Doctor.

In contrast to this view, one can point out the logical flaw in Moffat believing that *all* fans skeptical of the scenario of the Doctor becoming a woman must be won over in order for this seismic shift in the gendering of the show's hero to succeed on a decoding level. On a philosophical level, this is a form of absolutist thinking as, with any creative effort, whether it is a much-loved BBC SF show, a painting, a rock album, or a poem, not everyone will agree that the work is a valid—or acceptable—piece of art. Turning Moffat's comments upon themselves, one could point out that his demands for a lead-female Doctor encoding situation needing to satisfy everyone in *NüWho* fandom may be as uncompromising as the very "traditionalist" fans who may never accept nor support a woman as the heroic Time Lord.

Looking at the possibility from a decoding perspective, many *Doctor Who* fans are passionately divided upon this issue. For the more conservative members of fandom, the Doctor has always represented a stable masculine heroic role model. Thus, to switch the character's sex would be to destabilize this long-held decoded belief system. Alternatively, other progressively-minded fans believe the show represents a fertile encoded ground for a change in the Doctor's sex via the narrative trope of regeneration, a process during which every cell in the alien character's body undergoes change in order to give him a new appearance. Furthermore, since the show itself has first mentioned that a Time Lord can regenerate into either a male or female form when the Eleventh Doctor referred to his gender-switching Gallifreyan friend the Corsair in "The Doctor's Wife," fandom's curiosity to witness such a change onscreen had been piqued and stimulated by online blogs and fiction espousing such a scenario. Although Series Eight's example of Missy as a female incarnation of the formerly male Master satisfied this need for certain fans, other fans simply view this change as just another step in the inevitable encoding journey to regenerate the Doctor into a woman.

In Series Nine, Moffat once more reverses a Time Lord's gender via regeneration through the character of the General in "Hell Bent." When this high-ranking Gallifreyan military official regenerates from a white man, his eleventh incarnation, into a black woman for his twelfth persona, after the Doctor shoots him in order to escape with Clara from the extraction chamber, Moffat finally satisfies some fans' desire to witness an onscreen depiction of a male Time Lord regenerating into a female. On the one hand, Moffat doubles the import of this regeneration by adding race to the encoding quotient,[6] yet, on the other, he still places emphasis upon the fact that the regendering, like the Master-Missy transformation, has occurred through the body of a supporting character, not via the traditionally masculine body of the Doctor.

In regard to the casting of a female in the role of Doctor, Alyssa, a fan who runs the blog *Whovian Feminism*, asks, "[C]ould a woman portray the Doctor as deliberately unlikable as Peter Capaldi has been portraying the Twelfth Doctor? Would fans accept a rude, callous, grumpy, morally compromised Doctor portrayed by a woman? And could the production team deliberately market a woman portraying the Doctor that way?" One answer to these questions would be to speculate that perhaps a future *Doctor Who* production team would go for an opposite approach to the Twelfth Doctor's characterization by encoding a female Doctor who is sympathetic, cheerful, and moralistic. As a precedent, these characteristics could be applied to the Second, Fifth, Eighth, Tenth, and Eleventh Doctors, so the thought of a future female incarnation joining their ranks would not be too far of an intellectual stretch. Contradictorily, will any of the Doctor's traits—whether they are positive, negative, or somewhere in between—be strictly classified as masculine in the eyes of many fans? Alyssa likewise theorizes,

> When a woman becomes a Doctor, they won't just be introducing an unlikable female character on her own terms. They'll be introducing a female character as a version of a male character, creating a whole series of contradictory expectations for her. She'll be carrying the legacy of a character who has only been played by white men, and who has had a fairly consistent gendered dynamic with his largely

female companions. By simply existing, she'll be upending a lot of preconceptions about what characteristics and personality traits are inherent to men and women.

Perhaps the "contradictory expectations" that this blogger expects future fans to hold in regard to a female Doctor will add a new, vibrant life to the series, in both how the character is encoded in her heroic adventures and the ways in which fans will decode her characterization. More importantly, this blogger's socially progressive vision that the existence of a woman Doctor will overturn fandom's notions of male and female gendered traits in terms of what comprises a heroic Time Lord brings up a myriad of possibilities relating to the fluidic act of one's every day (and moment) gender formation. In this case, as much as a possible female Doctor could be encoded as embarking on a televised journey to exert her newfound feminine identity and heroic self, *Doctor Who* fans may be turning an analytical mirror upon themselves when they offer decoding views that support or resist this theorized radical regendering of the character through their critical and artistic cultural productions.

* * *

Returning to the constant of time in regard to *Doctor Who*, *Blake's 7*, *Red Dwarf*, and *Torchwood*, one, on a theoretical note, could mention Fredric Jameson's thoughts on the problems surrounding ending SF narratives:

> [I]n order for narrative to project some sense of a totality of experience in space and time, it must surely know some closure (a narrative must have an ending, even if it is ingeniously organized around the structural repression of endings as such). At the same time, however, closure or the narrative ending is the mark of that boundary or limit beyond which thought cannot go. The merit of SF is to dramatize this contradiction on the level of plot itself, since the vision of future history cannot know any punctual ending of this kind, at the same time that its novelistic expression demands some such ending [148].

In relation to *Red Dwarf*, a television show, Jameson's articulation of the problems surrounding crafting an ending to a futuristic narrative for a novel are quite applicable. In other words, how could Doug Naylor satisfyingly present a future Earth in the series' final episode? The *Red Dwarf* co-creator's potential extrapolation of this planet's state and the possible descendants of humanity three million years in the future thus serves as "a mark of that boundary or limit beyond which [viewers'] thought cannot go." Additionally, while it is one thing for Naylor (and Grant) to write about Lister's desire to return to an unseen future Earth throughout *Red Dwarf*'s ten seasons, it is another to display the fictitious reality of this scenario as neither the encoders nor the decoders possess a realistic frame of reference.

Another way of applying Jameson's philosophical slant on concluding a future narrative could be to say that *Red Dwarf*'s future is impossible to end due to the theoretical point that one cannot offer an ending for a time period that does not yet exist. However, the more direct conclusion one can make regarding the future of the *Red Dwarf* universe is that decoders, the fans who compose fiction and video productions, will inevitably be the ones who continue Lister and company's journey, regardless of whether or not Naylor encodes a finale that presents the Dwarfers finding Earth. Extended to the other BBC modules of fan-beloved SF television shows discussed in this work—*Doctor Who*, *Blake's 7*, and *Torchwood*—the idea that decoders are the ones who ultimately serve as the true stewards of these series' fantastical narratives is virtually indisputable. Regardless of whether or not these three shows will or may produce new "official" (i.e., canonical or rebooted) episodes that build upon the already televised adventures of the Doctor, Roj Blake, and Captain Jack in the future, the fans will probably be crafting their own complementary and contradictory literary, art, and video productions. As an extraordinary result, not only will these fandoms be celebrating and refining the gendered heroisms originating in these series as time inexorably unfolds in their lives but challenging and defining their own complex identities as well....

Appendix: Televised Works
(Listed in order of original transmission date)

Blake's 7

"The Way Back." *Blake's 7*. By Terry Nation. Dir. Michael Briant. Perf. Gareth Thomas, Michael Keating, and Sally Knyvette. BBC. 2 Jan. 1978. Television.

"Space Fall." *Blake's 7*. By Terry Nation. Dir. Pennant Roberts. Perf. Gareth Thomas, Paul Darrow, Michael Keating, and Sally Knyvette. BBC. 9 Jan. 1978. Television.

"Cygnus Alpha." *Blake's 7*. By Terry Nation. Dir. Vere Lorrimer. Perf. Gareth Thomas, Paul Darrow, Michael Keating, and Sally Knyvette. BBC. 16 Jan. 1978. Television.

"Time Squad." *Blake's 7*. By Terry Nation. Dir. Pennant Roberts. Perf. Gareth Thomas, Paul Darrow, Michael Keating, Sally Knyvette, and Jan Chappell. BBC. 23 Jan. 1978. Television.

"Seek–Locate–Destroy." *Blake's 7*. By Terry Nation. Dir. Vere Lorrimer. Perf. Gareth Thomas, Paul Darrow, Michael Keating, Sally Knyvette, and Jan Chappell. BBC. 6 Feb. 1978. Television.

"Pressure Point." *Blake's 7*. By Terry Nation. Dir. George Spenton-Foster. Perf. Gareth Thomas, Paul Darrow, Michael Keating, Sally Knyvette, and Jan Chappell. BBC. 6 Feb. 1979. Television.

"Star One." *Blake's 7*. By Chris Boucher. Dir. David Maloney. Perf. Gareth Thomas, Paul Darrow, Michael Keating, Sally Knyvette, and Jan Chappell. BBC. 3 Apr. 1979. Television.

"Aftermath." *Blake's 7*. By Terry Nation. Dir. Vere Lorrimer. Perf. Paul Darrow, Michael Keating, Jan Chappell, Josette Simon, and Steven Pacey. BBC. 7 Jan. 1980. Television.

"City at the Edge of the World." *Blake's 7*. By Chris Boucher. Dir. Vere Lorrimer. Perf. Paul Darrow, Michael Keating, Jan Chappell, Josette Simon, and Steven Pacey. BBC. 11 Feb. 1980. Television.

"Rumours of Death." *Blake's 7*. By Chris Boucher. Dir. Fiona Cumming. Perf. Paul Darrow, Michael Keating, Jan Chappell, Josette Simon, and Steven Pacey. BBC. 25 Feb. 1980. Television.

"Terminal." *Blake's 7*. By Terry Nation. Dir. Mary Ridge. Perf. Paul Darrow, Michael Keating, Jan Chappell, Josette Simon, and Steven Pacey. BBC. 31 Mar. 1980. Television.

"Sand." *Blake's 7*. By Tanith Lee. Dir. Vivienne Cozens. Perf. Paul Darrow, Michael Keating, Josette Simon, and Steven Pacey. BBC. 23 Nov. 1981. Television.

"Orbit." *Blake's 7*. By Robert Holmes. Dir. Brian Lighthill. Perf. Paul Darrow, Michael Keating, Josette Simon, and Steven Pacey. BBC. 7 Dec. 1981. Television.

"Warlord." *Blake's 7*. By Simon Masters. Dir. Viktors Ritelis. Perf. Paul Darrow, Michael Keating, Josette Simon, and Steven Pacey. BBC. 14 Dec. 1981. Television.

"Blake." *Blake's 7*. By Chris Boucher. Dir. Mary Ridge. Perf. Paul Darrow, Michael Keating, Josette Simon, Steven Pacey, and Gareth Thomas. BBC. 21 Dec. 1981. Television.

Doctor Who

"An Unearthly Child." *Doctor Who*. By Anthony Coburn. Dir. Waris Hussein. Perf. William Hartnell, William Russell, Jacqueline Hill, and Carole Ann Ford. BBC. 23 Nov.–14 Dec. 1963. Television.

"The Aztecs." *Doctor Who*. By John Lucarotti. Dir. John Crockett. Perf. William Hartnell, William Russell, Jacqueline Hill, and Carole Ann Ford. BBC. 23 May–13 June 1964. Television.

"The Dalek Invasion of Earth." *Doctor Who*. By Terry Nation. Dir. Richard Martin. Perf. William Hartnell, William Russell, Jacqueline Hill, and Carole Ann Ford. BBC. 21 Nov.–26 Dec. 1964. Television.

"The Romans." *Doctor Who*. By Dennis Spooner. Dir. Christopher Barry. Perf. William Hartnell, William Russell, Jacqueline Hill, and Maureen O'Brien. BBC. 16 Jan.–6 Feb. 1965. Television.

"The Chase." *Doctor Who*. By Terry Nation. Dir. Richard Martin. Perf. William Hartnell, William Russell, Jacqueline Hill, Maureen O'Brien, and Peter Purves. BBC. 22 May–26 June 1965. Television.

"Fury from the Deep." *Doctor Who*. By Victor Pemberton. Dir. Hugh David. Perf. Patrick Troughton, Frazer Hines, and Deborah Watling. BBC. 16 Mar.–20 Apr. 1968. Television.

"Spearhead from Space." *Doctor Who*. By Robert Homes. Dir. Derek Martinus. Perf. Jon Pertwee, Caroline John, and Nicolas Courtney. BBC. 3–24 Jan. 1970. Television.

"Colony in Space." *Doctor Who*. By Malcolm Hulke. Dir. Michael E. Briant. Perf. Jon Pertwee, Katy Manning, and Roger Delgado. BBC. 10 Apr.–15 May 1971. Television.

"The Three Doctors." *Doctor Who*. By Bob Baker and Dave Martin. Dir. Lennie Mayne. Perf. Jon Pertwee, Katy Manning, Patrick Troughton, William Hartnell, and Nicolas Courtney. BBC. 30 Dec. 1972–20 Jan. 1973. Television.

"The Green Death." *Doctor Who*. By Robert Sloman. Dir. Michael Briant. Perf. Jon

Pertwee, Katy Manning, and Nicolas Courtney. BBC. 19 May–23 June 1973. Television.

"The Time Warrior." *Doctor Who.* By Robert Holmes. Dir. Alan Bromly. Perf. Jon Pertwee, Elisabeth Sladen, and Nicholas Courtney. BBC. 15 Dec. 1973–5 Jan. 1974. Television.

"The Deadly Assassin." *Doctor Who.* By Robert Holmes. Dir. David Maloney. Perf. Tom Baker. BBC. 30 Oct.–20 Nov. 1976. Television.

"The Talons of Weng-Chiang." *Doctor Who.* By Robert Holmes. Dir. David Maloney. Perf. Tom Baker and Louise Jameson. BBC. 26 Feb.–2 Apr. 1977. Television.

"Destiny of the Daleks." *Doctor Who.* By Terry Nation. Dir. Ken Grieve. Perf. Tom Baker and Lalla Ward. BBC. 1–22 Sept. 1979. Television.

"City of Death." *Doctor Who.* By David Agnew. Dir. Michael Hayes. Perf. Tom Baker and Lalla Ward. BBC. 29 Sept.–20 Oct. 1979. Television.

"Shada." *Doctor Who.* By Douglas Adams. Dir. Pennant Roberts. Perf. Tom Baker and Lalla Ward. BBC. (never completed or broadcast due to industrial action). Television.

"Meglos." *Doctor Who.* By John Flanagan and Andrew McCulloch. Dir. Terence Dudley. Perf. Tom Baker and Lalla Ward. BBC. 27 Sept.–18 Oct. 1980. Television.

"Full Circle." *Doctor Who.* By Andrew Smith. Dir. Peter Grimwade. Perf. Tom Baker, Lalla Ward, and Matthew Waterhouse. BBC. 25 Oct.–15 Nov. 1980. Television.

"Logopolis." *Doctor Who.* By Christopher H. Bidmead. Dir. Peter Grimwade. Perf. Tom Baker, Matthew Waterhouse, Sarah Sutton, and Janet Fielding. BBC. 28 Feb.–21 Mar. 1981. Television.

"Castrovalva." *Doctor Who.* By Christopher H. Bidmead. Dir. Fiona Cumming. Perf. Peter Davison, Matthew Waterhouse, Sarah Sutton, and Janet Fielding. BBC. 4–12 Jan. 1982. Television.

"Four to Doomsday." *Doctor Who.* By Terence Dudley. Dir. John Black. Perf. Peter Davison, Matthew Waterhouse, Sarah Sutton, and Janet Fielding. BBC. 18–26 Jan. 1982. Television.

"Kinda." *Doctor Who.* By Christopher Bailey. Dir. Peter Grimwade. Perf. Peter Davison, Matthew Waterhouse, Sarah Sutton, and Janet Fielding. BBC. 1–9 Feb. 1982. Television.

"The Visitation." *Doctor Who.* By Eric Saward. Dir. Peter Moffatt. Perf. Peter Davison, Matthew Waterhouse, Sarah Sutton, and Janet Fielding. BBC. 15–23 Feb. 1982. Television.

"Earthshock." *Doctor Who.* By Eric Saward. Dir. Peter Grimwade. Perf. Peter Davison, Matthew Waterhouse, Sarah Sutton, and Janet Fielding. BBC. 8–16 Mar. 1982. Television.

"Time-Flight." *Doctor Who.* By Peter Grimwade. Dir. Ron Jones. Perf. Peter Davison, Sarah Sutton, and Janet Fielding. BBC. 22–30 Mar. 1982. Television.

"Arc of Infinity." *Doctor Who.* By Johnny Byrne. Dir. Ron Jones. Perf. Peter Davison, Sarah Sutton, and Janet Fielding. BBC. 3–12 Jan. 1983. Television.

"Snakedance." *Doctor Who*. By Christopher Bailey. Dir. Fiona Cumming. Perf. Peter Davison, Sarah Sutton, and Janet Fielding. BBC. 18–26 Jan. 1983. Television.

"Mawdryn Undead." *Doctor Who*. By Peter Grimwade. Dir. Peter. Moffat. Perf. Peter Davison, Sarah Sutton, Janet Fielding, and Mark Strickson. BBC. 1–9 Feb. 1983. Television.

"Terminus." *Doctor Who*. By Steve Gallagher. Dir. Mary Ridge. Perf. Peter Davison, Sarah Sutton, Janet Fielding, and Mark Strickson. BBC. 15–23 Feb. 1983. Television.

"Enlightenment." *Doctor Who*. By Barbara Clegg. Dir. Fiona Cumming. Perf. Peter Davison, Janet Fielding, and Mark Strickson. BBC. 1–9 Mar. 1983. Television.

"The Five Doctors." *Doctor Who*. By Terrance Dicks. Dir. Peter Moffatt. Perf. Peter Davison, Jon Pertwee, Patrick Troughton, Richard Hurndall, Tom Baker, and William Hartnell. BBC. 25 Nov. 1983. Television.

"Resurrection of the Daleks." *Doctor Who*. By Eric Saward. Dir. Matthew Robinson. Perf. Peter Davison, Janet Fielding, and Mark Strickson. BBC. 8–15 Feb. 1984. Television.

"Planet of Fire." *Doctor Who*. By Peter Grimwade. Dir. Fiona Cumming. Perf. Peter Davison, Mark Strickson, and Nicola Bryant. BBC. 23 Feb.–2 Mar. 1984. Television.

"The Caves of Androzani." *Doctor Who*. By Robert Holmes. Dir. Graeme Harper. Perf. Peter Davison and Nicola Bryant. BBC. 8–16 Mar. 1984. Television.

"The Twin Dilemma." *Doctor Who*. By Anthony Steven. Dir. Peter Moffatt. Perf. Colin Baker and Nicola Bryant. BBC. 22–30 Mar. 1984. Television.

"Vengeance on Varos." *Doctor Who*. By Philip Martin. Dir. Ron Jones. Perf. Colin Baker and Nicola Bryant. BBC. 19–26 Jan. 1985. Television.

"The Mark of the Rani." *Doctor Who*. By Pip and Jane Baker. Dir. Sarah Hellings. Perf. Colin Baker and Nicola Bryant. BBC. 2–9 Feb. 1985. Television.

"The Two Doctors." *Doctor Who*. By Robert Holmes. Dir. Peter Moffatt. Perf. Colin Baker, Patrick Troughton, Nicola Bryant, and Frazer Hines. BBC. 16 Feb.–2 Mar. 1985. Television.

"Timelash." *Doctor Who*. By Glen McCoy. Dir. Pennant Roberts. Perf. Colin Baker and Nicola Bryant. BBC. 9–16 Mar. 1985. Television.

"Revelation of the Daleks." *Doctor Who*. By Eric Saward. Dir. Graeme Harper. Perf. Colin Baker and Nicola Bryant. BBC. 23–30 Mar. 1985. Television.

"The Trial of a Time Lord." *Doctor Who*. By Robert Holmes, Philip Martin, Pip and Jane Baker. Dir. Nicholas Mallett, Ron Jones, and Chris Clough. Perf. Colin Baker, Nicola Bryant, and Bonnie Langford. BBC. 6 Sept.–6 Dec. 1986. Television.

"Time and the Rani." *Doctor Who*. By Pip and Jane Baker. Dir. Andrew Morgan. Perf. Sylvester McCoy and Bonnie Langford. BBC. 7–28 Sept. 1987. Television.

"Paradise Towers." *Doctor Who*. By Steven Wyatt. Dir. Nicholas Mallett. Perf. Sylvester McCoy and Bonnie Langford. BBC. 5–26 Oct. 1987. Television.

"Delta and the Bannermen." *Doctor Who*. By Malcolm Kohll. Dir. Chris Clough. Perf. Sylvester McCoy and Bonnie Langford. BBC. 2–16 Nov. 1987. Television.

"Dragonfire." *Doctor Who*. By Ian Briggs. Dir. Chris Clough. Perf. Sylvester McCoy, Bonnie Langford, and Sophie Aldred. BBC. 23 Nov.–7 Dec. 1987. Television.

"Remembrance of the Daleks." *Doctor Who*. By Ben Aaronovitch. Dir. Andrew Morgan. Perf. Sylvester McCoy and Sophie Aldred. BBC. 5–26 Oct. 1988. Television.

"The Happiness Patrol." *Doctor Who*. By Graeme Curry. Dir. Chris Clough. Perf. Sylvester McCoy and Sophie Aldred. BBC. 2–16 Nov. 1988. Television.

"Silver Nemesis." *Doctor Who*. By Kevin Clarke. Dir. Chris Clough. Perf. Sylvester McCoy and Sophie Aldred. BBC. 23 Nov.–7 Dec. 1988. Television.

"Battlefield." *Doctor Who*. By Ben Aaronovitch. Dir. Michael Kerrigan. Perf. Sylvester McCoy and Sophie Aldred. BBC. 6–27 Sept. 1989. Television.

"Survival." *Doctor Who*. By Rona Munro. Dir. Alan Wareing. Perf. Sylvester McCoy and Sophie Aldred. BBC. 22 Nov.–6 Dec. 1989. Television.

"Dimensions in Time." *Children in Need*. By John Nathan-Turner and David Roden. Dir. Stuart McDonald. Perf. Jon Pertwee, Tom Baker, Peter Davison. Colin Baker, and Sylvester McCoy. BBC. 26–27 Nov. 1993. Television.

"Doctor Who." *Doctor Who*. Dir. Geoffrey Sax. By Matthew Jacobs. Perf. Paul McGann, Sylvester McCoy, Eric Roberts, Daphne Ashbrook, and Yee Jee Tso. BBC/Fox. 14 May 1996. Television.

"Doctor Who and the Curse of Fatal Death." *Doctor Who*. By Steven Moffat. Dir. John Henderson. Perf. Rowan Atkinson, Julia Sawalha, Joanna Lumley, and Jonathan Pryce. BBC. 12 Mar. 1999. Television.

"Rose." *Doctor Who*. By Russell T Davies. Dir. Keith Boak. Perf. Christopher Eccleston, Billie Piper, Camille Coduri, and Noel Clarke. BBC. 26 Mar. 2005. Television.

"The Empty Child." *Doctor Who*. By Steven Moffat. Dir. James Hawes. Perf. Christopher Eccleston, Billie Piper, and John Barrowman. BBC. 21 May 2005. Television.

"The Doctor Dances." *Doctor Who*. By Steven Moffat. Dir. James Hawes. Perf. Christopher Eccleston, Billie Piper, and John Barrowman. BBC. 28 May 2005. Television.

"Boom Town." *Doctor Who*. By Russell T Davies. Dir. Joe Ahearne. Perf. Christopher Eccleston, Billie Piper, and John Barrowman. BBC. 4 June 2005. Television.

"Bad Wolf." *Doctor Who*. By Russell T Davies. Dir. Joe Ahearne. Perf. Christopher Eccleston, Billie Piper, and John Barrowman. BBC. 11 June 2005. Television.

"The Parting of the Ways." *Doctor Who*. By Russell T Davies. Dir. Joe Ahearne. Perf. Christopher Eccleston, Billie Piper, and John Barrowman. BBC. 18 June 2005. Television.

"Rise of the Cybermen." *Doctor Who*. By Tom MacRae. Dir. Graeme Harper. Perf. David Tennant, Billie Piper, and Noel Clarke. BBC. 13 May 2006. Television.

"The Age of Steel." *Doctor Who*. By Tom MacRae. Dir. Graeme Harper. Perf. David Tennant, Billie Piper, and Noel Clarke. BBC. 20 May 2006. Television.

"Love and Monsters." *Doctor Who*. By Russell T Davies. Dir. Dan Zeff. Perf. David Tennant and Billie Piper. BBC. 17 June 2006. Television.

"Army of Ghosts." *Doctor Who*. By Russell T Davies. Dir. Graeme Harper. Perf. David Tennant and Billie Piper. BBC. 1 July 2006. Television.

"Doomsday." *Doctor Who*. By Russell T Davies. Dir. Graeme Harper. Perf. David Tennant and Billie Piper. BBC. 8 July 2006. Television.

"Utopia." *Doctor Who*. By Russell T Davies. Dir. Graeme Harper. Perf. David Tennant, Freema Agyeman, and John Barrowman. BBC. 16 June 2007. Television.

"The Sound of Drums." *Doctor Who*. By Russell T Davies. Dir. Colin Teague. Perf. David Tennant, Freema Agyeman, and John Barrowman. BBC. 23 June 2007. Television.

"Last of the Time Lords." *Doctor Who*. By Russell T Davies. Dir. Colin Teague. Perf. David Tennant, Freema Agyeman, and John Barrowman. BBC. 30 June 2007. Television.

"Time Crash." *Doctor Who*. By Steven Moffat. Dir. Graeme Harper. Perf. David Tennant and Peter Davison. BBC. 16. Nov. 2007. Television.

"Journey's End." *Doctor Who*. By Russell T Davies. Dir. Colin Teague. Graeme Harper. Perf. David Tennant, Catherine Tate, Billie Piper, Freema Agyeman, John Barrowman, and Elisabeth Sladen. BBC. 5 July 2008. Television.

"The End of the Time: Part Two." *Doctor Who*. By Russell T Davies. Dir. Euros Lyn. Perf. David Tennant, John Simm, and Bernard Cribbins. BBC. 1 Jan. 2010. Television.

"The Eleventh Hour." *Doctor Who*. By Steven Moffat. Dir. Adam Smith. Perf. Matt Smith, Karen Gillan, and Arthur Darvill. BBC. 3 Apr. 2010. Television.

"The Big Bang." *Doctor Who*. By Steven Moffat. Dir. Toby Haynes. Perf. Matt Smith, Karen Gillan, Alex Kingston, and Arthur Darvill. BBC. 26 June 2010. Television.

"The Doctor's Wife." *Doctor Who*. By Neil Gaiman. Dir. Richard Clark. Perf. Matt Smith, Karen Gillan, and Arthur Darvill. BBC. 14 May 2011. Television.

"A Good Man Goes to War." *Doctor Who*. By Steven Moffat. Dir. Peter Hoar. Perf. Matt Smith, Karen Gillan, Arthur Darvill, and Alex Kingston. BBC. 4 June 2011. Television.

"Let's Kill Hitler." *Doctor Who*. By Steven Moffat. Dir. Richard Senior. Perf. Matt Smith, Karen Gillan, Arthur Darvill, Nina Toussaint-White, and Alex Kingston. BBC. 27 Aug. 2011. Television.

"Dinosaurs on a Spaceship." *Doctor Who*. By Chris Chibnall. Dir. Saul Metzstein. Perf. Matt Smith, Karen Gillan, and Arthur Darvill. BBC. 8 Sept. 2012. Television.

"The Name of the Doctor." *Doctor Who*. By Steven Moffat. Dir. Saul Metzstein. Perf. Matt Smith, Jenna-Louise Coleman, and Alex Kingston. BBC. 18 May 2013. Television.

"The Day of the Doctor." *Doctor Who*. By Steven Moffat. Dir. Nick Hurran. Perf. Matt Smith, David Tennant, Jenna Coleman, Billie Piper, and John Hurt. BBC. 23 Nov. 2013. Television.

"The Time of the Doctor." *Doctor Who*. By Steven Moffat. Dir. Jamie Payne. Perf. Matt Smith and Jenna Coleman. BBC. 25 Dec. 2013.Television.

"Deep Breath." *Doctor Who*. By Steven Moffat. Dir. Ben Wheatley. Perf. Peter Capaldi, Jenna Coleman, Matt Smith, and Michelle Gomez. BBC. 23 Aug. 2014. Television.

"Into the Dalek." *Doctor Who*. By Phil Ford and Steven Moffat. Dir. Ben Wheatley. Perf. Peter Capaldi, Jenna Coleman, and Samuel Anderson. BBC. 30 Aug. 2014. Television.

"Robot of Sherwood." *Doctor Who*. By Mark Gatiss. Dir. Paul Murphy. Perf. Peter Capaldi and Jenna Coleman. BBC. 6 Sept. 2014. Television.

"Listen." *Doctor Who*. By Steven Moffat. Dir. Douglas Mackinnon. Perf. Peter Capaldi, Jenna Coleman, and Samuel Anderson. BBC. 13 Sept. 2014. Television.

"The Caretaker." *Doctor Who*. By Gareth Roberts and Steven Moffat. Dir. Paul Murphy. Perf. Peter Capaldi, Jenna Coleman, Samuel Anderson, and Ellis George. BBC. 27 Sept. 2014. Television.

"Kill the Moon." *Doctor Who*. By Peter Harness. Dir. Paul Wilmshurst. Perf. Peter Capaldi, Jenna Coleman, Samuel Anderson, and Ellis George. BBC. 4 Oct. 2014. Television.

"Mummy on the Orient Express." *Doctor Who*. By Jamie Mathieson. Dir. Paul Wilmshurst. Perf. Peter Capaldi and Jenna Coleman. BBC. 11 Oct. 2014. Television.

"Flatline." *Doctor Who*. By Jamie Mathieson. Dir. Douglas Mackinnon. Perf. Peter Capaldi, Jenna Coleman, and Samuel Anderson. BBC. 18 Oct. 2014. Television.

"In the Forest of the Night." *Doctor Who*. By Frank Cottrell-Boyce. Dir. Sheree Folkson. Perf. Peter Capaldi, Jenna Coleman, Samuel Anderson, and Michelle Gomez. BBC. 25 Oct. 2014. Television.

"Dark Water." *Doctor Who*. By Steven Moffat. Dir. Rachel Talalay. Perf. Peter Capaldi, Jenna Coleman, Samuel Anderson, and Michelle Gomez. BBC. 1 Nov. 2014. Television.

"Death in Heaven." *Doctor Who*. By Steven Moffat. Dir. Rachel Talalay. Perf. Peter Capaldi, Jenna Coleman, Samuel Anderson, and Michelle Gomez. BBC. 8 Nov. 2014. Television.

"Last Christmas." *Doctor Who*. By Steven Moffat. Dir. Paul Wilmshurst. Perf. Peter Capaldi, Jenna Coleman, Nick Frost, and Samuel Anderson. BBC. 25 Dec. 2014. Television.

"The Magician's Apprentice." *Doctor Who*. By Steven Moffat. Dir. Hettie MacDonald. Perf. Peter Capaldi, Jenna Coleman, and Michelle Gomez. BBC. 19 Sept. 2015. Television.

"The Zygon Invasion." *Doctor Who*. By Peter Harness. Dir. Daniel Nettheim. Perf. Peter Capaldi, Jenna Coleman, and Ingrid Oliver. BBC. 31 Oct. 2015. Television.

"The Zygon Inversion." *Doctor Who*. By Peter Harness and Steven Moffat. Dir. Daniel Nettheim. Perf. Peter Capaldi, Jenna Coleman, and Ingrid Oliver. BBC. 7 Nov. 2015. Television.

"Face the Raven." *Doctor Who*. By Sarah Dollard. Dir. Justin Molotnikov. Perf. Peter Capaldi, Jenna Coleman, and Maisie Williams. BBC. 21 Nov. 2015. Television.

"Hell Bent." *Doctor Who*. By Steven Moffat. Dir. Rachel Talalay. Perf. Peter Capaldi, Jenna Coleman, Ken Bones, Maisie Williams, and T'nia Miller. BBC. 5 Dec. 2015. Television.

Red Dwarf

"The End." *Red Dwarf*. By Rob Grant and Doug Naylor. Dir. Ed Bye. Perf. Chris Barrie, Craig Charles, Danny John-Jules, and Norman Lovett. BBC. 15 Feb. 1988. Television.

"Future Echoes." *Red Dwarf*. By Rob Grant and Doug Naylor. Dir. Ed Bye. Perf. Chris Barrie, Craig Charles, Danny John-Jules, and Norman Lovett. BBC. 22 Feb. 1988. Television.

"Thanks for the Memory." *Red Dwarf*. By Rob Grant and Doug Naylor. Dir. Ed Bye. Perf. Chris Barrie, Craig Charles, Danny John-Jules, and Norman Lovett. BBC. 20 Sept. 1988. Television.

"Stasis Leak." *Red Dwarf*. By Rob Grant and Doug Naylor. Dir. Ed Bye. Perf. Chris Barrie, Craig Charles, Danny John-Jules, and Norman Lovett. BBC. 27 Sept. 1988. Television.

"Parallel Universe." *Red Dwarf*. By Rob Grant and Doug Naylor. Dir. Ed Bye. Perf. Chris Barrie, Craig Charles, Danny John-Jules, and Norman Lovett. BBC. 11 Oct. 1988. Television.

"Polymorph." *Red Dwarf*. By Rob Grant and Doug Naylor. Dir. Ed Bye. Perf. Chris Barrie, Craig Charles, Danny John-Jules, Robert Llewellyn, and Hattie Hayridge. BBC. 28 Nov. 1989. Television.

"The Last Day." *Red Dwarf*. By Rob Grant and Doug Naylor. Dir. Ed Bye. Perf. Chris Barrie, Craig Charles, Danny John-Jules, Robert Llewellyn, and Hattie Hayridge. BBC. 19 Dec. 1989. Television.

"Camille." *Red Dwarf*. By Rob Grant and Doug Naylor. Dir. Ed Bye. Perf. Chris Barrie, Craig Charles, Danny John-Jules, Robert Llewellyn, and Hattie Hayridge. BBC. 14 Feb. 1991. Television.

"DNA." *Red Dwarf*. By Rob Grant and Doug Naylor. Dir. Ed Bye. Perf. Chris Barrie, Craig Charles, Danny John-Jules, Robert Llewellyn, and Hattie Hayridge. BBC. 21 Feb. 1991. Television.

"White Hole." *Red Dwarf*. By Rob Grant and Doug Naylor. Dir. Ed Bye. Perf. Chris Barrie, Craig Charles, Danny John-Jules, Robert Llewellyn, and Hattie Hayridge. BBC. 7 Mar. 1991. Television.

"Dimension Jump." *Red Dwarf*. By Rob Grant and Doug Naylor. Dir. Ed Bye. Perf. Chris Barrie, Craig Charles, Danny John-Jules, Robert Llewellyn, and Hattie Hayridge. BBC. 14 Mar. 1991. Television.

"Holoship." *Red Dwarf*. By Rob Grant and Doug Naylor. Dir. Juliet May. Perf. Chris Barrie, Craig Charles, Danny John-Jules, Robert Llewellyn, and Hattie Hayridge. BBC. 20 Feb. 1992. Television.

"The Inquisitor." *Red Dwarf*. By Rob Grant and Doug Naylor. Dir. Juliet May and

Doug Naylor. Perf. Chris Barrie, Craig Charles, Danny John-Jules, Robert Llewellyn, and Hattie Hayridge. BBC. 27 Feb. 1992. Television.

"Terrorform." *Red Dwarf.* By Rob Grant and Doug Naylor. Dir. Juliet May. Perf. Chris Barrie, Craig Charles, Danny John-Jules, Robert Llewellyn, and Hattie Hayridge. BBC. 5 Mar. 1992. Television.

"Demons and Angels." *Red Dwarf.* By Rob Grant and Doug Naylor. Dir. Juliet May and Doug Naylor. Perf. Chris Barrie, Craig Charles, Danny John-Jules, Robert Llewellyn, and Hattie Hayridge. BBC. 19 Mar. 1992. Television.

"Back to Reality." *Red Dwarf.* By Rob Grant and Doug Naylor. Dir. Juliet May and Doug Naylor. Perf. Chris Barrie, Craig Charles, Danny John-Jules, Robert Llewellyn, and Hattie Hayridge BBC. 26 Mar. 1992. Television.

"Emohawk: Polymorph II." *Red Dwarf.* By Rob Grant and Doug Naylor. Dir. Andy de Emmony. Perf. Chris Barrie, Craig Charles, Danny John-Jules, and Robert Llewellyn. BBC. 28 Oct. 1993. Television.

"Out of Time." *Red Dwarf.* By Rob Grant and Doug Naylor. Dir. Andy de Emmony. Perf. Chris Barrie, Craig Charles, Danny John-Jules, and Robert Llewellyn. BBC. 11 Nov. 1993. Television.

"Tikka to Ride." *Red Dwarf.* By Doug Naylor. Dir. Ed Bye. Perf. Chris Barrie, Craig Charles, Danny John-Jules, and Robert Llewellyn. BBC. 17 Jan. 1997. Television.

"Stoke Me a Clipper." *Red Dwarf.* By Paul Alexander and Doug Naylor. Dir. Ed Bye. Perf. Chris Barrie, Craig Charles, Danny John-Jules, and Robert Llewellyn. BBC. 24 Jan. 1997. Television.

"Ouroboros." *Red Dwarf.* By Doug Naylor. Dir. Ed Bye. Perf. Chris Barrie, Craig Charles, Danny John-Jules, Robert Llewellyn, and Chloë Annett. BBC. 31 Jan. 1997. Television.

"Duct Soup." *Red Dwarf.* By Doug Naylor. Dir. Ed Bye. Perf. Craig Charles, Danny John-Jules, Robert Llewellyn, and Chloë Annett. BBC. 7 Feb. 1997. Television.

"Blue." *Red Dwarf.* By Kim Fuller and Doug Naylor. Dir. Ed Bye. Perf. Chris Barrie, Craig Charles, Danny John-Jules, Robert Llewellyn, and Chloë Annett. BBC. 14 Feb. 1997. Television.

"Nanarchy." *Red Dwarf.* By Paul Alexander, James Hendrie, and Doug Naylor. Dir. Ed Bye. Perf. Craig Charles, Danny John-Jules, Robert Llewellyn, Chloë Annett, and Norman Lovett. BBC. 7 Mar. 1997. Television.

"Back in the Red: Parts One–Three." *Red Dwarf.* By Doug Naylor. Dir. Ed Bye. Perf. Chris Barrie, Craig Charles, Danny John-Jules, Robert Llewellyn, Chloë Annett, and Norman Lovett. BBC. 18 Feb.–4 Mar. 1999. Television.

"Cassandra." *Red Dwarf.* By Doug Naylor. Dir. Ed Bye. Perf. Chris Barrie, Craig Charles, Danny John-Jules, Robert Llewellyn, Chloë Annett, and Norman Lovett. BBC. 11 Mar. 1999. Television.

"Krytie TV." *Red Dwarf.* By Doug Naylor and Paul Alexander. Dir. Ed Bye. Perf. Chris Barrie, Craig Charles, Danny John-Jules, Robert Llewellyn, Chloë Annett, and Norman Lovett. BBC. 18 Mar. 1999. Television.

"Pete: Parts One and Two." *Red Dwarf.* By Doug Naylor and Paul Alexander. Dir.

Ed Bye. Perf. Chris Barrie, Craig Charles, Danny John-Jules, Robert Llewellyn, Chloë Annett, and Norman Lovett. BBC. 25 Mar.–1 Apr. 1999. Television.

"Only the Good…" *Red Dwarf*. By Doug Naylor. Dir. Ed Bye. Perf. Chris Barrie, Craig Charles, Danny John-Jules, Robert Llewellyn, Chloë Annett, and Norman Lovett. BBC. 5 Apr. 1999. Television.

"Back to Earth." *Red Dwarf*. By Doug Naylor. Dir. Doug Naylor. Perf. Chris Barrie, Craig Charles, Danny John-Jules, Robert Llewellyn, and Chloë Annett. Dave. 10–12 Apr. 2009. Television.

"Trojan." *Red Dwarf*. By Doug Naylor. Dir. Doug Naylor. Perf. Chris Barrie, Craig Charles, Danny John-Jules, and Robert Llewellyn. Dave. 4 Oct. 2012. Television.

"Fathers & Suns." *Red Dwarf*. By Doug Naylor. Dir. Doug Naylor. Perf. Chris Barrie, Craig Charles, Danny John-Jules, and Robert Llewellyn. Dave. 11 Oct. 2012. Television.

"Entangled." *Red Dwarf*. By Doug Naylor. Dir. Doug Naylor. Perf. Chris Barrie, Craig Charles, Danny John-Jules, and Robert Llewellyn. Dave. 25 Oct. 2012. Television.

"Dear Dave." *Red Dwarf*. By Doug Naylor. Dir. Doug Naylor. Perf. Chris Barrie, Craig Charles, Danny John-Jules, and Robert Llewellyn. Dave. 1 Nov. 2012. Television.

"The Beginning." *Red Dwarf*. By Doug Naylor. Dir. Doug Naylor. Perf. Chris Barrie, Craig Charles, Danny John-Jules, and Robert Llewellyn. Dave. 8 Nov. 2012. Television.

Torchwood

"Everything Changes." *Torchwood*. By Russell T Davies. Dir. Brian Kelly. Perf. John Barrowman, Eve Myles, Burn Gorman, Naoko Mori, and Gareth David-Lloyd. BBC. 22 Oct. 2006. Television.

"Day One." *Torchwood*. By Chris Chibnall. Dir. Brian Kelly. Perf. John Barrowman, Eve Myles, Burn Gorman, Naoko Mori, and Gareth David-Lloyd. BBC. 22 Oct. 2006. Television.

"Cyberwoman." *Torchwood*. By Chris Chibnall. Dir. James Strong. Perf. John Barrowman, Eve Myles, Burn Gorman, Naoko Mori, and Gareth David-Lloyd. BBC. 5 Nov. 2006. Television.

"Greeks Bearing Gifts." *Torchwood*. By Toby Whithouse. Dir. Colin Teague. Perf. John Barrowman, Eve Myles, Burn Gorman, Naoko Mori, and Gareth David-Lloyd. BBC. 26 Nov. 2006. Television.

"Out of Time." *Torchwood*. By Catherine Tregenna. Dir. Alice Troughton. Perf. John Barrowman, Eve Myles, Burn Gorman, Naoko Mori, and Gareth David-Lloyd. BBC. 17 Dec. 2006. Television.

"Combat." *Torchwood*. By Noel Clarke. Dir. Andy Goddard. Perf. John Barrowman, Eve Myles, Burn Gorman, Naoko Mori, and Gareth David-Lloyd. BBC. 24 Dec. 2006. Television.

"Captain Jack Harkness." *Torchwood.* By Catherine Tregenna. Dir. Ashley Way. Perf. John Barrowman, Eve Myles, Burn Gorman, Naoko Mori, and Gareth David-Lloyd. BBC. 1 Jan. 2007. Television.

"Kiss Kiss, Bang Bang." *Torchwood.* By Chris Chibnall. Dir. Ashley Way. Perf. John Barrowman, Eve Myles, Burn Gorman, Naoko Mori, and Gareth David-Lloyd. BBC. 16 Jan. 2008. Television.

"Adam." *Torchwood.* By Catherine Tregenna. Dir. Andy Goddard. Perf. John Barrowman, Eve Myles, Burn Gorman, Naoko Mori, and Gareth David-Lloyd. BBC. 13 Feb. 2008. Television.

"Reset." *Torchwood.* By J. C. Wilsher. Dir. Ashley Way. Perf. John Barrowman, Eve Myles, Burn Gorman, Naoko Mori, and Gareth David-Lloyd. BBC. 13 Feb. 2008. Television.

"Dead Man Walking." *Torchwood.* By Matt Jones. Dir. Andy Goddard. Perf. John Barrowman, Eve Myles, Burn Gorman, Naoko Mori, and Gareth David-Lloyd. BBC. 20 Feb. 2008. Television.

"A Day in the Death." *Torchwood.* By Joseph Lidster. Dir. Andy Goddard. Perf. John Barrowman, Eve Myles, Burn Gorman, Naoko Mori, and Gareth David-Lloyd. BBC. 27 Feb. 2008. Television.

"Something Borrowed." *Torchwood.* By Phil Ford. Dir. Ashley Way. Perf. John Barrowman, Eve Myles, Burn Gorman, Naoko Mori, and Gareth David-Lloyd. BBC. 5 Mar. 2008. Television.

"Adrift." *Torchwood.* By Chris Chibnall. Dir. Mark Everest. Perf. John Barrowman, Eve Myles, Burn Gorman, Naoko Mori, and Gareth David-Lloyd. BBC. 19 Mar. 2008. Television.

"Fragments." *Torchwood.* By Chris Chibnall. Dir. Jonathan Fox Bassett. Perf. John Barrowman, Eve Myles, Burn Gorman, Naoko Mori, and Gareth David-Lloyd. BBC. 21 Mar. 2008. Television.

"Exit Wounds." *Torchwood.* By Chris Chibnall. Dir. Ashley Way. Perf. John Barrowman, Eve Myles, Burn Gorman, Naoko Mori, and Gareth David-Lloyd. BBC. 4 Apr. 2008. Television.

"Day One." *Torchwood: Children of Earth.* By Russell T Davies. Dir. Euros Lyn. Perf. John Barrowman, Eve Myles, Gareth David-Lloyd, and Kai Owen. BBC. 6 July 2009. Television.

"Day Three." *Torchwood: Children of Earth.* By Russell T Davies and James Moran. Perf. John Barrowman, Eve Myles, Gareth David-Lloyd, and Kai Owen. Dir. Euros Lyn. BBC. 8 July 2009. Television.

"Day Four." *Torchwood: Children of Earth.* By John Fay. Dir. Euros Lyn. Perf. John Barrowman, Eve Myles, Gareth David-Lloyd, and Kai Owen. BBC. 9 July 2009. Television.

"Day Five." *Torchwood: Children of Earth.* By Russell T Davies. Dir. Euros Lyn. Perf. John Barrowman, Eve Myles, and Kai Owen. BBC. 10 July 2009. Television.

"The New World." *Torchwood: Miracle Day.* By Russell T Davies. Dir. Bharat Nalluri. Perf. John Barrowman, Eve Myles, Mekhi Phifer, Alexa Havins, Kai Owen, and Bill Pullman. BBC/Starz. 8 July 2011. Television.

"Rendition." *Torchwood: Miracle Day.* By Doris Egan. Dir. Billy Gierhart. Perf. John Barrowman, Eve Myles, Mekhi Phifer, Alexa Havins, Kai Owen, and Bill Pullman. BBC/Starz. 15 July 2011. Television.

"Dead of Night." *Torchwood: Miracle Day.* By Jane Espenson. Dir. Billy Gierhart. Perf. John Barrowman, Eve Myles, Mekhi Phifer, Alexa Havins, Kai Owen, and Bill Pullman. BBC/Starz. 28 July 2011. Television.

"The Categories of Life." *Torchwood: Miracle Day.* By Jane Espenson. Dir. Guy Ferland. Perf. John Barrowman, Eve Myles, Mekhi Phifer, Alexa Havins, Kai Owen, and Bill Pullman. BBC/Starz. 5 Aug. 2011. Television.

"Immortal Sins." *Torchwood: Miracle Day.* By Jane Espenson. Dir. Gwyneth Horder-Payton. Perf. John Barrowman, Eve Myles, Mekhi Phifer, Alexa Havins, Kai Owen, and Bill Pullman. BBC/Starz. 19 Aug. 2011. Television.

"The Blood Line." *Torchwood: Miracle Day.* By Russell T Davies and Jane Espenson. Dir. Billy Gierhart. Perf. John Barrowman, Eve Myles, Mekhi Phifer, Alexa Havins, Kai Owen, and Bill Pullman. BBC/Starz. 9 Sept. 2011. Television.

Chapter Notes

Introduction

1. *NüWho* showrunner Russell T Davies wrote *Damaged Goods*, published in 1996 as part of Virgin's *New Adventures*, a more mature-audience-themed series of original *Doctor Who* novels that continued the story of a post–"Survival" Seventh Doctor and Ace. Paul Cornell and Gareth Roberts, who have also written for *NüWho*, likewise contributed novels to this range, and Robert Shearman, who penned *Jubilee*, a 2003 Big Finish CD featuring the Sixth Doctor, adapted the script as "Dalek" for Series One. Additionally, Davies's successor, Steven Moffat, wrote the short story "Continuity Errors" for Virgin's *Decalog 3: Consequences* (1996), and "Doctor Who and the Curse of Fatal Death," a 1999 Red Nose Day charity sketch.

2. However, at this point, *Red Dwarf XI* and *XII* will be respectively airing on Dave in 2016 and 2017.

3. For example, major stars depart a production, new producers or writers take a series in a direction that is not embraced by fans, or repetitive storylines and/or static characterizations bore audiences.

4. I mean paradoxical in the sense that writers occasionally contradict one another's characterizations or storylines.

5. Currently, only *Doctor Who* and *Red Dwarf* are still in production.

6. Slash fiction is a genre of fan writing that takes two characters of the same sex and adds a romantic subtext to their relationship and/or delineates them having sex.

Chapter One

1. Of course, literally speaking, the table could be round, or there may be no table at all if the scriptwriter is composing upon a notebook positioned upon his or her lap.

2. Interestingly, the opening image of the fiftieth anniversary *Doctor Who* tale, "The Day of the Doctor," which aired on November 23, 2013, exactly fifty years from the original transmission of "An Unearthly Child," offers an image of a male police officer patrolling a London street near the fictitious 76 Totters Lane address for I.M. Foreman's junkyard. Granted, showrunner Steven Moffat's writing of a male actor to realize this part works as a clever homage to the man who played the original officer. But a certain maleness has been reinforced in this scene, which begins in black and white and drifts into the modern warm colors of high-definition television, as the contemporary officer strolls across the scene with an authoritative swagger. One can only wonder, then, how this scene would have played out if a female had been cast in this brief yet important role during the encoding process.

3. In "The Five Doctors," *Classic Who's* multi–Doctor twentieth anniversary special, the First Doctor (played by Richard Hurndall as a replacement for the deceased William Hartnell) is reunited with Susan in Gallifrey's Death Zone. Disappointedly, neither of them references the fact that he stranded her on Earth many years earlier.

4. Davison was the youngest actor to play the role until twenty-six-year-old Matt Smith began recording scenes as the Eleventh Doctor in July 2009 for Series Five.

5. In the next chapter, the 1980s *Doctor Who* encoding representations of the lead character's costumes across three incarnation will be further discussed.

6. For television, one can reference *Buck Rogers* and *Star Trek: The Next Generation*, and, regarding film, one could mention a number of SF-fantasy films featuring such stars as Harrison Ford, Kurt Russell, and Arnold Schwarzenegger.

7. On this note, once can think of Indiana Jones, James Bond, Michael Knight (of

Knight Rider), and *Blake's 7*'s Avon and Tarrant.

8. *Classic Who* is the term I am employing to refer to the twenty six seasons comprising the original run of *Doctor Who* (1963–89).

9. *Doctor Who Bulletin* respectively provided these headlines on issues #49 (Nov. 1987), #51 (Jan. 1988), and #58 (Sept. 1988).

10. With the media success of the modern series, the British police box has more than ever entered the public consciousness and imagination. A full-scale police box shell was the object used by fans for the 2011 iteration of the ongoing Caltech-MIT feud between engineering students. (See: http://hacks.mit.edu/Hacks/by_year/2010/tardis/) The MIT students had planned on placing a replica of the TARDIS exterior upon Baxter Hall, a Caltech building, but they were initially thwarted by campus security, who were unfamiliar with the politics of their friendly feud. Later, in true *Doctor Who* fashion, in the sense that the Doctor sometimes forms unlikely alliances with his enemies, most noticeably, the Master, to achieve a greater heroic goal, the two schools' students combined efforts in ensuring that the replica was completely assembled upon the school building's roof. On the subject of replicas, fan-generated conventions often combine fan efforts in building police box shells, and many fans have utilized online fan blueprints to build the beloved object for their homes and backyards. In one case, a fan who frequently dressed up as the Tenth Doctor was buried in a TARDIS-style police box coffin. See: http://www.dailymail.co.uk/news/article-1191224/Dr-Who-lookalike-sent-Tardis-style-coffin.html

11. In *Classic Who*, UNIT is the acronym for United Nations Intelligence Taskforce.

12. Shaped like a large, portable transparent cube in which his inner electronic workings are exposed to his users, Orac, a supercomputer, who has a male voice and personality derived from his creator, Dr. Ensor, dualistically possesses a feminine shape (i.e., he is vaginal in design). In terms of orientation, both males (Blake and Avon) and a notable female, Servalan, turn toward Orac in their respective desires to harness his power.

13. Even Vila, an unlikely romantic hero, is given his chance to express his heterosexual identity in the Series C episode "City at the Edge of the World," in which he woos Kerril, a repentant criminal.

14. Servalan actually survives the Liberator's destruction by teleporting off the ship, as revealed in the following series.

15. J.J. Abrams's *Star Trek* 2009 reboot smartly retained the classic encoded design of the Original Series and movie series Enterprise in its design of the newest iteration of the ship. Likewise, Syfy's 2003 reboot of *Battlestar Galactica* echoed the original series' design for the titular ship. In both instances, fan criticism was kept to a minimum due to encoded design choices that practiced fidelity to the original, iconic shapes for these fan-adored vessels.

16. If the BBC had commissioned a fifth series of *Blake's 7*, then script editor Chris Boucher claims that at least Avon would have been revealed to have survived the finale.

17. At the same time, the Tenth Doctor and companion Donna Noble were the best of friends, without any romantic tension occurring between them.

Chapter Two

1. The DWAS (The Doctor Who Appreciation Society) gave JN-T this title/award in July 1982.

2. Baker and Ward's romance culminated in a brief, well-publicized marriage.

3. He does seem to quietly enjoy the female scientist Todd's companionship in "Kinda."

4. On this note, Colin Baker and Nicola Bryant star together as a married couple in *The Airzone Solution*, a 1993 fan-produced film featuring Baker, Davison, and McCoy playing different roles in an SF setting. Additionally, Jon Pertwee makes a cameo appearance at the end of the production.

5. For an in-depth discussion of Nathan-Turner's controversial sexual life during this era, one can refer to Richard Marson's biography of the man, *JN-T: The Life & Scandalous Times of John Nathan-Turner*.

6. Fans criticized Nathan-Turner for casting comedy actress Beryl Reid in "Earthshock," comedian Ken Dodd in "Delta and the Bannermen," and the comedic duo Hale and Pace in "Survival." But the most notorious piece of stunt casting occurred when Nathan-Turner chose former child star Bonnie Langford to play Melanie Bush, companion to the Sixth and Seventh Doctors.

7. Former *Doctor Who* producer Barry Letts served as Nathan-Turner's executive producer (or BBC-mandated "overseer") for this season only.

8. Young viewers had been frightened by a drowning sequence in "The Deadly Assas-

sin" and a giant rat eating a woman in "The Talons of Weng-Chiang."

9. Lionheart Television International were the BBC's USA distributors.

10. Jon Pertwee and Patrick Troughton played the Third and Second Doctors.

11. Colin Baker, Sylvester McCoy, and Paul McGann played the Sixth, Seventh, and Eighth Doctors.

12. One of the Curator's lines in particular, in which he tells the Eleventh Doctor that he has revisited some of his past faces—but only "the old favorites," could potentially be construed by fans as Moffat's way of saying that the Fifth, Sixth, and Seventh Doctors, since they are absent from "The Day of the Doctor," are not part of this privileged club.

13. The Master's treatment of Adric in "Castrovalva" easily lends itself to slash fan fiction productions.

14. Writer Christopher H. Bidmead based the title of the story and the town itself upon the M.C. Escher lithograph print, "Castrovalva," which features the Abruzzo village of Castrovalva, which is positioned atop a sheer slope. When the town starts to unravel in "Castrovalva's" third and fourth episodes, Escher's famous depiction of space being distorted in his other works (i.e., people and creatures walking upside down and sideways in buildings whose architecture connects and folds in upon itself) is also applied to the visual storytelling. In short, Bidmead and the designers of "Castrovalva" have decoded Escher's works and encoded them into *Doctor Who*.

15. This production simply goes by the title *Doctor Who*.

16. Debuting in the conclusion of the *NüWho* Series Seven finale, "The Name of the Doctor," the War Doctor is a regeneration of the show's lead character who fought in the Time War but choose not to call himself the Doctor. He exists between the Eighth and Ninth Doctors.

17. The Doctor's phallus can be posited as enigmatic in the sense that viewers have never seen televised evidence of the Time Lord having sexual relations with any of his companions (or even River Song), despite several textual references in *Classic* and *NüWho* to him being a grandfather and father.

18. At this point in time, Waterhouse is also an openly gay man. During his tenure on the show as Adric, however, this was not public knowledge.

19. As an example, Tom Baker, who had objected to Waterhouse's casting and character, can be seen acting without making eye with his costar in many of their season eighteen scenes together.

20. Waterhouse also rejoined his *Doctor Who* castmates, Peter Davison, Janet Fielding (Tegan) and Sarah Sutton (Nyssa) in recording two 2014 Big Finish audio dramas set during their time together on the show, "Psychodrome" and "Iterations of I."

21. In the cliffhanger to part one of "Mawdryn Undead," Turlough, at the Black Guardian's urging, attempts to smash in the Doctor's head, but, in part two's resolution, the explosion of a machine the Time Lord is tinkering with throws the two backward, forming a scenario that thematically echoes the First Doctor's behavior in episode three of "An Unearthly Child," when he tries to kill an injured caveman whom he believes is slowing down his escape from other violent cave people until Ian stops him. With both instances, the audience pays witness to alien male antiheroes having their fear-motivated murderous impulses halted, which grants them the rare opportunity to discover and embrace a more traditional heroism that relies on intellect and ingenuity in order to find a solution to a problematic situation.

22. On this contractual requirement, Davison claims, "I didn't really realise ... that when I was being cast, I was sort of being turned into a gay icon—that's why [Nathan-Turner] insisted on highlights in my hair" (Marson 157).

23. Timberlake won a Grammy for "Best Dance Recoding."

24. "Neutral" likewise imagines Tegan being married to the Sixth Doctor, whom the Fifth becomes after surviving an assassination attempt by the Master, and the couple having two children.

25. Sevateem is the tribal name for the descendants of the Survey Team 6 from the Mordee Expedition.

26. "Mindwarp" is the Target Books, BBC Video, and preferred fan title for episodes 5–8 of "The Trial of a Time Lord."

27. The Valeyard, representing an evil distillation of the Doctor somewhere between his twelfth and final regeneration, definitely presents a more cynical, troubled future representation of the Time Lord.

28. Ironically, as an adult, Chibnall has written for *Torchwood* and *NüWho*, for which he will begin serving as showrunner in 2018.

29. This statement is relayed in Cartmel's *Script Doctor: The Inside Story of Doctor Who 1986–89* and Richard Marson's *JN-T: The Life & Scandalous Times of John Nathan-Turner*.

30. While not a strict cancellation of the show, in late February 1985, the BBC had given *Doctor Who* an eighteen-month hiatus between the airing of its twenty-second and twenty-third seasons.

31. The concluding sentence of Gray's thought reads, "To study the anti-fan, then, is to study what expectations and what values structure media consumption" (73).

32. Omega originally appeared in "The Three Doctors" (1973) and later in "Arc of Infinity" (1983).

33. Although Nathan-Turner had managed to secure an agreement with Grade that Baker could appear in the first four episodes of season twenty-four in order to film a regeneration story, the actor declined the offer, claiming professional reasons.

34. Andrew Cartmel, the new script editor, had been forced by Nathan-Turner to work with the Bakers' script, which had been commissioned by Nathan-Turner before Cartmel's appointment. Cartmel relates his aversion to "Time and the Rani" and his conflict with the Bakers in the first few chapters of *Script Doctor*.

35. To facilitate this process, Cartmel distributed two Alan Moore texts in particular, *Halo Jones* and *Watchmen*, which feature postmodern approaches to storytelling and characterization, to his potential script writers, asking them to consider the visionary comic book writer's conception of nonlinear time when working on their own scripts.

36. Rezzies is a play on the word "residents."

37. For an intertextual connection to this analysis, see Marc Schuster's and my application of language theory to "Paradise Towers" in "Red Kangs Are Best: Language Games in the Whoniverse," chapter seven of our book collaboration, *The Greatest Show in the Galaxy: The Discerning Fan's Guide to Doctor Who* (McFarland, 2007).

38. In the beginning of part three, when he repeats his actions by breaking into Tilda and Tabby's apartment, Pex inadvertently succeeds in rescuing Mel from being their dinner, thus finally proving his heroic worth.

39. In *Doctor Who*, the Autons, who debuted in "Spearhead from Space" (1970), are the faceless, plastic foot soldiers that are part of the Nestene Consciousness.

40. Cartmel himself, in *Script Doctor*, refers to Tilda and Tabby as "lesbian cannibals" (61).

41. The Chief Caretaker initially believes the Doctor to be the Great Architect, and so he wants him executed.

42. Kroagnon is the bodiless true Great Architect of Paradise Towers who had been trapped in the building's basement.

43. The other season twenty-four stories are "Time and the Rani," "Delta and the Bannermen," and "Dragonfire."

44. Concerning "Silver Nemesis," which was written by Kevin Clarke, Cartmel, who instituted what became known in fan circles as "The Cartmel Master Plan," claims, "[It] is notable for doing a generally successful job of ushering in the new, more mysterious, powerful and shadowy Doctor that I was aiming towards. It presents the Doctor as a calculating chess player, manipulating events in an intricate strategy that cuts across centuries. I was tired of the notion of the Doctor as a mere Time Lord amongst other Time Lords" (155). Regardless of Cartmel's invigorating decision to go against Nathan-Turner's former mindset to pay frequent nods to the show's past, *Doctor Who*'s ratings were near an all-time low during this and the following season.

45. The Doctor also decries the threat of nuclear Armageddon in part four of season twenty-six's opening tale, "Battlefield."

46. The Doctor's playful words serve as a quietly incendiary counterargument to then–Prime Minister Margaret Thatcher's position on gay lifestyles.

47. The most noticeable postmodern, subversive corporate aspect of "The Happiness Patrol" can be seen in the figure of the despotic Helen A's henchman, the Kandy Man, a murderous cybernetic chef who bears more than a passing resemblance to candy confectioner Bassett's trademarked character, Bertie Bassett, who is made up of licorice allsorts.

48. Additionally, Moffat writes an uncharacteristic easily irritated Fifth Doctor, and he has the Tenth Doctor comment that this former self possesses a "frowny face"—an observation that does not ring true when one considers the younger Davison's consistently sensitive, patient performance during his three-season tenure in the role.

49. For several years, he had been attending the fan-run Gallifrey One *Doctor Who* conventions that are held in Los Angeles around February.

50. The evil snakelike Mara appears in "Kinda" and "Snakedance," and the Time Lord joke references "Arc of Infinity."

51. This comment, I realize, is subject to argument. Davison indeed told the actors involved with the filming of his production that they may not be paid. However, the special

has been included on the Blu-ray *Doctor Who* fiftieth anniversary box set compilation, so I assume that all of the actors involved were monetarily compensated for their efforts.

52. Although Bob Baker and Dave Martin's original script for "The Three Doctors" had more heavily featured Hartnell, it had to be rewritten due to his physical illness.

53. Tom Baker's Fourth Doctor only appears via inserted stock footage from "Shada," the strike-affected original closing story for season seventeen.

54. Humorously, K9, the Fourth Doctor's robotic dog, has been included in this grouping.

Chapter Three

1. The initial four-hour *Battlestar Galactica* miniseries aired on Syfy in December 2003, and *NüWho* premiered its first episode, "Rose," on March 26, 2005.

2. From a theoretical economic standpoint, accompanying DVD/digital, syndication, and ancillary merchandise sales for a *Blake's 7* reboot could potentially guarantee a return on an initial corporate broadcaster investment.

3. For example, the Doctor, in either *Classic* or *NüWho*, can periodically defeat recurring enemies such as the Master, Daleks, or Cybermen in ways that could work as their final appearances. In regard to Syfy's *Battlestar Galactica* series, its finale depicted the human survivors establishing a lasting peace with their enemies, the cybernetic Cylons.

4. In the case of the *Battlestar Galactica* reboot, however, this reimagined version of the 1977 original, and its spin-off, *Caprica*, featured content (i.e., violence and sex scenes) geared at a more mature audience.

5. On a political level, Blake could perhaps be seen as representing the oppressed British citizen of a post-punk, "No Future," 1978 England, who wishes for a better government that stimulates the economy by providing jobs, not welfare, to its citizenry. On a more far-reaching global level, Blake could also embody the oppressed citizen of any given major empire, regardless of their operating capitalistic or communist ethos.

6. Gan is also envisioned as the "Little John" of the Robin-Hood-like Blake's group.

7. This number includes Zen.

8. Even before Servalan is introduced, a model shot of Space Command, a round, rotating outer space hub for the Federation with a middle circle, arguably hints, in a phenomenological sense, that its shape is oriented toward a female leader, one who is both powerful and sexual.

9. Claiming he is a soldier, Travis simply commanded a field medic to patch him up in this manner instead of having cosmetic surgery.

10. Costume designer Barbara Lane comments, "The Mutoids were the ones with the brains on top of their heads. I wanted to make it look as though the brains were a peculiar shape, so the contours of the cranium took the shape of the brain, and the helmet was that shape because it took on the shape of the head underneath. Of course you had to be pretty good-looking to wear one of those" (qtd. in Nazzaro and Wells 63–64).

11. However, Gan did die in "Pressure Point," a casualty of Blake being tricked by Servalan and Travis to attack the long-empty, former location of Star One on Earth.

12. This blog, a follow-up to the Perrymans' other blog, *Adventures with the Wife in Space: Living with Doctor Who*, offers an episode-by-episode analysis of *Blake's 7*, which they share with their own supporter-fans/casual readers through transcripts of their conversations, podcasts, video commentary on their own Web site and via *Facebook* and *Twitter* postings.

13. In addition, while not a live-action production, a twenty-two episode *Star Trek* animated series utilizing the vocal talents of all of the original cast, except for Walter Koenig, aired on NBC in 1973.

14. Defining this term, Henry Jenkins writes, "The 'post–Gauda Prime' story constitutes one of the dominant genres of *Blake's 7* fan writing, represented by multiple examples in almost every zine; some zines even feature only 'fifth season' stories. Fans offer diverse explanations for the survival of one or more of the protagonists from the massacre of the fourth series' final episode. Common devices include the suggestion that the events were faked by Blake as a loyalty test for Avon and his crew, that the man Avon killed was Blake's clone or that most of the crew was shot with stun guns rather than lethal weapons" (164–65).

15. I have placed quotation marks around the word, since Terry Nation had approved *Afterlife* as a sequel to *Blake's 7*, but, years later in 2013, with Paul Darrow's Big Finish novel *Lucifer*, which I will be discussing in this section, the canonicity of Attwood's work has been overturned. Regardless of whose book is regarded as a true continuation of *Blake's 7*'s saga, both works' narratives would

be naturally negated by any televised sequel to the events of "Blake."

16. In *Enterprising Women*, Camille Bacon-Smith provides a definition of hurt-comfort storytelling: "In [this] subset of stories, one member of the hero dyad is wounded, or occasionally, ill, and his companion comforts the wounded party. If both heroes are hurt or ill, they comfort each other.... A hurt-comfort story may precipitate a sexual relationship or occur within the context of an ongoing sexual relationship. Alternatively, no sexual tie need be present at all" (261).

17. The opening sequence for this production presents a CGI-rendering of the Icarus flying around space and a logo that combine elements from both *Blake's 7*'s Series A and D's title credits.

18. Unfortunately, this is the cliffhanger point where this ambitious fan production ends, with no other installments yet being filmed.

19. As an example, Servalan, at the end of "Rumours of Death," sensually rubs a gun against Avon's face and instructs him to tell his Liberator friends to teleport him up to the ship with the cruel intention of sending them a corpse. Fortunately for Avon, Servalan is distracted by a dying officer, and her prey is safely teleported away from her.

20. As stated earlier, Avon shoots his former lover, Anna Grant, who had betrayed him, in "Rumours of Death." Also, he guns down Klyn in "Blake." Ironically, Klyn was played by Janet Lees-Price, who later married Darrow.

21. In a dream sequence, Blake asks Avon, "Why did you kill me?"

22. This city had been constructed in the seventeen or so years that had passed since the events of "Blake."

23. On how he would have written Avon if *Blake's 7* had been commissioned a fifth series, script editor Chris Boucher reveals, "I would have tried ... to make Avon over into a hero, and make over his personality as well, so that he would have become Blake. In effect recreating what he'd destroyed, and if you really wanted to play games with it, Avon would now actually be called Blake, for some specific reason or other." Apparently, Alan Stevens, who co-interviewed Boucher in 1992 and co-wrote *The Logic of Empire* in 1998, had applied Boucher's potential direction for Avon to the audio production's narrative.

24. The shorter time span of approximately twenty-two minutes is employed by American sitcom producers in order to allow for the inclusion of commercials to fill out the thirty minutes of airplay allotted for a particular episode.

25. However, "City at the Edge of the World," a Series C episode, does thrust Vila into the unlikely masculine heroic spotlight, temporarily encoding him as a capable, virile male as he both romances Kerril and utilizes his lock-picking skills to help them stay one step ahead of the villain, Bayban the Butcher (who, incidentally, is played by future Sixth Doctor Colin Baker).

26. Freeman, on an aca-fan note, pitch perfectly channels the anxious face that Michael Keating would perform as Vila during tense moments in *Blake's 7*.

27. Alternatively, perhaps the obvious point is that the characters—both rebels and villains—are taking a rest from their ongoing conflict in this parallel universe that looks like our reality, hence they are temporarily not obligated to chase after/run from/fight one another.

28. Camille Bacon-Smith offers a history of *Blake's 7* fandom's production of slash efforts in America and Paul Darrow's reaction to those sexual decodings of his character in *Enterprising Women* (34–37).

29. Big Finish is geared toward producing audios that capitalize on the nostalgic value of older BBC and ITV telefantasy shows, a list which includes *Doctor Who*, *Survivors*, *The Avengers*, and *Sapphire and Steel*.

30. Some of these Big Finish CD productions include *Blake's 7: The Classic Audio Adventures* and *Blake's 7: The Liberator Chronicles*.

Chapter Four

1. For instance, the cliffhanger ending to *Red Dwarf VIII*'s final episode, "Only the Good...," (1999) is never properly resolved, naturally irritating fans over the years. This situation even prompts Naylor to write joking dialogue in *Red Dwarf X*'s finale, "The Beginning" (2012), when Rimmer is verbally halted by the rest of the crew from revealing a denouement to the former episode's dangling plotline.

2. In particular, Lister is an avid fan of the London Jets, a futuristic zero-gravity football team.

3. Most *Red Dwarf* episodes are told within a half-hour timeframe while *Back to Earth*'s running time is over an hour long.

4. There was a three year gap between the airing of *Red Dwarf VI*'s final episode in December 1993 and *Red Dwarf VII*'s first in January 1997.

Notes—Chapter Four

5. The film's writer, Doug Naylor, does eventually incorporate a few elements from the unproduced work's script into "The Beginning."
6. Three million years is the time it took for the radioactive contamination from an explosion that killed the crew to safely dissipate on the ship.
7. He was placed in this state for refusing to reveal the whereabouts of his pregnant cat, Frankenstein.
8. For *Red Dwarf I*, Cat, who is evolved from Lister's pregnant cat, fills this role.
9. This is where Lister wished to live with Kochanski and his cat.
10. Both this pregnancy and Lister later giving birth to twin boys offscreen, between *Red Dwarf II* and *III*, fulfill the vision of Lister presenting his newborn babies to his past self during the conclusion to the *Red Dwarf I* episode "Future Echoes."
11. Throughout this chapter, I will be employing the term "Dwarfers," which has been frequently applied in professional and fan writing in regard to the *Red Dwarf* cast.
12. *Classic Who*'s final episode, part three of season twenty-six's "Survival," would air on December 6, 1989.
13. I can equally theorize that a BBC Two show's ratings were not as important as a series airing on the primary channel, BBC One, hence a series such as *Red Dwarf* had room to creatively develop and find its audience.
14. At this time, a typical *Doctor Who* episode could run twenty-two to twenty-five minutes while a *Red Dwarf* episode would fill a full half hour.
15. In particular, a pair of season twenty-two Sixth Doctor stories, "Vengeance on Varos" and "Timelash," feature first episodes that contain extended scenes in the TARDIS, where, to the detriment of their individual narratives, the Doctor bickers with his assistant, Peri.
16. This is the imperfect version of Red Dwarf's computer, created by Kryten's triplicator.
17. In particular, a "sperm-in-law," alternative version of Lister in "The Inquisitor," a psi-moon that patterns itself after Rimmer's tortured psyche in "Terrorform," and the High and Low aspects of the crew in "Demons and Angels" serve as the means to character development in a season that frequently delves into the realms of SF-fantasy and adventure.
18. Cat, for instance, becomes a full-fledged hero as his feline-like reflexes and heightened sense of smell make him indispensable to the crew as Starbug's pilot.

19. This is a half-domesticated polymorph that has been spayed at birth.
20. Rimmer's light bee is a small device that floats inside of him and projects his holographic image.
21. In the episode "Duct Soup," for example, Kochanski's sympathetic understanding of Lister's claustrophobia helps her to distract him from their situation of being trapped together in Starbug's small ventilation duct system.
22. In her memoir *Random Abstract Memory*, Hattie Hayridge comments on the portion of the *Red Dwarf* studio audience who were fans when she played the role of Holly in *Red Dwarf II–V* (1989–92): "As *Red Dwarf* progressed through the years the studio audience was made up more and more of dedicated fans—people who had not only sent off for tickets but had queued, cajoled, begged and gate-crashed for them. There was even talk of ticket touts outside the studio gates" (217).
23. Naturally, a live audience cannot watch the show's model work/special effects scenes being created by BBC (or other) technicians, as these shots, which are inserted later on in the editing process, are usually quite time-consuming.
24. To better explain, a rock concert most likely involves a portion of its audience being under the influence of alcohol or illegal substances, which could easily fuel a more frenzied communal reaction to a live band performance.
25. This is the commercial name for a collection of blooper-reel botched performances from the *Red Dwarf* cast.
26. During the video cassette era, the *Red Dwarf* "Smeg Ups" were marketed as a separate product apart from the regular season episodic releases.
27. *Felis sapiens* is Grant and Naylor's name for the evolved cat race from which Cat hails.
28. One can likewise apply this fact to American SF television airing at that time.
29. This argument is given further weight since she never came close to carrying out her goal of killing Servalan.
30. This plot development occurs at the end of the two-part Series Two story "Rise of the Cybermen" and "The Age of Steel" (2006).
31. In "Stasis Leak," the fourth episode of *Red Dwarf II*, however, a Lister from five years in the future is seen marrying Kochanski and honeymooning with her at the Ganymede Holiday Inn. Since this future occur-

rence is never mentioned again in the series, one can argue that it has been ignored by writers Rob Grant and Doug Naylor in order to retain the thrust of Lister's romantic quest for Kochanski or, on an aca-fan theoretical note, as an alternate future timeline that is never realized. Also, *Red Dwarf: Back to Earth* reveals that the alternative Kochanski, who had been introduced in the *Red Dwarf VII* episode "Ouroboros," and Lister had at some point become lovers. With both situations, nevertheless, the present-day Lister does not successfully woo Kochanski on-screen.

32. On the note of *Red Dwarf*'s dating, the first season of the show says that Lister hails from the twenty-first century, but *Red Dwarf III* amends this fact to the twenty-third. Grant and Naylor had initiated this change in their novelization of the show, *Better than Life*, rationalizing that humans would need a few more centuries to properly travel into deep space.

33. This device creates two copies of anything placed within its field: one pure, the other tainted. It also temporary destroys Red Dwarf until the crew reassembles the machine by finding its parts on the High and Low versions of the ship.

34. Dr. Frank N. Furter is the lead villain in the 1975 SF rock musical film *The Rocky Horror Picture Show*.

35. The "H" is short for hologram.

36. Burden comments that Barrie "realized that out of all of [his castmates], even though he looked the most ridiculous, he looked really hysterically funny, so he went for it" ("Heavy Science").

37. Even though all of *Red Dwarf VII*'s episodes were not recorded before a live audience, they were later screened to a group of viewers in order for the producers to record a non-diegetic laugh track.

38. *Red Dwarf VII*'s concluding episode, "Nanarchy," had ended with the Dwarfers being reunited with Holly, who has been restored to the original Jupiter Mining Corporation factory setting for his male persona and a nanobot-reconstructed Red Dwarf.

39. This is in reference to the NBC television show *Bewitched*'s Darrin, who was played by two actors, Dick York and Dick Sargent, during the course of the show's 1964–72 run.

40. This is the result of him being in service for over three million years.

41. In the *Red Dwarf II* episode "Thanks for the Memory," he drunkenly confesses to Lister that when he was alive he had experienced a brief sexual liaison with Yvonne McGruder, Red Dwarf's female boxing champion. However, the hologrammatic Rimmer would finally experience sex with a fellow hologram, Nirvanah Crane, an officer abroad the holoship Enlightenment, in *Red Dwarf V*'s "Holoship."

42. This fact is revealed in "DNA," a *Red Dwarf IV* episode.

43. As a pleasure GELF, Camille is genetically engineered to appear as the fantasy version of whatever her beholder desires her to become. In reality, she is a large green blob.

44. They had found the time drive on the Gemini 12, a derelict ship, in "Out of Time."

45. Along with the rest of the Dwarfers, Kryten is serving a two-year prison sentence as a result of their actions in the opening episodes of *Red Dwarf VIII*, "Back in the Red: Parts One–Three."

46. This scene actually mocks a real-life situation Naylor experienced during his many attempts to secure funding for a *Red Dwarf* movie.

47. Included on disc two of the *Red Dwarf VII* DVDs is this video-recorded faux-ceremony, titled "Red Dwarf Fan Film Awards," which an additional title card claims is "Live from Albert's hall." In the video, Doug Naylor, dressed in a tuxedo, presents awards for two distinguished entries from the competition: "Best Dramatic Reconstruction of Our Attempts to Get Funding for the *Red Dwarf* Movie" and "Best *Red Dwarf* Film Featuring a Genetic Mutant Played by a Male Human Body Part."

48. For my analysis of this story, I will be referring to the director's cut of *Back to Earth*, which smoothly edits together all three episodes and includes additional footage.

49. The actor has also starred as cab driver Lloyd Mullaney from 2005 to the present on *Coronation Street*, a long-running ITV soap opera.

50. This character looks and acts like *Blade Runner*'s Dr. Eldon Tyrell, the creator of the replicants.

51. In *Blade Runner*, the rogue replicant Zhora crashes through panes of glass as Rick Deckard repeatedly shoots at her.

52. In contrast to the male Despair Squid, the female of this alien species emits a toxic to her victims that generates a pleasure-inducing yet ultimately deadly hallucination.

53. Retroactively, *Back to Earth* is now considered by Doug Naylor to be *Red Dwarf*'s ninth series.

54. Naylor had inadvertently agreed to a budget with Dave that initially did not include the cost of filming the episodes before a live studio audience.

55. In *Back to Earth*, the hallucinatory hologram Katerina does not share in the Dwarfers' adventure on the fake Earth of 2009, while Kochanski is a cynical manifestation of Lister's fears that he will not be reunited with her at some point in the future.

56. In this case, going against Lister and Rimmer's frantic warnings, she pushes the wrong buttons, which end up opening the airlock to the vacuum of space.

57. The tone of his voice at this moment is reminiscent of Ace Rimmer's deeper masculine inflections.

58. This *Seventh-Seal*-like personification of Death had appeared before Rimmer telling him that his life was over.

59. This inflexible fan desire can be viewed as a manifestation of the Continuum of Nostalgic Continuity's occasional lethargic pull.

Chapter Five

1. *Buffy the Vampire Slayer* aired on The WB and UPN from March 10, 1997, until May 20, 2003, and *Angel* aired on The WB from October 5, 1999, to May 19, 2004.

2. I should also mention that *Blake's 7*'s first episode, "The Way Back," presents a scene in which Blake's defense attorney, Tel Varon, is depicted in bed with his wife, Maja.

3. The exact episode order for these five episodes are as follows: "The Empty Child," "The Doctor Dances," "Boom Town," "Bad Wolf," and "The Parting of the Ways."

4. As a counterargument to this position, one can bring up the ending of the Series Two episode "Something Borrowed." Returning to the Hub after taking part in the adventure surrounding Gwen and Rhys's wedding day, Jack nostalgically pulls out a metal box and looks at an old black-and-white photo (date unknown) that shows him on one of his (many?) wedding days with a young, unnamed woman. In addition, *Children of Earth*'s first episode, "Day One," reveals that Jack has a daughter, Alice, as a result of his past relationship with fellow Torchwood team member Lucia Moretti, who died in 2006. At the same time, this heterosexual romance is only relayed through dialogue occurring between Jack and Alice, not in the form of a flashback. Therefore, in both instances that depict Jack as being involved in hetero marriages, these relationships are simply conveyed to viewers through photos and exposition that predominantly encode an offscreen rendering of Jack's romantic attraction to women.

5. Conversely, Gwen's affair with Owen is non-heteronormative since it threatens to destabilize her relationship with Rhys, who wishes to have a strictly monogamous relationship with her.

6. This detail is further emphasized as Dr. Tanizaki, a cybernetics expert whom Ianto has secretly contacted, inspects Lisa, commenting, "Her breathing and hearing appears completely cybernetic, and yet there's also bare flesh" as he lasciviously rubs the palm of his hand over her belly and the surrounding metal and then grips her right breastplate.

7. Respectively, these two-part *Nü Who* episodes are "Rise of the Cybermen"/"The Age of Steel" and "Army of Ghosts"/"Doomsday."

8. Some *Torchwood* fans have theorized that Lisa's breastplate is only an underlayer of the complete metallic shell that forms the exterior appearance of a Cyberman.

9. Interestingly, Owen now wears glasses to signify his bookish persona while Tosh, for some unexplained reason, no longer wears them.

10. In *Torchwood* and *Doctor Who*, the Void is the infinite nothingness between dimensions.

11. For a photo reference of Jaq Harkness's costume, see: https://femmelords.files.wordpress.com/2013/04/0418131818d.jpg

12. In *Female Masculinity*, Halberstam points out, "[F]ar from being an imitation of maleness, female masculinity actually affords us a glimpse of how masculinity is constructed as masculinity. In other words, female masculinities are framed as the rejected scraps of dominant masculinity in order that male masculinity may appear to be the real thing" (1).

13. These aliens have been named the 456 by the British after the radio frequency they utilize to communicate with humanity.

14. These episode are "Reset," "Dead Man Walking," and "A Day in the Death."

15. While *Nü Who* Series Three presented Martha as romantically pining after an uninterested Tenth Doctor, the two characters never engaged in sexually suggestive verbal play. In "Reset," a *Torchwood* Series Two episode, however, Martha indeed playfully jokes with Gwen via double-entendre-encoded language that the two of them "must be the only two people on the planet" who have not made love to him. Later in the episode, she shares a similar sexually suggestive conversa-

tion in the Hub's medical lab with Ianto as they obliquely discuss how he "dabbles" with Jack. In an online review of "Reset," Billie Doux writes, "Martha Jones fit[s] in at Torchwood like she'd been there forever. In fact, I think Martha worked better on *Torchwood* than she did on *Doctor Who*. She was obsessed with everyone else's sex life just like the rest of the Torchies. She tromped all over Owen, and then they got along like a house afire. Maybe that's what every woman should do with Owen. That is, if he weren't dead." In my aca-fan opinion, Doux is correct in writing that Martha comes off as a more rounded, confident character on *Torchwood*, one who works better as a member of a team of specialists who respect her skills and abilities rather than as the patriarchal and emotionally unresponsive Tenth Doctor's human sidekick.

16. Jack does reveal to Alice that he has found a gray hair.

17. At one point in "Day Three," during a scene set inside an abandoned Torchwood warehouse, where the team is hiding out, Clem McDonald performs a similar act of "outing" Ianto as he asks Gwen, "[W]ho's the queer?" prompting Ianto to angrily respond, "Oy! It's not 1965 anymore." Nonetheless, Clem adds that he can tell Ianto is queer because he can "smell it." Gwen and Rhys's shared embarrassed amused reaction to Clem's words subsequently encodes the scene with a heterosexist vibe, as their guilty smiling glances reinforce Ianto's status as an Othered sexual being.

18. With his July 12, 2009 entry on his blog, *the pen is mightier than the spork*, Moran writes that he is grateful for the positive feedback he has received concerning *Children of Earth*. However, in reaction to the more negative messages, he writes, "Unacceptable. Some have been spewing insults and passive aggressive nonsense. Accusing me of deliberately trying to mislead, lie, and hurt people. Telling me I hate the fans, that I'm laughing at them, that I used them, that I'm slapping people in the face, that I've 'killed' the show, that I'm a homophobe, that I want to turn the fan base away and court new, 'cooler' viewers, even that I'm hurting depressed people with dark storylines. Asking me to pass on vitriolic, hateful messages to people I love and respect. Not cool."

19. Edelman continues, "[T]he Child who might choose a provocative book from the shelves of the public library; the Child, in short, who might find an enjoyment that would nullify the figural value, itself imposed by adult desire, of the Child as unmarked by the adult's adulterating implication in desire itself; the Child, that is, made to image, for the satisfaction of adults, an Imaginary fullness that's considered to want, and therefore to want for, nothing" (21).

20. This is my shorthand for Edelman's involved reworking of the Lacanian Symbolic, Real, and Imaginary.

21. Clement McDonald was rejected by the 456 during their original abduction of orphaned children in Scotland, 1965 because his brain emits a frequency that is painful to the aliens. As a result of this experience, Clem had gone mad and has been in and out of psychiatric facilities for over four decades.

22. John Frobisher had appointed Agent Johnson to hunt down Torchwood.

23. The 456 ambassador's constant thrashing of its large alien tentacles against its survival environment in Thames House demonstrates volatile mood swings that are akin to those experienced by a human drug addict who needs a constant supply of an illicit substance.

24. After Jack was exterminated by the Daleks in the *NüWho* episode "The Parting of the Ways," a time-vortex empowered Rose resurrected him, making him nearly immortal.

25. The Blessing is a mysterious organic being forming a pole of the Earth spanning from Shanghai to Buenos Aires and is somehow connected to all of humanity and their status as mortal beings. "The Blood Line" reveals that the Family, a group of three families who desire to achieve a new world order, had poured Jack's immortal blood, which they had earlier procured in 1927, into the Blessing. As a result, the now-corrupted Blessing spreads this new genetic template throughout the world's population.

26. Simultaneously, Rex either ignores or, due to the urgency of his mission and personal situation, does not focus upon his CIA colleague Esther Drummond's unstated—yet implied—romantic feelings for him. In this sense, however, his attitude toward Esther reverses the troubling discourse present in BBC SF television in which minority heroic characters have been rejected by their white counterparts.

27. At the same time, Gwen, by the conclusion of *Miracle Day*, once more remains *Torchwood*'s last-woman-standing survivor. This token status takes on an even more heteronormative shading when one considers that Gwen, Rhys, and Anwen form a family unit that is arguably encoded to represent

the fears and anxieties of the viewer who has children. For a potent example of how Gwen's commitment to her heteronormative lifestyle outweighs her loyalty to Jack, one can refer to the seventh episode of *Miracle Day*, "Immortal Sins." This episode shows Gwen knocking out, tying up, and driving Jack to a rendezvous point in Mesa, California in order to deliver him to a group of mysterious people who are holding her daughter, husband, and mother hostage in Wales. During the drive, Gwen tells Jack she had enjoyed all they have experienced together in Torchwood and that she knows he thinks she would never hand him over to their enemies since she loves him. Then, she tearfully exclaims, "This is about my daughter, and I swear, for her sake, I will see you killed like a dog right in front of me if means her back in my arms."

28. This is Rex's nickname for Jack based upon the Captain's World War II jacket.

29. Mekhi Phifer is the actor who plays Rex Matheson.

Chapter Six

1. Technically, this is his thirteenth persona, if one takes the War Doctor into consideration. However, due to the fact that the BBC officially refers to this version of the Time Lord as the Twelfth Doctor, for the sake of consistency (and my aca-fan sanity), I will be referring to the character in this manner.

2. Beginning with the image of clock cogs arranged in an overlapping circular manner in a smoke-filled atmosphere, the title sequence soon gives way to a brightly lit spiral of a clock face with Roman numerals that have Gallifreyan symbols behind them. With these last two images—that of the Roman and Gallifreyan language—one can argue that they represent a patriarchal encoding of the Twelfth Doctor, as these respective societies, real and fictitious, are male-dominated. Later, after the TARDIS emerges from one clock face spiral and travels into another, the second clock face spirals apart as Peter Capaldi and Jenna Coleman's names fill the screen, and then the image of the Twelfth Doctor's intensely staring eyes, which are transposed against an outer space background, dominate it. Thus, the visual encoding of a strong-willed, masculine leading Time Lord is relayed to the show's viewers before the *Doctor Who* logo, some spinning planets/turning clockwork, the TARDIS once again, and the episode title/writer's name close out the sequence.

3. Respectively, Ford co-authored "Into the Dalek" with Moffat, Gatiss penned "Robot of Sherwood," Roberts co-wrote "The Caretaker," and Cottrell-Boyce scripted "In the Forest of the Night."

4. One can mention the case of teenage fan Andrew Smith, who was commissioned by *Classic Who* script editor Christopher H. Bidmead to write "Full Circle" for season eighteen.

5. Refining this statement, Burgess and Green continue that *YouTube* is "a space in which individuals can represent their identities and perspectives, engage with the self-representations of others, and encounter cultural difference" (81).

6. As a possible nod to *NüWho*'s Mexican fans, the Series Eight episode "Kill the Moon" references a four-man Mexican mineral survey team who established a base on the moon, Minera Luna San Pedro, but had disappeared in 2039. While the example of this privately-financed base does not envision a future Mexican government as being economically capable of spearheading a lunar expedition, it successfully provides a positive depiction of Mexican citizens as astronauts and scientists.

7. See chapter three for my discussion of Hyde's "gift economy."

8. As a contrast to Clara's response to the older Twelfth Doctor in "Deep Breath," one can bring up his reaction to a seemingly older version of his companion in the 2014 Christmas special, "Last Christmas." Near the end of the episode, the Doctor is reunited with an elderly Clara in her future home, where she tells him that she has experienced a fulfilling life. This situation, however, is soon revealed to be a Dream-Crab-induced scenario. After the Doctor and Clara finally wake up, he is overjoyed to see that she is still young, and the two resume traveling together aboard the TARDIS. Nevertheless, does this moment show that the two friends subscribe to a lopsided power dynamic in which the virtually immortal man only accepts his mortal female companion in her younger form? Of course, one can rationalize that only a younger Clara has the energy to travel with the Doctor, unlike the vision of her older self who had been created by her dreaming mind. Alternatively, from a gendered perspective, one could decode this variable as being sexist in the mindset that this older-appearing Doctor only enjoys traveling with an attractive younger female.

9. Conversely, it is perhaps too speculative to expect that the Doctor, who travels the totality of time and space, would even begin to put this lifestyle aside and subscribe to the

nine-to-five reproductive, childrearing, and labor demands inherent in a legitimate heteronormative lifestyle.

10. According to xXdreameaterXx, aspirin can be fatal to Time Lords, hence the Doctor's need to seek out alternative alien medications in this story.

11. On the subject of being the joint oldest Doctor (with William Hartnell, who played the First Doctor), Peter Capaldi comments in an interview with the *Doctor Who Team*, "I think too much is made of my age. Who cares? Doctor Who is over 2,000 years old...."

12. Strax, a member of the Paternoster Gang, along with Madame Vastra and Jenny, is a Sontaran nurse who is indebted to the Doctor for once saving his life.

13. For this aca-fan, who was reading this book around the age of twelve, not all of Tulloch and Alvarado's academic speak made sense, but I was intrigued by their comparisons of *Classic Who*'s first and nineteenth seasons thematic and character parallels. Their thoughts, in turn, gave me the beginnings of a finer analytical lens through which I could enjoy my adolescent viewing of the show.

14. During Series Seven, the Eleventh Doctor gave Clara this term of endearment in reference to the mystery concerning her multiple selves.

15. Captain Lundvik is the commanding astronaut of a 2019 mission to blow up the Moon with nuclear bombs because its increasing gravity has been adversely affecting the Earth.

16. Clara had befriended Rigsy, a graffiti artist, in "Flatline."

17. Perhaps Courtney can indeed be considered a character who possesses an extraordinary element to her, since, concerning her future, the Doctor reveals to Clara in "Kill the Moon" that the energetic school girl will one day become the president of the United States.

18. However, I am not entirely correct when I consider the spectacle of the Twelfth Doctor falling from the exploded UNIT aircraft, Boat One, in the Series Eight climax, "Death in Heaven." As he plummets toward the Earth, the Doctor, in his best James-Bond manner, steers his body toward the TARDIS, which is falling beneath him, and successfully enters it in order to halt their shared descent toward the ground.

19. Mickey returns in the Series Four episode, "Journey's End," and he is later seen as married to Martha Jones in the Tenth Doctor's final episode, "The End of Time: Part Two."

20. Seb is actually an AI-interface that was created by Missy to interact with deceased individuals in the Nethersphere.

21. Osgood had previously appeared in "The Day of the Doctor," where she revealed her adulation of UNIT's famous scientific advisor, the Doctor. Visually, her wearing of the Fourth Doctor's long colorful scarf in that episode and her donning of an outfit similar to the Eleventh Doctor's in "Death in Heaven" work as a meta nod to *Nü Who*'s female cosplaying fans. Moffat's killing of the character, however, has been interpreted by some viewers as his symbolic sadistic destruction of the quintessential female fan. As an example, fan blogger MaryAnn Johanson complains, "Killing her off is just cruel and pointless ... especially after the Doctor hinted that she would get a chance to travel with him. Another potentially really great companion, one who would have loved traveling with him, eliminated." Fortunately for fans, Osgood returned in the Series Nine two-parter, "The Zygon Invasion"/"The Zygon Inversion," but the fact of whether or not she is the original human version of the character or her Zygon duplicate has been purposely obfuscated by writers Peter Harness and Steven Moffat.

22. "Kitty," the original version of "Mickey," written by Mike Chapman and Nicky Chinn and performed by the UK music group Racey, is about a woman. With this thought in mind, it is interesting to note that Legs Nose Robinson's version of Basil's adaptation once more restores a women as the subject of the song.

23. Regarding fan reaction to the Master's regendering as Missy, many *Nü Who* fans have celebrated Moffat's bold direction for the character. However, on her blog, Amy Walker astutely addresses the fans who do not support Moffat's and Gomez's female Master: "For all those people who are complaining that The Master is now a woman and are quitting the series. Good. The rest of us don't want you. If a character that belongs to a species that changes their bodies when they're dying becoming female disturbs you, then there's something wrong with you. One value this show fosters is that no matter what species people are, what their outward appearance is, they're still people with decent personalities and people you can care about, a message that we should all adopt in the real world. What if it was a black Master, or Asian? Would that be terrible then too? What happens eventually when the Doctor changes gender?"

Conclusion

1. The Xbox Live service deal is called a rumor by the Web site *Giant Freakin Robot*: http://www.giantfreakinrobot.com/scifi/blakes-7-happened-roboot-series-html

2. The exceptions, of course, were the Series C finale, "Terminal," which features a drugged Avon hallucinating a vision of an injured Blake, and Series D's final episode, "Blake," which features the resistance leader himself.

3. In this episode, Blake sports a notable scar running down his face from his left eye.

4. Conversely, would both new and old *Blake's 7* fans wish for the rebooted Avon to eventually replace Blake as the show's central character?

5. To see these three pieces of *Blake's 7* production art on the *Nerdist* Web site, go to: http://nerdist.com/exclusive-concept-art-for-long-simmering-blakes-7-series/

6. With "Let's Kill Hitler," a *NüWho* Series Six episode, Moffat had previously encoded Mels, the second incarnation of River Song, as a young black woman.

Works Cited

Ahmed, Sara. *Queer Phenomenology: Orientations, Objects, Others*. Durham: Duke University Press, 2006. Print.
The Airzone Solution. By Nicholas Briggs. Dir. Bill Baggs. Perf. Colin Baker, Nicola Bryant, Peter Davison, Sylvester McCoy, and Jon Pertwee. BBV, 1993. VHS.
Alyssa. "An Unlikeable Doctor." *Whovian Feminism*. Tumblr, 12 Mar. 2015. Web. 25 Mar. 2015.
Anderson, Kyle. "Exclusive: Concept Art for Long-Simmering *Blake's 7* Series." *Nerdist*. Nerdist, 7 Aug. 2014. Web. 15 Apr. 2015.
Aragon, Rick. "The Hypocrisy of the Doctor." *Gallifrey Exile*. Blogger, 9 Oct. 2014. Web. 9 Mar. 2015.
Asher-Perrin, Emily. "STDs Are Forever? *Torchwood: Miracle Day*—'Dead of Night.'" Torwww. Macmillan, 25 July 2011. Web. 22. Feb. 2015.
Attwood, Tony. *Blake's 7: Afterlife*. London: Target, 1984. Print.
"Back from the Dead—Series VII" Prod. Helen Norman. Dir. Andrew Ellard. *Red Dwarf VII*. BBC Video, 2005. DVD. Disc 3.
Bacon-Smith, Camille. *Enterprising Women: Television Fandom and the Creation of Popular Myth*. Philadelphia: University of Pennsylvania Press, 1992. Print.
Bakhtin, M.M. *The Dialogic Imagination*. Ed. Michael Holquist. Trans. Caryl Emerson and Michael Holquist. Austin: University of Texas Press, 1981. Print.
Barrowman, John. "Is everything bad that happens on *Torchwood* Captain Jack's fault? We asked John Barrowman!" Interview by Charlie Jane Anders. *io9*. io9, 1 Aug. 2011. Web. 22 Feb. 2015.
_____, and Carole E. Barrowman. *Anything Goes: The Autobiography*. London: Michael O'Mara Books, 2008. Print.
Bersani, Leo. *Homos*. Cambridge: Harvard University Press, 1995. Print.
Bignell, Jonathan, and Andrew O'Day. *Terry Nation*. Manchester: Manchester University Press, 2004. Print.
Blade Runner. Dir. Ridley Scott. Perf. Harrison Ford, Rutger Hauer, Sean Young, and Edward James Olmos. Warner Bros., 1982. Film.
Blake's Junction 7. By Tim Plester. Dir. Ben Gregor. Perf. Mark Heap, Martin Freeman, Raquel Cassidy, and Peter Tuddenham, Mackenzie Crook, and Johnny Vegas. B7 Enterprises, 2005. DVD.
"Blake's Legend (Blake's 7 fan spin-off)." Chris Kirk. *YouTube*. YouTube, 6. June 2013. Web. 10 Nov. 2014.
Boucher, Chris. "Chris Boucher Interview." Interview by Alan Stevens and Anthony Brown. *Magic Bullet*. Kaldor City, n.d. Web. 18 Nov. 2014.
Bourdieu, Pierre. *Distinction: A Social Critique of the Judgment of Taste*. Trans. Richard Nice. Cambridge: Harvard University Press, 1984. Print.
Bradford, K. Tempest. "Invisible Bisexuality in *Torchwood*." *Apex Magazine*. Apex Publications. 4 Mar. 2014. Web. 3 Feb. 2015.
Burgess, Jean, and Joshua Green, eds. *YouTube: Online Video and Participatory Culture (Digital Media and Society Series)*. London: Polity, 2009. Print.
Butler, Judith. *Bodies That Matter: On the Discursive Limits of "Sex."* New York and London: Routledge, 1993. Print.
_____. *Gender Trouble*. New York and London: Routledge, 1999. Print.

Campbell, Joseph. *The Hero with a Thousand Faces*. New Jersey: Princeton University Press, 1973. Print.

Capaldi, Peter. "Peter Capaldi Interview." Interview by the *Doctor Who* Team. *BBC*. BBC, 13 Aug. 2014. Web. 13 Apr. 2015.

Cartmel, Andrew. *Script Doctor: The Inside Story of Doctor Who 1986–89*. Great Britain: Miwk Publishing, 2013. Print.

castrovalva9. "Saving Adric." *A Teaspoon and an Open Mind: A Doctor Who Fan Fiction Archive*. whofic.com, 12 Dec. 2013. Web. 1 Oct. 2014.

Clarance, Leon. Blog comment. "Exclusive: Concept Art for Long-Simmering *Blake's 7* Series," by Kyle Anderson. *Nerdist*. Nerdist, 7 Aug. 2014. Web. 15 Apr. 2015.

Cook, Greg. "A Review of John Nathan-Turner's Tenure." *The Doctor Who Ratings Guide: By Fans, For Fans*. PageFillers.com, 5 Jan. 2000. Web. 19 Oct. 2014.

Darrow, Paul. *Lucifer*. London: Big Finish Productions, 2013. Print.

———. *You're Him, Aren't You?—An Autobiography*. London: Big Finish Productions, 2006. Print.

Davidson, Andy, Chris Orton, Andrew Orton, Robert Hammond, and Matthew West. *Wallowing in Our Own Weltschmerz: An Auton Guide to the Stories Behind the Stories of the Seventh Doctor*. Great Britain: Miwk Publishing, 2014. Print.

Davison, Peter. "I Thought I Was Too Young to Play the Doctor!" Ed. Peter Haining. *Doctor Who—A Celebration: Two Decades Through Time and Space*. London: W. H. Allen, 1983. 67–69. Print.

de Certeau, Michel. *The Practice of Everyday Life*. Trans. Steven F. Rendall. Berkeley: University of California Press, 1988. Print.

"*Doctor Who*: Earth Conquest—The World Tour." *Doctor Who—The Complete Series Eight*. Prod. Alison Severs, Julia Kenyon, and Julia Nocciolino. Dir. Jim Demuth and Posy Dixon. BBC Video, 2014. DVD. Disc. 1.

"Doctor Who Peter Davison message to Gallifrey One." clodman4's channel. *YouTube*. YouTube, 16 Mar. 2010. Web. 25 Oct. 2014.

"Dr Who lookalike has time-travelling funeral in Tardis-style coffin." *Daily Mail*. Associated Newspapers Ltd., 6 June 2009. Web. 28 Mar. 2015.

Doux, Billie. "*Torchwood*: Reset." *Doux Reviews*. Blogger, n.d. Web. 28 Feb. 2015.

Duffett, Mark. *Understanding Fandom: An Introduction to the Study of Media Fan Culture*. New York and London: Bloomsbury, 2013. Print.

Eco, Umberto. *Faith in Fakes: Travels in Hyperreality*. Trans. William Weaver. London: Vintage, 1998. Print.

Edelman, Lee. *No Future: Queer Theory and the Death Drive*. Durham: Duke University Press, 2004. Print.

Escobar, Joe. "'The Logic of Empire' Review." *Magic Bullet*. Kaldor City, n.d. Web. 14 Nov. 2014.

fairyd123. "*Torchwood*—Exit Wounds Review." *fairyd123's journal*. Dreamwidth Studios, 5 Apr. 2008. Web. 28 Jan. 2015.

finmagik. "The final intimacy." *A Teaspoon and an Open Mind: A Doctor Who Fan Fiction Archive*. whofic.com, 16 Feb. 2008. Web. 24 Sept. 2014.

The Five(ish) Doctors Reboot. Prod. Georgia Tennant. Dir. Peter Davison. Perf. Peter Davison, Sylvester McCoy, and Colin Baker. BBC Red Button. BBC, 23 Nov. 2013. Web. 24 Oct. 2014.

Foster, Dave. "*Red Dwarf VII*." *The Digital Fix*. Poisonous Monkey Ltd., 4 Nov. 2005. Web. 2 Jan. 2015.

"FreemantleMedia International Launches Georgeville TV's Remake of Cult Series *Blake's 7* to MIPTV Buyers." *FreemantleMedia*. FreemantleMedia Ltd., 8 Apr. 2013. Web. 19 Apr. 2015.

Gomez, Michelle. "Devil Woman!" Interview by Benjamin Cook. *Doctor Who Magazine*. (#480) Winter 2014/15: 14–17. Print.

Grade, Michael. "Michael Grade Interview." *BBC*. BBC. 26 Apr. 2005. Web. 30 Sept. 2014.

"Grand Designs: Inside the Hub." *Torchwood: The Official Magazine Yearbook*. London: Titan Books, 2008. Print. 14–20.

Gray, Jonathan. "New Audiences, New Textualities: Anti-Fans and Non-Fans." *International Journal of Cultural Studies*. 6.1 (2003): 64–81. Print.

gt52. "Blue Christmas." *Archive of Our Own*. Organization for Transformative Works, 25 Dec. 2014. Web. 5 Jan. 2015.

Halberstam, Judith. *Female Masculinity*. Durham: Duke University Press, 1998. Print.

———. *In a Queer Time & Place: Transgender Bodies, Subculture Lives*. New York: New York University Press, 2005. Print.

Hall, Stuart. "Encoding/decoding." *Culture, Media, Language.* Ed. Stuart Hall, Dorothy Hobson, Andrew Lowe, and Paul Willis. London and New York: Routledge, 1992. Print.
Hanshaw, Billy. "Interview: Billy Hanshaw on Series 8's Title Sequence." Interview by Connor Johnston. *Doctor Who TV.* Doctor Who TV, 1 Sept. 2014. Web. 18 Mar. 2015.
Haraway, Donna. "A Cyborg Manifesto: Science, Technology, and Socialist-Feminism in the Late Twentieth Century," in *Simians, Cyborgs, and Women: The Reinvention of Nature.* New York and London: Routledge, 1991. Print.
HayamaRei. "Not easy to get rid of." *Archive of Our Own.* Organization for Transformative Works, 8 Jan. 2015. Web. 9 Feb. 2015.
Hayridge, Hattie. *Random Abstract Memory.* London: Penguin Books, 1997. Print.
"Heavy Science—Series V." Prod. Helen Norman. Dir. Andrew Ellard. *Red Dwarf V.* BBC Video, 2004. DVD. Disc 2.
Helford, Elyce Rae. "Reading Masculinities in the 'Post-Patriarchal' Space of *Red Dwarf.*" *Foundation: The Review of Science Fiction* 64 (1995): 20–31. Print.
Hills, Matt. *Fan Cultures. (Sussex Studies in Culture and Communication).* London and New York: Routledge, 2002. Print.
Howarth, Chris, and Steve Lyons. *Red Dwarf Programme Guide* (2nd Rev. Ed.). London: Virgin, 1997. Print.
Husserl, Edmund. *Ideas: General Introduction to Pure Phenomenology.* Trans. W. R. Boyce Gibson. New York: Collier Books, 1967. Print.
Hutcheon, Linda, with Siobhan O'Flynn. *A Theory of Adaptation* (2nd Rev. Ed.). London and New York: Routledge, 2013. Print.
Hyde, Lewis. *The Gift: Creativity and the Artist in the Modern World* (25th Anniversary Edition). New York: Vintage Books, 2007. Print.
ionlylurkhere. "The Appliance of Science" *LiveJournal.* LiveJournal, n.d. Web. 11 Feb. 2015.
Jameson, Fredric. "Progress Versus Utopia; Or, Can We Imagine the Future?" *Science Fiction Studies* 9 (1982): 147–58. Print.
Jaq Harkness. "Captain Jaq Harkness. And who are you?" *FemmeLords.* WordPress, 19 Apr. 2013. Web. 2 Feb. 2015.
jedsocrazy. "The slime's coming home!" "*Red Dwarf*: 'The Beginning': Episode Fan Reviews." tvwww. CBS Interactive Inc., 9 Nov. 2012. Web. 3 Jan. 2015.
Jenkins, Henry. *Convergence Culture: Where Old and New Media Collide.* (Rev. Ed.). New York: New York University Press, 2008. Print.
____. *Textual Poachers: Television Fans and Participatory Culture.* (Rev. Ed.). New York and London: Routledge, 2013. Print.
____, Sam Ford, and Joshua Green. *Spreadable Media.* New York: New York University Press, 2013. Print.
JeromeWetzelTV. "'The Blood Line' concludes *Torchwood: Miracle Day.*" *The TV King.* Zupsa Ltd., 11 Sept. 2011. Web. 5 Mar. 2015.
Johanson, MaryAnn. "*Doctor Who* blogging: 'Death in Heaven.'" *flickfilosopher.* WordPress. 9 Nov. 2014. Web. 17 Apr. 2015.
Johnson, Dorf. "The Twelfth Doctor: A Bad Man with a Box?" *Doctor Who TV.* Doctor Who TV, 17 Mar. 2015. Web. 24 Mar. 2015.
Juneau, Jason P. "Blake's 7—Afterlife." *Hermit.org.* Hermit.org, n.d. Web. 12 Nov. 2014.
Kibble-White, Graham. "The DWM Review: 'The Caretaker.'" *Doctor Who Magazine.* (#479) Dec. 2014: 67–68. Print.
"Kill the Moon—Review." *TARDIS Archives.* WordPress, 4 Oct. 2014. Web. 9 Mar. 2015.
Killick, Jane. *Stasis Leaked Complete: The Unofficial Behind the Scenes Guide to Red Dwarf.* United Kingdom: Elly Books, 2012. Print.
koloSigma1. "*Doctor Who*—The Fifth Doctor and Turlough are Bringing Sexy Back." *YouTube.* YouTube, 28 Dec. 2009. Web. 4 Oct. 2014.
Koski, Genevieve, Chris Mincher, Josh Modell, Noel Murray, Keith Phipps, Leonard Pierce, and Tasha Robinson. "The Darrin Effect: 20 jarring cases of recast roles." *A.V. Club.* The Onion Inc., 14 July 2008. Web. 3 Jan. 2015.
Legs Nose Robinson. "'Hey Missy'—*Doctor Who* Parody *Spoilers* [Hey Mickey]—by Legs Nose Robinson." *YouTube.* YouTube, 13 Nov. 2014. Web. 10 Mar. 2015.
Leigh, Gary, ed. *The DWB Interview File: The Best of the First 100 Issues No. 2.* London: DWB, 1994. Print.
Llewellyn. Robert. *The Man in the Rubber Mask.* London: Unbound, 2013. Print.

"The Making of *Back to Earth*: Part Two." *Red Dwarf: Back to Earth* (The Director's Cut). Prods. Jo Howard and Helen Norman. Dir. Andrew Ellard. BBC Video, 2009. DVD. Disc 2.

Mann, Richard. "*Red Dwarf: Back to Earth* review." *4 out of 10*. WordPress, 15 Apr. 2009. Web. 8 Dec. 2014.

Marshall, Jackie. "Love in a Cold Climate." *Licence Denied: Rumblings from the Doctor Who Underground*. Ed. Paul Cornell. London: Virgin, 1997. 56–59. Print.

Marson, Richard. *JN-T: The Life & Scandalous Times of John Nathan-Turner*. United Kingdom: Miwk Publishing, 2013. Print.

Martin, Daniel. "Jack of Hearts." *Gay Times*. Oct. 2006: 40. Print.

Matt. Blog post. "Exclusive: Concept Art for Long-Simmering *Blake's 7* Series," by Kyle Anderson. *Nerdist*. Nerdist, 7 Aug. 2014. Web. 15 Apr. 2015.

Meek, Jon. "Doctor Why Bother?" *Doctor Who TV*. Doctor Who TV, 8 Mar. 2015. Web. 28 Mar. 2015.

MissSarahG1. "*Torchwood* Series 5—Operation Cardiff Cleanup." *FanFiction*. WordPress, 7 June 2014. Web. 27 Feb. 2015.

Moffat, Steven. "*Doctor Who's* [sic] Missy and River Song are Steven Moffat's way of prepping for a female Doctor." Interview by Chris E. Hayner. *Zap2it*. Zap2it/Tribune Broadcasting, 17 Dec. 2014. Web. 14 Mar. 2015.

_____. "Second Time Around." Interview by Tom Spilsbury. *Doctor Who Magazine*. (#484) Apr. 2015: 12–21. Print.

Moran, James. "Stepping back." *the pen is mightier than the spork*. Blogger, 12 July 2009. Web. 28 Feb. 2015.

Mori, Naoko. "Interview with *Torchwood* star Naoko Mori." Interview by Carole Gordon. *Eclipse Magazine*. WordPress, 1 Jan. 2007. Web. 2 Feb. 2015.

Morley, Chris. "Doctor Who: 5 Reasons The Five-Ish Doctors Reboot Was Great Fun." *Musings of a Mild Mannered Man*. WordPress, 2 Dec. 2013. Web. 10 Oct. 2014.

"The Movie: Yeah, No, Yeah, No." Prod. Kirk Northrop. Dir. Ian Symes. Narr. Austin Ross. Perf. Seb Patrick, John Hoare, Tanya Jones, and Jonathan Capps. Featured in "Fan Films." *Red Dwarf VII*. BBC Video, 2006. DVD. Disc 2.

Muir, John Kenneth. *A Critical History of Doctor Who on Television*. Jefferson: McFarland, 1999. Print.

_____. *A History and Critical Analysis of Blake's 7, the 1978–1981 British Television Space Adventure*. Jefferson: McFarland, 2006. Print.

Naylor, Doug. "From a Dwarf to a Giant." Interview by Leah Holmes. *SFX Collection 22: Best of British*. 2005: 84–87. Print.

_____. *Red Dwarf VIII*. London: Virgin, 1999. Print.

Nazzaro, Joe, and Sheelagh Wells. *Blake's 7: The Inside Story*. Great Britain: Virgin, 1997. Print.

"*Open Air*." Host. Pattie Coldwell. BBC. 8 Dec. 1986. *Doctor Who*: "The Trial of a Time Lord": Parts 13–14: "The Ultimate Foe." Dir. Chris Clough. BBC Video, 2008. DVD.

Newspapers Ltd, 6 June 2009. Web. 28 Mar. 2015.

Orman, Kate. "*Torchwood* and Rape." *News From the House of Sticks*. LiveJournal, 2 Nov. 2006. Web. 2 Feb. 2015.

Oshiro, Mark. "Mark Watches '*Torchwood*: *Children of Earth*': Day Four." *Mark Watches*. WordPress, 21 July 2011. Web. 27 Feb. 2015.

Parsley the Lion. "*Blake's Junction 7* DVD Review." *Den of Geek*. Den of Geek, 22 Jan. 2008. Web. 31 Oct. 2014.

"Part Five." Prod. Simon Berman. *Doctor Who*: "Earthshock." Dir. Peter Grimwade. BBC Video, 2004. DVD.

Pearce, Jacqueline. "Interview with Jacqueline." Interview by Alan Stevens and Alistair Lock. *Magic Bullet*. Kaldor City, n.d. Web. 3 Dec. 2014.

_____. "Jacqueline Pearce." Interview by Peter Linford. Leigh 165–70.

Perryman, Neil, and Sue Perryman. "Series 4 Overview." *Adventures with the Wife and Blake*. The Wife and Blake, 30 Sept. 2014. Web. 20 Nov. 2014.

"Peter Davison Video—Opening Ceremonies Gallifrey 22." nerdchik. *YouTube*. YouTube, 18 Feb. 2011. 25 Oct. 2014.

Pixley, Andrew. "*The Five(ish) Doctors—Reboot*." *Doctor Who Magazine Special Edition #38—The Year of the Doctor: The Official Guide to Doctor Who's 50th Anniversary*. Aug. 2014: 80–87. Print.

Rawson-Jones, Ben. "Davies: 'Buffy', 'Angel' inspired 'Torchwood.'" *Digital Spy*. Hearst Magazines UK. 17 Oct. 2006. Web. 3 Feb. 2015.
Red Dwarf: Back to Earth (The Director's Cut). By Doug Naylor. Dir. Doug Naylor. Perf. Craig Charles, Chris Barrie, Danny John-Jules, and Robert Llewellyn. BBC Video, 2009. DVD.
RomanatorX. "*Red Dwarf* Review, Series II, Episode 6, "Parallel Universe." *RomanatorX's Geek Centre*. BlogSpot, 5 July 2013. Web. 20 Jan. 2015.
RoseCathy. "Nadir." *Archive of Our Own*. Organization for Transformative Works, 6 Dec. 2014. Web. 5 Jan. 2015.
Quizzical Pussy. "The 51st Century and The Future of Sex." *Doctor Her*. Doctor Her, 4 Apr. 2012. Web. 28. Jan. 2015.
Sandifer, Philip. "Outside the Government: Adam." *Philip Sander Writer*. Philip Sandifer: Writer. Blogger, 30 Oct. 2013. Web. 25 Feb. 2015.
Saward, Eric. "The Revelations of a Script Editor." Interview by *Starburst*. Starburst. (#97) Sept. 1986: 16–19. Print.
Sedgwick, Eve Kosofsky. *Epistemology of the Closet*. Berkeley: University of California Press, 1990. Print.
shawnlunn2002. "Light in the Darkness Written by Joseph Lidster Directed by Andy Goddard." tvwww. CBS Interactive Inc., 5 June 2011. Web. 16 Feb. 2015.
Star Wars: Episode IV: A New Hope. Dir. George Lucas. Perf. Mark Hamill, Harrison Ford, Carrie Fisher, Peter Cushing, and Alec Guinness. 20th Century Fox, 1977. Film.
Stevens, Alan. "Alan Stevens' Comments." *Hermit.org*. Hermit.org, n.d. Web. 12 Nov. 2014.
____, and David Tulley. *The Logic of Empire*. Perf. Paul Darrow, Peter Tuddenham, Trevor Cooper, Tracy Russell, Ian Reddington, Jacqueline Pearce, and Gareth Thomas. Magic Bullet Productions, 1998. Audiocassette.
"The Tank—Series VIII." Prod. Helen Norman. Dir. Andrew Ellard. *Red Dwarf VIII*. BBC Video, 2005. DVD. Disc 3.
TARDIS on building 7, great dome, and beyond." *Interesting Hacks to Fascinate People: The MIT Gallery of Hacks*. IHTFP Hack Gallery, 2011. Web. 21 Mar. 2015.
tardisjournal. "I Love a Man in a Uniform." *Archive of Our Own*. Organization for Transformative Works, 27 Apr. 2013. Web. 11 Feb. 2015.
The_AG. "The crew triplicate the ship and meet sides of themselves they never would have met." "*Red Dwarf*: 'Demons & Angels': Episode Fan Reviews." tvwww. CBS Interactive Inc., 11 May 2010. Web. 1 Jan. 2015.
Thomas, Gareth. "Gareth Thomas." Interview by Brian J. Robb. Leigh 162–63.
Timberlake, Justin. "SexyBack." *Future Sex/Love Sounds*. Zomba Recordings/Sony BMG Music Entertainment, 2006. CD.
Tom and Lorenzo. "Doctor Who: Flatline." *Tom + Lorenzo: Fabulous & Opinionated*. Tom and Lorenzo.com. 19 Oct. 2014. Web. 25 Mar. 2015.
"*Torchwood: Miracle Day* Episode 10 'The Blood Line' Review." *Whedonopolis*. Whedonopolis, 9 Sept. 2011. Web. 27 Feb. 2015.
ToryTigress92. "Neutral." *FanFiction*. WordPress, 5 Jun 2009. Web. 23 Oct. 2014.
"Trials and Tribulations." Prod. Ed Stradling. *Doctor Who*: "The Trial of a Time Lord": Parts 13–14: "The Ultimate Foe." Dir. Chris Clough. BBC Video, 2008. DVD.
Tulloch, John, and Manuel Alvarado. *Doctor Who: The Unfolding Text*. New York: St. Martin's Press, 1983. Print.
Undie Girl. "*Doctor Who* 8x10 Review: In the Forest Of the Night." *The Geekiary*. The Geekiary, 26 Oct. 2014. Web. 30 Mar. 2015.
Walker, Amy. "An Old Foe Returns in a New Form." *Trans-Scribe*. Blogger, 1 Nov. 2014. Web. 24 Mar. 2015.
Walsh, Eris. "*Doctor Who* Deep Breath: She-Geeks Series 8 Premiere Review." *Krewe Du Who*. Krewe Du Who. 27 Aug. 2014. Web. 13 Apr. 2015.
Warner, Michael. *The Trouble with Normal: Sex, Politics, and the Ethics of Queer Life*. Cambridge: Harvard University Press, 2000. Print.
Warren, Martin. "Bothersome Otherness." *Queers Dig Time Lords: A Celebration of Doctor Who by the LGBTQ Fans Who Love It*. Ed. Sigrid Ellis and Michael Damian Thomas. Illinois: Mad Norwegian Press, 2013. 140–49. Print.
Wharton, David. "Blake's 7: Whatever Happened To That Reboot Series, Anyway?" *Giant Freakin Robot*. 1 Nov. 2013. Web. 16 Mar. 2015.

wildw. "Disappointing." "*Blake's Junction 7* (Short 2005)," by IMDb. *IMDb*. IMDb, 17 Apr. 2008. Web. 4 Nov. 2014.
Wolverson, E.G. "The Twin Dilemma." *The History of the Doctor*. Doctor Who Reviews, 2009. Web. 19 Sept. 2014.
Wright, Mark. "When Worlds Collide..." *Doctor Who Magazine*. (#478) Nov. 2014: 62–66. Print.
"Writing a Final Visitation." Prod. John Kelly. *Doctor Who*: "The Visitation." Dir. Peter Moffatt. BBC Video, 2005. DVD.
xXdreameaterXx. "The Blue Pill." *Archive of Our Own*. Organization for Transformative Works, 6 Mar. 2015. Web. 1 Apr. 2015.
yonderdarling. "Locked in Orbit." *Archive of Our Own*. Organization for Transformative Works, 30 Dec. 2014. Web. 24 Mar. 2015.
Zenia. "Gauda Prime: A fairytale." *Hermit.org*. Hermit.org, n.d. Web. 1 Nov. 2014.

Index

Abrams, J.J. 4, 32, 246
aca-fan 42, 79, 87, 110, 159, 168, 250, 252, 254–56
Ace 44, 60, 68, 110, 207, 224, 245
Adam 155–56
Adams, Douglas 46
adaptation theory 17–18, 71, 99–100
Adrian 209
Adric 48–49, 51–54, 73–74, 214, 247
Ahmed, Sara 22
Ainley, Anthony 71
The Airzone Solution 246
alternate universe (AU) 166
Alvarado, Manuel 39, 202, 206, 256
Alyssa 230–32
Alzarius 48
AMC 225
Anders, Charlie Jane 176
Andy 118
Angel 147, 164, 253
Annett, Chloë 118, 131–32
anti-fans 64–65, 79, 114, 248
antihero 31, 35, 50–51, 58, 79–80, 88–90, 94, 96, 106, 147–48, 160–62, 164, 179, 196–98, 202, 205, 212, 247; *see also* heroic quest
Aragon, Rick 210
Argo 21
Asher-Perrin, Emily 182
Ashildr 8, 206
Atkinson, Rowan 103
Attwood, Tony 89–90, 93–95, 249
Autons 248
A.V. Club 132
The Avengers 250
Avon, Kerr 11, 15, 29–34, 81–82, 84–91, 93–102, 104–6, 116, 123, 140, 145, 148, 224–25, 246, 249–50, 257
Avon, Tor 89

B7 Enterprises 34, 92–93, 97, 140
Bacon-Smith, Camille 250
Baker, Bob 249
Baker, Colin 5–6, 43, 47, 50, 57–58, 61, 65, 71–78, 140, 229, 246–48, 250
Baker, Jane 63, 65, 248
Baker, Pip 63, 65, 248
Baker, Tom 43, 45–49, 71, 75, 190, 246–47, 249
Bakhtin, Mikhail 19–20
Barrie, Chris 108, 121, 124, 127, 129, 252
Barrowman, John 149–50, 163, 168–69, 176
Bartikovsky, Katerina 138, 253
Basil, Toni 217, 256
Bassett, Bertie 248
Batman 36
Battlestar Galactica 3, 32, 79, 227, 246, 249
Bayban the Butcher 250
BBC: BBC America 170, 189, 202; BBC One 38, 113, 170, 178, 184, 202, 251; BBC Red Button 5, 72; BBC/Starz 14, 38, 147, 184, 223; BBC Three 149, 154, 181, 184; BBC Two 34, 38, 109–10, 113–14, 116, 118, 126, 130, 149, 154, 165, 184, 251; BBC Wales 7–8, 75
Becker, Howard S. 2
Bersani, Leo 165–67
Better Than Life 252
Bewitched 252
Bibby, Mel 35
Bidmead, Christopher H. 46, 247, 255
Big Finish 7, 12, 106, 245, 247, 249–50
Bignell, Jonathan 84
bisexual erasure 172–73
Black Guardian 54, 247
Blade Runner 138, 140, 252
Blake, Roj 11, 14–15, 28–32, 34, 40, 80–87, 90–91, 94–98, 101, 105–6, 116, 134, 141, 145, 197, 221, 224–27, 232, 246, 249–50, 253, 257
Blake's Junction 7 33, 97–105, 140–41, 215
Blake's Legend 91–93
Blake's 7 (episodes): "Aftermath" 99; "Blake" 7, 33, 82, 86–91, 93–95, 97, 105,

224–25, 250, 257; "City at the Edge of the World" 246, 250; "Cygnus Alpha" 82; "Orbit" 89, 101; "Pressure Point" 99, 249; "Rumours of Death" 86, 250; "Sand" 149; "Seek–Locate–Destroy" 82; "Space Fall" 81–82; "Star One" 81, 85, 87, 197; "Terminal" 31, 86, 105, 257; "Time Squad" 82; "Warlord" 87; "The Way Back" 28, 80–81, 97, 112, 197, 225, 253
Blake's 7: Afterlife 89–90, 93, 95, 249
The Blessing 178–79, 254
Blue Box Boy 53
Blue Midget 144
Blur 165
Boat One 215, 217, 256
Boeshane Peninsula 155
Bond, James 245, 256
Boneless 204
Booth, Paul 9
Borad 60
Boucher, Chris 29, 84, 246, 250
Bourdieu, Pierre 61–62
Brad 181–82
Bradford, K. Tempest 172–73
Broadbent, Jim 103
Bron, Eleanor 46
Brown, Perpugilliam "Peri" 27, 44, 55, 58–61, 251
Bryant, Nicola 60, 246
Buck Rogers 114, 245
Buffy the Vampire Slayer 72, 95, 147, 164, 253
Burden, Howard 127, 252
Burgess, Jean 188, 255
Bush, Melanie 44, 60, 66–67, 246, 248
Butler, Judith 104, 215–16

Cabina, Susie 178–79
Cally 29, 82, 84, 91–92, 99, 102, 145
Caltech-MIT feud 246
Cameca 25
Camille 135, 252
Campbell, David 25
Campbell, Joseph 13–14, 28, 80–81, 111, 130, 161, 201
Canaries 130–31, 135
Canterbury, Tim 100
Capaldi, Peter 17, 39, 47, 77, 187, 189, 191, 194–95, 208, 214, 230, 255–56
Caprica 249
Cardiff 3, 16, 37–38, 74, 148, 150–51, 161–62, 164–65, 170, 172, 185, 223–24
Cardiff Rift 174, 223–24
Caretakers 65, 67
Carter, Alice 171–72, 253–54
Carter, Steven 170–72, 175–76, 178
Cartmel, Andrew 65, 68–69, 247–48
Cartmel Master Plan 248
Carys 148, 150–51, 157

Cassandra 130–31
Castrovalva 49, 247
castrovalva9 53
Cat 15, 35, 108–9, 111–12, 115–16, 118–19, 123–26, 130, 133, 135, 142, 145, 251; *see also* Dibbley, Duane; The Padré
Chapman, Mike 256
Charles, Craig 123–25, 129, 140
Cheetah People 224
Chesterton, Ian 24–26, 68, 202, 207–8
Chibnall, Chris 4, 63, 228, 247
Chief Caretaker 67, 248
The Child 175–76, 254; *see also* reproductive futurism
Children in Need 69, 103
Chinn, Nicky 256
chronolock 206
Clarance, Leon 226–27
Clarke, Kevin 248
Cleese, John 46
Coal Hill School 24, 39, 186, 202–3, 206–9, 211
Colasanto, Angelo 150
Coldwell, Pattie 62–63
Coleman, Jenna 8, 189, 255
Continuum of Nostalgic Continuity (CNC) 3–5, 7–8, 13, 16–17, 27, 32, 42, 47, 57, 74–76, 79, 97, 99, 105–6, 194, 222, 224, 226, 253
Cook, Greg 77
Cooper, Gwen 16, 36–37, 148–49, 151, 153–57, 171, 173, 175, 179–82, 212, 223–24, 253–55
Copley, Dr. Aaron 158
Cornell, Paul 245
Coronation Street 140, 252
The Corsair 230
cosplay 13, 16, 19, 28, 38, 100, 138, 168–69, 189, 256
Costello, Suzie 151
Cottrell-Boyce, Frank 187, 255
Crane, Nirvanah 149, 252
Crawford, Sim 143
Creation 42
Crook, Mackenzie 34, 100, 104, 215
Crozier 60
The Curator 47, 247
Cybermen 51, 53, 68, 71, 152–53, 208, 212–14, 217, 249, 251, 253
Cygnus Alpha 81
Cylons 249

Daleks 25, 46, 56, 60, 68, 150, 197–98, 201, 203, 245, 249, 254–55
Danes, Oswald 174, 178–79, 212
Danny 180–81
Darrin 252
Darrow, Paul 7, 85–86, 94–96, 98, 249–50

Dave 111, 123, 138–39, 141, 143–44, 222, 245, 253
Davidson, Andy 66
Davies, Rhiannon 172–73, 180
Davies, Russell T 5, 23, 37, 39, 43, 47, 49–50, 70–71, 77, 147–48, 150–51, 162, 172–73, 176, 178, 181, 184–86, 224, 245
Davison, Peter 5–7, 26–28, 43, 47–50, 54, 57, 70–78, 140, 245–48
Death 145, 253
Death Zone 74, 245
de Certeau, Michel 1–2, 18–19
Deckard, Rick 252
Delos 207
Despair Squid 118, 125, 141, 252
Dibbley, Duane 118, 125; see also Cat
DIO 28
Divergent 227
DIY 1, 28, 169, 221
The Doctor: First Doctor 14, 17, 24, 68, 74, 80, 147, 202–3, 206–7, 245, 247, 256; Second Doctor 46, 49, 74–75, 201, 230, 247; Third Doctor 15, 26, 46, 49, 74, 103, 217, 219, 247; Fourth Doctor 28, 43–49, 51, 103, 190, 203, 249, 256; Fifth Doctor 5, 26–27, 39, 42–44, 46, 48–51, 53, 55–57, 70–71, 74–76, 78, 103, 203, 210, 230, 247–48; Sixth Doctor 15, 27, 42–44, 47, 50, 57–59, 61, 74–78, 103, 229, 245–47, 250–51; Seventh Doctor 27, 42–44, 47, 49, 51, 60, 64–65, 67–68, 75–78, 103, 207, 245–47; Eighth Doctor 49, 72, 230, 247; War Doctor 50–51, 74, 247, 255; Ninth Doctor 39, 47, 50–51, 53, 57, 70, 77, 123, 128, 146, 148–49, 208, 247; Tenth Doctor 17, 39, 47, 50–51, 53, 57, 70–71, 74–75, 77, 103, 123, 187, 194, 199, 201, 208, 212–13, 217, 227, 230, 246, 248, 253–54, 256; Eleventh Doctor 17, 22–23, 39–40, 47, 50–51, 53, 74–75, 77, 103, 149, 189, 192–95, 198–99, 201, 203, 227, 230, 245, 247, 256; Twelfth Doctor 8, 17, 23, 39, 47, 51, 77, 104, 187, 189, 191–97, 199, 201–3, 206, 208–10, 214–15, 218, 227–28, 230, 255–56
Doctor Who (episodes): "The Age of Steel" 251, 253; "Arc of Infinity" 203, 248; "Army of Ghosts" 253; "The Aztecs" 25, 202, 207; "Bad Wolf" 253; "Battlefield" 248; "The Big Bang" 40; "Boom Town" 253; "The Caretaker" 206–9, 255; "Castrovalva" 26, 48–49, 51, 247; "The Caves of Androzani" 52, 60; "The Chase" 26, 208; "City of Death" 46; "Colony in Space" 217; "The Dalek Invasion of Earth" 25; "Dark Water" 104, 208, 212–14, 217–18; "The Day of the Doctor" 5, 47, 50, 71–77, 140, 201, 245, 247, 256; "The Deadly Assassin" 246–47; "Death in Heaven" 200, 208, 212–13, 215, 217–18, 256; "Deep Breath" 191–94, 196–97, 200, 214, 218, 255; "Delta and the Bannermen" 246, 248; "Destiny of the Daleks" 46; "Dimensions in Time" 103; "Dinosaurs on a Spaceship" 51; "The Doctor Dances" 50, 149, 162, 253; "Doctor Who" (1996) 49; "Doctor Who and the Curse of the Fatal Death" 103, 245; "The Doctor's Wife" 40, 215, 230; "Doomsday" 253; "Dragonfire" 248; "Earthshock" 48, 51–52, 246; "The Eleventh Hour" 40; "The Empty Child" 149, 253; "The End of the Time: Part Two" 213, 217, 256; "Enlightenment" 54, 56; "Face the Raven" 201, 206; "The Five Doctors" 46–47, 56, 74, 245; "Flatline" 204, 256; "Four to Doomsday" 51; "Full Circle" 51, 255; "Fury from the Deep" 49; "A Good Man Goes to War" 23; "The Green Death" 15; "The Happiness Patrol" 68, 248; "Hell Bent" 8, 201, 206, 230; "In the Forest of the Night" 211, 255; "Into the Dalek" 197, 255; "Journey's End" 57, 256; "Kill the Moon" 203, 206–7, 255–56; "Kinda" 246, 248; "Last Christmas" 255; "Last of the Time Lords" 168–69; "Let's Kill Hitler" 257; "Listen" 196; "Logopolis" 48, 203; "Love and Monsters" 70; "The Magician's Apprentice" 219; "The Mark of the Rani" 43; "Mawdryn Undead" 54–55, 210, 247; "Meglos" 75; "Mummy on the Orient Express" 198; "The Name of the Doctor" 247; "Paradise Towers" 65, 67–68, 248; "The Parting of the Ways" 128, 150, 253–54; "Planet of Fire" 54–55, 60; "Remembrance of the Daleks" 68; "Resurrection of the Daleks" 56, 203; "Revelation of the Daleks" 60; "Rise of the Cybermen" 251, 253; "Robot of Sherwood" 255; "The Romans" 207; "Rose" 208, 249; "Shada" 46, 249; "Silver Nemesis" 68, 248; "Snakedance" 248; "The Sound of Drums" 168–69; "Spearhead from Space" 248; "Survival" 224, 245–46, 251; "The Talons of Weng-Chiang" 247; "Terminus" 48, 54; "The Three Doctors" 74–75, 248–49; "Time and the Rani" 65, 248; "Time Crash" 28, 70–71; "Time-Flight" 52, 56, 203, 206; "The Time of the Doctor" 193; "The Time Warrior" 26; "Timelash" 60, 251; "The Trial of a Time Lord" 15, 60–62, 247; "The Twin Dilemma" 58–59; "The Two Doctors" 60; "An Unearthly Child" 11, 23–25, 39, 202, 206, 245, 247; "Utopia" 168; "Vengeance on Varos" 60, 251; "The Visitation" 49–50; "The Zygon Invasion" 256; "The Zygon Inversion" 256

Doctor Who Appreciation Society (DWAS) 62–64, 246
Doctor Who Bulletin 27, 64, 246
"*Doctor Who*: Earth Conquest—The World Tour" 189
Doctor Who Magazine 209
Doctor Who Restoration Team 53
The Doctor Who Team 256
Dodd, Ken 246
Dog 112
Dollard, Sarah 206
Doux, Billie 254
drag 104, 126, 168, 215–16; see also kinging
Dream Crabs 255
Drummond, Esther 148, 182–83, 254
Duffett, Mark 120–21

E-Space 52
EastEnders 103
Eccleston, Christopher 70
Eco, Umberto 20
Edelman, Lee 174–76, 254
Edgington, Professor 143, 253
Elise 96
emohawk 118, 251; see also Polymorph
encoding/decoding 1, 9, 12–14, 17, 20, 22, 28, 187
encoding/decoding/encoding (EDE) 2–5, 7, 9, 41, 50, 53, 95, 186–87, 191
Enlightenment 252
Ensor, Dr. 246
Enterprise 29, 35, 45, 88, 246
Esa 91–93
Escher, M.C. 247
Escobar, Joe 96–97
Eternals 56
Everdeen, Katniss 227

Facebook 107, 122, 249
fairyd123 159, 161–62
The Family 183, 254
fan fiction 7, 34, 53, 59–60, 88, 95, 99, 110, 127, 129–30, 156, 166–67, 174, 189, 218, 223, 227, 247; see also hurt-comfort; slash
fanboy auteur(s) 4–5
Fay, John 18, 173–74
Federation 14–15, 28–29, 31–33, 79–93, 95–97, 101–2, 104–6, 134, 148, 197, 221, 224–26, 249
felis sapiens 123, 133, 251
female masculinity 169, 253
Fielding, Janet 73, 247
Fiji 112, 251
finmagik 59
Fire Escape 66
The Five(ish) Doctors Reboot 5–7, 28, 34, 47, 71–77, 99, 140

Ford, Harrison 245
Ford, Phil 187, 255
Ford, Sam 187
Foreman, Susan 24–26, 44, 202–3, 206–7, 245
Foster, Bran 28
Foster, Dave 120
The 456 170–73, 175–78, 253–54
Frankenstein 111, 251
Freeman, Martin 100, 250
FreemantleMedia 225
Freudian psychoanalysis 29, 49, 159; see also psychoanalytical lens
Frobisher, John 171, 254
Fuller, Kim 128–29
Furter, Dr. Frank N. 126, 252

Gaiman, Neil 40
Gallifrey 14, 40, 44, 56, 74, 201, 218–19, 245
Gallifrey One 5–6, 72–73, 168, 248
Game of Thrones 15
Gan, Olag 29, 82, 99, 101, 145, 249
Ganymede Holiday Inn 251
Gatiss, Mark 187, 255
Gauda Prime 87, 89, 91, 95–96, 105
GELF 135, 252
Gemini 12 252
gender parody 104, 216
The General 230
Geraghty, Lincoln 6
Giant Freakin Robot 257
gift economy 92, 190, 255
Gold, Murray 75
Golden Fleece 21, 201
Gomez, Michelle 214–15, 217, 256
Gordon, Carole 154
Grade, Michael 61, 63, 65, 229, 248
Grant, Anna 86, 250
Grant, Hugh 103, 137
Grant, Richard E. 103
Grant, Rob 34–35, 108–10, 112, 116, 118–20, 124–28, 132, 134, 145, 231, 251–52
Gray 155, 159, 161
Gray, Jonathan 1–2, 64–65, 248
Green, Joshua 187–88, 255
Gregor, Ben 99–100
Greif, Stephen 83
Grimes, Rick 225
Grogan, Clare 132
gt52 129–30
Gus 198
Gwynne, Owain 3

Habiba, Lois 171
habitus 61
Halberstam, Judith 168–69, 253
Hale and Pace 246
Half-Face Man 196–97, 214

Index

Hall, Stuart 1–2, 12, 20, 22, 41
Hallett, Lisa 152–54, 253
Halo Jones 248
Hand of Omega 68; see also Omega
Hanshaw, Billy 187–91
Haraway, Donna 133–35, 153
Harkness, Captain Jack 14, 16–17, 36–38, 50, 128, 145, 148–50, 153–85, 212, 221, 223–24, 232, 253–55
Harkness, Captain Jacqueline "Jaq" 168, 253
Harness, Peter 256
Harper, Dr. Owen 36, 148–49, 151–62, 170, 179, 183–85, 253–54
Hart, Captain John 38, 148, 161, 164–70
Hartnell, William 14, 17, 24, 39, 58, 74, 80, 147, 202, 208, 245, 249, 256
Harvey, Colin B. 3
HayamaRei 174
Hayner, Chris E. 227
Hayridge, Hattie 35, 117–18, 251
Heap, Mark 98, 100
Helen A 248
Helford, Elyce Rae 116–17, 124
Heriot, Zoe 214
heroic quest(s) 3, 8, 11, 13–17, 27, 35–36, 38–41, 45, 74, 76, 80, 86, 97, 107–9, 111, 118, 134, 141, 146, 222, 224–25; see also antihero
heteronormative 16, 22–26, 33, 35, 37, 55, 129, 135, 167–68, 170–71, 173–74, 176, 180, 183, 192, 211, 214, 253–56; see also homonormative
heterosexist 125–26, 175, 180–81, 183, 254
Highs 126, 251–52; see also Lows
Hills, Matt 3, 5–6, 69
Hilly 109, 113, 116; see also Holly
Hinchcliffe, Philip 46
Holly 35, 108–9, 111–13, 115–19, 126, 130, 133, 137–38, 145, 251–52; see also Hilly
Hollywood 100, 137, 185
Holmes, Diane 160
Holmes, Leah 136
Holmes, Robert 89
holo-whip 127
homonormative 164; see also heteronormative
Hood, Robin 199–200, 208, 249
Howarth, Chris 35, 118, 125
Hub 36–38, 148, 151–52, 154–55, 161, 165–66, 170, 173, 175, 223–24, 253–54
Hudson, June 44
The Hunger Games 227
Hurndall, Richard 245
hurt-comfort 91, 250; see also fan fiction; slash
Husserl, Edmund 21–22
Hutcheon, Linda 17–18, 71–74, 99–100
Hyde, Lewis 92–93, 190, 255

Icarus 91, 93, 250
Idris 40
Image 225
Imperial Star Destroyer 34
ionlylurkhere 156–57
Ireland, Andrew 7
ITV 250, 252
Ixta 207

J-Lo 137
Jameson, Fredric 231–32
Janto 166, 174
Jason 21
Jector 92
jedsocrazy 144
Jek, Sharaz 60
Jenkins, Henry 1–2, 4, 19, 42, 89, 187–88, 249
Jenny 23, 192, 197, 256
JeromeWetzelTV 184
Jim and Bexley 125
Jobel 60
Johanson, MaryAnn 256
John-Jules, Danny 121, 123–25
Johnson, Agent 175, 254
Johnson, Derek 4–5
Johnson, Dorf 199
Johnston, Connor 190
Jones, Bethan 2
Jones, Ianto 17–18, 36–38, 148–57, 164–67, 172–75, 179–80, 184–85, 253–54
Jones, Indiana 245
Jones, Martha 39, 123–24, 150, 159, 171, 179, 212–13, 223, 253–54, 256
jouissance 175–76, 178–79
Jovanka, Tegan 26–27, 44, 48–49, 51–52, 54–57, 59, 71, 73, 202–3, 206, 247
Juarez, Dr. Vera 182–83
Juneau, Jason P. 89
Jupiter Mining Corporation 35, 111, 252

K9 28, 249
Kandy Man 248
Kangs 65–67, 248
Katie 160
Kearns, Laura 4
Keating, Michael 250
Keenan, Gareth 100
Kelso 96
Kerril 246, 250
Kibble-White, Graham 209
Kickstarter 88
Kill Crazy 135
Killick, Jane 34
kinging 168–70; see also drag
Kirk, Captain James T. 29, 35, 45, 88, 92
"Kitty" 217, 256
Kiv, Lord 60
Klyn 250

Knight, Michael 245
Knight Rider 246
Knyvette, Sally 31
Kochanski, Kristine 22, 35–36, 108–9, 113, 118–19, 123–25, 128, 130–32, 135–38, 140, 143, 145, 153, 212, 251–53
Koenig, Walter 249
koloSigma1 55
Korell 89–90, 93
Koski, Genevieve 131–32
Kroagnon 67, 248
Kryten 15, 35, 108, 116–17, 119, 121, 126, 130–31, 133–36, 142, 144–45, 251–52

Lacanian psychoanalysis 175, 254; *see also* psychoanalytical lens
Lambert, Verity 14
Lane, Barbara 83, 249
Langford, Bonnie 246
Lazar's Disease 48
Leela 59
Lees-Price, Janet 250
Legs Nose Robinson 217–18, 256
Lethbridge-Stewart, Brigadier Alistair Gordon 210
Letts, Barry 246
LGBTQ 16, 23, 129, 150, 162, 164, 167, 170, 181
Liberator 15, 28–33, 40, 81–82, 84–87, 90–91, 93, 99, 106, 226–27, 246, 250
light bee 119, 251
Limb, Roger 75
Linford, Peter 84
The Lion, the Witch and the Wardrobe 21
Lionheart Television International 46, 247
Lister, Dave 15, 22, 34–36, 108–16, 118–19, 123–35, 137–45, 147, 153, 163, 200, 212, 222–23, 231–32, 250–53; *see also* Lister, Deb; Spanners
Lister, Deb 112; *see also* Lister, Dave
live studio audience 108, 110, 119–23, 130, 136, 138, 142–43, 251–53
Llewellyn, Robert 121–22
Lock, Alistair 95
The Logic of Empire 7, 95–97, 250
The London 80–81
London Jets 250
Lorrimer, Vere 7
Lovett, Norman 35, 117–18, 124
Lows 117, 126–29, 251–52; *see also* Highs
Lucifer 94–95, 249
Lumley, Joanna 103
Lundvik, Captain 203, 256
Lury, Celia 3
Lusk 91–93
Luxton, Julian 37
Lydon 96
Lyons, Steve 35, 118, 125

Magda 94
Maggie 160
Maloney, David 29
Mann, Richard 139
Mara 71, 248
Mariner 56
Marshall, Jackie 56
Marson, Richard 58, 246–47
Marsters, James 164, 169
Martin, Daniel 150
Martin, Dave 249
Mary 154, 156
The Master 8, 48–49, 51–52, 71, 104, 168–69, 186, 214–19, 224, 227–28, 230, 246–47, 249, 256; *see also* Missy
Matheson, Rex 148, 178–84, 223, 254–55
Matt 226
McCoy, Sylvester 5–6, 47, 50, 65, 71–78, 140, 246–47
McDonald, Clement 175, 254
McGann, Paul 6, 47, 72–73, 247
McGruder, Yvonne 252
Meek, Jon 197
Mellanby, Dayna 31, 84, 86–87, 92, 99, 102, 123, 145
Mels 257; *see also* Pond, Melody; Song, River
"Mickey" 117, 256
Millennium Falcon 35
Minera Luna San Pedro 255
The Miracle 178–80
MissSarahG 1, 223–24
Missy 8, 104, 186, 200, 208, 212–19, 227, 230, 256; *see also* The Master
Moffat, Steven 4, 8, 23, 28, 39–41, 43, 47, 50, 70–72, 74, 76–77, 103, 162, 186–89, 193–95, 202, 206–7, 216, 219, 227–30, 245, 247–48, 255–57
Monarch 51
Moore, Alan 248
Moran, James 18, 173–74, 185, 254
Moretti, Lucia 253
Mori, Naoko 154, 159
Morley, Chris 75–76
The Mother 178–79
Muir, John Kenneth 46–47, 87
Mullaney, Lloyd 252
Murray-Leach, Roger 29–30, 106, 226
Mutoids 83, 249

nanobots 36, 130, 252
Narnia 21
Nathan-Turner, John 5, 16, 23, 27, 42–51, 54, 56–59, 61–66, 68–69, 71–72, 74–78, 113, 137, 202, 228, 246–48
Nation, Terry 29, 79–80, 82, 249
Naylor, Doug 4, 16, 34–35, 108–12, 116, 118–22, 124–29, 131–32, 134, 136–43, 145, 221–22, 231–32, 250–53

Nazzaro, Joe 29–30, 83, 249
NBC 79, 227, 249, 252
Necros 59–60
Nemesis statue 68
Nerdist 226, 257
Nethersphere 212–14, 256
New Adventures 245
Newman, Sydney 14
Nitro 9 68
Noble, Donna 246
Noddy 139
Nut Hutch 15
Nyssa of Traken 26–27, 44, 48–49, 51–52, 54–55, 71, 73, 202–3, 206, 214, 247

O'Day, Andrew 84
The Office 100
Oldsters 65
Omega 65, 74, 248; see also Hand of Omega
Open Air 62–63
Orac 29, 86, 89, 93–95, 101, 246
Orient Express 198
Orman, Kate 151
Osgood 215–16, 256
Oshiro, Mark 173
Oswald, Clara 8, 23, 39, 186, 192–206, 208, 211–13, 218–19, 227, 230, 255–56

The Padré 125; see also Cat
Paradise Towers 65–66, 248
Parsley the Lion 102
Paternoster Gang 256
PBS 46
Pearce, Jaqueline 7, 84, 92, 95, 98, 104, 215
Perkins 199
Perryman, Neil 88, 249
Perryman, Sue 88, 249
Pertwee, Jon 46, 49, 74, 219, 246–47
Peterfield, Lyn 180
Pex 65–67, 248
The Pharm 158
Pharos Project 48
phenomenology 6, 20–22, 25, 29–32, 37, 40, 193, 249
Phifer, Mekhi 184, 255
Pierce, General Austin 177
Pink, Danny 23, 39, 186, 196, 200, 202–3, 205, 207–14
Pixley, Andrew 73
poaching 1–2, 18
Polymorph 126; see also emohawk
Pond, Amy 23, 39–40, 149
Pond, Melody 149; see also Mels; Song, River
Poppins, Mary 214
post–Gauda Prime story 7, 88–91, 93, 97, 105, 224, 249

posthuman condition 15, 22–23, 83, 109, 132, 140, 144, 146, 208, 221
post-life existence 134, 144, 158, 160–61, 179, 184, 214
postmodernism 41, 43, 46, 50–51, 67–68, 72, 76, 87, 98, 101, 105, 108, 138–43, 146, 197, 200, 248
Powers, Austin 169
Prior, Beatrice "Tris" 227
Prix 143
psi-moon 251
psychic paper 204
psychoanalytical lens 40, 50, 58, 90, 94, 104, 159; see also Freudian psychoanalysis; Lacanian psychoanalysis
PTSD 38–39, 146, 186

Quantum Shade 206
queer closet 37, 76
queer death drive 175–76
queered 28, 44, 60, 83, 129, 135, 177, 183, 211, 215
Quell, Captain 198–99
Quizzical Pussy 163

Racey 256
Rai 83
Rassilon 201; see also Tomb of Rassilon
Rawson-Jones, Ben 147
Rebel Blockade Runner 34
Red Dwarf (episodes): "Back in the Red: Parts One-Three" 130–31, 252; "Back to Reality" 118, 125; "The Beginning" 144–45, 250–51; "Blue" 128–29, 163; "Camille" 135; "Cassandra" 130–31; "Dear Dave" 144; "Demons and Angels" 117, 126–28, 130, 251; "Dimension Jump" 116, 125; "DNA" 252; "Duct Soup" 251; "Emohawk: Polymorph II" 118; "The End" 35, 111, 113, 130, 141, 144; "Entangled" 143; "Fathers & Suns" 143–44; "Future Echoes" 251; "Holoship" 144, 149, 252; "The Inquisitor" 251; "Krytie TV" 131, 135–36; "The Last Day" 116; "Nanarchy" 252; "Only the Good..." 131, 136, 145, 250; "Ouroboros" 119, 252; "Out of Time" 252; "Parallel Universe" 109, 112, 115–16, 120, 222; "Pete: Parts One and Two" 131, 135–36; "Polymorph" 126; "Stasis Leak" 251; "Stoke Me a Clipper" 119, 128, 145; "Terrorform" 251; "Thanks for the Memory" 115, 252; "Tikka to Ride" 135; "Trojan" 122–23, 143–44; "White Hole" 117
Red Dwarf (ship) 21–22, 34–36, 111, 114–15, 118, 124, 128, 130–31, 133, 138–39, 143–44, 251–52
Red Dwarf: Back to Earth 7–8, 36, 110, 124, 138–43, 145, 200, 250, 252–53

Index

redecoding 1–2
regendering 3, 8, 216, 219, 222, 227–31, 256
Reid, Beryl 246
replicants 140, 252
reproductive futurism 174–76; *see also* The Child
Restal, Vila 11, 29, 82, 86–87, 89, 96, 101–2, 105, 115, 145, 246, 250
Resurrection Glove 151, 158, 160
Rezzies 66–67, 248
Rigsy 206, 256
Rimmer, Ace 116, 118–19, 125, 128–29, 145, 253; *see also* Rimmer, Arnold
Rimmer, Arlene 112; *see also* Rimmer, Arnold
Rimmer, Arnold 14–15, 35, 108–16, 118–19, 124–31, 133–34, 139, 141–45, 149, 163, 200, 250–53; *see also* Rimmer, Ace; Rimmer, Arlene
Rimmer, Howard 144
Robb, Brian J. 85
Roberts, Gareth 187, 245
The Rocky Horror Picture Show 252
Romana 28, 43, 46, 59, 214
RomanatorX 112
RoseCathy 127
Ross 198
Ross, Sharon Marie 6, 8
Russell, Kurt 245
Russell, William 208

Sackhoff, Katee 227
St. Paul's Cathedral 218
Sandifer, Philip 155
Sandvoss, Cornel 4
Sapphire and Steel 59, 250
Sargent, Dick 252
Sato, Toshiko 36, 148–49, 151, 153–59, 161–62, 170, 182–85, 253
Saward, Eric 49, 51, 54, 58–59, 62–63
Schuster, Marc 248
Schwarzenegger, Arnold 245
Scorpio 28, 33, 35, 84, 87, 89, 91, 99
Scott, Suzanne 4
Seb 213, 256
Sedgwick, Eve Kosofsky 172, 181
Servalan 11, 15, 29, 31–34, 59, 82–87, 89, 92–98, 102, 104, 106, 110, 123, 149, 163, 215, 246, 249–51
Sevateem 59, 247
The Seventh Seal 253
SFX 139
shawnlunn2002 159
Shearman, Robert 245
Shockeye 60
Shontalle 92–93
Showrunner Dream 4
Sil 60
Simm, John 71, 168–69

Simon, Josette 123
Simulant 144–45
sinthomosexual 174–79, 212
Sisko, Benjamin 223
Skovox Blitzer 208
Skywalker, Luke 35
slash 15, 28, 44, 53, 55, 60, 90–91, 105, 129–30, 156, 166–67, 245, 247, 250; *see also* fan fiction; hurt-comfort
Slave 33
S/M 59, 67, 83, 129, 164–67, 169
Smegheads 11
Smith, Andrew 255
Smith, Matt 17, 47, 72, 77, 194, 245
Smith, Mickey 123, 153, 208, 213, 223, 256
Smith, Ricky 123
Smith, Sarah Jane 59
Solo, Han 33, 92
Song, River 103, 227, 247, 257; *see also* Mels; Pond, Melody
sonic screwdriver 31, 40, 49–50, 103, 201, 204
sonic shades 201
Soolin 84, 86–87, 92, 145
Space Command 249
Space Corps 125
Space World 91
Spanners 125; *see also* Lister, Dave
Spears, Bridget 171
spectrox toxaemia 52
Spilsbury, Tom 228
Spock 35, 88
square gun 50
Stannis, Jenna 29, 31, 81–82, 84, 91–92, 99, 145
Star One 85, 197, 249
Star Trek 29, 32, 34, 42, 45, 79, 88, 92, 106, 114, 137, 223, 245–46, 249
Star Wars 4, 31, 33–34, 92, 98, 114
Starbuck, Lieutenant 3, 227
Starbug 35, 118, 128–30, 133, 135, 139, 251
Starburst 62
Starz 14, 38, 147, 178, 181, 184, 223; *see also* BBC/Starz
Stevens, Alan 7, 95–97, 250
Stewart, Patrick 137
Strax 197, 256
Survivors 250
Sutton, Sarah 73, 247
Syfy 32, 80, 106, 225, 227, 246, 249
Symes, Ian 137

Tabby 67, 248
TaftKirk Productions 92
Tanizaki, Dr. 253
TARDIS 21–28, 30, 38–41, 46, 48–49, 51–52, 59, 68, 75–76, 114–15, 190, 193, 195,

Index

198–201, 203–4, 206–8, 211–12, 246, 251, 255–56
TARDIS Archives 207
tardisjournal 166–67
Target Books 89, 247
Tarrant, Del 31, 86–87, 101, 145, 149, 246
Tennant, David 17, 47, 70, 72–73, 187
Terileptil 49
Terminal 87, 90
Terminus 48
Terra Alpha 68
Thatcher, Margaret 31, 68, 126, 248
The_AG (online fan reviewer) 127–28
They Walk Among Us! (comic book store) 139
Thomas, Edward 37
Thomas, Gareth 7, 31, 85, 95
Thoros Beta 60
3W Institute 212, 218
Tilda 67, 248
Timberlake, Justin 55, 247
Time Agency 149, 166
time drive 135, 252
Time Lords 38, 51, 56, 60, 71, 77, 134, 195, 201, 217, 219, 248, 256
Time War 51, 74, 146, 193, 217, 247
Titan 3 58
Todd 246
Tom and Lorenzo 205
Tomb of Rassilon 74; *see also* Rassilon
"Tongue Tied" 124
Torchwood (episodes) "Adam" 154–56, 160; "Adrift" 37, 148, 165; "Captain Jack Harkness" 150; "Combat" 157, 160; "Cyberwoman" 152–53, 164; "A Day in the Death" 150, 158, 160, 253; "Day One" 148, 150–51, 157; "Dead Man Walking" 158, 253; "Everything Changes" 36, 147, 149, 151, 160, 162; "Exit Wounds" 38, 159, 161, 183–84; "Fragments" 160; "Greeks Bearing Gifts" 154, 156; "Kiss Kiss, Bang Bang" 164–65, 169; "Out of Time" 160; "Reset" 158, 160, 253–54; "Something Borrowed" 253
Torchwood: Children of Earth: "Day One" 170–71, 173, 175, 180, 223, 253; "Day Three" 171, 177, 254; "Day Four" 18, 171, 173–74; "Day Five" 170, 172, 174, 176–78
Torchwood: Miracle Day: "The Blood Line" 147, 178–79, 183, 254; "The Categories of Life" 183; "Dead of Night" 178, 181–82; "Immortal Sins" 150, 255; "The New World" 179; "Rendition" 150, 180–81
ToryTigress92 56–57
Totters Lane 245
Traken 48, 203
Travis 11, 15, 82–85, 104, 106, 163, 249
Trenzalore 193
Tribe of Gum 24
triplicator 126, 251–52
Troughton, Patrick 46, 74, 247
Tuddenham, Peter 7, 91, 95, 101
Tulley, David 7, 95, 97
Tulloch, John 39, 202, 206, 256
Turlough 54–55, 247
Twitter 78, 122, 249
Tyler, Rose 39, 57, 103, 123, 150, 153, 208, 254
Tyrell, Dr. Eldon 252

Undie Girl 211–12
UNIT 28, 210, 215–17, 219, 246, 256
UPN 253

Vader, Darth 98
Valeyard 60, 247
Varon, Maja 253
Varon, Tel 80, 253
Vastra, Madame 23, 192, 197, 256
Vegas, Johnny 100
Veneer, Commander 92
Viagra 195–96
Victoria, Queen 223
Virgin 245
Void 156, 253

Walker, Amy 256
The Walking Dead 225
Walsh, Eris 194
Ward, Lalla 43, 246
Warner, Michael 163–64
Warren, Martin 44–45
Watchmen 248
Waterhouse, Matthew 51–53, 73–74, 247
The WB 253
Weevils 157, 160
Wells, Sheelagh 29–30, 83, 249
Whedonopolis 179
Wicked Witch of the West 21
wildw 102
Williams, Anwen 254–55
Williams, Graham 46, 48
Williams, Maisie 8
Williams, Rebecca 1, 7
Williams, Rhys 148, 151, 155, 180, 212, 253–54
Williams, Rory 23, 149
The Wizard of Oz 21
Wolf, Mark J.P. 3–4
Wolverson, E.G. 58
Woods, Courtney 39, 186, 202–3, 206–7, 256
Wragg, Peter 34
Wright, Barbara 24–26, 202–3, 206–8
Wright, Mark 58
Wyatt, Stephen 65

X Files 2
Xbox Live service 106, 225, 257
Xenon Base 33
xXdreameaterXx 195–96, 256

yonderdarling 218–19
York, Dick 252
Youngsters 65
YouTube 18, 55, 78, 93, 187–88, 190, 217, 255
Yrcanos, King 60

Zen 29–30, 33, 82, 91, 93, 249
Zenia 90–91
Zero Room 26
Zhora 252
Zygons 76, 256

www.ingramcontent.com/pod-product-compliance
Ingram Content Group UK Ltd.
Pitfield, Milton Keynes, MK11 3LW, UK
UKHW041929140426
5217IPUK00014B/390